Help with Housing Costs:

Guide to Housing Benefit

2017-18

Sam Lister and Martin Ward

Guide to Housing Benefit
Peter McGurk and Nick Raynsford, 1982-88
Martin Ward and John Zebedee, 1988-90

Guide to Housing Benefit and Community Charge Benefit
Martin Ward and John Zebedee, 1990-93

Guide to Housing Benefit and Council Tax Benefit
John Zebedee and Martin Ward, 1993-2003
John Zebedee, Martin Ward and Sam Lister, 2003-1[
Sam Lister and Martin Ward, 2012-13

Guide to Housing Benefit and Council Tax Rebates
Sam Lister and Martin Ward, 2013-14

Guide to Housing Benefit
Sam Lister and Martin Ward, 2014-17

Help with Housing Costs: Guide to Housing Benefit
Sam Lister and Martin Ward, 2015-18

Sam Lister is policy and practice officer at the Chartered Institute of Housing (email: *sam.lister@cih.org*) and a founding director of Worcester Citizens Advice Bureau and Whabac. He has specialised in housing benefit and social security since 1993.

Martin Ward is an independent consultant and trainer on housing and benefit related matters (e-mail: *mward@knowledgeflow.org.uk*). He has provided consultancy services and training for several national organisations as well as many local authorities and large and small housing providers across the UK since 1982.

ISBN 978-0-9934984-4-2

Edited and typeset by Davies Communications *(www.daviescomms.com)*

Printed by The Russell Press Ltd, Nottingham
(www.russellpress.com)

Preface

This guide explains the rules about housing benefit as they apply from 1st April 2017, using the information available on that date.

We welcome comments and criticisms on the contents of our guide and make every effort to ensure it is accurate. However, the only statement of the law is found in the relevant Acts, regulations, orders and rules (chapter 1).

This guide has been written with the help and encouragement of many other people. Much material remains as written by John Zebedee. This year we thank the following in particular:

Linda Davies and Peter Singer (editing and production), Philip Cairns (DFC) Peter Meehan, Julia Service (Housing Systems), the Welfare Reform Club and John Zebedee as well as staff from the Department for Work and Pensions and the Rent Service. Their help has been essential to the production of this guide.

Sam Lister and Martin Ward

May 2017

List of tables

Table		Page

Table		Page

Abbreviations

The principal abbreviations used in the guide are given below.

CTB	Council tax benefit
CTC	Child tax credit
CTR	Council tax rebate
DHP	Discretionary Housing Payment
DLA	Disability living allowance
DFC	The Department for Communities in Northern Ireland
DWP	The Department for Work and Pensions in Great Britain
EP	Extended payment
ESA	Employment and support allowance (including ESA(C) and ESA(IR))
ESA(C)	Contributory employment and support allowance
ESA(IR)	Income-related employment and support allowance
GB	England, Scotland and Wales
GLHA	The DWP guidance local housing allowance
GM	The DWP HB/CTB Guidance Manual
HB	Housing benefit
HMRC	Her Majesty's Revenue and Customs
HMCTS	Her Majesty's Courts and Tribunals Service
IB	Incapacity benefit
IS	Income support
JSA	Jobseeker's allowance (including JSA(C) & JSA(IB))
JSA(C)	Contribution-based jobseeker's allowance
JSA(IB)	Income-based jobseeker's allowance
NI	Northern Ireland
NIHE	The Northern Ireland Housing Executive
OG	The DWP HB/CTB Overpayments Guide
PIP	Personal independence payment
RRS	The planned new rate rebate scheme in Northern Ireland
SDA	Severe disablement allowance
SI	Statutory instrument
SMI	Support for Mortgage Interest
SPC	State pension credit (including guarantee credit and savings credit)
SR	Statutory rules (Northern Ireland)
SSI	Scottish Statutory Instrument
UC	Universal credit
UK	England, Scotland, Wales and Northern Ireland
WTC	Working tax credit

Key to footnotes

Each reference applies to Great Britain only unless otherwise stated.
If prefixed by 'NI' (e.g. NIAA) it applies to Northern Ireland only.

AA	The Social Security Administration Act 1992 [section number]
AC	Appeal Cases, published by The Incorporated Council of Law Reporting for England and Wales, London
All ER	All England Law Reports, published by Butterworths
art	Article number
BC	Borough Council
BMLR	Butterworths Medico-Legal Reports
CA	Court of Appeal for England and Wales
CBA	The Social Security Contributions and Benefits Act 1992 [section number]
CC	City Council
ChD	High Court (England and Wales) Chancery Division
COD	Crown Office Digest, published by Sweet & Maxwell
CPR	The Housing Benefit and Council Tax Benefit (Consequential Provisions) Regulations 2006, SI No 217 [regulation number]
CPSA	The Child Support, Pensions and Social Security Act 2000 [section number]
CS	Court of Session, Scotland
DAR	The Housing Benefit and Council Tax Benefit (Decisions and Appeals) Regulations 2001, SI No 1002 [regulation number]
DAR99	The Social Security and Child Support (Decisions and Appeals) Regulations 1999, SI No 991 [regulation number]
DC	District Council
DFA	The Discretionary Financial Assistance Regulations 2001, SI No 1167 [regulation number]
ECJ	European Court of Justice
EEA	The Immigration (European Economic Area) Regulations 2006, SI No 1003 [regulation number (UK reference)]

EWCA Civ	Court of Appeal Civil Division for England & Wales (neutral citation)
EWHC Admin	High Court for England & Wales, Administrative Court (neutral citation)
FTPR	The Tribunal Procedure (First-tier Tribunal) (Social Entitlement Chamber) Rules 2008, SI No 2685 [rule number]
HB	The Housing Benefit Regulations 2006, SI No 213 [regulation number]
HB60+	The Housing Benefit (Persons who have attained the age for state pension credit) Regulations 2006, SI No 214 [regulation number]
HBRB	Housing Benefit Review Board
HC (Admin)	High Court for England and Wales, Administrative Court
HL	House of Lords
HLR	Housing Law Reports, published by Sweet & Maxwell
IAA99	Immigration and Asylum Act 1999 [section number (UK reference)]
LBC	London Borough Council
MBC	Metropolitan Borough Council
NIAA	The Social Security Administration (Northern Ireland) Act 1992 [section number]
NICBA	The Social Security Contributions and Benefits (Northern Ireland) Act 1992 [section number]
NICPR	The Housing Benefit (Consequential Provisions) Regulations (Northern Ireland) 2006, SR No 407 [regulation number]
NICPSA	The Child Support, Pensions and Social Security Act (Northern Ireland) 2000 [section number]
NIDAR	The Housing Benefit (Decisions and Appeals) Regulations (Northern Ireland) 2001, SR No 213 [regulation number]
NIDAR99	The Social Security and Child Support (Decisions and Appeals) Regulations (Northern Ireland) 1999, SR No 162 [regulation number]
NIDFA	The Discretionary Financial Assistance Regulations (Northern Ireland) 2001, SR No 216 [regulation number]
NIED	The Housing Benefit (Executive Determinations) Regulations (Northern Ireland) 2008, SR No 100 [regulation number]
NIHB	The Housing Benefit Regulations (Northern Ireland) 2006, SR No 405 [regulation number]

NIHB60+	The Housing Benefit (Persons who have attained the age for state pension credit) Regulations (Northern Ireland) 2006, SR No 406 [regulation number]
NISR	Statutory Rules of Northern Ireland (equivalent to Statutory Instruments in GB)
NISSCPR	The Social Security Commissioners (Procedure) Regulations (Northern Ireland) 1999, SR No 225 [regulation number]
NIWRO	The Welfare Reform (Northern Ireland) Order 2015, SI 2015 No 2006
QBD	High Court (England and Wales) Queens Bench Division
reg	regulation [regulation number]
ROO	In England and Wales, The Rent Officers (Housing Benefit Functions) Order 1997, SI 1984; in Scotland, The Rent Officers (Housing Benefit Functions) (Scotland) Order 1997, SI 1995 [in both cases followed by article number or schedule and paragraph number]
sch	Schedule
SI	Statutory Instrument [year and reference number]
SLT	Scots Law Times, published by W. Green, Edinburgh
SO	The Income Related Benefits (Subsidy to Authorities) Order 1998, SI No 562
SR	Statutory rules [year and reference number (apply to NI only)]
SSWP	Secretary of State for Work and Pensions
TCEA	Tribunals, Courts and Enforcement Act 2007 [section number]
UCTP	Universal Credit (Transitional Provisions) Regulations 2014, SI No 1230 [regulation number]
UKHL	House of Lords, UK case (neutral citation)
UKSC	Supreme Court (neutral citation)
UTPR	The Tribunal Procedure (Upper Tribunal) Rules 2008, SI No 2698 [rule number]
WLR	Weekly Law Reports, published by The Incorporated Council of Law Reporting for England and Wales, London
WRA	The Welfare Reform Act 2012

Chapter 1 **Introduction**

- ■ Summary of HB and how it is changing: see paras 1.5-19.
- ■ Using this guide (benefit figures, terminology and references): see paras 1.20-27.
- ■ How HB is administered: see paras 1.28-35.
- ■ HB law, guidance and proper decision-making: see paras 1.36-58.

1.1   Welcome to this guide, which describes housing benefit (HB) throughout the UK. The guide is used by administrators, advisers, people claiming HB, landlords and appeal tribunals.

1.2   HB helps you pay your rent anywhere in the UK, and your rates in Northern Ireland. About five million people get HB: see table 1.1.

1.3   For working age claims, HB is gradually being replaced by universal credit (see para 1.15). You can find full details about UC etc in *Help With Housing Costs Volume 1: Universal Credit and Council Tax Rebates,* the companion to this guide.

1.4   The rules in this guide apply from 1st April 2017. The next edition will give the rules from 1st April 2018. Recent and expected changes to the HB scheme are summarised in table 1.2. For basic definitions of the main terminology used in this guide see table 1.4.

Table 1.1 **Key HB statistics**

HB claims in Great Britain on 1st November 2016	
Number of cases	4,550,616
Average weekly payment	£95.92
Composition of HB caseload in Great Britain on 1st November 2016	
In receipt of passport benefit	61.0%
Claimants aged 65+	27.7%
Local authority tenants	28.3%
Housing association tenants	40.8%
Private tenant LHA cases	27.0%
Private tenant non-LHA cases	3.7%
HB caseload in Northern Ireland on 1st August 2014	
Number of cases	166,600
Housing Executive tenants	40.5%
Housing Association tenants	16.6%
Private tenants	42.9%

■ Source: DWP, Single Housing Benefit Extract (SHBE); DFC Statistics and Research Agency.

Table 1.2 **Summary of HB changes from 2016**

1st Apr 2016 SI 2015/1857	Backdating of working age claims in Great Britain reduced from six months to one month (paras 5.54-55).
1st May 2016 SI 2015/1857	Abolition of family premium for new claims in Great Britain (para 12.19).
31st May 2016 NISR 2016/46 NISR 2016/55 NISR 2016/178	Extension of benefit cap to Northern Ireland with transitional protection (para 6.22).
30th Jun 2016 NISR 2016/230	Minor changes to rules about superseding decisions in Northern Ireland when claimant or member of their family receives personal independence payment.
28th Jul 2016 SI 2016/624	In Great Britain, HB for absences outside the UK limited to four weeks (paras 3.57-66).
4th Aug 2016 SI 2016/743	New rules in Great Britain introduced about assessing postgraduate master's degree student loans (table 22.2).
5th Sep 2016 NISR 2016/310	Abolition of family premium and reduction in working age backdating to one month introduced in Northern Ireland.
7th Nov 2016 SI 2016/909 NISR 2016/375	The benefit cap is reduced, but no longer applies to people getting carer's allowance or guardian's allowance (para 6.24, table 6.5).
16th Jan 2017 NISR 2016/432	Scope of discretionary housing payments in Northern Ireland extended to allow for the abolition of the family premium, capping of the eligible rent under the LHA rules and reduced awards due to the benefit cap.
30th Jan 2017 NISR 2017/1	Rules about absences from the UK (see 28th July 2016) introduced in Northern Ireland.
20th Feb 2017 NISR 2016/326 NISR 2016/432 NISR 2017/1	Extension of social renter size criteria ('bedroom tax') to Northern Ireland, and of private and social renter size rules relating to armed forces absences, foster parents and disabled children (paras 8.15, 11.15, 11.21 and 11.33).
1st Apr 2017 SI 2017/213 20th Apr 2017 NISR 2017/70	Changes to size criteria rules to implement UK Supreme Court judgment (para 11.20) and take account of couples who cannot share a bedroom due to disability (para 11.32) and to allow an extra bedroom for children who require an overnight carer (para 11.25).
1st/3rd Apr 2017 SI 2016/1179 SI 2017/260	Uprating of applicable amounts for pension age claims and non-dependant deductions for all claims. Applicable amounts for working age claims (except premiums for caring and disability)

NISR 2017/9 NISR 2017/56	and LHA figures for all claims (except selected LHA rates benefiting from targeted affordability funding) remain frozen at April 2015 levels – probably until April 2020 (tables 6.4, 12.1, paras 9.23-24).
3rd Apr 2017 SI 2017/204 NISR 2017/51	Work-related activity component abolished for new claims with transitional rules for existing claims. Other consequential changes arising from abolition.
3rd Apr 2017 SI 2017/329	In Great Britain rules about treatment of compensation payments from government trusts for infected blood products extended to include new Scottish scheme (paras 6.16, 13.36-37 and 15.42).
6th Apr 2017 SI 2017/376	In Great Britain, personal allowances for children/young persons limited to two, but only for new claims or new born children. Work-related activity component reduced to nil (paras 12.12, 12.18).
6th April 2017 SI 2017/422 NISR 2017/66	Introduction of bereavement support payments for deaths occurring after 5th April 2017. Disregarded as income and capital (table 13.1 and para 15.51).
10th Apr 2017 SI 2017/174 NISR 2017/62	Pensions paid by any government to victims of Nazi persecution treated in same way as those paid by German and Austrian Governments (implements UT ruling [2014] UKUT 187 (AAC)).
11th May 2017 NISR 2017/79	Two child limit to personal allowances applies in Northern Ireland to mirror rules in Great Britain (see 6th April 2017).

Planned changes

- May 2017 onwards, in Northern Ireland expected alignment of regulations with Great Britain (work-related activity component, compensation payments relating to infected blood products from Scottish NHS).

- Starting September 2017, the extension of the UC scheme to Northern Ireland and introduction of a new rate rebate scheme for UC claimants (paras 2.5 and 19.2).

- From April 2018, freezing applicable amounts for working age claims for a further two years (para 12.3).

- By late 2018, all areas in the UK areas are expected to be UC 'full service' areas, where UC replaces HB (except in specified supported accommodation) and the passport benefits for all new working age claims (paras 2.4-12)

- April 2019, LHA rates will set the maximum eligible rent for all social renter claims, including supported accommodation. Separate top up fund for supported housing (outside of HB) to be devolved to the national governments and in England to local authorities.

- During 2019-22, the expected transfer of existing working age HB and passport benefit claimants to UC, with some kind of transitional protection

- During 2018-21, the gradual transfer of existing working age HB and passport benefit claimants to UC.

Table 1.3 **State benefits before and after the changes**

	Before	**After**
Help with living costs	JSA/ESA/IS/SPC	UC/SPC
Help with mortgage interest	JSA/ESA/IS/SPC	UC/SPC
Help with rent[1]	HB	UC/SPC
Help with rates in Northern Ireland[2]	HB	RRS
Help with council tax[3]	CTB	CTR

1. HB for rent continues for many claimants (paras 2.4-8). It will also continue for specified supported accommodation (para 2.13) until it is either absorbed into UC at some later date or replaced by a separate scheme in its own right administered by local authorities.
2. HB for rates in Northern Ireland continues for 2017-18, but is expected to be superseded later in 2017 by a new rate rebate scheme (RRS) for UC claimants.
3. CTB was replaced by CTR on 1st April 2013.

The HB scheme

1.5　　Many people can get HB towards their rent, and/or in Northern Ireland rates. Chapters 2 and 3 give the details about whether you are eligible for HB. This section summarises how much HB you are awarded and other key rules including the changes to HB.

The amount of your HB

1.6　　The main rules about the amount of your HB are as follows:

(a)　your HB is based on your 'eligible rent', and/or in Northern Ireland 'eligible rates': see para 1.7;

(b)　if you are on a passport benefit (para 1.9), you qualify for maximum HB;

(c)　if you are not on a passport benefit, your HB depends on how much income and capital you (and your partner) have: see chapters 13 to 15;

(d)　if you are not on a passport benefit, it also depends on your 'applicable amount', which reflects your (and your family's) basic living needs: see chapters 4 and 12;

(e)　your HB can be reduced if you have one or more 'non-dependants' in your home. These are adults who are expected to contribute towards your housing costs: see chapters 4 and 6;

(f)　if you are working age your HB can be reduced if the total income from your HB, out-of-work benefits, child tax credits and child benefit exceeds 'the benefit cap': see chapter 6.

Chapter 6 gives the full HB calculation.

Eligible rent and rates

1.7   The council works out your eligible rent and rates as follows:

(a) in most social sector lettings, your eligible rent equals the rent payable on your home (reduced in certain cases if the home is larger than you need), apart from any charges included in the rent for services which HB cannot meet (chapter 8);

(b) in most private sector lettings, your eligible rent is a fixed 'local housing allowance' figure depending on where you live and the size of accommodation you need (chapter 8);

(c) in Northern Ireland, eligible rates equal the rates payable on your home (chapter 19).

The passport benefits

1.8   The 'passport benefits' (para 1.9) can help you meet basic living needs (such as food and heating) and also, if you are not in rented housing, your mortgage interest: see chapter 24.

1.9   The 'passport benefits' are:

(a) income-based jobseeker's allowance (JSA(IB));

(b) income-related employment and support allowance (ESA(IR));

(c) income support (IS); and

(d) guarantee credit (part of state pension credit).

How to get HB

1.10   In England, Scotland and Wales you can claim HB from your local council, or in Northern Ireland from the relevant government agency (para 1.28). Chapter 5 explains how to claim and chapter 17 describes how your HB can change.

Payments of HB

1.11   If you qualify for HB it is paid as:

(a) a rent rebate if you rent from the council or the Northern Ireland Housing Executive (para 16.16);

(b) a rent allowance if you rent from any other landlord (para 16.18);

(c) a rate rebate towards rates in Northern Ireland (para 19.18).

If you are overpaid you may have to repay it: see chapter 18.

Information and appeals about HB

1.12   The council must send you a decision notice about your HB claim, about any later changes to it, and about any overpayments: see chapter 16.

1.13   You can ask the council to reconsider its decision about HB, and/or appeal to an independent tribunal: see paras 16.67 onwards. This includes decisions about how much HB you are awarded, how it was calculated, when it starts, backdating (para 5.50) and overpayments.

Landlords and HB

1.14   If your HB is a rent allowance (para 1.11), it can be paid to your landlord in some situations instead of you. The rules about this, and about your and your landlord's rights, are in paras 16.34-66.

Universal credit and changes to HB

1.15　　For working age claims (para 1.23), universal credit (UC) is gradually replacing:

(a) HB for rent, unless you live in specified supported accommodation (para 2.13);

(b) the passport benefits JSA(IB), ESA(IR) and IS; and

(c) the tax credits CTC and WTC.

For the current rules about whether you can get UC or HB, see paras 2.4-14.

1.16　　UC can help with basic living needs (such as food and heating) and rent (whether you are working or not), childcare costs (if you are working) and mortgage interest (if you are a homeowner and not working). It doesn't help with council tax or rates, but you can get council tax or rate rebates separately (paras 1.18-19). For full details see Help with Housing Costs Volume 1.

State pension credit and changes to HB

1.17　　For pension age claims (para 1.23), state pension credit (SPC) will also change from a date to be decided, but not before 2018, to include help with rent (as well as mortgage interest as at present). A 'housing credit' element will include this, and the rules are expected to be similar to UC.

Council tax rebates in Great Britain

1.18　　Council tax rebates (CTR) are separate from both HB and UC. You may be able to get CTR from the council towards your council tax whether or not you are on HB or UC (paras 1.29-30). For full details see *Help With Housing Costs Volume 1*.

The rate rebate scheme in Northern Ireland

1.19　　A new rate rebate scheme (RRS) is being introduced alongside the roll-out of UC (first phase expected from 25th September 2017: table 1.2). It is separate from both HB and UC and is only for people claiming UC. For full details see *Help with Housing Costs Volume 1*. For anyone else in Northern Ireland, HB for rates continues: see chapter 19.

Using this guide

1.20　　The HB rules in this guide apply from 1st April 2017. For changes during 2016 and 2017, see table 1.2.

HB and other benefit figures

1.21　　The HB figures in this guide (e.g. in tables 6.4 and 12.1) apply from:

(a) Monday 3rd April 2017 for HB for rent if your rent is due weekly or in multiples of weeks;

(b) Saturday 1st April 2017 for HB for rent in all other cases and for HB for rates in all cases.

1.21　　AA 150(10); NIAA 132(1); HB 79(3); HB60+ 59(3); NIHB 77(5); NIHB60+ 57(5)

The figures for most other benefits (appendix 2) apply from week commencing Monday 10th April 2017 (except tax credits which change on Thursday 6th April), but affect your HB from 1st or 3rd April 2017 (para 17.44).

Terminology used in this guide

1.22 Table 1.4 summarises the main terms used in this guide.

Table 1.4 **HB terminology**

Housing benefit

Housing benefit means any kind of HB for rent or (in Northern Ireland) rates.

Rent rebate, rent allowance and rate rebate

A rent rebate means HB for rent (in the form of a reduction in rent) for a council tenant or NIHE tenant. A rent allowance means HB for rent (in the form of a cash payment) for anyone else. A rate rebate means HB for rates in Northern Ireland.

Tenant

A tenant includes any kind of rent-payer (for example a licensee).

Eligible rent and eligible rates

Your eligible rent and rates are the amount of rent and rates HB can meet.

Local housing allowance

LHAs are the main way of working out eligible rent for private sector tenants.

Social sector and private sector tenants

If you rent from the council, the NIHE or a housing association you are usually a social sector tenant. If you rent from any other landlord you are usually a private sector tenant.

Claimant and family

A claimant is someone who is making a claim for HB or someone who is getting HB. Your claim includes your family if you have one. For family terminology (partner, child, young person, etc) see table 4.1. For whether your claim counts as working age or pension age see paras 1.23-25.

Council and authority

These both mean the public authorities that administer HB. They also administer CTR.

DWP and HMRC

The Department for Work and Pensions administers most other state benefits, including UC, SPC and the passport benefits. But HM Revenue and Customs administers tax credits, child benefit and guardian's allowance.

Guarantee credit and savings credit

These are the two kinds of state pension credit (SPC). You are on SPC if you are awarded either of them. You are on guarantee credit if you are awarded it with or without savings credit. You are on savings credit if you are awarded it without guarantee credit.

'Pension age' vs 'working age' claims for HB

1.23 Some HB rules are different between pension age and working age claims, for example in relation to backdating (paras 5.50-58) and the assessment of income and capital (chapters 13-15).

1.24 The main dividing line is the qualifying age for state pension credit (SPC). The law refers to people below that age as being 'working age', people above it as 'pension age'. The qualifying age for SPC is increasing from 60 (before April 2010) to 66 (from April 2020). During the 2017-18 benefit year it rises from 63¾ to 64½, and during 2018-19 from 64½ to 65⅓ (in each case approximately). A complete list of qualifying ages is given in appendix 3.

1.25 However, people on JSA(IB), ESA(IR), IS or universal credit (UC) are counted as 'working age' for HB purposes regardless of their actual age. Table 1.5 shows whether you count as 'working age' or 'pension age'.

Table 1.5 **Pension age or working age claim**

Single claimant/lone parent

■ under SPC age   Working age HB claim

■ at or over SPC age:

 ■ not on JSA(IB)/ESA(IR)/IS/UC   Pension age HB claim

 ■ on JSA(IB)/ESA(IR)/IS/UC   Working age HB claim

Couple/polygamous marriage

■ both/all under SPC age   Working age HB claim

■ at least one at or over SPC age:

 ■ neither on JSA(IB)/ESA(IR)/IS/UC Pension age HB claim

 ■ one on JSA(IB)/ESA(IR)/IS/UC Working age HB claim

■ Appendix 3 gives a complete list of the qualifying ages for state pension credit ('SPC age').

Abbreviations and footnotes

1.26 The tables at the front of this guide give:

(a) a list of the abbreviations used in the text; and

(b) a key to the abbreviations used in the footnotes.

The footnotes throughout this guide refer to the law governing HB. All the references are to the law as amended.

1.27 For example, the footnote for table 1.5 refers to regulation 5 of the Housing Benefit Regulations 2006, regulation 5 of the Housing Benefit (Persons who have attained the qualifying age for state pension credit) Regulations 2006, and regulation 5 of the two Northern Ireland equivalents, all four of which are similar.

T1.5 HB 5; HB60+ 5; NIHB 5; NIHB60+ 5

Administering the HB scheme

Who administers the HB scheme

1.28   HB was first introduced throughout the UK in 1982-83. There are different arrangements for administering it in different parts of the UK:

(a) in areas in England with two layers of local government (county and district/borough), HB is administered by the district/borough councils – also known as the local housing authority;

(b) in the rest of Great Britain (areas with one layer of local government), HB is administered by English unitary authorities and London boroughs (including the Common Council of the City of London), Welsh county and county borough councils, and Scottish local councils;

(c) in Northern Ireland, HB for rent and rates is administered for tenants by the Northern Ireland Housing Executive (NIHE), and HB for rates is administered for owners by the Land and Property Services. More details and exceptions are in table 1.6.

1.29   In Great Britain (except as described in paras 1.30-32), you claim HB from the council in the area where you live (para 5.8). The same council also administers CTR, and you can often claim both benefits on a single application form.

Table 1.6 **Which agency administers HB in Northern Ireland**

Land and property services	**Northern Ireland Housing Executive (NIHE)**
Owner occupiers	NIHE tenants
Partners of sole owners	Housing association tenants
Former partners of sole owners	Tenants of private landlords
Former non-dependants of sole owners	People with a life interest
	People in co-ownership schemes
	People in rental purchase schemes

■ The same agency also administers rate relief and lone pensioner allowance.

Out-of-area council tenants

1.30   If a council owns properties outside its area (as is reasonably common in London), the tenants there claim HB from their landlord council – but claim CTR from the council in the area where they live.

Arranging for someone else to administer HB

1.31   Councils in Great Britain may arrange for HB (but not CTR) to be administered on their behalf by another council or by a number of councils jointly. This is very common.

1.28   AA 134(1),(1A),(1B),(2), 139(1),(2), 191; NIAA 126(2),(3)

1.31   AA 134 (1A),(5), 191

1.32   Councils can contract out the administration of HB (and CTR) to private companies (in other words, pay them to do part or all of their work). They do this under the Deregulation and Contracting Out Act 1994 and the Contracting Out (Functions of Local Authorities: Income-related Benefits) Regulations 2002/1888. When contractors make decisions on claims, they must submit a daily 10% random sample of claims for the council to check.

Good administration

1.33   Under the Local Government Act 1999 councils in England and Wales are required to provide the best value they can, achieve continuous improvement and publish their plans for how they will perform.

1.34   The DWP sets councils 'performance indicators' relating to HB (checks on how well they do their work). The key indicators are:

(a) 'speed of processing' – which is the average time to process claims and changes to entitlement; and

(b) a 'right benefit' indicator – which is the number of changes to entitlement in a year.

The DWP has the power to inspect councils and report on their administration generally and on the prevention and detection of fraud (but no inspections have been carried out since 2012). The HB Good Practice Guide provides guidance to help councils manage their services efficiently and is available online [www].

Maladministration

1.35   In individual cases of bad administration by your council, you (or someone else) can complain to the Local Government Ombudsman. Guidance on how to complain, what constitutes maladministration, and recent Ombudsman's reports on HB (and CTR and CTB), are available online [www].

HB law

Acts of Parliament

1.36   The Acts giving the basic rules of the HB scheme are the Social Security Contributions and Benefits Act 1992, the Social Security Administration Act 1992 and their Northern Ireland equivalents, and also (as regards decision-making and appeals) the Child Support, Pensions and Social Security Act 2000 (appendix 1).

1.37   The Data Protection Act 1998 controls the use of, and access to, information about an individual held on a computer or any other retrievable filing system. This Act does not stop disclosure when other law requires it (section 35 of the Act) but authorities are under a duty to protect personal information (GM chapter D3).

1.34   AA 139A-139H
        www.gov.uk/government/publications/housing-benefit-review-local-authority-good-practice-guide

1.35   www.lgo.org.uk (England), www.ombudsman-wales.org.uk (Wales)
        www.spso.org.uk (Scotland), https://nipso.org.uk (Northern Ireland)

1.38 Other Acts affecting HB include the Immigration and Asylum Act 1999 (e.g. s115 about migrants), Northern Ireland Act 1998 (section 87) and the Northern Ireland (Welfare Reform) Act 2015 (making the social security system UK-wide), the Human Rights Act 1998, various anti-discrimination laws, the Deregulation and Contracting Out Act 1994 and the Local Government Act 1999.

Regulations, orders and rules

1.39 The regulations, orders and rules giving the detail of the HB scheme are all passed under the Acts mentioned above and are listed in Appendix 1. They are known technically as Statutory Instruments (SIs) and in Northern Ireland as Statutory Rules (SRs).

Obtaining the law

1.40 The public has the right to see copies of the relevant legal material (plus details of any local scheme: para 13.18) at the council's principal office.

1.41 The Acts, regulations, orders and rules are available online [www]. (For the consolidated legislation in Northern Ireland, see the DWP's The Law Relating to Social Security, volume 8 parts 1 and 2 (also called 'the blue volumes') which are available online [www].) The Child Poverty Action Group's annual publication, CPAG's Housing Benefit and Council Tax Reduction Legislation, also contains all the law in Great Britain plus a detailed commentary including references to case law.

Proper decision-making

1.42 This section explains how the council (or the relevant government agency in Northern Ireland) should go about making decisions on HB by working through the following steps:

(a) identifying what the relevant facts are in any particular case;

(b) properly considering the evidence that does exist, if the facts are in doubt or in dispute;

(c) establishing the facts 'on the balance of probability' if this is necessary;

(d) correctly interpreting the relevant law and applying it to the facts of the case; and

(e) arriving at decisions that can be understood in terms of the relevant facts and law.

Relevant facts

1.43 The only facts which are relevant to the council are those which affect the HB scheme:

(a) sometimes the facts are clear and not in dispute. For example, it may be agreed by the claimant and the council that the claimant has a grown-up son living with him;

(b) sometimes facts are unclear or are in dispute. For example, the claimant may say the son is not living with him (but other things suggest he is);

(c) sometimes there is no evidence of the facts at all. For example, the claimant may have left all of the 'your household' section of his HB application form blank.

1.41   www.legislation.gov.uk
        www.communities-ni.gov.uk/services/law-relating-social-security (Northern Ireland)

1.44   The law uses two ideas to deal with uncertainty about the facts: 'burden of proof' and 'balance of probability'.

Burden of proof

1.45   The 'burden of proof' is based on the idea that it is up to someone to prove their side of a dispute. It is used when there is something that has to be shown to be the case in order for HB law to apply at all. Two examples are:

(a)   when a claimant first makes a claim for HB, there is at the outset no evidence – and so it is for the claimant to support the claim by supplying the council with all the evidence it reasonably requires (para 5.13);

(b)   when the council says that a recoverable HB overpayment has occurred, the council must have evidence to support this (paras 18.1-15).

1.46   The 'burden of proof' is also used when a decision cannot be made by the 'balance of probability' because there is no evidence either way, or the evidence that does exist is exactly balanced. In these cases the side with the burden loses unless they can supply evidence that adjusts the balance of probability in their favour.

Balance of probability

1.47   The 'balance of probability' is based on the idea that in the end a decision has to be made or nothing would ever get done. It is used when there is a disagreement about the facts. In such a case, the council must consider the available evidence to decide what the true position is. The evidence each way must be weighed up and the 'facts' of the case are those supported by the greater weight of evidence. There does not have to be absolute certainty. It is because HB decisions are matters of civil law that the appropriate test is the 'balance of probability' (not 'beyond reasonable doubt', which is a test used in criminal law).

Applying the law

1.48   The HB scheme is governed by law passed by Parliament (paras 1.36-39). The starting point for applying the law is that it means exactly what it says – though many words have special meanings in HB (as described in this guide) and precedents can affect how the law is interpreted (para 1.50).

1.49   Having worked out which piece of law applies and what it means, it must then be applied to the case in hand. For example, whether or not a claimant's son counts as a non-dependant can only be answered by considering the legal definition of 'non-dependant' and applying it to the facts. Part of the definition is that the person must 'normally reside' with the claimant. So if the facts are that the son normally resides somewhere else but visits the claimant from time to time, then as a matter of law he cannot be a non-dependant.

Precedents from courts and Upper Tribunals

1.50   When there are 'precedents' (also called 'case law'), these should be followed. A 'precedent' is a binding decision by a court or an Upper Tribunal on a case which is relevant to the case in hand. For example, in deciding whether a person 'normally resides' with a claimant (para 1.49) there is a precedent in the decision Kadhim v Brent LBC (para 4.31) which may well have a bearing on other cases. Generally speaking, precedents from one part of the UK are regarded as binding in other parts of the UK (for example Great Britain precedent is taken into account in Northern Ireland: C001/03-04(HB)); and precedents from other parts of the social security system may be binding on similar HB decisions (e.g. on backdating: para 5.56).

1.51 Case law from the courts is given throughout this guide, and the full legal citation and details of how to find the transcript online are found in the footnote to the appropriate paragraph. Most Upper Tribunal decisions are available online [www]. Since 1st January 2010 Upper Tribunal decisions are cited using the 'neutral citation' (e.g. [2011] UKUT 136 AAC; the file reference (e.g. CH/3853/2001) is used for older decisions.

Judgment and discretion

1.52 Sometimes a decision about HB requires the council to use its judgment. The law uses terms like 'reasonable', 'appropriate', 'good cause' or 'special circumstances' to show that the council has a judgment to make. Examples of judgments are:

(a) whether it is 'reasonable' for the council to award HB on two homes in the case of a person who has fled violence (para 3.43);

(b) how much it is 'appropriate' to restrict the rent in exempt accommodation (para 10.15);

(c) whether a claimant has 'good cause' for a late claim (para 5.56);

(d) whether a claimant has 'special circumstances' for their delay in notifying an advantageous change in circumstances (para 17.14).

1.53 And sometimes a decision about HB allows the council to use its discretion. A discretion differs from a judgment in the sense that an authority may choose what to do. The law usually says that a council 'may' do something to show that it has a discretion. Examples of discretion are:

(a) whether to award discretionary housing payments (para 25.4);

(b) whether to recover a recoverable overpayment of HB (para 18.27);

(c) in some situations whether to pay HB to a landlord (para 16.42).

Judicial review

1.54 When using judgment or discretion, councils are bound by the principles of administrative law evolved by the courts. If they ignore these they can be challenged by applying to the High Court (or in Scotland the Court of Session) for 'judicial review'. Examples of when a challenge may be successful are if the council:

(a) fails to consider each case on its merits, instead applying predetermined rules;

(b) takes into account matters which it ought not to consider;

(c) does not consider matters which it ought to take into account; or

(d) reaches a conclusion that no reasonable council could have come to (what is reasonable here means rational rather than what is the best decision).

1.51 www.osscsc.gov.uk/aspx/default.aspx (Great Britain for decisions before January 2016)
https://www.gov.uk/administrative-appeals-tribunal-decisions (Great Britain decisions after January 2016)
www.communities-ni.gov.uk/services/northern-ireland-digest-case-law (Northern Ireland)

1.55　　　For more on judicial review, see Judicial Review Proceedings, Jonathan Manning, Robert Brown and Sarah Salmon, Legal Action Group; or Judicial Review in Scotland, Tom Mullen and Tony Prosser, Wiley.

DWP guidance

1.56　　　The DWP (Department for Work and Pensions) is the central government department responsible for HB policy. It publishes guidance on the scheme which is often very useful and is referred to throughout this guide. But (like this guide itself) it is guidance, not law: CH/3853/2001.

1.57　　　DWP guidance includes the following:

- Housing Benefit and Council Tax Benefit Guidance Manual (GM);
- Subsidy Guidance Manual;
- HB Overpayments Guide (OG);
- Guidance on Discretionary Housing Payments;
- circulars in the 'A' series (about adjudication and operations);
- circulars in the 'F' series (about fraud);
- circulars in the 'S' series (about statistics and subsidy);
- circulars in the 'G' series (about general matters); and
- circulars in the 'U' series (about urgent matters).

1.58　　　The manuals are available online [www] as are the 'A', 'S', 'G' and 'U' circulars ('G' and 'U' circulars are also known as bulletins). The 'F' circulars are not available to the public. Strictly speaking, DWP circulars do not apply to Northern Ireland although the relevant government agencies there generally accept the validity of 'A' circulars (unless the law in Northern Ireland is different).

1.58　　www.gov.uk/government/collections/housing-benefit-claims-processing-and-good-practice-for-local-authority-staff

Chapter 2 **Who can get HB**

- Basic conditions: see paras 2.1-3.
- People who fall within the UC scheme: see paras 2.4-14.
- Other people excluded from HB: see paras 2.15-26.
- Liability to pay rent: see paras 2.27-39.
- Contrived lettings and other exclusions from HB: see paras 2.40-59.

Basic conditions

2.1   To get HB, you must meet the conditions in table 2.1. Once you are awarded HB, your HB continues until you no longer meet them all, at which point it stops (para 17.41).

Table 2.1 **Basic conditions for HB**

HB for rent:

  (a) the payments for your dwelling must count as 'rent' for HB purposes (table 7.1).

  (b) you must be liable (or treated as liable) to make the payments (paras 2.27);

  (c) you must occupy the dwelling as your home (chapter 3);

  (d) you must not be excluded from getting HB (para 2.2);

  (e) you must make a valid claim and provide relevant information and evidence (chapter 5);

  (f) your capital must not (unless you are on guarantee credit) exceed £16,000 (paras 15.2-4);

  (g) your income and any non-dependant deductions that apply to you must not be too high to qualify (paras 6.2-6); and

  (h) your weekly entitlement must be at least 50p (para 6.7).

HB for rates:

- you must be liable for rates on a dwelling in Northern Ireland (chapter 19); and
- you must meet conditions (c) to (g) above.

2.2   You may be excluded from getting HB for rent if:

  (a) you fall within the UC scheme (para 2.4-14);

  (b) you are a care leaver aged under 18 (paras 2.15-18);

  (c) you are a full-time student (para 2.19);

T2.1   AA 1(1),(1A),(1B); CBA 130(1),(4), 134(1),(4); NIAA 1(1),(1A),(1B); NICBA 129(1), 130(1),(3)

(d) you are a migrant or recent arrival to the UK (paras 2.20-25);

(e) you are a member of a religious order (para 2.26);

(f) the payments you make don't count as rent (paras 2.27, 7.4 and table 7.2);

(g) you are treated as not liable for rent because you have a contrived or other letting excluded from HB (paras 2.28-59).

Exclusions (a), (c) and (d) can also apply to HB for rates.

2.3   In the future, changes to the SPC scheme are also likely to affect who can get HB (para 1.17).

People who fall within the UC scheme

2.4   This section summarises the current rules about who can get universal credit (UC), and explains how these affect your entitlement to HB. It only applies if you (or your partner) are under state pension credit age (para 1.24).

UC areas

2.5   The rules about whether you can get UC or HB differ between UC 'full service' areas (also called 'digital service' areas) and UC 'live service' areas:

(a) since 25th April 2016, everywhere in Great Britain is either a full service area or live service area, and live service areas are being converted to full service areas during 2016-18;

(b) in Northern Ireland UC is expected to be introduced from September 2017 on a 'full service' basis only.

You can get more information about your area online [www].

2.6   You can claim UC if you:

(a) live in a full service area and meet the basic conditions (para 2.7); or

(b) live in a live service area and meet the basic conditions and the gateway conditions.

You are awarded UC if you meet the financial conditions – for example, your capital must not exceed £16,000 and your income must be low enough to qualify. You can then continue to get UC even if you live in (or move to) a live service area and don't meet the gateway conditions.

The UC basic and gateway conditions

2.7   The basic conditions for UC are given in detail in *Help with Housing Costs Volume 1*. The main ones are that:

(a) you (or your partner if you are in a couple) must be below state pension credit age (para 1.24);

(b) if you are aged 16 or 17 or are a student or migrant, you must be in an eligible group;

(c) you can't get UC if you are a prisoner, hospital detainee or member of a religious order (but single prisoners can continue getting UC for housing costs during their first six months in prison).

2.5   www.gov.uk/government/publications/universal-credit-national-expansion

The gateway conditions can vary between live service areas, but in many areas you have to be a single jobseeker.

UC claims, payments and assessment periods

2.8   You claim UC from the DWP (Department for Work and Pensions) in Great Britain and the DFC (Department for Communities) in Northern Ireland. It is awarded for 'assessment periods' of one month (normally beginning on the same day of each month) and is paid in arrears. Most changes in your circumstances take effect from the beginning of the assessment period in which they occur.

Claims for HB

2.9   In UC full service areas (para 2.5), you can't make a claim for HB during any period in which you meet the UC basic conditions (para 2.7). This applies whether or not you are on UC, and regardless of your financial circumstances. Table 2.2 summarises who can make a claim for HB. And for specified supported accommodation see para 2.13.

2.10   In UC live service areas (paras 2.5) you can't make a claim for HB during any period in which you meet the UC basic conditions (para 2.7) and:

(a)   you are on UC; or

(b)   you have claimed UC or become a couple with someone already on UC, and are waiting for a decision or appeal about whether you qualify; or

(c)   less than six months have passed since:

- you claimed UC but didn't qualify, or

- your UC stopped,

due to the level of your earned income (during these six months you can be re-awarded UC without having to make a claim).

Otherwise you can make a claim for HB – even if you meet the UC basic conditions. And for specified supported accommodation, see para 2.13.

Table 2.2	**Who can make a claim for HB in a UC full service area**

If you live in a UC full service area (para 2.5) you can make a claim for HB if any of the following apply to you.

(a)   You are a single claimant or lone parent and are over SPC age (para 1.24).

(b)   You are a couple and both over SPC age.

(c)   You live in specified supported accommodation (para 2.13 and table 2.3).

(d)   You are a student who is eligible for HB (table 22.1) but you don't meet the UC basic

---

2.9-10   AA 1(4)(za); UCTP 5(1), 6; UC commencement orders

T2.2   AA 1(4)(za); UCTP 5(1),(2)(a); UC commencement orders

conditions. For example, you have limited capability for work (para 12.25) or have a UK grant which includes an amount for deafness, but don't receive DLA or PIP.

(e) You are a prisoner who is eligible for HB under the rules about temporary absences (paras 3.48-52) but don't meet the UC basic conditions. For example, you claim HB after going to prison or because your UC has stopped after six months in prison.

Notes:

- As a general rule, you should be able to make a claim for HB whenever the DWP says you don't meet the UC basic conditions.

- The full rules for (d) and (e) are very detailed, and the UC basic conditions are explained in chapter 2 of *Help with Housing Costs Volume 1*.

- If you live in a UC live service area, see para 2.10.

- If you are already on HB, see para 2.11.

Continuing awards of HB

2.11   If you are already on HB (in either a UC full service or live service area) you can continue getting it. But if you meet the UC basic conditions (para 2.7), your HB 'terminates' (ends) in the following situations:

(a) if you make a claim for UC, your HB ends on the day before the date of your UC claim, or (if UC waiting days apply to you) the end of the waiting days;

(b) if you become a couple with someone already on UC, your HB ends on the day before the first day of your partner's UC assessment period in which you became a couple, or (if you move out of your home) the day described in table 17.3;

(c) if you move to a UC full service area where HB is administered by a different authority, your HB ends on the day described in table 17.3.

The examples illustrate these. But for specified supported accommodation see para 2.13.

2.12   In all the situations in para 2.11, if you don't qualify for UC or your UC ends, you can claim HB again unless the rules in paras 2.9-10 prevent you from doing so.

Examples: Ending HB when you fall within the UC scheme

1. A claim for UC

Mary rents her home and is on HB. On 19th July 2017 she claims and qualifies for UC, but waiting days apply to her so her UC starts seven days later, on 26th July.

- The last day of Mary's HB is Tuesday 25th July (para 2.11).

2. Becoming a couple with someone already on UC

Jack and Jill each rent their home. Jack is on HB. Jill is on UC and her assessment periods begin on the 7th of each month. They become a couple on 19th July, and qualify jointly for UC from 7th July (the first day of the UC assessment period).

2.12   UCTP 5(2)(b), 7,8

- Their UC includes housing costs for whichever is now their normal home from 7th July.

- If Jill moves in with Jack on 19th July, the last day of Jack's HB is Thursday 6th July (para 2.11).

- If Jack moves in with Jill on 19th July, the last day of Jack's HB is Sunday 23rd July (table 17.3).

3. Moving to a UC full service area

Tom rents his home and is on HB. He meets the conditions for claiming UC but has not chosen to. On 19th July 2017 he moves to a rented home in a UC full service area where his HB is administered by a different authority.

- The last day of Tom's HB on his old home is Sunday 23rd July (table 17.3).

- He can't claim HB on his new home (para 2.9) but can claim UC there.

HB for supported accommodation

2.13   You can claim and continue getting HB on specified supported accommodation (table 2.3) whether or not you are on UC. If you move out of specified supported accommodation while you are on UC, or your UC stops while you live there, see paras 17.29-31.

Table 2.3 **Supported accommodation types**

In this table CSS means 'care, support or supervision'; see also notes to this table for further details.

(a) Exempt accommodation

- your accommodation is provided by one of the not-for-profit landlord types in para 10.4(b) and you are provided with CSS that meets the additional condition in para 10.5; or

- you live in resettlement accommodation that meets the condition in para 10.6.

(b) General supported accommodation

- your accommodation is provided by one of the not-for-profit landlord types in para 10.4(b); and

- you get CSS from the accommodation provider or someone else (it need not be commissioned or provided by your landlord); and

- you were admitted into the accommodation in order to meet a need for CSS.

(c) Domestic violence refuges

- your accommodation is provided by one of the not-for-profit landlord types in para 10.4(b) or an authority that administers HB (para 1.28); and

---

2.13   UCTP 5(2)(a)

T2.3   HB 2(1) definitions: 'hostel', 'housing association', 'voluntary organisation', 75H

- the building (or relevant part of it) is wholly or mainly used as non-permanent accommodation for people who have left their home as a result of domestic violence; and
- the accommodation is provided to you for that reason.

See notes for definition of domestic violence.

(d) Local authority hostels

- the building must be owned or managed by an authority which administers HB; and
- you get CSS from the accommodation provider or someone else; and
- the building provides non-self-contained domestic accommodation with meals or adequate food-preparation facilities; and
- it is not a care home, residential home or independent hospital (table 7.2).

Notes:

- Care, support or supervision (CSS): See the first part of table 10.1. The cases there are about exempt accommodation, and are also likely to apply to types (b) and (d) (but in types (b) and (d) it need not be provided by the landlord).
- In exempt accommodation the accommodation provider must be your immediate landlord (para 10.4), and this is also likely to be the case for general supported accommodation and domestic violence refuges.
- Domestic violence is defined as including 'controlling or coercive behaviour, violence, or psychological, physical, sexual, emotional, financial or other abuse, regardless of the gender or sexuality of the victim'.

HB appeals

2.14 If the authority says you can't make a claim for HB (paras 2.9-10), this isn't a 'decision on a claim'. So you can't appeal to a tribunal about this but may be able to challenge it by judicial review (para 1.54). If the authority ends your HB (para 2.11), you can appeal to a tribunal about this (para 16.81).

Other people excluded from HB

Care leavers aged under 18

2.15 You can't get HB for rent if you:

(a) are aged 16 or 17;

(b) are a care leaver (para 2.17); and

(c) have never had a successful family placement (para 2.18)

This is because social services are responsible for looking after you.

2.15-17 Children Act 1989 sch 2 para 19B; Children (Leaving Care) Act 2000 s6; Children (Leaving Care) Act (Northern Ireland) 2002 s6; SI 2001/2874 (E); SSI 2004/747 (S); SI 2001/289, SI 2004/1732 (W); NISR 2005/221

2.16　Other care leavers can get HB (except as described in para 2.2), and in these cases the eligible rent rules can be more generous to you (paras 9.20 and 10.47).

2.17　For the above rule (para 2.15), you are a care leaver if:

(a)　social services looked after you for one or more periods beginning after you reached 14 (and in Scotland they accommodated you or supervised you following a children's hearing);

(b)　one of these periods continued past your 16th birthday; and

(c)　the periods totalled at least 13 weeks, or (except in Scotland) would have done apart from the fact that on your 16th birthday you were in hospital or detained in an institution under a court order.

But periods of up to four weeks aren't counted towards the 13 weeks if you spent them in respite care and returned at the end to the care of your parent(s) or the person with parental responsibility for you.

2.18　A successful family placement (para 2.15) means one that was arranged by social services and:

(a)　in England, Wales or Northern Ireland, was with a family, lasted for a continuous period of at least six months (whether or not it began while you were in care or afterwards) and didn't end as a result of breaking down;

(b)　in Scotland, was with a member of your family aged 18 or over, or with the person who was looking after you before you went into care.

Full-time students

2.19　If you are a full-time student you cannot get HB for rent or rates unless you fall within certain eligible groups (para 22.9 and table 22.1). All the student rules are in chapter 22.

Migrants and recent arrivals

2.20　To get HB for rent or rates, you must meet one of the conditions summarised in paras 2.21-25. These are very unlikely to stop you getting HB if you are a UK national and only leave the UK for short holidays. For full details see *Help with Housing Costs Volume 1*.

2.21　If you are a national of the Common Travel Area (CTA), you can only get HB if you:

(a)　are habitually resident in the CTA, or

(b)　are present in the UK as a result of your deportation, removal or expulsion from another country.

2.22　The CTA means the UK (England, Scotland, Wales and Northern Ireland), the Republic of Ireland, the Channel Islands and the Isle of Man.

2.23　If you are a national of any other country in the European Economic Area (EEA), you can only get HB if you:

(a)　are a worker or self-employed, or retain that status while out of work, or

---

2.18　SSI 2004/747; NISR 2005/324 reg 2(2)

2.19　HB 54,56; NIHB 51,53

2.20-25　HB 10; HB60+ 10; NIHB 10; NIHB60+ 10

(b)   are a family member of one of the above, or

(c)   have a permanent right of residence.

2.24   If you are a national of any other country, you can only get HB if you have been granted:

(a)   leave to be in the UK which allows you to have 'recourse to public funds', or

(b)   refugee status following an application you made for asylum, or

(c)   humanitarian protection, discretionary leave, or leave under the 'Destitution Domestic Violence Concession'

and you must also be habitually resident in the CTA.

2.25   The EEA means (apart from countries in the CTA) Austria, Belgium, Bulgaria, Cyprus, Czech Republic, Denmark, Estonia, Finland, France, Germany, Greece, Hungary, Iceland, Italy, Latvia, Lichtenstein, Lithuania, Luxembourg, Malta, Netherlands, Norway, Poland, Portugal, Romania, Slovakia, Slovenia, Spain, Sweden and (for HB purposes) Switzerland.

Members of religious orders

2.26   You can't get HB if you are a member of a religious order and are fully maintained by it (apart from any payments you make for your accommodation). This applies for example to monks or nuns in enclosed orders. The DWP (GM A3.257) points out that members of religious communities (as opposed to religious orders) are often eligible for HB since they frequently do paid work or retain their own possessions.

Liability to pay rent

2.27   The general rule is that to be eligible for HB you must be liable (have a legal obligation or duty) to pay rent for the home (or be treated by the authority as so liable). For the types of payment that count as or do not count as 'rent' and its meaning in HB law see paras 7.2-4 and tables 7.1 and 7.2.

The nature of liability for rent

2.28   Liability for rent arises under a tenancy, but for HB includes any kind of 'periodical payments' made in return for the right to occupy a dwelling (para 2.27). There is no requirement for a written agreement (GM A3.50): word of mouth alone may be sufficient: R v Poole BC ex p Ross. The landlord normally has a sufficient legal interest in the dwelling to grant you the letting, but circumstances can arise where a landlord does not have such an interest but nevertheless can still create a liability upon which HB is payable (CH/2959/2006 paras 21-22).

2.29   Most landlords would expect to end the agreement if a tenant does not pay and large arrears may suggest that there is no genuine liability: CH/1849/2007. But the fact that there has been no payment of the rent 'even for an extensive period, does not of itself mean there is no legal liability': [2010] UKUT 43 AAC; and nor is this necessarily implied by the fact that the rent actually changing hands is less than the rent on the tenancy agreement.

2.26   HB 9(1)(j); HB60+ 9(1)(j); NIHB 9(1)(j); NIHB60+ 9(1)(j)

2.30   It is not possible in law for you to grant a tenancy to yourself: Rye v Rye; neither can liability arise under a tenancy 'granted' to you if you already have the right to occupy that dwelling. For example, if you are one of a couple and are joint owners of a property and your partner leaves, your partner cannot 'grant' a tenancy to you as the remaining occupier.

2.31   If you are unable to act, or are aged under 18, you may have someone appointed to act for you (paras 5.5-7). If you don't and are incapable of understanding the agreement you are entering (lack capacity), this can make the agreement void under Scottish law following a 'transaction by transaction approach' to deciding legal capacity: [2012] AACR 20; but does not do so in the rest of the UK: CH/2121/2006 and [2012] UKUT 12 (AAC).

Illegal and unlawful tenancies and sub-tenancies

2.32   Sub-tenancies created in breach of a clause in the head lease not to sublet or assign the tenancy do not prevent the assignment or sub-letting from being valid between the head tenant and sub-tenant: Governors of Peabody Donation Fund v Higgins (not a HB case). Such lettings are unlawful rather than illegal and expose the head tenant to eviction for breach of the agreement. Given that there is a legal liability for rent it seems that these lettings are eligible for HB, unless it is also a letting to which paragraphs 2.40-59 apply.

2.33   An illegal letting is one in which its creation would necessarily involve committing a criminal offence. An example is where a landlord lets a dwelling knowing it to be in contravention of a Housing Act prohibition order. In contrast to unlawful contracts, illegal contracts are generally not binding and so would not be eligible for HB. Where a letting was not illegal when it was created (e.g. prior to a prohibition order) it seems likely that it remains binding until the end of the next rental period.

Treating you as liable to make payments even when you are not

2.34   If you fit one of the descriptions below (paras 2.35-39) you may be eligible for HB even though you are not liable for rent etc (so long as you meet the other conditions: table 2.1). The law says that you are 'treated as liable to make payments'.

You are the liable person's partner

2.35   If you are in a couple (or in a polygamous marriage) and only your partner is liable for rent, the authority should normally treat you as liable to make payments. For example, if your partner is the liable person and a full-time student who is not eligible for HB (para 22.11) and you are not liable for rent because your name is not on the tenancy agreement, you can nevertheless be treated as liable and therefore eligible for HB.

Former partners and others when the liable person is not paying the rent

2.36   If the liable person is not paying the rent, the authority should treat you as liable if you have to make payments in order to continue living in the home and you are:

2.27   CBA 130(1)(a); NICBA 129(1)(a); HB 8(1)(a); NIHB 8(1)(a); NIHB60+ 8(1)(a)

2.28   R v Poole BC ex p Ross, QBD 05/05/95 28 HLR 351

2.30   Rye v. Rye [1962] A.C. 496

2.32   Governors of the Peabody Donation Fund v Higgins 20/06/83 CA (1983) 1 WLR 1091, 10 HLR 82

2.35   HB 8(1)(b); HB60+ 8(1)(b); NIHB 8(1)(b); NIHB60+ 8(1)(b)

(a)   the liable person's former partner (current partners are covered instead by the rule in para 2.35); or

(b)   someone else the authority considers it reasonable to treat as liable. An example might be a son or daughter left in occupation where the tenant is now living in a care home or independent hospital.

Examples: Treated as liable to pay rent

Megan has been deserted by her partner Ffion. Although Megan is not the tenant, the landlord will allow her to remain in the property if she continues to pay the rent. The authority should treat Megan as liable if her former partner is not paying.

Logan is the son of a council tenant. He takes over responsibility for paying the rent while his father is working abroad. Logan should be treated as liable to make payments if it is reasonable to do so.

2.37   This rule helps someone who could perhaps arrange to become the tenant (but who has not done so) remain in their home. It can be used if the liable person has been absent for too long to get HB (para 3.30), or has left permanently, and a partner or other person remains. The liable person need not be an individual; they could be a company or other body (R(H) 5/05) – including, presumably, the executors of a deceased tenant. If you claim under this rule you still need to meet the requirements relating to national insurance numbers (para 5.16): [2013] UKUT 321 (AAC). The test of reasonableness does not apply to you if you are a former partner of the liable person: for you, the rule is automatic. For anyone else claiming under this rule, the test of reasonableness applies. In particular, if the only reason the liable person is not paying is that they are excluded from HB (paras 2.40-59) then it may not be reasonable to award HB to you (CSHB/606/2005).

When your rent is waived in return for work you do on the home

2.38   If your rent is waived by your landlord the authority should still treat you as liable – but only:

(a)   if the waiver is reasonable compensation for reasonable repairs or redecoration work actually carried out by you; and

(b)   for up to eight weeks in respect of any one waiver of liability.

Rent already paid or varied

2.39   If you have already paid your rent wholly or partly in advance you are nonetheless treated as liable for it over the period it is due. If your rent liability is varied during that period you are treated as liable for the revised amount due.

2.36   HB 8(1)(c); HB60+ 8(1)(c); NIHB 8(1)(c); NIHB60+ 8(1)(c)

2.38   HB 8(1)(d); HB60+ 8(1)(d); NIHB 8(1)(d); NIHB60+ 8(1)(d)

2.39   HB 8(2); HB60+ 8(2); NIHB 8(2); NIHB60+ 8(2)

Contrived lettings and other exclusions from HB

2.40 The rest of this chapter describes the circumstances in which you cannot get HB, even though you are in fact liable for rent. The law does this by saying that you are treated as not liable to make payments. The term 'contrived' does not appear in HB legislation but it is commonly used for the lettings described in para 2.59.

Non-commercial agreements

2.41 You are not eligible for HB if the agreement under which you occupy the accommodation is not on a commercial basis. In reaching its decision the authority must consider whether the agreement contains terms which are not legally enforceable. The regulations do not define what constitutes a commercial basis and how each should be decided but this has been considered by the courts and tribunals. Table 2.4 provides a summary of the case law and guidance.

Table 2.4 **Non-commercial agreements**

- *General principles in reaching a decision on commerciality:* Each case must be decided on its facts and is a matter of judgment (R(H) 1/03) but the concept is 'notoriously imprecise and difficult' (CH/2491/2007). An arrangement is non-commercial if the main basis on which it is made is not commercial even if the original purpose was commercial, so long as the reasons for the change can be identified: CH/3497/2005.

- *Relevant matters to be taken into account:* These are not limited to the financial relationship: all the terms of the agreement should be considered (R v Sutton LBC ex parte Partridge). The important factor is whether the arrangements are 'arms length' or more akin to arrangements between close relatives contributing towards their keep or household expenses: R v Sheffield HBRB ex parte Smith.

- *Sham legal agreements:* The true factual basis of the arrangements is what matters: if they indicate that the letting is a 'truly personal arrangement' then it will be non-commercial even though the written documents give the appearance of legal liability: CH/3282/2006.

- *Lettings to family members and/or people with disabilities:* A letting by a parent to a disabled child could be commercial. While a family arrangement may indicate that the letting is non-commercial it is one factor and not decisive. The fact that the landlord might not evict but accept a lower rent if HB was not awarded is not evidence that it is non-commercial but bowing to the inevitable. Proper weight should be given to all factors and focusing on one aspect only (such as care and support) is grounds for appeal (CH/296/2004). However, more recent decisions

---

2.41   HB 9(1)(a),(2); HB60+ 9(1)(a),(2); NIHB 9(1)(a),(2); NIHB60+ 9(1)(a),(2)

T2.4   R v Sutton LBC ex p Partridge QBD 04/11/94 28 HLR 315; R v Sheffield HBRB ex p Smith QBD 08/12/94 28 HLR 36;
        R v Poole HBRB ex p Ross QBD 05/05/95 28 HLR 351

have described the law as 'ill-suited to providing humane outcomes in these cases' and have sometimes found these arrangements to be non-commercial (CH/1096/2008 and CH/2491/2007).

- *Lettings to former foster children:* The DWP (HB/CTB A30/95) advised that arrangements for paying rent (e.g. when the child reaches age 18) should generally be treated as commercial.

- *Personal friendship between the parties:* Of itself this cannot turn a commercial arrangement into a non-commercial one (R v Poole BC ex parte Ross and CH/4854/2003). Nor can the fact that the claimant cared for the landlord after an accident: [2009] UKUT 13 AAC.

- *Arrangements that take into account the claimant's religion:* If an arrangement has all the characteristics of something that is non-commercial, the fact it takes into account the religious beliefs of the claimant cannot make it commercial. Nor does this fact infringe their right to freedom of religion (R(H) 8/04).

Landlord is a close relative residing in the dwelling

2.42   If your landlord is your or your partner's 'close relative' (para 2.43), and the landlord also resides in the dwelling (para 2.45), you are not eligible for HB.

2.43   A 'close relative' is:

(a)   a parent, step-parent or parent-in-law; or

(b)   a brother or sister; or

(c)   a son, son-in-law, daughter, daughter-in-law, step-son, step-daughter; or

(d)   a partner of any of the above.

2.44   The terms 'brother' and 'sister' include 'half-brothers' and 'half-sisters' ([2016] UKUT 517 (AAC)), but not 'step-brothers' or 'step-sisters'.

2.45   For your landlord to count as 'residing in' the same dwelling as you (para 2.42), it is not necessary to share all the accommodation, merely some essential living accommodation: CH/542/2006. Similarly, if you have exclusive possession of one room in a house, this does not mean that the landlord is not residing with you: CH/3656/2004. Despite the slight difference of wording, the definition of 'residing with' (para 4.29) also applies here (GM A3.238).

Renting a former joint home from an ex-partner

2.46   If you separate from your partner and your liability is to your former partner for accommodation that you both occupied when you were together then you are treated as not liable and thus not eligible for HB. This rule also applies if your liability is to your partner's former partner and is in respect of accommodation they both occupied before they separated.

2.42   HB 9(1)(b); HB60+ 9(1)(b); NIHB 9(1)(b); NIHB60+ 9(1)(b)

2.43   HB 2(1) definition: 'close relative'; HB60+ 2(1); NIHB 2(1); NIHB60+ 2(1)

2.46   HB 9(1)(c); HB60+ 9(1)(c); NIHB 9(1)(c); NIHB60+ 9(1)(c)

2.47 The rule applies if the informal shared living arrangements changed but the dwelling overall did not, for example, if you are a tenant and you form a relationship with your landlord but then revert to being a tenant. This exclusion does not constitute discrimination under the Human Rights Act: R (Painter) v Carmarthenshire County Council HBRB and [2011] UKUT 301 (AAC).

Responsibility for your landlord's child

2.48 You are not eligible for HB if you, or your partner, are responsible for the landlord's child (i.e. someone under the age of 16). The DWP (GM A3.269) emphasises that 'responsibility for a child' means more than 'cares for'.

2.49 This rule is difficult to interpret as it blurs certain established concepts so far as means-tested benefits are concerned. It appears to apply where the 'landlord' is the parent, or has adopted a child, but where the child is nevertheless considered to be part of your family for JSA(IB), IS or HB purposes. This rule has been found not to be contrary to the Human Rights Act: R v Secretary of State for Social Security, ex parte Tucker.

Certain trusts

2.50 A trust is an arrangement whereby the legal ownership (title) of property is separated from its benefits (such as the right to live in it or get an income from it). The title is held by the trustees who ensure that its benefits are delivered for use by someone else, 'the beneficiary'.

2.51 You are not eligible for HB if your landlord is a trustee of a trust of which one of the following is a trustee or a beneficiary:

(a)   you or your partner;

(b)   your or your partner's close relative (para 2.43) if the close relative 'resides with' (para 4.29) you; or

(c)   your former partner or your partner's former partner.

'Beneficiary' here means someone who could benefit from the trust by occupying the property in question: [2009] UKUT 7 (AAC).This disentitlement does not apply however where you are able to satisfy the authority that the liability was not intended to be a means of taking advantage of the HB scheme.

2.52 You are not eligible for HB if your landlord is a trustee of a trust of which your child or your partner's child is a beneficiary. Unlike in the previous paragraph, this rule has no exception.

2.47   R (Painter) v Carmarthenshire County Council HBRB & Anor [2001] EWHC Admin 308 04/05/01
           www.bailii.org/ew/cases/EWHC/Admin/2001/308.html

2.48   HB 9(1)(d); HB60+ 9(1)(d); NIHB 9(1)(d); NIHB60+ 9(1)(d)

2.49   R v Secretary of State for Social Security, ex p Tucker 08/11/01 [2001] EWCA Civ 1646
           www.bailii.org/ew/cases/EWCA/Civ/2001/1646.html

2.51   HB 9(1)(e),(3); HB60+ 9(1)(e),(3); NIHB 9(1)(e),(3); NIHB60+ 9(1)(e),(3)

2.52   HB 9(1)(f); HB60+ 9(1)(f); NIHB 9(1)(f); NIHB60+ 9(1)(f)

Renting from a company of which you are a director or an employee

2.53   You are not eligible for HB if your landlord is a company of which one of the following is a director or an employee;

(a) you or your partner;

(b) your or your partner's close relative (para 2.43) if the close relative 'resides with' (para 4.29) you; or

(c) your former partner or your partner's former partner.

This disentitlement does not apply however where you are able to satisfy the authority that the liability was not intended to be a means of taking advantage of the HB scheme. Note also that this rule does not apply if you are employed by a company and rent from a director of the company (since a director is not the company itself).

2.54   The DWP advises (GM para A3.271) that a 'company' means a registered company. This can be checked online with Companies House for any part of the UK [www].

Former non-dependants

2.55   You are not eligible for HB if:

(a) you were, at any time before the creation of the liability, a non-dependant of someone who resided in the dwelling; and

(b) that person continues to reside in the dwelling.

This disentitlement does not apply however where you are able to satisfy the authority that the liability was not intended to be a means of taking advantage of the HB scheme.

Former owners (sale and rent back or mortgage rescue)

2.56   You are not eligible for HB if:

(a) you or your partner previously owned the dwelling (including owning it on a long lease: table 7.2); and

(b) owned it within the last five years (even if you subsequently moved out and then back in: CH/3698/2008).

This disentitlement does not apply however where you are able to satisfy the authority that you or your partner could not have continued to live in the dwelling without giving up ownership. Good advice on this is given in DWP circular HB/CTB A5/2009 in the light of the increasing number of these cases, also known as 'sale and rent back' cases.

2.57   Whether you could have remained in the dwelling is a practical test based on fact – and in exceptional cases this can include your perceptions if the stress of the situation you were in forced a quick sale: R(H) 6/07. Authorities are entitled to examine why you gave up ownership and what other options you might have had, such as getting work to finance the mortgage, taking in a tenant, etc: CH/1586/2004. You are not expected to act irresponsibly

---

2.53   HB 9(1)(e),(3); HB60+ 9(1)(e),(3); NIHB 9(1)(e),(3); NIHB60+ 9(1)(e),(3)

2.54   www.gov.uk/get-information-about-a-company

2.55   HB 9(1)(g),(3); HB60+ 9(1)(g),(3); NIHB 9(1)(g),(3); NIHB60+ 9(1)(g),(3)

2.56   HB 9(1)(h),(ha); HB60+ 9(1)(h),(ha); NIHB 9(1)(h),(ha); NIHB60+ 9(1)(h),(ha)

(e.g. using a credit card to pay mortgage arrears): CH/2340/2008. You may have had no real choice if a mortgage lender would have sought possession and a housing association used a mortgage rescue scheme to buy the property and rent it back to you (GM A3.282-286).

Tied accommodation

2.58   You are not eligible for HB if your or your partner's occupation of the dwelling is a condition of employment by the landlord. The DWP advises (GM A3.291) that this test should not be taken to mean 'as a result of the employment'. A retired employee, for example, may continue to live in previously tied accommodation but this would no longer be as a condition of employment by the landlord, and so this rule would not prevent eligibility for HB.

Contrived liability

2.59   You are not eligible for HB if the authority is satisfied that your liability 'was created to take advantage of the HB scheme' (usually called a 'contrived' tenancy). The regulations do not describe what constitutes a contrived tenancy but this has been considered by the courts and tribunals. Table 2.5 provides a summary of the case law and further guidance can be found in GM paragraphs A3.310-319.

Table 2.5 **Case law on contrived liabilities**

- *Liability and taking advantage of the HB scheme:* These are separate considerations and should not be confused: CSHB/718/2002.

- *The circumstances and intentions of both parties are relevant:* The authority must consider these before reaching a conclusion that the liability is contrived. Particular consideration should be given to the consequences if HB is not paid. If it seems unlikely that the landlord will ask you to leave so that the dwelling can be re-let then this is evidence that the liability is contrived: R v Sutton HBRB ex p Keegan.

- *Letting to relatives:* Except where the liability is excluded from HB by one of the other provisions in this section (paras 2.42-58), accommodation provided by a parent to their children is not of itself evidence of a contrived liability: R v Solihull HBRB ex p Simpson.

- *Letting to people on low incomes generally:* The mere fact that you could not afford the rent cannot be taken as evidence that the liability is contrived although in extreme cases a high rent may support that contention. Before the authority can reach a conclusion that the liability is contrived there must be clear evidence that this is so; it cannot merely be inferred (Solihull case).

- *Letting to people on low incomes to make a profit:* There is no objection to landlords doing this and landlords may even organise their affairs to 'maximise the amounts

---

2.58   HB 9(1)(i); HB60+ 9(1)(i); NIHB 9(1)(i); NIHB60+ 9(1)(i)

2.59   HB 9(1)(l); HB60+ 9(1)(l); NIHB 9(1)(l); NIHB60+ 9(1)(l)

T2.5   R v Sutton HBRB ex p Keegan 15/05/92 QBD 27 HLR 92
          R v Solihull HBRB ex p Simpson 03/12/93 QBD 26 HLR 370 & 05/05/94 CA 27 HLR 41
          R v Manchester CC ex p Baragrove Properties 15/03/91 QBD 23 HLR 337

payable by HB'. In doing so 'the size of the charges and the profit [that results] are relevant [...] only in so far as they show abuse' (see next bullet): CH/39/2007.

■ *Charging higher rents to groups outside the normal rent restriction rules:* These types of arrangement may be a factor in considering whether the liability has been created to take advantage of the scheme. For example, lettings to vulnerable tenants (para 10.22); or complex arrangements designed to take advantage of specific rules such as 'exempt accommodation' (paras 10.3-8) (R v Manchester CC ex p Baragrove Properties; CH/3933/2006 and CH/136/2007).

Chapter 3 **Occupying your home**

- ■ Your home and when you can get HB there: see paras 3.1-9.
- ■ When you can get HB on two homes: see paras 3.10-15.
- ■ Moving home and when you can get HB after moving out or before moving in: see paras 3.16-28.
- ■ When you can get HB during an absence from home: see paras 3.29-56.
- ■ When you can get HB during an absence abroad: see paras 3.57-66.

Your home

3.1　　You can only get HB on a dwelling in the UK which you occupy as a home. This chapter explains the rules about this and table 3.1 gives a summary. You must also be liable for rent and meet the other conditions in chapter 2. For HB for rates in Northern Ireland, see chapter 19.

Your normal home

3.2　　Unless one of the later rules in this chapter applies to you, you can only get HB on your normal home. This is the dwelling which is 'normally occupied as a home' by:

(a) you; or

(b) you and your family (CH/2521/2002) – if you have a family (para 4.2).

3.3　　Occupying somewhere as your home has its ordinary meaning. It usually means somewhere you live. Just having the right to live there or paying rent there is not enough, and it doesn't include accommodation you occupy for a holiday or business purposes.

3.4　　If you have more than one dwelling, they are all taken into account in deciding which is your normal home, including dwellings outside the UK. This means looking at all the relevant facts including how much time you, or you and your family, spend in each of them. But a partner, child or young person is not taken into account if they have a different normal home from yours (paras 4.20-22) either in the UK or abroad (GM para A3.356). And if you do have dwellings both in the UK and abroad, deciding which is your normal home is not restricted to considering where your 'centre of interests' is (CH/1786/2005).

What is a dwelling

3.5　　A dwelling is 'any residential accommodation, whether or not consisting of the whole or part of a building and whether or not comprising separate and self-contained premises'. In other words it means just about any kind of accommodation used for living in.

3.1　　CBA 130(1)(a); NICBA 129(1)(a)

3.2　　HB 7(1); HB60+ 7(1); NIHB 7(1); NIHB60+ 7(1)

3.4　　HB 7(1),(2); HB60+ 7(1),(2); NIHB 7(1),(2); NIHB60+ 7(1),(2)

3.5　　CBA 137(1) definition: 'dwelling'; NICBA 133(1)

Short-term accommodation

3.6   Somewhere can be your normal home for just a short period. If it is, you can get HB there. This can apply if you move around a lot or are staying in a hostel, refuge, etc.

Night shelters

3.7   A night shelter may or may not count as your home. If it doesn't, you can't get HB there. There is no general rule about this. Instead, it depends on the particular facts in your case. If you are allowed to stay overnight but have to leave in the morning taking all your belongings with you, and have no right to stay in any part of the shelter or generally (in the sense that if you turn up late and it is full you will be turned away), then you don't occupy it as your home and can't get HB ([2013] UKUT 65 (AAC)).

Repairs to your normal home

3.8   If you have to stay somewhere temporary because essential repairs are being done to your normal home:

   (a)   you can get HB on your temporary home if:

   ▪   you are liable for rent there, but

   ▪   you aren't liable for rent or mortgage interest on your normal home (e.g. because your landlord has moved you out and has stopped charging rent on it, or because you own it outright or live there rent-free with relatives);

   (b)   otherwise you can only get HB on your normal home (and only if you are liable for rent there).

Students and trainees

3.9   There are further rules about which home you can get HB on if you are a student or trainee (paras 22.12-17).

Table 3.1 **Your home, two homes, moving home and absences from home**

This table summarises which home or homes you can get HB on. For further conditions and time limits (when they apply) see the paras referred to.

Your home

You can get HB on:

   ▪   your normal home (paras 3.2-7)

Or you may be able to get HB on:

   ▪   temporary accommodation while your normal home is being repaired (para 3.8)

   ▪   term-time accommodation if you are a single student or trainee (para 22.13)

3.8   HB 7(4); HB60+ 7(4); NIHB 7(4); NIHB60+ 7(4)

Two homes

You may be able to get HB on two homes if:

- you have a large family (para 3.11)
- you couldn't avoid liability for rent on your old home (para 3.21)
- you are waiting for your new home to be adapted for a disability (para 3.25)
- you are absent from your normal home because of fear of violence (para 3.43)
- you are a student or trainee in a couple (para 22.14)

Moving home

You may be able to get HB on your old home after moving out if:

- you couldn't avoid liability for rent there (para 3.21)

Or you may be able to get HB on your new home before moving in if:

- you are waiting for it to be adapted for a disability (para 3.24)
- you are waiting for local welfare assistance (para 3.26)
- you are waiting to leave hospital or a care home (para 3.28)

Absences from home

You may be able to get HB during an absence from home if:

- you are trying out a care home or independent hospital (para 3.36)
- you are staying in hospital or a care home or are receiving or providing care (para 3.40)
- you are absent because of fear of violence (para 3.42)
- you are a prisoner on remand or on bail (para 3.48)
- you are a sentenced prisoner (para 3.49)
- you are a student or trainee (para 22.15)
- you are absent for other reasons (para 3.34)

But if your absence is abroad see para 3.57.

HB on two homes

3.10 This section explains when you can get HB on two homes at the same time. In any other situation you can only get HB on one home (para 3.4).

Large families

3.11 You can get HB on two homes if your family (para 4.2) is so large that a local housing authority has housed you in both of them. There is no time limit. Any council that administers HB is a local housing authority. The DWP advises that the council must have provided the two homes for you but does not need to own them (GM para A3.660).

3.11   HB 7(6)(c); HB60+ 7(6)(c); NIHB 7(6)(c); NIHB60+ 7(6)(c)

Other rules

3.12   You may be able to get HB on two homes for a limited period if:

(a) you have moved home and could not avoid being liable for rent on your old home (para 3.21);

(b) you are waiting to move into a new home while it is being adapted for a disability (para 3.25);

(c) you are temporarily absent from your normal home because of fear of violence (para 3.43); or

(d) you are in a couple and you or your partner are a student or trainee (para 22.14).

Occupying two dwellings as one home

3.13   It is also possible to get HB on two dwellings which you occupy as one home (even if you don't meet the conditions in paras 3.11-12). This can be the case when two flats are knocked together to make one home, even if they are rented from different landlords (CH/1895/2008), or when statutory overcrowding would otherwise occur (R(H) 5/09 para 22; CH/4018/2007). The Court of Appeal has approved of similar situations in relation to JSA(IB) (SSWP v Miah reported as R(JSA) 9/03).

Getting HB on two homes

3.14   You need to tell the council you are claiming for two homes, and if HB for them is administered by different councils you need to make two claims (one for each home). If you aren't eligible for HB on two homes, you are still eligible for HB on your normal home (paras 3.2-4 and 3.17).

3.15   HB for two homes is calculated as follows:

(a) add together the two eligible rents;

(b) then make any non-dependant deductions only once;

(c) then deduct 65% of any excess income (para 6.8) only once.

This applies whether the calculation is done by one council or by two councils working together ([2011] UKUT 5 (AAC) paras 23,33). If you start or stop qualifying for HB on two homes, your HB changes on the exact day (para 17.25).

Moving home

3.16   When you move home your HB usually changes on the date of your move (table 17.3). You may also be able to get HB:

(a) on your old home after you move out if you could not avoid being liable for rent there (paras 3.20-23); or

---

3.12   HB 7(6)(a),(b),(d),(e); HB60+ 7(6)(a),(b),(d),(e); NIHB 7(6)(a),(b),(d),(e); NIHB60+ 7(6)(a),(b),(d),(e)

3.15   HB 79(2A)(b),(2B), 80(9); HB60+ 59(2A)(b),(2B), 61(9); NIHB 77(3)(b),(4), 78(10); NIHB60+ 57(3)(b),(4), 59(10)

(b)   on your new home before you move in if you are:

- waiting for adaptations for a disability (paras 3.24-25),
- waiting for local welfare assistance (paras 3.26-27), or
- waiting to leave hospital or a care home (para 3.28).

The date of your move

3.17   The date of your move means the day your normal home changes rather than the date on a letting agreement etc (R(H) 9/05), and in most cases this is straightforward. But in R(H) 9/05 a claimant aged 87 had ended her old tenancy and her family had moved her furniture and possessions into her new home. Although she was unable to move at the last moment because she was taken ill, she was held to be 'normally occupying' her new home.

Getting HB when you move home

3.18   You should tell the council about your move, and if HB for your old and new homes is administered by different councils (or you weren't on HB at your old home) you need to make a claim for your new home. To get HB after you move out (paras 3.20-23) you also need to tell the council about this.

3.19   To get HB before you move in (paras 3.24-28) you need to tell the council or make a claim (para 3.18) before the date of your move. If you make a claim but the council says you don't qualify at that stage, you should claim again within four weeks after the date of your move. Your date of claim then counts as being on the day you made the first claim. In all cases, the HB for this period can't be paid until you have moved in (and can't be paid at all if you don't move in).

Unavoidable liability for rent

3.20   You can get HB on your old home for up to four weeks after the date you move out of it if:

(a)   you have moved into a new dwelling (para 3.22) – this can include a hospital, care home or prison (paras 3.41 and 3.51);

(b)   you continue to be liable for rent on your old home; and

(c)   this liability could not reasonably have been avoided (para 3.23).

But if you left your old home because of fear of violence (para 3.45) you only have to meet conditions (b) and (c) – in other words you can qualify if you haven't got anywhere to live yet or don't want to say where it is.

3.21   You can get HB on both your old and new homes for up to four weeks after the date of your move if:

(a)   you have moved into your new home (para 3.22);

(b)   you are liable for rent on both homes; and

(c)   liability on two homes could not reasonably have been avoided (para 3.23).

3.19   HB 7(8)(b),(9); HB60+ 7(8)(b),(9); NIHB 7(8)(b),(9); NIHB60+ 7(8)(b),(9)

3.20   HB 7(7),(10); HB60+ 7(7),(10); NIHB 7(7),(10); NIHB60+ 7(7),(10)

3.21   HB 7(6)(d); HB60+ 7(6)(d); NIHB 7(6)(d); NIHB60+ 7(6)(d)

This is sometimes called the 'overlapping HB rule'. It doesn't apply if you are staying somewhere temporary while repairs are being done (para 3.8). For further details about HB on two homes see paras 3.14-15.

3.22   If you have a family (para 4.2) you only count as having moved into your new home (for the rules in paras 3.20-21) if they have moved in too; preparing it for occupation is not enough (CH/1911/2006 para 19). But this does not apply to someone who is no longer a member of your family (e.g. a partner you are separating from).

3.23   Whether your liability for rent 'could not reasonably have been avoided' is decided by looking at all the relevant facts, including any alternatives that were open to you (CH/4546/2002). For example, the council might ask whether you gave notice to your old landlord, or could have done earlier than you did. Your circumstances don't have to have been 'exceptional', but if they were this can mean you qualify (GM para A3.682).

Examples: Liable for rent on a former home

1. HB on both old and new homes ('overlapping HB')

Barnaby (already on HB) is living in privately rented accommodation. His rent is due monthly and notice of one month is due if he wishes to leave.

On Thursday 27th April 2017, Barnaby is invited to view a housing association property (in the same local authority area) which he is then offered and accepts. The housing association insists that the tenancy must start on Monday 1st May. On Friday 28th April Barnaby writes to his old landlord giving notice. The landlord insists that Barnaby must pay to the end of May. Barnaby moves in to his housing association home on Monday 1st May.

The authority accepts that Barnaby meets all the conditions for HB on both homes (para 3.21) and awards HB from Monday 1st May for the new address and until Sunday 30th May at the old address; so HB is awarded for both homes for four weeks.

2. HB on a former home

Mildred is on HB and living in housing association accommodation. Her rent is due on Mondays and notice of four weeks is due if she wishes to leave.

On Friday 30th June 2017 Mildred's brother is found to be seriously ill and Mildred decides to go as soon as possible and live in his house to look after him. She decides to give up her housing association tenancy and gives her notice in on Monday 3rd July to expire on Sunday 30th July 2017. She moves out of her housing association tenancy on Wednesday 5th July, handing the keys back the same day.

The authority accepts that Mildred meets all the conditions for HB on the address she has left (para 3.20) and awards HB on the housing association tenancy up till the end of the tenancy (covering three weeks and five days from the day she left till the end of her liability).

3.24   HB 7(8)(c)(i); HB60+ 7(8)(c)(i); NIHB 7(8)(c)(i); NIHB60+ 7(8)(c)(i);
        R (Mahmoudi) v Lewisham [2014] EWCA 284 www.bailii.org/ew//cases/EWCA/Civ/2014/284.html

Waiting for adaptations for a disability

3.24   You can get HB on your new home for up to four weeks before the date you move into it if:

   (a)   your liability for rent there has begun;

   (b)   you are waiting for it to be adapted to meet your disablement needs or those of a member of your family (para 4.2); and

   (c)   your delay in moving in is necessary and reasonable.

Adapting your new home means making it more suitable for your or your family member's disablement needs, so it can include furnishing or redecoration as well as changes to its fabric or structure (R (Mahmoudi) v Lewisham LBC).

3.25   You can get HB on both your old and new homes for up to four weeks before the date of your move if:

   (a)   you are liable for rent on both of them; and

   (b)   you meet the conditions in para 3.24 (b) and (c).

For further details about HB on two homes see paras 3.14-15.

Waiting for local welfare assistance

3.26   You can get HB on your new home for up to four weeks before the date you move into it if:

   (a)   your liability for rent there has begun;

   (b)   you are waiting for local welfare assistance (para 25.34) to help with the move or with setting up home;

   (c)   you or your partner have reached state pension credit age (para 1.24) or qualify for a working age component or disability premium (paras 12.20-32), or your family includes a child under 6 or a child or young person who qualifies for a disabled child premium (para 12.34); and

   (d)   your delay in moving in is reasonable.

3.27   You can't get HB on your old home at the same time. So if you are liable for rent on both your old and new homes, you can only get HB on whichever counts as your normal home (paras 3.4 and 3.17).

Waiting to leave hospital or a care home

3.28   You can get HB on your new home for up to four weeks before the date you move into it if:

   (a)   your liability for rent there has begun;

   (b)   you are waiting to leave hospital or a care home or independent hospital (table 7.2); and

   (c)   your delay in moving is reasonable (e.g. your stay in hospital is longer than expected).

3.25   HB 7(6)(e); HB60+ 7(6)(e); NIHB 7(6)(e); NIHB60+ 7(6)(e)

3.26   HB 7(8)(c)(ii); HB60+ 7(8)(c)(ii); NIHB 7(8)(c)(ii); NIHB60+ 7(8)(c)(ii)

3.28   HB 7(8)(c)(iii),(18); HB60+ 7(8)(c)(iii),(18); NIHB 7(8)(c)(iii),(18); NIHB60+ 7(8)(c)(iii),(18)

Absences from home

3.29   This section explains when you can get HB during an absence from your normal home (paras 3.2-6). The rules also apply to absences from another home you can get HB on (in the situations in paras 3.8, 3.11 and 22.13-14). But for absences abroad see paras 3.57-66, and for absences of a member of your family see paras 4.23-25 and 11.15.

3.30   You may be able to get HB:

(a) for up to 13 weeks during any temporary absence (paras 3.34-35); or

(b) for up to 13 weeks if you are trying out a care home or independent hospital (paras 3.36-37); or

(c) for up to 52 weeks during certain temporary absences (paras 3.38-48).

If you don't qualify, someone else in your home may be able to get HB during your absence (paras 2.34-37).

General conditions about absences

3.31   You only qualify for HB during an absence if:

(a) you intend to return to your normal home (paras 3.32);

(b) you are liable for rent there; and

(c) the part you normally occupy hasn't been rented out (by you or your landlord) to someone else.

For how the length of your absence is counted, see paras 3.53-56.

Intending to return

3.32   Whether and when you intend to return to your normal home is decided by looking at all the relevant facts, including:

(a) what you intend, rather than what a relative or official intends for you; and

(b) whether you will be able to return. Wanting to return is not enough if your return is impossible, e.g. because it is clear that you won't be able to leave hospital or a care home (CSHB/405/2005 para 30).

If you change your mind about returning, see paras 3.53-56.

Getting HB during an absence

3.33   You should tell the council if your absence is likely to affect your HB (para 17.3). And if you weren't on HB before you left your normal home (e.g. because your income was higher then) you need to make a claim.

3.29   HB 7(11)-(13),(14)-(17),(18) definition: 'main dwelling'; HB60+ 7(11)-(13),(14)-(17); NIHB 7(11)-(13),(14)-(17),(18); NIHB60+ 7(11)-(13),(14)-(17),(18)

3.31   HB 7(11)(b),(c),(13)(a),(b),(16)(a),(b); HB60+ 7(11)(b),(c),(13)(a),(b),(16)(a),(b); NIHB 7(11)(b),(c),(13)(a),(b),(16)(a),(b); NIHB60+ 7(11)(b),(c),(13)(a),(b),(16)(a),(b)

3.33   HB 88(1); HB60+ 69(1),(6)(c); NIHB 84(1); NIHB60+ 65(1),(4)(c)

Temporary absences up to 13 weeks

3.34   You can get HB on your normal home for up to 13 weeks during any temporary absence. For example you could be on holiday, working or looking for work, or a sentenced prisoner (para 3.49).

3.35   You must intend to return to your normal home (paras 3.31-32), and the time limit works in two ways:

  (a)   the maximum period for getting HB is 13 weeks; and

  (b)   your absence must be unlikely to be longer than 13 weeks (paras 3.53-56).

Trial periods in a care home or independent hospital

3.36   You can get HB on your normal home for up to 13 weeks if you are trying out a care home or independent hospital (table 7.2).

3.37   You must intend to return to your normal home (paras 3.31-32), but only if the place you are trying turns out not to suit you, and the time limit works as follows:

  (a)   the maximum period for getting HB on the place you are trying out is 13 weeks;

  (b)   if you try out more than one place, the 13 weeks starts again for each one (even if you don't return to your normal home between them);

  (c)   you don't have to say how long your absence is likely to be;

  (d)   but (a) and (b) only apply until your total absence (for these or other reasons) reaches 52 weeks.

If you decide to stay, see para 3.41.

Example: Trying out a care home and then deciding to stay there

Betella rents her home and has been on HB for a while. She goes into a care home for a six-week trial period to see if it suits her. Betella remains eligible for HB.

In the fourth week of her trial period, Betella decides that this is the care home for her and gives four weeks' notice to her former landlord. The authority is satisfied that Betella could not reasonably have avoided the liability at her old address. She remains eligible for HB for the additional four-week period.

3.34-35 HB 7(13); HB60+ 7(13); NIHB 7(13); NIHB60+ 7(13)

3.36-37 HB 2(1) definitions: 'care home', 'independent hospital', 7(11),(12),(18); HB60+ 2(1), 7(11),(12),(18); NIHB 2(1), 7(11),(12),(18); NIHB60+ 2(1), 7(11),(12),(18)

Temporary absences up to 52 weeks

3.38   You can get HB on your normal home for up to 52 weeks during a temporary absence if:

(a)   you are in hospital or a care home or receiving or providing care (paras 3.40-41);

(b)   you are absent because of fear of violence (paras 3.42-46);

(c)   you are a prisoner on remand or on bail (para 3.48); or

(d)   you are a student or trainee (para 22.15).

3.39   You must intend to return to your normal home (paras 3.31-32), and the time limit works in two ways:

(a)   the maximum period for getting HB is 52 weeks; and

(b)   your absence must be unlikely to be longer than 52 weeks, or in exceptional circumstances unlikely to be substantially longer than this (paras 3.53-56).

The DWP advises that your absence is likely to be 'substantially' longer than 52 weeks if it is likely to be longer than 15 months, and that 'exceptional circumstances' can include an unanticipated event (e.g. a relapse in hospital) that delays your return (GM para A3. 5.32).

In hospital or a care home or receiving or providing care

3.40   You can get HB on your normal home for up to 52 weeks (para 3.39) during a temporary absence if:

(a)   you are a patient in hospital or a similar institution;

(b)   you are receiving medical treatment or medically approved care or convalescence;

(c)   your absence is because your partner or child is receiving medical treatment or medically approved convalescence;

(d)   you are providing medically approved care to someone;

(e)   your absence is to care for a child whose parent or guardian is away from their home to receive medical treatment or medically approved care; or

(f)   you are receiving care in a care home or independent hospital (table 7.2), e.g. during a period of respite care (but for trial periods see paras 3.36-37).

3.41   If you move into any of the above accommodation (rather than going there temporarily), you may be able to get HB on your old home for up to four weeks after you move (para 3.20). If you qualify for HB during a trial period (paras 3.36-37) this means up to four weeks after the trial period ends (R(H) 4/06). When you leave hospital or a care home, you may be able to get HB on your new home for up to four weeks before you move in (para 3.28).

3.38-39   HB 7(16)(a)-(c),(d)(i),(17); HB60+ HB 7(16)(a)-(c),(d)(i),(17); NIHB HB 7(16)(a)-(c),(d)(i),(17); NIHB60+ HB 7(16)(a)-(c),(d)(i),(17)

3.40   HB 2(1) definitions: 'care home', 'independent hospital', 7(16)(c)(ii),(iii),(v)-(vii),(ix),(17),(18);
        HB60+ 2(1), 7(16)(c)(ii),(iii),(v)-(vii),(ix),(17),(18);
        NIHB 2(1), 7(16)(c)(ii),(iii),(v)-(vii),(ix),(17),(18); NIHB60+ 2(1), 7(16)(c)(ii),(iii),(v)-(vii),(ix),(17),(18)

3.41   HB 7(7),(8)(c)(iii); HB60+ 7(7),(8)(c)(iii); NIHB 7(7),(8)(c)(iii); NIHB60+ 7(7),(8)(c)(iii)

Fear of violence

3.42   You can get HB on your normal home for up to 52 weeks (para 3.39) if you are temporarily absent from it because of fear of violence (paras 3.45-46).

3.43   You can get HB on both your normal home and your temporary home for up to 52 weeks (para 3.39) if:

(a) you are temporarily absent from your normal home because of fear of violence (paras 3.45-46);

(b) you are liable for rent on both homes; and

(c) awarding HB on both of them is reasonable.

For further details about HB on two homes see paras 3.14-15.

3.44   The rule in para 3.43 works differently if:

(a) you get UC towards your rent or other housing costs on one home (either your normal home or your temporary home); and

(b) the other one is supported accommodation (para 2.13).

In this case you can only get HB on the supported accommodation for up to 52 weeks, and only if awarding both HB and UC for housing costs is reasonable.

3.45   The above rules (and the rule in para 3.64) only apply if you have left your normal home, and remain absent from it, because of:

(a) fear of violence happening in it, whoever this would be from (including someone not living there); or

(b) fear of violence happening outside it, but in this case only if it would be from someone who was a member of your family (para 4.2).

In either case, this could be fear of violence towards you or another member of your family. No violence needs to have actually happened, but the council can take account of whether your fear of it was and is 'reasonably held' (CH/1237/2004 para 18). If your fear of violence doesn't met these conditions, you can get HB for up to 13 weeks during a temporary absence (paras 3.34-35).

3.46   The rules in paras 3.42-44 (and para 3.64) only apply if you intend to return to your normal home (para 3.32). It is enough if you intend to return once it becomes safe to do so, e.g. if you are taking steps to remove the person you fear the violence from.

3.47   If you don't intend to return, you can get:

(a) HB on your new home even if it is somewhere short-term (so long as it counts as your normal home: paras 3.2-7); and

(b) HB for up to four weeks on the home you have left if you could not avoid being liable for rent there (paras 3.20-23).

3.42   HB 7(16)(c)(x),(17); HB60+ 7(16)(c)(x),(17); NIHB 7(16)(c)(x),(17); NIHB60+ 7(16)(c)(x),(17)

3.43   HB 7(6)(a); HB60+ 7(6)(a); NIHB 7(6)(a); NIHB60+ 7(6)(a)

3.44   HB 7(6)(a); HB60+ 7(6)(a); NIHB 7(6)(a); NIHB60+ 7(6)(a)

3.45-46 HB 7(6)(a),(16)(c)(x); HB60+ 7(6)(a),(16)(c)(x); NIHB 7(6)(a),(16)(c)(x); NIHB60+ 7(6)(a),(16)(c)(x)

Both (a) and (b) apply whether or not your fear of violence meets the conditions in para 3.45. If it does meet those conditions, (b) applies even if you haven't got anywhere to live yet.

Examples: Fear of violence

1. Morgana gets HB on her council flat. Her partner lives with her and he begins to threaten her with violence. She goes to stay in a refuge, but she intends to return to her flat and has got her parents to tell her ex-partner to leave.

She can get HB for up to 52 weeks on her flat because she intends to return. She can also get HB on the refuge (para 3.43).

2. After four months in the refuge, Morgana goes to stay with her parents. She still intends to return to her flat and her solicitor has written to her ex-partner instructing him to leave. A month after that she decides she won't return to her flat.

She can continue to get HB on her flat until she decides not to return to it (paras 3.43 and 3.56).

Prisoners on remand or on bail

3.48   You can get HB on your normal home for up to 52 weeks (para 3.39) during a temporary absence if you are a prisoner:

(a)   on remand; or

(b)   bailed to live in a bail or probation hostel (table 7.2) or anywhere else (e.g. a relative's home).

This means most prisoners on remand can get HB. But for prisoners on bail the time limit includes time you spent in prison.

Sentenced prisoners

3.49   You can get HB on your normal home for up to 13 weeks (paras 3.34-35) during a temporary absence if you are serving a sentence in prison, hospital or any other kind of custody. Your absence must be unlikely to be longer than 13 weeks, and this time limit is strict (CH/1986/2009). But it takes account of factors that affect your release, including:

(a)   any remission you qualify for. So you are likely to meet the time limit if your sentence is less than six months, or ten months if you are entitled to home detention curfew;

(b)   any likelihood of release on parole. If a parole hearing is delayed, the date it should take place is more relevant than when it actually takes place (CH/2638/2006).

For DWP guidance see GM paras A3.512-518.

3.47   HB 7(1),(2),(6)(d),(7),(10); HB60+ 7(1),(2),(6)(d),(7),(10); NIHB 7(1),(2),(6)(d),(7),(10); NIHB60+ 7(1),(2),(6)(d),(7),(10)

3.48   HB 7(16)(c)(i),(16A),(17); HB60+ 7(16)(c)(i),(16A),(17); NIHB 7(16)(c)(i),(16A),(17); NIHB60+ 7(16)(c)(i),(16A),(17)

3.49   HB 7(13); HB60+ 7(13); NIHB 7(13); NIHB60+ 7(13)

3.50   If you were on remand before you were sentenced:

(a)   para 3.48 applies until you are sentenced, so if you qualified for HB while on remand you don't have to pay it back;

(b)   para 3.49 applies from when you are sentenced, but you only qualify if your total absence from home (including your time on remand) is unlikely to be longer than 13 weeks (CH/499/2006).

3.51   If your absence is likely to be longer than 13 weeks, you may be able to get HB on your old home for up to four weeks after you move out of it (para 3.20). If you qualified for HB while on remand, this means up to four weeks after you are sentenced.

Example: Remand and conviction

Gabriel has been getting HB for a while. He is then arrested and detained on remand pending his trial. The authority should assume that Gabriel will be absent for no more than 52 weeks. He therefore remains eligible for HB.

Fifteen weeks later Gabriel is tried, found guilty, and sentenced to a term of one year's imprisonment. Although he will serve only six months in prison (after remission), and although the 15 weeks he has been on remand count towards this, his total absence from home now exceeds 13 weeks. Gabriel's eligibility for HB under the temporary absence rule ends. The fact that he has been sentenced is a change in his circumstances (chapter 17). (But the HB he was awarded for his 15 weeks on remand was nonetheless correctly paid.) If, however, the necessary conditions are met (paras 3.20 and 3.51) Gabriel may be entitled to a further four weeks of HB.

Prisoners on temporary release

3.52   If you are on temporary release from prison or a bail or probation hostel, you count as still being absent from your normal home. The rules in paras 3.48-51 apply as though you were still in prison or the hostel.

Counting the length of your absence

3.53   The time limits for each kind of absence are given earlier throughout this (and the following) sections:

(a)   for all absences, there is a maximum period for which you can get HB;

(b)   except for trial periods in a care home or independent hospital, there is also a time limit for the likely length of your absence.

3.54   The time limits refer to absences which are continuous (R v Penwith HBRB ex parte Burt). Your absence begins when you leave your normal home and ends when you return to it. If you go away again, this starts a new absence with a new time limit. The DWP advises that returning for just a few hours is not enough (so your absences before and after count as one absence) and returning for at least 24 hours can be enough (GM para A3.460). But if you go

---

3.51   HB 7(7); HB60+ 7(7); NIHB 7(7); NIHB60+ 7(7)

3.52   HB 7(14)-(15); HB60+ 7(14)-(15); NIHB 7(14)-(15); NIHB60+ 7(14)-(15)

3.54   R v Penwith DC HBRB ex p Burt 26/02/90 QBD 22 HLR 292

away frequently and only return for short periods, your home could stop counting as your normal home so your HB could stop. And if you are a prisoner on temporary release you still count as absent (para 3.52).

Decisions about your absence

3.55   The council decides whether you qualify for HB when you leave your normal home and also during your absence (CH/1237/2004 para 12). The DWP advises councils to check this regularly in appropriate cases (GM para A3.631).

3.56   If you are awarded HB, changes in your intention to return (paras 3.31-32), or in the likely length of your absence (CH/1237/2004 para 12), count as changes of circumstances. So your HB stops if and when:

(a)   you stop intending to return to your normal home or being able to; or

(b)   your absence (unless you are trying out a care home or independent hospital) becomes likely to be longer than the time limit; or

(c)   you reach the time limit for getting HB.

But HB for the period before then counts as properly paid, so you don't have to repay it (GM para A3. 632).

Examples: Getting a job and counting the length of an absence

1. Mordred gets HB on a privately rented flat. He gets a contract to work for one term as a cleaner at a school. It is too far for him to commute and he stays rent-free with a friend for the whole of the term.

He can get HB on his flat because his absence is unlikely to be longer than 13 weeks (para 3.34), but his new income is taken into account.

2. Mordred (who still qualifies for HB) gets a year's contract to work at the school. He goes back to his flat for each of the school holidays.

He can continue to get HB on his flat because each absence is less than 13 weeks (para 3.54).

3. Mordred then gets a permanent contract at the school. He keeps his flat on, but removes most of his possessions from it and stops going back in the holidays.

He stops qualifying for HB on his flat because his absence is now likely to be longer than 13 weeks. Even if he returns occasionally to the flat, it is unlikely to count as his normal home so he can't get HB there (paras 3.54-56).

Absences abroad

3.57   This section explains when you can get HB on your normal home (paras 3.2-6) during an absence abroad. The rules also apply to getting HB on another home during an absence abroad (in the situations in paras 3.8, 3.11 and 22.13-14). But for absences of a family member see paras 4.23-25 and 11.15.

3.58   This rules in this section apply only to absences from Great Britain that began after 27th July 2016 or, in Northern Ireland, absences from Northern Ireland that began after 29th January 2017. Absences that began earlier fall within the rules in paras 3.29-56.

3.59   During a temporary absence abroad, you may be able to get HB:

(a)   for up to four weeks (paras 3.60-61); or

(b)   for up to eight weeks following someone's death (3.62-63); or

(c)   for up to 26 weeks in certain situations (paras 3.64-65).

In each case you must intend to return to your normal home and must meet the other conditions in paras 3.31-33.

Absences abroad for up to four weeks

3.60   You can get HB on your normal home for up to four weeks during a temporary absence abroad if:

(a)   you are providing medically approved care to someone;

(b)   your absence is to care for a child whose parent or guardian is away from their home to receive medical treatment or medically approved care;

(c)   you are receiving care in a care home or independent hospital, e.g. during period of respite care (but if you are receiving care somewhere else see paras 3.64-65);

(d)   you are a prisoner on remand or on bail;

(e)   you are a student or trainee (para 22.15); or

(f)   you are absent for any other reason, e.g. on holiday, working or looking for work.

'Care home', 'independent hospital', 'on remand' and 'on bail' aren't defined in HB law for countries outside the UK. It would therefore be reasonable to interpret them in an appropriate way.

3.57   HB 7(13C)-(13G),(16),(16A),(17C),(17D),(18) definition: 'main dwelling'; HB60+ 7(13C)-(13G),(16),(16A),(17C),(17D),(18); NIHB 7(13C)-(13G),(16),(17C),(17D),(18); NIHB60+ HB 7(13C)-(13G),(16),(16A),(17C),(17D),(18)

3.58   SI 2016/624; NISR 2017/1 reg 5

3.61   You must intend to return to your normal home (paras 3.31-32), and the time limit works in two ways:

  (a)   the maximum period for getting HB is four weeks; and

  (b)   your absence must be unlikely to be longer than four weeks, or:

  ▪   in exceptional circumstances, and

  ▪   only if your absence falls within para 3.60(a)-(e),

  is unlikely to be substantially longer than this (paras 3.39 and 3.53-56).

Absences abroad for up to eight weeks

3.62   You can get HB on your normal home for up to eight weeks during a temporary absence abroad if your absence is in connection with the death of:

  (a)   your partner;

  (b)   a child or young person you are responsible for; or

  (c)   a close relative (para 2.43) of you or one of the above;

and it would be unreasonable to expect you to return within the first four weeks.

3.63   You must intend to return to your normal home (paras 3.31-32), and the time limit works in two ways:

  (a)   the maximum period for getting HB is eight weeks; and

  (b)   your absence must be unlikely to be longer than this (paras 3.39 and 3.53-56).

Absences abroad for up to 26 weeks

3.64   You can get HB on your normal home for up to 26 weeks during a temporary absence abroad if:

  (a)   you are a patient in hospital or similar institution;

  (b)   you are receiving medical treatment or medically approved care or convalescence;

  (c)   you are absent because of fear of violence (paras 3.45-46);

  (d)   you are a member of HM armed forces (regular or reserve) posted overseas to perform your duties;

  (e)   you are a mariner with a UK contract of employment; or

  (f)   you are a continental shelf worker in UK, EU or Norwegian waters.

3.61   HB 7(13C)-(13G),(16)(c)(i),(iv)-(vi),(viii),(ix),(d)(iii),(16A),(17D),(18);
         NIHB 7(13C)-(13G),(16)(c)(i),(iv)-(vi),(viii),(ix),(d)(iii),(16A),(17D),(18)
         HB60+ HB 7(13C)-(13G),(16)(c)(i),(iv)-(vi),(viii),(ix),(d)(iii),(16A),(17D),(18);
         NIHB60+ HB60+ HB 7(13C)-(13G),(16)(c)(i),(iv)-(vi),(viii),(ix),(d)(iii),(16A),(17D),(18)

3.62-63 HB 7(13C),(13E); HB60+ 7(13C),(13E); NIHB 7(13C),(13E); NIHB60+ 7(13C),(13E)

3.64-65 HB 7(13A),(13B),(17A),(17B); HB60+ 7(13A),(13B),(17A),(17B);
         NIHB 7(13A),(13B),(17A),(17B); NIHB60+ 7(13A),(13B),(17A),(17B)

3.65 You must intend to return to your normal home (paras 3.31-32), and the time limit works in two ways:

(a) the maximum period for getting HB is 26 weeks; and

(b) your absence must be unlikely to be longer than 26 weeks, or:

- ■ in exceptional circumstances, and

- ■ only if your absence falls within para 3.64(a)-(d),

unlikely to be substantially longer than this (paras 3.39 and 3.53-56).

Absences partly abroad

3.66 If only part of your absence from your normal home is abroad:

(a) the rules about absences in Great Britain only apply while you are in Great Britain, but their time limits continue to run while you are abroad;

(b) the rules about absences abroad only apply while you are abroad, and their time limits only run while you are abroad;

(c) but if the time limit for your absence abroad runs out while you are abroad, you can't get HB (even if you return to Great Britain) until you return to your normal home or to a new normal home in Great Britain.

Example: An absence partly abroad

Atilla gets HB in Great Britain. He leaves his home because his partner has been violent to him. He stays with relatives in Great Britain for ten weeks, then with his parents abroad for 30 weeks, then with his relatives in Great Britain for ten weeks. Then he returns to his home, which he has intended to do throughout his absence.

While he is staying with relatives in Great Britain, he can get HB (para 3.42). And while he is staying with his parents abroad, he can get HB (para 3.64). He can't get HB during the remainder of his absence abroad, nor during his subsequent stay with his relatives in Great Britain (para 3.66). But he can claim HB again when he returns to his home.

Chapter 4 **The people in your home**

- Your family: see paras 4.2-3.
- Couples: see paras 4.4-13.
- Children and young persons: see paras 4.14-19.
- Household membership: see paras 4.20-25.
- Non-dependants: see paras 4.26-32.
- Carers, lodgers, joint tenants and others: see paras 4.33-50.

4.1 This chapter explains how the people in your home affect your HB. They are divided into:

(a) you and your family; and

(b) other people, including foster children, non-dependants, carers, lodgers and joint tenants.

Your family

4.2 For HB purposes, your 'family' does not always mean the same as in day-to-day life. It means only the following members of your household:

(a) your partner if you are in a couple (or partners in a polygamous marriage); and/or

(b) each child or young person you or your partner are responsible for.

Table 4.1 gives a summary of the terminology.

4.3 You and the members of your family are included when the council decides your applicable amount (para 12.3) and the size of accommodation you need (para 11.10). And your partner's income and capital is included with yours (paras 13.2 and 15.2).

Table 4.1 **Family terminology**

Family

Your HB is based on you and the following members of your 'family':

- your partner if you are in a couple (or partners in a polygamous marriage); and/or
- each child or young person you or your partner are responsible for.

Single claimant

You are a 'single claimant' if you do not have a partner, and are not responsible for any children or young persons.

4.2   CBA 137(1) definition: 'family'; NICBA 133(1)

Lone parent

You are a 'lone parent' if you do not have a partner, and are responsible for one or more children or young persons.

Couple

You are a 'couple' if you are two people who are married or in a civil partnership or living together as a couple (see paras 4.4-13), whether or not you are responsible for any children or young persons.

Polygamous marriage

You are in a 'polygamous marriage' if you (or your husband or wife) are married to more than one person under the law of a country that permits this, whether or not you are responsible for any children or young persons.

Claimant and partner

If you are in a couple or polygamous marriage, only one of you is the 'claimant' (para 5.3). The other one (or each of the others) is your 'partner'.

Child and young person

A 'child' is someone under the age of 16. A 'young person' is someone aged 16 to 19 who is in or has recently left secondary education or approved training (para 4.16 and table 4.2).

Examples: Families and other occupiers

1. Laurel and Oliver are a married couple who rent their home. They have two daughters aged 15 and 21 living with them, a foster son aged 14, and a lodger who rents a room from them. Laurel claims HB.

Laurel is the claimant, with Oliver as her partner. Oliver and the younger daughter are the members of Laurel's family (para 4.2). The older daughter is Laurel's non-dependant (para 4.26). Their foster son and lodger are not included in their family and are not non-dependants (table 4.4).

2. Stanley and Hardeep are living together as a couple and rent their home. Hardeep's son aged 7 lives with them and so does Hardeep's adult sister. Stanley claims HB.

Stanley is the claimant, with Hardeep as his partner. Hardeep and his son are the members of Stanley's family. Hardeep's sister is Stanley's non-dependant.

Couples

4.4   This section explains who counts as a couple. If you are in a couple your partner is a member of your family (paras 4.2-3). If you are in a polygamous marriage (table 4.1) you don't count as a couple but your partners are included in the same way.

T4.1   CBA 137(1) – defs: 'child', 'couple', 'family'; NICBA 133(1); HB 2(1) – defs: 'child', 'claimant', 'couple', 'lone parent', 'partner', 'polygamous marriage', 'single claimant', 19; HB60+ 2(1), 19; NIHB 2(1), 17; NIHB60+ 2(1), 17

4.5 You are a couple for HB purposes if you are two people who are:

(a) married or in a civil partnership; or

(b) living together as though you were married or in a civil partnership (paras 4.8-12).

You must also be members of the same household (paras 4.20-22) – whether you are married/civil partners (CIS/72/1994) or living together ([2004] UKUT 17 (AAC)). If your partner is temporarily absent see paras 4.23-25.

4.6 If your relationship has ended, you are no longer a couple if you now maintain separate households. In deciding this, your shared understanding that your relationship has ended and your actual living arrangements are more important than whether you still share responsibilities and financial arrangements (CIS/72/1994), but by itself a shared understanding may not be enough if you are still married/civil partners (CIS/2900/1998).

4.7 Someone who no longer counts as your partner (paras 4.5 and 4.25) is not included in your applicable amount. Their income and capital is not included with yours, but income you receive from them is counted as maintenance (table 13.6). If they still live in your dwelling they fall within one of the other descriptions in this chapter (for example they might be your joint tenant or a non-dependant) and the effect on your HB follows from that.

Living together as a couple

4.8 The law doesn't give a fixed definition of:

(a) living together as though you were a married couple, or

(b) living together as though you were civil partners;

except to say that these are decided in the same way.

4.9 The decision about this is made by looking at:

(a) your purpose in living together (Crake and Butterworth v the Supplementary Benefits Commission); and

(b) (if your purpose is unclear) your relationship and living arrangements.

For example, living together for 'care, companionship and mutual convenience' doesn't necessarily mean you are a couple (R(SB) 35/85). The later sections of this chapter illustrate the other ways in which two people can live in the same dwelling.

4.10 What matters is your relationship as a whole (R(SB) 7/81), taking account of the following factors (Crake case; [2013] UKUT 505 (AAC)):

(a) whether you share the same household;

(b) the emotional element of your relationship;

(c) whether you publicly acknowledge you are a couple;

(d) the stability of your relationship;

(e) your financial arrangements;

(f) whether you have a sexual relationship;

(g) whether you share responsibility for a child.

4.5   CBA 137(1) definition: 'couple'; NICBA 133(1); HB 2(1) definition: 'couple'; HB60+ 2(1); NIHB 2(1); NIHB60+ 2(1)

4.8   CBA 137(1) definition: 'couple', (1A); NICBA 133(1),(1A)

4.9   Crake and Butterworth v SBC 21/07/80 QBD [1982] All ER 498

4.11   The factors in para 4.10 can have different importance in different situations. None of them is conclusive by itself (GM C1 annex A para A1.02) unless you do not share a household (paras 4.20-24). But (b) and (c) were emphasised in [2014] UKUT 17 (AAC), which held that a 'committed loving relationship must be established and publicly acknowledged' (since marriage and civil partnership are a public commitment). In that case the parties' denial that they had an emotional relationship 'itself seriously undermined the notion that there is such a relationship'.

4.12   Detailed advice about living together cases is in volume 3 ch 11 of the DWP Decision Maker's Guide [www]. Guidance on the questions councils should ask is in GM C1 annex A paras A1.07-10.

DWP decisions about couples

4.13   If you have claimed a passport benefit (para 1.9) the council is likely to accept the DWP's decision about whether you are a couple. But:

(a)   if the DWP decided you are in a couple, the council must make its own decision about this if you say the DWP is wrong (R(H) 9/04);

(b)   if the DWP awarded you a passport benefit on the basis that you aren't in a couple, the council should accept this unless it has evidence of fraud which the DWP is unaware of and hasn't considered (CH/4014/2007).

Children and young persons

4.14   This section explains who counts as a child or young person and when they are included in your family.

4.15   A 'child' means someone who is aged under 16.

4.16   A 'young person' means someone who meets all the following conditions:

(a)   they are aged 16 or more but under 20;

(b)   they meet the conditions for child benefit to be paid for them (table 4.2) – in practice it is almost always enough if child benefit is actually being paid for them;

(c)   they are not a care leaver aged 16 or 17 (paras 2.15-18); and

(d)   they are not themself on JSA(IB), ESA(IR), IS or UC.

4.17   A child or young person is included in your family (paras 4.2-3) if:

(a)   you or your partner are responsible for them – in other words they normally live with you (paras 4.18-19); and

(b)   they do not fall within any of the exceptions in table 4.3.

They must also be a member of your household (paras 4.20-22) – but this is usually the case if they meet the above conditions. If a child or young person is temporarily absent, see paras 4.23-25.

4.12   www.gov.uk/government/publications/decision-makers-guide-vol-3-subjects-common-to-all-benefits-staff-guide

4.15   CBA 137(1) definition: 'child'; NICBA 133(1); HB 2(1) definition: 'child'; HB60+ 2(1); NIHB 2(1); NIHB60+ 2(1)

4.16   HB 19; HB60+ 19; NIHB 17; NIHB60+ 17

4.17   CBA 137(1) definition: 'family'; NICBA 133(1)

Responsibility for a child or young person

4.18 You are 'responsible' for a child or young person if they are 'normally living' with you. This is usually straightforward. For example they could be your son or daughter, adopted by you, a step-child, a grandchild, or any other child or young person (whether related to you or not); so long as they normally live with you.

4.19 Each child or young person can only be the responsibility of one person (or one couple) at any one time. This is the person they 'normally' live with, whether or not that person gets child benefit for them. But if this is unclear, or they spend equal time in different households (e.g. when parents have separated), they are the responsibility of:

(a) the person who gets child benefit for them; or

(b) if no-one gets child benefit, the person who has claimed it for them; or

(c) if no-one has claimed it (or more than one person has), the person who has 'primary responsibility' for them.

See table 4.3(e) for children and young persons who do not normally live with you.

Table 4.2 **Who is a young person**

Someone aged 16 or more but under 20 is a 'young person' (para 4.16) during any or all of the following periods (the periods in which child benefit can be paid for them):

(a) Until the 31st August following their 16th birthday (in all cases, whether or not they are in education, training or work).

(b) While they are undertaking a course of education which:

- is not above GCE A level or equivalent (national standard level 3) [www]; and

- takes up more than 12 hours per week on average during term-time of tuition, practical work, supervised study or taking examinations; and

- they began before their 19th birthday.

(c) While they are between two courses which meet the above conditions. But this only applies if they are enrolled on and actually start the second course.

(d) While they are undertaking approved training which is not provided under an employment contract. This includes many kinds of employment preparation course etc [www].

(e) From when they leave the above education or training until the last day of August, November, February or May, whichever comes first. This is called the 'child benefit terminal date'.

4.18   HB 20(1); HB60+ 20(1); NIHB 18(1); NIHB60+ 18(1)

4.19   HB 20(2),(3); HB60+ 20(2),(3); NIHB 18(2),(3); NIHB60+ 18(2),(3)

T4.2   HB 19; HB60+ 19; NIHB 17; NIHB60+ 17
       https//www.gov.uk/what-different-qualification-levels-mean
       www.hmrc.gov.uk/manuals/ccmmanual/ccm18035.htm

(f)   If they are aged 16 or 17, from when they leave the above education or training until the end of the 20th whole week after that. This is called the 'child benefit extension period'. But it only applies if:

- they are not in remunerative work; and
- they are registered for work, education or training with the Careers Service or Connexions Service; and
- an application is made, within three months of the end of the education or training, for child benefit to continue during this period.

For exceptions, see para 4.16 and table 4.3.

Table 4.3 Children and young persons who are not included in your family

The following are not included in your family (para 4.17), your applicable amount (para 12.3), or the 'size criteria' (the size of accommodation you need: paras 11.10 and 11.13).

Fostering and adoption

Fostering is also called 'boarding out' or 'kinship care'.

(a)   A child or young person who is placed with you or your partner as a foster child or prior to adoption.

- But they can affect the size criteria (paras 11.21-22).
- And they are included in your family, your applicable amount and the size criteria when you actually adopt them – if they normally live with you (paras 4.17-19).

(b)   A child or young person who is placed with someone else as a foster child or prior to adoption.

Local authority care

This is also called 'being looked after by a local authority'.

(c)   A child or young person who is in local authority care and is not living with you.

- But they are included in your family, your applicable amount and the size criteria in any benefit week in which they live with you for part or all of that week, if it is reasonable to do so – e.g. if they are visiting you under local authority supervision (GM paras C1.120, C1.150).

T4.3(a)   HB 21(3),(6); HB60+ 21(3),(6); NIHB 19(3),(6); NIHB60+ 19(3),(6)

T4.3(b)   HB 21(4)(b),(c); HB60+ 21(4)(b)(c); NIHB 19(4)(b),(c); NIHB60+ 19(4)(b)(c)

T4.3(c)   HB 21(4)(a),(5),(6); HB60+ 21(4)(a),(5),(6); NIHB 19(4)(a),(5),(6); NIHB60+19(4)(a),(5),(6)

Living with you but not a young person

(d) Someone aged 16 or more who lives with you but doesn't count (or no longer counts) as a young person (para 4.16 and table 4.2).

- But they usually count as a non-dependant (para 4.26).
- And they are included in the size criteria (para 11.10(b),(e)).

Not normally living with you

(e) A child or young person who doesn't live with you, or doesn't normally live with you (para 4.19), even if they spend some time with you.*

- But they are included in your family, your applicable amount and the size criteria if they are only temporarily absent (para 4.24).
- And if they normally live with another occupier of your dwelling, see paras 4.32, 4.39, 4.46 and 4.48-49.

* Exclusion from applicable amount: [2013] UKUT 642 (AAC), [2014] UKUT 223 (AAC);
from social sector size criteria: [2015] UKUT 34 (AAC);
from private sector size criteria: R v Swale HBRB ex parte Marchant, [2010] UKUT 208 (AAC).

Household membership

4.20 Someone can only be included in your family if you are members of the same 'household' (paras 4.5 and 4.17). Other HB rules also refer to household membership (e.g. about joint tenants: para 4.45).

4.21 Rather than being defined in the law, a household has its ordinary meaning. It means a domestic arrangement involving two or more people who live together as a unit (R(IS) 1/99), even when they have a reasonable level of independence and self-sufficiency (R(SB) 8/85). It requires a settled course of daily living rather than visits from time to time (R(F) 2/81). And a person can't be a member of two or more households at the same time (R(SB) 8/85).

4.22 You are not members of the same household if you have:

(a) separate homes in different dwellings (R(SB) 4/83); or

(b) separate households within the same dwelling (CIS/072/1994).

So if you keep your eating, cooking, food storage, finances (including paying your housing costs), living space and family life separate, you are unlikely to be members of the same household.

T4.3(d)   HB 19; HB60+ 19; NIHB 17; NIHB60+ 17

T4.3(e)   HB 20; HB60+ 20; NIHB 18; NIHB60+ 18

T4.3(*)   R v Swale HBRB ex p Marchant 9/11/99 CA 32 HLR 856

4.20   CBA 137(1) definition: 'family'; NICBA 133(1)

Absences of family members

4.23   Paras 4.24-25 explain the rules about absences of family members. Different rules apply if you (the claimant) are absent from your home (para 3.29) or a non-dependant is (para 4.31).

4.24   A partner, child or young person who is temporarily living away from you continues to be included in your household and in your family. So they are included in your applicable amount, and normally included when the council decides the size of accommodation you need (paras 11.10-11). They could be on holiday, working or looking for work, studying or training (e.g. a child/young person at boarding school or a partner taking a course), in hospital or receiving or providing care, in prison, and so on.

4.25   But they stop being included if:

(a)   they don't intend to resume living with you (this is usually looked at in the same way as in para 3.32); or

(b)   their absence is likely to be longer than 52 weeks, unless there are exceptional circumstances and it is unlikely to be substantially longer than this.

'Exceptional circumstances' includes being in hospital and other situations where they have no control over the length of their absence. 'Substantially' longer than 52 weeks is likely to mean longer than 15 months (GM para A3.532).

Non-dependants

4.26   A 'non-dependant' is someone who:

(a)   normally resides with you (paras 4.29-31); and

(b)   does not fall within any of the exceptions in table 4.4.

For example, an adult daughter, son, relative or friend is usually a non-dependant if they live with you on a non-commercial basis. (See also paras 4.41 and 4.47 for special cases.)

4.27   If you have one or more non-dependants you may get less HB – this is called a non-dependant deduction (para 6.9 and tables 6.3 and 6.4). Non-dependants are not included in your applicable amount, but they are included when the council decides the size of accommodation you need (para 11.10).

4.28   Non-dependants can't get HB themselves (paras 2.27 and 2.40). But they may be able to get HB if they take over paying your rent because you aren't paying it (paras 2.36-37).

4.24   HB 21(1); HB60+ 21(1); NIHB 19(1); NIHB60+ 19(1)

4.25   HB 21(2); HB60+ 21(2); NIHB 19(2); NIHB60+ 19(2)

4.26   HB 3; HB60+ 3; NIHB 3; NIHB60+ 3

Normally residing with you

4.29   Someone is only a non-dependant if they 'normally reside' with you (or you 'normally reside' with them). Paras 4.30-31 give the two parts to this rule.

4.30   They must actually share some accommodation with you. Sharing just a bathroom, toilet or communal area is not enough. They must share accommodation beyond that, e.g. a kitchen or living room. (Communal areas mean halls, corridors, stairways, etc: para 8.53.)

4.31   You must also have the sort of relationship that means you 'normally reside' with each other in the ordinary sense (Khadim v Brent LBC). For example:

(a)   a temporary visitor is not a non-dependant (CH/4004/2004), unless and until residing with you becomes the normal arrangement (CH/3935/2007);

(b)   a short absence (e.g. a holiday) is unlikely to stop someone counting as a non-dependant.

For sons and daughters who are absent in the armed forces, see table 6.3 and para 11.15.

If a non-dependant has a family of their own

4.32   If your non-dependant has their own family, each of them counts as your non-dependant (paras 4.27-28) if they normally reside with you. But:

(a)   there is only one deduction for a non-dependant couple instead of two (para 6.18);

(b)   there is no deduction for any non-dependants aged under 18 (or for many others: para 6.11 and table 6.3);

(c)   a non-dependant's child or young person counts as a member of your own family (instead of being a non-dependant) if they meet the conditions for this (paras 4.14-19).

Example: Three generations living together

■   Gloria's daughter aged 15 lives with her, as does the daughter's baby. Gloria gets child benefit for them both. The council decides that Gloria is responsible for them both, and includes both in Gloria's family (and thus in her applicable amount).

■   Later, (after leaving school) the daughter claims income support for herself. The council decides that the daughter and baby now form a separate family, and so excludes them from Gloria's family (and applicable amount).

In both cases, the daughter and baby are included in deciding the size of accommodation Gloria needs. In the second situation the daughter and baby are Gloria's non-dependants (paras 4.26 and 4.32).

4.29   HB 3(1); HB60+ 3(1); NIHB 3(1); NIHB60+ 3(1)

4.30   HB 3(4), sch 1 para 8; HB60+ 3(4), sch 1 para 8; NIHB 3(4), sch 1 para 8; NIHB60+ 3(4), sch 1 para 8

Table 4.4 **People who are not your non-dependants**

None of the following count as your non-dependants (para 4.26):

(a) Members of your family (paras 4.2-25).

(b) Children and young persons who are a foster child, placed for adoption, or in local authority care (table 4.3(a)-(c)).

(c) Carers you pay a voluntary or charitable organisation for (para 4.33).

(d) Lodgers of yours (paras 4.36-41).

(e) Joint tenants of yours (paras 4.42-47).

(f) Separate tenants of your landlord (para 4.48).

(g) Your landlord (para 4.49).

(h) People who normally reside with someone in (d) to (g) (see the paras referred to above).

(i) Anyone else who doesn't normally reside with you (paras 4.29-31).

Other people in your home

Carers provided by a charitable or voluntary organisation

4.33   A carer who lives in your home doesn't count as a non-dependant if:

(a) they are living with you to look after you or your partner;

(b) they are employed or engaged by a charitable or voluntary organisation (not a public or local authority); and

(c) the organisation makes a charge to you or your partner for this.

No deduction is made from your HB for them. But if your dwelling is their home, they are included when the council decides the size of accommodation you need (para 11.10(e)).

T4.4(a)   HB 3(2)(a),(b); HB60+ 3(2)(a),(b); NIHB 3(2)(a),(b); NIHB60+ 3(2)(a),(b)

T4.4(b)   HB 3(2)(c); HB60+ 3(2)(c); NIHB 3(2)(c); NIHB60+ 3(2)(c)

T4.4(c)   HB 3(2)(f); HB60+ 3(2)(f); NIHB 3(2)(f); NIHB60+ 3(2)(f)

T4.4(d)   HB 3(2)(e)(i); HB60+ 3(2)(e)(i); NIHB 3(2)(e)(i); NIHB60+ 3(2)(e)(i)

T4.4(e)   HB 3(2)(d); HB60+ 3(2)(d); NIHB 3(2)(d); NIHB60+ 3(2)(d)

T4.4(f)   HB 3(1),(4); HB60+ 3(1),(4); NIHB 3(1),(4); NIHB60+ 3(1),(4)

T4.4(g)   HB 3(2)(e)(ii); HB60+ 3(2)(e)(ii); NIHB 3(2)(e)(ii); NIHB60+ 3(2)(e)(ii)

T4.4(h)   HB 3(1),(2)(e)(iii); HB60+ 3(1),(2)(e)(iii); NIHB 3(2)(e)(iii); NIHB60+ 3(2)(e)(iii)

T4.4(i)   HB 3(1); HB60+ 3(1); NIHB 3(1); NIHB60+ 3(1)

4.33   HB 3(2)(f); HB60+ 3(2)(f); NIHB 3(2)(f); NIHB60+ 3(2)(f)

Other carers

4.34   Any other carer who lives in your home falls within one of the other descriptions in this chapter, and the effect on your HB follows from that. For example they could be your family member, non-dependant, joint tenant, landlord, etc. If you employ them see para 4.50.

4.35   If you or your partner have overnight care from one or more carers who don't live in your home, this can affect the size of accommodation you need (paras 11.23-29). But no deduction is made from your HB for them.

Lodgers

4.36   A lodger is someone who is liable to pay you or your partner rent, on a commercial basis, in order to live in your home. (We use 'lodger' in this guide because HB law doesn't have a straightforward term for this.) The following rules apply separately for each lodger you have.

4.37   The HB rules divide lodgers into two kinds:

   (a) lodgers whose rent includes meals (para 4.38), sometimes called boarders; and

   (b) lodgers whose rent doesn't include meals, sometimes called sub-tenants.

In either case, they might have people who normally reside with them rather than with you (e.g. their family members or non-dependants).

4.38   A lodger's rent counts as including meals if:

   (a) 'at least some meals' are provided as part of the letting agreement between you (e.g. breakfast every day is enough);

   (b) they are cooked or prepared by you or someone else, but not by the lodger or a member of their family; and

   (c) they are cooked/prepared and consumed in your home or in associated premises.

4.39   Your lodger, and the people who normally reside with them, affect your HB as follows:

   (a) part of the rent you receive from them counts as your income, and the way this is done means you are usually better off if you provide meals than if you don't (table 13.7);

   (b) they are included when the council decides the size of accommodation you need (para 11.10(c),(e));

   (c) they are not included in your applicable amount; and

   (d) they are not your non-dependants (table 4.4).

The lodger can make their own claim for HB and – if they do – the people who reside with them are taken into account in their claim.

4.36   HB 3(2)(e)(i); HB60+ 3(2)(e)(i); NIHB 3(2)(e)(i); NIHB60+ 3(2)(e)(i)

4.37   HB sch 5 paras 22,42; HB60+ sch 5 paras 9,10; NIHB sch 6 paras 23,44; NIHB60+ sch 6 paras 10,11

4.38   HB sch 5 para 42(2); HB60+ 2(1) definition: 'board and lodging accommodation'; NIHB sch 6 para 44(2); NIHB60+ 2(1)

Example: A claimant whose lodger also claims HB

Fred rents his home from a commercial landlord. It has three bedrooms and he rents (sub-lets) two of these to Barney, one for Barney and one for Barney's son Dino, aged 8. Fred is working and he claims HB. Barney is on JSA(IB) and he also claims HB.

Fred's HB

Fred is the claimant, Barney is his lodger (para 4.36), and Dino is Barney's child. So Fred is a single claimant. The rent Barney pays is taken into account as Fred's income (table 13.7). The LHA figure for a three-bedroom dwelling is used to calculate Fred's HB, because Barney and Dino live in his dwelling as his home (para 11.10), as well as Fred.

Barney's HB

Barney is the claimant, Dino is his child, and Fred is his landlord. So Barney is a lone parent. The LHA figure for a two-bedroom dwelling is used to calculate Barney's HB (paras 9.16-17), because just he and his son are taken into account.

Distinguishing lodgers from non-dependants

4.40   The difference between lodgers and non-dependants is that:

(a) a lodger has a commercial relationship with you, and is liable to make payments which usually count as 'rent' in the HB sense (table 7.1);

(b) a non-dependant doesn't have a commercial relationship with you, whether or not they contribute towards your housing costs.

Even if a non-dependant has exclusive occupation (e.g. of their bedroom) this doesn't make them a lodger, because there are 'many examples… of family arrangements and acts of friendship or generosity not… giving rise to a tenancy even when exclusive occupation is given' ([2012] UKUT 114 (AAC)).

When a lodger counts as a non-dependant

4.41   A lodger who has a 'contrived' or other letting for which HB can't be paid (paras 2.40-59) counts instead as a non-dependant. For example if you rent out part of your home to a close relative (para 2.43) they count as a non-dependant not a lodger.

Joint tenants

4.42   A joint tenant is someone who is jointly liable to pay the rent on your home. They could be jointly liable with you, your partner, or both of you. The following rules apply separately for each joint tenant you have.

4.41   HB 3(3); HB60+ 3(3); NIHB 3(3); NIHB60+ 3(3)

4.42   HB 3(2)(d); HB60+ 3(2)(d); NIHB 3(2)(d); NIHB60+ 3(2)(d)

4.43 The HB rules divide joint tenants into two kinds:

(a) joint tenants who are a member of your family, e.g. your partner or a young person; and

(b) joint tenants who aren't a member of your family, e.g. a relation or friend who jointly rents your home as your house-sharer or flat-sharer.

Joint tenants who are a member of your family

4.44 A joint tenant who is a member of your family is just included in your family, and the effect on your HB follows from that (paras 4.2-3).

Joint tenants who are not a member of your family

4.45 A joint tenant who is not a member of your family might:

(a) share your household (paras 4.20-22); or

(b) maintain a separate household from you.

In either case, they might have people who normally reside with them rather than with you (e.g. their family members or non-dependants).

4.46 The joint tenant, and the people who normally reside with them, affect your HB as follows:

(a) they affect what your share of the eligible rent on your home is (paras 8.12, 9.7-8 and table 10.5);

(b) they are included when the council decides the size of accommodation you need (paras 8.26, 10.13 and 11.10) as follows:

- in social sector, exempt accommodation and rent referral cases, this applies whether they share your household or maintain a separate household, but

- in private sector (LHA) cases, this applies only if they share your household (para 9.7);

(c) they are not included in your applicable amount;

(d) they are not your non-dependants (table 4.4) – except in the case of a non-dependant who normally resides with both you and your joint tenant (para 6.19).

The joint tenant can make their own claim for HB and – if they do – the people who reside with them are taken into account in their claim. For examples see chapters 7 to 10.

When a joint tenant counts as a non-dependant

4.47 A joint tenant who has a 'contrived' or other letting for which HB can't be paid (paras 2.40-49) counts instead as a non-dependant. For example if you and a friend are renting from a resident landlord who is the friend's close relative (para 2.43) the friend counts as either your or your landlord's non-dependant, depending on who they normally reside with (paras 4.29-31).

4.47 HB3(3); HB60+ 3(3); NIHB 3(3); NIHB60+ 3(3)

Separate tenants of your landlord

4.48   If you live in a dwelling which is rented out in separate lettings, the other tenants aren't included when the council decides the size of accommodation you need, and don't affect the amount of your HB in any way. The same applies to people who normally reside with them rather than with you (e.g. their family members or non-dependants).

Resident landlords

4.49   If you have a resident landlord, they aren't included when the council decides the size of accommodation you need, and don't affect the amount of your HB in any way. The same applies to people who normally reside with them rather than with you (e.g. their family members, non-dependants or any other member of their household).

Employees

4.50   If you employ someone who lives in your dwelling as their home (e.g. a nanny, an au pair, or a carer who does not fall within para 4.33):

(a)   they are included when the council decides the size of accommodation you need (para 11.10(e));

(b)   they may count as a non-dependant (paras 4.26-32), but in practice they usually don't unless they work for you free of charge (GM para C1.185);

(c)   they don't affect your HB in any other way.

4.48   HB 3(1),(4); HB60+ 3(1),(4); NIHB 3(1),(4); NIHB60+ 3(1),(4)

4.49   HB 3(2)(e)(ii),(iii); HB60+ 3(2)(e)(ii),(iii); NIHB 3(2)(e)(ii),(iii); NIHB60+ 3(2)(e)(ii),(iii)

Chapter 5 **Claims**

- Making a claim: see paras 5.1-12.
- Information and evidence: see paras 5.13-21.
- Complete and incomplete claims: see paras 5.22-27.
- When HB starts: see paras 5.28-49.
- Backdating: see paras 5.50-58.

Making a claim

5.1   HB can only be awarded if a claim is made. This section explains who makes the claim and how it is made. If you move while you are on HB, see also paras 17.22 and 17.30-31.

Who makes the claim

5.2   The general rule is that you make the claim yourself, but:

   (a) if you are in a couple (or in a polygamous marriage) one of you makes the claim: see paras 5.3-4;

   (b) if you are unable to act, someone can make the claim on your behalf: see paras 5.5-7.

Claims by couples

5.3   If you are a couple (or in a polygamous marriage) your HB claim covers both (or all) of you. But only one of you is the claimant. HB application forms usually make this clear by referring to 'you' (the claimant) and 'your partner'. It is up to you to choose which one of you is the claimant. Your choice does not usually affect your HB, but in some circumstances it can. We explain throughout this guide whenever it could affect:

   (a) your eligibility for HB (e.g. paras 20.12, 22.11); or

   (b) the amount of your HB (e.g. paras 5.54, 12.5-7).

If you can't agree which one of you is the claimant, the council chooses for you.

Swapping who is the claimant in a couple

5.4   You should ask the council to let you swap who is the claimant if you would be better off doing so (para 5.3). The law does not give specific rules about this, but in practice the council is likely to agree (GM paras BW3.143 and BW3.305) and may require you to complete a new HB application form. You can ask for a reconsideration if the council doesn't agree (para 16.75).

5.1   AA 1,5; NIAA 1,5

5.3   CBA 134(2); HB 82(1); HB60+ 63(1); NIHB 80(1); NIHB60+ 61(1)

If you are unable to act

5.5   Someone can make a claim on your behalf if you are unable, for the time being, to act. They take over all rights and responsibilities in relation to your HB claim.

5.6   If one of the following has been appointed to act for you, the council must accept a claim from them:

(a) a receiver or deputy appointed by the Court of Protection;

(b) an attorney;

(c) in Scotland, a judicial factor or other guardian;

(d) in Northern Ireland, a controller appointed by the High Court; or

(e) a person appointed by the DWP to act on your behalf in connection with some other benefit.

5.7   In any other case, the council may accept a written request from an individual over 18, or a firm or organisation, to be your 'appointee' – for example, a friend or relative, a social worker or solicitor. In doing this the council should take account of any conflict of interests. Once appointed, an appointee has all the rights and responsibilities that would normally belong to you. Either the council or the appointee can terminate the appointment by giving four weeks' written notice.

Claiming HB from the council

5.8   Claims for HB are made to the council – or to someone acting on its behalf (paras 1.31-32, and see also para 5.9). Many councils accept HB claims by telephone or online; and if you claim this way the council can require you to approve a written statement of a telephone claim, or keep written or electronic records of an online claim. In all other cases, HB claims must be in writing on the council's own form (or any other format it decides to accept) and sent to a 'designated office', which can be the council's benefit office, a county council office, a social landlord's address, etc. Application forms must be provided free of charge and give the address of every designated office and optionally an online address. You can ask anyone you like to help you fill in an application form.

Claiming HB via the DWP

5.9   Claims for HB can be made via the DWP in conjunction with a claim for JSA, ESA, IS, pension credit, or IB when it is linked to a former claim (but not UC: para 5.10). These claims are made by telephone to a DWP 0800 number (para 24.15). During the call, you are asked whether you wish to claim HB and if you do information relevant to HB is collected. The information is verified by the DWP if possible at an interview (which can be fast tracked if there is the threat of an eviction) or by post. The DWP then sends the council an electronic 'LAID' (local authority input document, known as 'LACI' in ESA cases), even if you do not qualify for the DWP benefit or withdraw your claim for it. The LAID/LACI is a computer generated claim form with your answers filled in. The DWP also sends the council a 'customer statement' (e.g. about DWP benefits you qualify for: para 5.18).

5.5   HB 82(6); HB60+ 63(6); NIHB 80(6); NIHB60+ 61(6)

5.8   HB 2(1), 83; HB60+ 2(10, 64; NIHB 2(1), 81; NIHB60+ 2(1), 62

5.9   HB 2(1),83(4),111; HB60+ 2(1),64(5),(5B),92; NIHB 2(1),81(4), NIHB60+ 2(1),62(5).(5B)

5.10   The following are the main exceptions to the above procedure:

(a) You cannot claim HB via the DWP in conjunction with a claim for UC, so if you are claiming UC and live in specified supported accommodation (para 2.13 and table 2.3) you should claim HB direct from the council.

(b) If you make a 'fast track' telephone claim to the DWP (e.g. because you know you wish to claim JSA(C) only), you are not invited to claim HB during the call, so you should claim HB direct from the council.

(c) If you phone the DWP to make a 'rapid reclaim' for JSA or ESA (i.e. within 12 weeks of a previous award ending) the DWP should post you an HB form (HBRR1) and you should send it to the council.

(d) If you claim a DWP benefit other than by telephone (e.g. ESA or pension credit) the DWP should post you an HB form (HCTB1) and you should send it to the council. The DWP also uses form HCTB1 in this way (marked 'CMS contingency') when its computer is unable to accept telephone claims.

Amending or withdrawing a claim

5.11   Before the council makes a decision on your claim, you can:

(a) amend it: the amendment is treated as having been made from the outset;

(b) withdraw it: the council is then under no duty to decide it.

5.12   A claim may be amended by telephone or in writing – to the council, or to the DWP if the claim was made to them. A claim may be withdrawn by telephone if it was made by telephone; otherwise it must be withdrawn in writing.

Information and evidence

5.13   You are responsible for providing 'certificates, documents, information and evidence' which are 'reasonably required by the authority in order to determine... entitlement' to HB. This applies when you make a claim (para 5.22), and also during the course of an award (paras 17.17 and 17.59). The council can ask you to attend an interview, but must not insist on this: R v Liverpool CC ex parte Johnson No. 2. Evidence should be obtained direct from a third party only with your written agreement (GM para D3.400), but this is usually given in the declaration made in connection with a claim.

5.14   The law does not specify (except as described in paras 5.15-16) what information and evidence is required in relation to particular matters. In practice councils require evidence about household members and their status, income and capital (for claimants not on a passport benefit), occupation of the dwelling (when appropriate), rent (in rent allowance cases), and other matters. Councils usually expect you to provide original documents rather than copies, but can also accept evidence in electronic formats (circular HB G1/2016) e.g. if you print out payslips or bank statements yourself. In written claims, your signature is a reasonable requirement, and many councils also require your partner's signature.

5.11   HB 87; HB60+ 68; NIHB 83; NIHB60+ 64

5.13   AA 5(1); NIAA 5(1); HB 83(1),86(1),(1A); HB60+ 64(2),67(1),(1A); NIHB 81(1),82(1),(1A); NIHB60+ 62(2),63(1),(1A); R v Liverpool CC ex p Johnson (No 2) 31/10/94 QBD [1995] COD 200

Information you need not disclose

5.15   The council must not require any information or evidence whatsoever about the following types of payment, whether they are made to you, your partner or non-dependant:

(a)   compensation payments from the government sponsored trust funds for people infected by NHS blood products or the London Bombings Relief Charitable Fund, and in certain cases payments derived from those sources (para 15.42);

(b)   payments in kind of capital from a charity or from the above sources;

(c)   payments in kind of income (table 13.9(k)) from any source.

National Insurance numbers

5.16   You must either provide your National Insurance (NI) number, and your partner's if you are in a couple, along with information or evidence establishing this; or provide information or evidence enabling it to be ascertained; or make an application for an NI number and give information or evidence to assist with this – even if it is highly improbable that one will be granted: CH/4085/2007. There are two exceptions:

(a)   the rule does not apply to you or your partner if you are claiming HB in respect of a hostel (para 7.22);

(b)   the rule does not apply in certain cases if your partner is a foreign national (para 20.14).

Matters relating to the provision of an NI number are appealable, including the evidence needed to ascertain one: CH/1231/2004; and the consequences in an HB decision of a refusal to allocate one: 2009 UKUT 74 (AAC).

If you are on a passport benefit, etc

5.17   If you have been lawfully awarded a passport benefit (table 6.1) or universal credit by the DWP, this is binding on the authority as proof that (at the relevant dates) you fulfil the income-related conditions for receiving maximum HB (paras 6.2 and 13.3): R v Penwith DC ex parte Menear and R v South Ribble Council HBRB. If you have been refused a passport benefit or universal credit, this is not binding on the authority: [2013] UKUT 245 (AAC). But If you have been lawfully awarded savings credit, certain figures are binding (para 13.15).

Information gathered by the DWP

5.18   The law requires the council to use information relevant to HB, without verifying its accuracy, if it is supplied by the DWP and relates to a claim for or an award of: attendance allowance, bereavement allowance, bereavement payment, carer's allowance, disability living allowance, employment and support allowance, incapacity benefit, income support, jobseeker's allowance, retirement pension, state pension credit, universal credit, widowed parent's allowance or winter fuel payment. But the council need not use information which is more than 12 months old, nor if the council has reason to believe that the information has changed since the DWP obtained it.

5.15   HB 86(2),(4); HB60+ 67(2),(4); NIHB 82(2),(4); NIHB60+ 63(2),(4)

5.16   AA1(1A); NIAA 1(1A); HB 4; HB60+ 4; NIHB 4; NIHB 60+ 4; R v Penwith ex p Menear 11/10/91 QBD 24 HLR 115;
            R v South Ribble HBRB ex p Hamilton 24/01/00 CA [2000] EWCA Civ 518 www.bailii.org/ew/cases/EWCA/Civ/2000/518.html

5.18   SI 2007/2911; NISR 2007/467

5.19   In practice, the DWP verifies the evidence relevant to a claim for HB made via the department (paras 5.9-10) – but there are exceptions (for example, the DWP does not usually verify capital if the claimant says it is below £6,000). The DWP advises that councils 'should accept' that it has 'taken the appropriate action' in relation to such evidence (CMS Guide for local authorities, March 2010).

Nil income claims, etc

5.20   No-one is required to claim HB via the DWP (even when that is the normal procedure: para 5.9); in some situations you may need to claim HB from the council while waiting for a DWP benefit to be assessed. The DWP recommends councils 'do not ask the [claimant] to provide information and evidence that you know will be collected by [the DWP] unless the claim is urgent' (CMS Guide for local authorities, March 2010). However, if there is evidence of your actual circumstances, it is not reasonable (para 5.13) to delay assessing HB to wait for a DWP decision. If you have no income and your capital is below £6,000/£10,000, you qualify for maximum HB (paras 6.2 and 15.4) regardless of what the DWP decides: for example if you are living off voluntary payments from friends or relatives, or payments in kind, or your savings.

5.21   Similarly, no-one can be compelled to claim a DWP benefit; in some situations you may prefer to claim HB without doing so (perhaps because you are living off savings or the kinds of payment mentioned above). The council has no power to refuse your claim for HB because it thinks you 'ought' to be on a DWP benefit.

Complete and incomplete claims

What is a claim

5.22   Making a claim (also sometimes called 'lodging' a claim) means telling the council/NIHE you want HB. You can do this by:

    (a) following the procedures in para 5.8 or (for claims via the DWP) para 5.9;

    (b) telephoning or writing to the council to say you want to claim; or

    (c) ticking a box on a leaflet etc provided by the council or other organisation that indicates you want to claim, and giving or sending this to the council (or DWP if you are also claiming a passport benefit) (CP/3447/2003).

But the council can't award you HB unless you 'complete' your claim (paras 5.23-26 and 5.33-34).

What is a complete claim

5.23   Your HB claim is complete (it is also sometimes called an 'effective' or 'valid' claim) if it is made:

    (a) in writing or online (para 5.8) and is on an application form approved by the council and completed in accordance with the instructions on the form – including any instructions to provide information and evidence;

5.23   AA 1,5,6; NIAA 1,5; HB 83(1),(4C),(9); HB60+ 64(2),(5D),(10); NIHB 81(1),(4C),(9); NIHB60+ 62(2),(5D),(10)

(b) in some other written form which the council accepts as sufficient in the circumstances of a particular case or class of cases, having regard to whether the information and evidence provided with it is sufficient;

(c) by telephone (paras 5.8-9) and you provide the information and evidence required to decide the claim.

Dealing with incomplete claims

5.24   Your HB claim is incomplete (it is also sometimes called a 'defective' claim) if it is received by the council (or DWP if appropriate) but does not meet the conditions given above (para 5.22). The council should give you the opportunity of doing whatever is needed to complete your claim. In the case of a claim via the DWP, however, the DWP may do this (but if it does not, the council must). Depending on the circumstances, this could mean that:

(a) the council sends you a claim form (or a supplementary form);

(b) the council returns a form to you for completion; or

(c) the council or the DWP requests information and evidence (or further information and evidence) from you.

In all cases, the council must also inform you of the duty to notify relevant changes of circumstances which occur, and say what these are likely to be.

5.25   You must be allowed at least one month to provide what is required (para 5.30), and must be allowed longer if it is reasonable to do so. In the case of telephone claims, the law specifically permits more than one reminder, and the month is counted from the last such reminder. In the case of written and online claims, some councils send a reminder, allowing a further period for the reply. In all these cases, if you do what is required within the time limit, your HB claim is treated as having been complete from the outset. This is the case even if it took the council a long time to ask you to complete your claim (CP/3447/2003).

Deciding incomplete claims

5.26   Once you have completed your claim it must be decided by the council as described in para 16.2. Even if you don't complete your claim, it must be decided by the council, and in such cases the council may:

(a) decide that you are not entitled to HB because you do not satisfy the conditions of entitlement, as you have not provided the necessary information or evidence; or

(b) make a negative inference (which means 'assume the worst') in order to make its decision. For example, if a claimant's bank statement shows that he withdrew £20,000 three weeks ago, and he refuses to explain this, it might be reasonable to decide that his capital remains £20,000.

In each case, you may appeal to a tribunal (para 16.81).

5.24   HB 83(4D)-(4E); (6)-(9), 86(1)-(3); HB60+ 64(5E)-(5F) (7)-(9), 67(1)-(3);
        NIHB 81(4D)-(4E), (6)-(9), 82(1)-(3); NIHB60+ 62(4D)-(4E), (7)-(9),63(1)-(3)

5.26   HB 83(4F),89; HB60+ 64(5G),70; NIHB 85; NIHB60+ 66

Claims not received

5.27   The council has no duty to decide a claim that was not received – for example an application form which is lost in the post. An (attempted) telephone claim in which you do not answer all the questions, or do not approve a written statement if requested to do so (para 5.8), is treated as 'not received' – but in this case the council may nonetheless decide it. An (attempted) online claim which the council's computer does not accept or which is not in the form approved (para 5.8) is treated as 'not received'. In all these cases, if you claim HB again, the council should consider whether the conditions for backdating are met (para 5.50).

When HB starts

Overview

5.28   The rest of this chapter is about when your HB starts. It explains:

(a)   what counts as your 'date of claim' (para 5.32);

(b)   when your first day of entitlement is (para 5.45); and

(c)   when your HB is backdated (para 5.50).

Duration of award

5.29   There is no fixed limit to an award of HB. Your entitlement may change if there is a change in your circumstances etc (para 17.1). Otherwise it simply continues until you:

(a)   stop being entitled – for example, if you gain too much capital or income or transfer onto UC (para 2.11); or

(b)   fail to respond to a request for information or evidence and then the award is terminated (para 17.75).

Definition of 'month'

5.30   Many of the rules in this guide refer to allowing someone a 'month' to do something in connection with a claim, etc. This means a calendar month, and the month is counted as follows (R(IB) 4/02):

(a)   if the council issues a letter on 26th June inviting you to provide something, you have provided it within a month if you get it to the council by the end of 26th July;

(b)   if the council issues a letter on 31st January asking you to provide something, you have provided it within a month if you get it to the council by the end of 28th (or 29th) February.

Things sent out by the council (such as requests for information or evidence, decision letters) are counted in the law as being sent out on the date of posting. Things received by the council (such as claims, information and evidence) are counted in the law as being received on the date of receipt. In the case of online communications, this means the date recorded by the computer as the date of sending or receipt unless the council reasonably directs otherwise.

5.27   HB 83(4),(4B),(4C) sch 11 paras 2(7),4; HB60+ 64(5),(5C),(5D) sch 10 paras 2(7),4;
            NIHB 81(4),(4B),(4C) sch 11 paras 2(7),4; NIHB60+ 62(5),(5C),(5D) sch 10 paras 2(7),4

5.30   HB sch 11 para 4; HB60+ sch 10 para 4; NIHB sch 11 para 4; NIHB60 sch 10 para 4; DAR 2; NIDAR 2

Definition of 'benefit week'

5.31   Many of the rules in this guide refer to a 'benefit week'. A benefit week always begins on a Monday and ends on the following Sunday.

Date of claim

5.32   The rules about what counts as your 'date of claim' are summarised in table 5.1 (and were confirmed in R(H) 9/07). Further details follow.

Table 5.1 **Date of claim for HB: summary**

Situation	Date of claim
You asked for a form (or notified an intention to claim) and return it, properly completed, within one month of when it was sent out or longer if reasonable (paras 5.33-34)	The day you asked for the form (or notified the intention to claim)
The claim is made within one month of your partner's death or your and your partner's separation, and your partner was on HB at the time (paras 5.35-36)	The day of the death or separation
You or your partner were awarded JSA(IB), ESA(IR), IS, guarantee credit or UC and the claim for HB is received within one month of when the claim for that benefit was received (paras 5.37-40)	The first day of your or your partner's entitlement to JSA(IB), ESA(IR), IS, guarantee credit or universal credit
You or your partner are on JSA(IB), ESA(IR), IS, guarantee credit or UC, and the claim for HB is received within one month of you or your partner first becoming liable for rent or rates (paras 5.41-42)	The first day of your or your partner's liability for rent or rates
In any other case (para 5.43)	The day the HB claim is received

Note: One month means a calendar month (para 5.30) and (except in the first situation) can't be extended. But see para 5.50 for backdating.

Notifying an intention to claim

5.33   This rule applies if:

(a)   you notified your intention to claim HB to the council or DWP;

(b)   the council or DWP gave or sent you an application form; and

(c)   you returned the form no more than one month after it was given or sent to you, or longer if reasonable.

5.31   HB 2(1); HB60+ 2(1); NIHB 2(1); NIHB60+ 2(1)

5.32   HB 83(5); HB60+ 64(6); NIHB 81(5); NIHB60+ 62(6)

5.33   HB 83(5)(d); HB60+ 64(6)(d); NIHB 81(5)(d); NIHB60+ 62(6)(d)

5.34 In this case, your date of claim for HB is the day you notified your intention to claim to the office in question. You can do this 'by any means' (which includes telephoning, emailing, writing, texting, visiting or sending a friend: CIS/2726/2005).

Example: Date of claim following notice of an intention to claim

On Thursday 22nd June 2017, a claimant realises she might qualify for HB and telephones the authority to ask to claim. The authority sends an application form out that very day. She posts it back and it reaches the authority on Friday 14th July 2017.

Her date of claim is Thursday 22nd June 2017 and (unless the week-one-yes rule applies: para 5.46) the first day of her entitlement to HB is the following Monday, 26th June 2017.

Claims following death or separation

5.35 This rule applies if:

(a) you claim HB no more than one month after your partner's death or your separation; and

(b) your partner was on HB at the time of the death or separation.

5.36 In this case, your date of claim for HB is the date of the separation or death in question, the intention being that there should be no gap in entitlement to HB.

Claims following an award of a passport benefit

5.37 This rule applies if:

(a) you or your partner claim and are awarded a passport benefit (JSA(IB), ESA(IR), IS or guarantee credit); and

(b) your HB claim is received by the council or the DWP no more than one month after the passport benefit claim was received by the DWP.

5.38 In this case, your date of claim for HB is the first day of that entitlement to the passport benefit. If your passport benefit is backdated, this means the day it is backdated to. In the case of JSA(IB) and ESA(IR) it means the first 'waiting day'.

Claims following an award of universal credit

5.39 This rule can only arise in relation to HB for specified supported accommodation (para 2.13). It applies if:

(a) you are awarded UC; and

(b) your HB claim is received by the council (not the DWP) no more than one month after:

■ the date the UC claim was received by the DWP, or

■ if UC is awarded without a claim, the date the DWP sent you notice of the UC award. This can occur when you become a couple or stop being a couple while you

---

5.35   HB 83(5)(c); HB60+ 64(6)(c); NIHB 81(5)(c); NIHB60+ 62(6)(c)

5.37   HB 83(5)(a); HB60+ 64(6)(a); NIHB 81(5)(a); NIHB60+ 62(6)(a)

5.39   HB 83(5)(aa)

are on UC; or in UC live service areas when you become entitled to UC within six months of being told you don't qualify because of the level of your earned income (para 2.10(c)).

5.40   In this case, your date of claim for HB is the first day of that entitlement to UC.

Becoming liable for rent or rates while on a passport benefit or UC

5.41   This rule applies if:

(a) you or your partner are receiving a passport benefit (table 6.1) or universal credit; and

(b) you or your partner become liable for rent or rates for the first time; and

(c) your HB claim is received by the council or the DWP no more than one month after the new liability begins.

5.42   In this case, your date of claim for HB is the first day of that new liability for rent or rates. For UC claimants moving into specified supported accommodation, see also para 17.31.

Other claims

5.43   If none of the earlier rules applies, your date of claim for HB is the day your claim is received by the council or the DWP (paras 5.8-10). For this rule only, 'council' includes a county council as well as the council administering HB. See also paragraph 5.50 for backdating.

Advance claims

5.44   You may make an advance claim for HB:

(a) up to 17 weeks before you reach pension credit age (para 1.24); or

(b) up to 17 weeks before an event which makes you entitled to HB (pension age claimants); or

(c) up to 13 weeks before an event which makes you entitled to HB (working age claimants); or

(d) up to eight weeks before you become liable for rates (HB for rates only).

In (a) to (c) your date of claim for HB is fixed so that your HB begins on the Monday following the birthday or event in question. In (d) your date of claim is the first day of liability for rates. Rules (c) and (d) do not, however, apply if you are a migrant or new arrival who is ineligible for HB (chapter 20).

5.41   HB 83(5)(b); HB60+ 64(6)(b); NIHB 81(5)(b); NIHB60+ 62(6)(b)

5.43   HB 83(5)(e); HB60+ 64(6)(e); NIHB 81(5)(e); NIHB 62(6)(e)

5.44   HB 83(10),(11); HB60+ 64(11),(12); NIHB 81(10),(11); NIHB60+ 62(11),(12)

First day of entitlement

The general rule

5.45 The general rule is that your first day of entitlement to HB is the Monday following your 'date of claim' (paras 5.32-44). Even if your date of claim is a Monday, your first day of entitlement is the following Monday. The exceptions follow.

The week-one-yes rule

5.46 The week-one-yes rule applies only if you or your partner become liable for rent or rates in the benefit week (para 5.31) containing your 'date of claim', and you move in during or before that week (para 3.17).

5.47 In this case, your HB begins in that week (rather than on the following Monday). Your first day of entitlement is:

(a) the day you or your partner become liable for rent or rates; or

(b) the day you move in, if this is later ([2014] UKUT 411 (AAC)).

This rule 'enables HB awards to match a period of occupancy' (GM para A6.81). See the following examples.

The rule for certain dwellings with daily rents

5.48 This rule only applies if you are liable to pay your rent on a daily basis to:

(a) a hostel (para 7.22); or

(b) any other accommodation in which you have been placed as a homeless person and which is board and lodging accommodation, accommodation licensed to the authority, or short-term leased accommodation (with a lease of no more than ten years) outside the authority's housing revenue account.

5.49 In this case, there is no time limit on when you may claim, and your HB is always awarded back to when you moved into the accommodation. In other words, your first day of entitlement to HB is always the day you moved in. In practice, this rule is likely to be needed only for short periods (as leaving it any longer may mean you are no longer available to provide the information and evidence necessary for your claim).

5.45   HB 76(1); HB60+ 57(1); NIHB 74(1); NIHB60+ 55(1)

5.46   HB 76(2),80(3)(a); HB60+ 57(2); 61(4)(a); NIHB 74(2),78(4)(a); NIHB60+ 55(2), 59(4)(a)

5.48   HB 76(3)-(5); HB60+ 57(2)-(4); NIHB 74(3)-(5); NIHB60+ 55(2)-(4)

Examples: First day of entitlement

The general rule

A man claims HB because his income has reduced (not because he is moving home).

- If his date of claim is Thursday 5th October 2017, his first day of entitlement is Monday 9th October 2017.

- If his date of claim is Monday 16th October 2017, his first day of entitlement is Monday 23rd October 2017.

The week-one-yes rule

A woman claims HB on her new home, and her date of claim is Friday 10th March 2017.

- If she became liable for rent there on Monday 6th March 2017 and moved in that day, her first day of entitlement is Monday 6th March 2017.

- If she became liable for rent there on Wednesday 8th March 2017 and moved in that day, her first day of entitlement is Wednesday 8th March 2017. (In her first benefit week she gets five-sevenths of a week's HB.)

- If she became liable for rent there on Monday 6th March 2017 but didn't move in until Saturday 11th March 2017, her first day of entitlement is Saturday 11th March 2017. (In her first benefit week she gets two-sevenths of a week's HB.)

- All the above apply whether her rent is due weekly, fortnightly, monthly, etc.

- But if she was getting HB from the same council at her old home, see instead table 17.3.

Backdating

5.50   This section explains how HB can be backdated to cover periods in the past:

(a) for pension age HB claims, backdating for up to three months is automatic (para 5.52);

(b) for working age HB claims, backdating requires you to have good cause and can be for up to one month (para 5.54).

5.51   For both age groups:

(a) it is your date of claim which is backdated, and your first day of entitlement is worked out from that (paras 5.45-47);

(b) you can get backdated HB even if you aren't currently entitled to HB, or even if you moved home during the backdated period (but if your old address was in a different council's area you are likely to have to apply separately to it);

(c) your HB during the backdated period is calculated using the rules that applied then; and

(d) you are awarded HB only for the parts of the backdated period in which you qualify.

But basing a claim for HB on a claim which was (on the balance of probability) received by the council or DWP (paras 5.8-9 and 5.22), but was then mislaid or not acted on, is not backdating (because in fact a claim was made). And for hostels etc where your rent is due daily, see instead paras 5.48-49.

Backdating HB for pension age claims

5.52 For all pension age claims (paras 1.23-25), your claim for HB covers any period in the three months before the day your claim is actually received (or the day you notified your intention to claim, so long as you followed that up within the relevant time limits: paras 5.33-34) – but only back to the day you reached pension credit age, or the day you became liable for rent or rates, if these are later.

5.53 You do not have to ask for this rule to apply, and do not have to have 'good cause' (or any reason whatsoever): the rule applies automatically in all cases.

Backdating HB for working age claims

5.54 For working age claims (paras 1.23-25), your HB is backdated if you (the claimant):

(a) request this in writing (e.g. on the HB application form or separately later); and

(b) 'had continuous good cause' (paras 5.56-57) for your failure to claim or to ask for your claim to be backdated.

If you meet these conditions your HB must be backdated for one month before your written request or (if shorter) for whatever period you had good cause. 'One month' means a calendar month (para 5.30).

HB if your passport benefit is backdated

5.55 If you are claiming a passport benefit (table 6.1) as well as HB:

(a) your passport benefit is backdated for up to three months if you have continuous good cause for your delay in claiming it;

(b) you count as having claimed HB on the date your passport benefit is backdated to (paras 5.37-38);

(c) so your HB starts from three months earlier too.

This is separate from the HB backdating rules, so you don't have to ask for your HB to be backdated for (c) to apply. And the one month time limit on backdating working age HB doesn't stop your HB being awarded for that period.

Examples: Backdating

1. A pension age claimant

A pension age claimant claims HB on Friday 13th October 2017. He would have been entitled if he had claimed at any time in the last year. His HB claim is automatically backdated for three months, so:

- ■ his date of claim for HB is Thursday 13th July; and
- ■ his HB begins on the following Monday, 17th July.

5.52   HB60+ 64(1),(1A); NIHB60+ 62(1),(1A)

5.54   HB 83(12),(12A); NIHB 81(12),(12A)

2. A working age claimant

A working age claimant claims HB on Friday 13th October 2017, and (at the same) asks for his HB to be backdated. The council agrees she has good cause for the past month, so:

- her date of claim is Wednesday 13th September; and
- her HB begins the following Monday, 18th September.

3. A working age claimant whose passport benefit is backdated

A working age claimant claims both JSA(IB) and HB on Friday 13th October 2017, and (at the same time) asks for his HB to be backdated. The DWP agrees he has good cause for the past three months, so:

- his JSA(IB) begins on Thursday 13th July;
- his date of claim for HB is Thursday 13th July; and
- his HB begins the following Monday, 17th July.

Note:

Each claimant's HB begins up to a week earlier if the week-one-yes rule applies (para 5.46).

'Good cause'

5.56   Good cause has been explained by tribunals and courts right back to the late 1940s, and this case law is binding: CH/5221/2001. Table 5.2 summarises cases of particular importance to HB.

5.57   The case law shows that you are likely to have good cause if:

(a) you were so ill (physically or mentally) or otherwise unable to act that you could not claim and could not ask someone to claim for you;

(b) someone you should have been able to rely on (such as the council, the DWP, an advice agency and possibly others) advised you that you could not get HB when in fact you could;

(c) there were good reasons for you not believing you could claim, amounting to more than just not thinking or not caring; or

(d) some external factor prevented you from making a claim (e.g. failure of the postal services, imprisonment).

But the council's decision about good cause must be based on your individual circumstances, and you may have good cause in other situations.

5.58   When you request backdating you should tell the council why you consider you have good cause, and the council can ask for information and evidence about this (para 5.13). You don't have to use the terms 'backdating' and 'good cause' so long as you make it clear you are asking for HB for a past period (CH/3402/2005). Disputes about good cause are appealable to a First-tier Tribunal (para 16.81) – and also to an Upper Tribunal (para 16.89) because they are regarded as questions of law (R(SB) 39/91) as well as fact.

Table 5.2 **Backdating working age HB: good cause case law**

- *Reasonableness:* Good cause includes 'any fact that would probably have caused a reasonable person to act as the claimant did' (CH/4501/2004 approving C.S. 371/49). What is 'reasonable' is objective rather than subjective ([2010] UKUT 64 (AAC)).

- *Ignorance of rights and attempts to ascertain them:* Claimants are expected to take reasonable steps to ascertain what their rights may be, but 'cannot always be assumed to have an understanding of public administration' C.S. 371/49). Though ignorance of itself is not good cause, it may be a factor to take into account since the law does not 'require a person to be acquainted with the "rules and regulations"' ([2010] UKUT 64 (AAC)).

- *A mistaken belief reasonably held:* Good cause can include a firmly held misunderstanding which amounts to a mistaken belief reasonably held, particularly when the claimant has not been careless or attempted to obtain benefit they are not entitled to (CH/4501/2004 approving earlier cases). This could include believing that you don't have to pay housing costs (and so don't have to claim HB) if you are on a passport benefit (CH/4501/2004), or that you can't get HB if you haven't paid national insurance contributions (CH/2198/2008).

- *Illness:* Good cause is related not to the severity or seriousness of an illness but to the resulting incapability of the claimant to claim (CH/5135/2001).

- *Mental incapacity:* In deciding good cause, a mentally disabled person is treated as having their mental age not their chronological age (CH/393/2003).

- *Inability to speak English:* By itself, an inability to speak English is not normally good cause (CH/3579/2003).

- *Not receiving a document from the council:* Good cause can include non-receipt of a document from the council (e.g. requesting information and evidence) if this meant your HB stopped and you have reapplied (CH/3402/2005).

- *Misleading or incorrect advice and other factors:* Case law about other benefits is binding on HB (CH/5221/2001). Misinformation on an official website such as gov.uk can be misadvice and amount to good cause ([2015] UKUT 616(AAC)).

- *Who has to have good cause:* Only you (the claimant) have to show good cause, not for example, your partner (CH/3817/2004).

- *Good cause and qualifying for HB:* If you have good cause your claim is backdated even if you only qualify for HB for part of the backdated period (CH/1237/2004). But the council doesn't have to consider whether you have good cause if you don't qualify for any of the backdated period (CH/996/2004).

- *Claims or requests for HB that aren't acted on:* If you made a claim for HB or told the council (or DWP) you wanted to claim (para 5.22) but the council did not act on this, your HB is awarded based on the date you did so, without this counting as 'backdating' your HB (CP/3447/2003).

Chapter 6 **Calculating HB**

- How HB is calculated: see paras 6.1-8.
- Non-dependant deductions: see paras 6.9-20.
- The HB benefit cap: see paras 6.21-33.
- Converting figures to weekly amounts: see paras 6.34-38.

How to calculate HB

6.1   This chapter explains how much HB you qualify for. To calculate this, work through the steps in paras 6.2-8. The calculation is summarised in table 6.2.

Maximum benefit

6.2   The starting point for all HB calculations is your weekly 'maximum benefit'. This is:

(a) your weekly eligible rent – and/or rates in Northern Ireland;

(b) minus any non-dependant deductions which apply.

See chapter 7-11 for how your eligible rent is worked out, and chapter 19 for eligible rates. Paragraphs 6.9 onwards give the amounts of the non-dependant deductions and explain when they apply.

People on a passport benefit or universal credit

6.3   You qualify for maximum benefit (para 6.2) if:

(a) you are on a passport benefit (table 6.1); or

(b) you are on universal credit (this can only apply if you live in specified supported accommodation: para 2.13 and table 2.3).

In the case of (a), the law says that your income is treated as being nil.

Other people

6.4   If you aren't on a passport benefit or universal credit:

(a) your HB is based on your income and applicable amount, as described in paras 6.5-6;

(b) but you don't qualify for HB if your capital is over £16,000.

6.2   CBA 130(1),(3), 130A; NICBA 129(1),(3), 129A; HB 70; HB60+ 50; NIHB 68; NIHB60+ 48

6.3   CBA 130(3)(a), NICBA 129(3)(a); HB 2(3),(3A),(3B), sch 5 paras 4,5, sch 6 paras 5,6; HB60+ 2(3),(3A), 26;
          NIHB 2(3),(3A),(3B), sch 6 paras 4,5, sch 7 paras 5,6; NIHB60+ 2(3),(3A), 24

6.4   CBA 130(3), 134(1); NICBA 129(3), 130(1); HB 43; HB60+ 28; NIHB 40; NIHB60+ 26

Table 6.1 **Passport benefits**

You count as being 'on a passport benefit' if you are:

■ on guarantee credit (or would qualify but for the minimum payment rule: para 24.25)

■ on income support – IS

■ on income-based jobseeker's allowance – JSA(IB)

■ on income-related employment and support allowance – ESA(IR)

■ entitled to JSA(IB) or ESA(IR) but not receiving it because of a sanction

■ in the 'waiting days' before your JSA(IB) or ESA(IR) start – or would start apart from a sanction (this is confirmed in circular HB U1/2015)

■ subject to a restriction in your JSA(IB) or IS as a result of breaching a community order.

Other people

6.5   If you have no income, or your income is less than or equal to your applicable amount, you qualify for maximum benefit (para 6.2).

Income and excess income

6.6   If your income is more than your applicable amount, the difference between the two is called 'excess income'. You qualify for maximum benefit (para 6.2) minus a percentage of this excess income. The percentage – also called a 'taper' – is:

(a)   65% in calculating HB for rent;

(b)   20% in calculating HB for rates in Northern Ireland.

Minimum benefit

6.7   If the amount of HB calculated as above is less than the 'minimum benefit' figure, then it is not awarded. For HB for rent the figure is 50p per week. There is no minimum figure for HB for rates in Northern Ireland.

Other calculation rules

6.8   The amount of HB can be reduced to recover an overpayment (para 18.41) or administrative penalty (para 18.73). For working age claims, HB is also subject to a benefit cap (para 6.21).

T6.1   CBA 130(1),(3)(a),130A; NICBA 129(1),(3)(a),129A; HB 2(3),(3A),(3B) sch 5 paras 4,5, sch 6 paras 5,6; HB60+ 2(3),(3A), 26; NIHB 2(3),(3A) sch 6 paras 4,5, sch 7 paras 5,6; NIHB60+ 2(3),(3A), 24

6.5   CBA 130(3)(a); NICBA 129(3)(a)

6.6   CBA 130(3)(b); NICBA 129(3)(b); HB 71; HB60+ 51; NIHB 69; NIHB60+ 49

16.7   HB 75; HB60+ 56; NIHB 73; NIHB60+ 54

Table 6.2 **Amount of HB: summary**

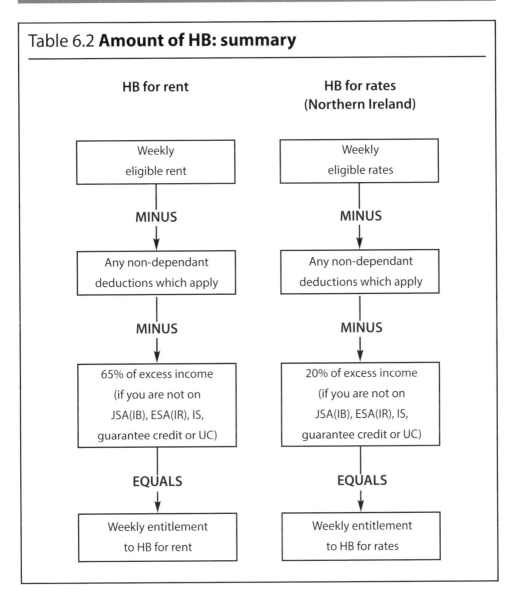

HB for rent	HB for rates (Northern Ireland)
Weekly eligible rent	Weekly eligible rates
MINUS	MINUS
Any non-dependant deductions which apply	Any non-dependant deductions which apply
MINUS	MINUS
65% of excess income (if you are not on JSA(IB), ESA(IR), IS, guarantee credit or UC)	20% of excess income (if you are not on JSA(IB), ESA(IR), IS, guarantee credit or UC)
EQUALS	EQUALS
Weekly entitlement to HB for rent	Weekly entitlement to HB for rates

Examples: Calculating HB

Claimant on a passport benefit

A claimant is on a passport benefit (JSA(IB), ESA(IR), IS or guarantee credit). She has no non-dependants. Her eligible rent is £105.00 per week.

Claimants on a passport benefit get maximum benefit – which equals their eligible rent.

Eligible rent equals weekly HB	£105.00

Claimant not on a passport benefit

A couple are not on JSA(IB), ESA(IR), IS, guarantee credit or UC. They have no non-dependants. Their joint weekly income exceeds their applicable amount by £20.00. Their eligible rent is £130.00 per week.

Claimants with excess income get maximum benefit minus a percentage of their excess income.

Eligible rent	£130.00
minus 65% of excess income (65% x £20.00)	£13.00
equals weekly HB	£117.00

Claimant on ESA(IR) with working non-dependant

A claimant is on ESA(IR). Her eligible rent is £100.00 per week. Her 26-year-old son lives with her. He earns £450 per week gross for a 35-hour week.

Claimants on ESA(IR) get maximum benefit, which in this case involves a non-dependant deduction. The son works at least 16 hours per week and the level of his gross income means the highest deduction applies in HB (table 6.4).

Eligible rent	£100.00
minus non-dependant deduction	£95.45
equals weekly HB	£4.55

Claimant on ESA(IR) with non-dependant on JSA(IB)

The son in the previous example loses his job and starts receiving JSA(IB).

The calculation is as above, except that now the lowest deduction applies in HB (table 6.4).

Eligible rent	£100.00
minus non-dependant deduction	£14.80
equals weekly HB	£85.20

Non-dependant deductions

6.9   This section explains the deductions that are made if you have one or more non-dependants. The deductions are made from your eligible rent (and/or rates in Northern Ireland) in the calculation of your HB (para 6.2). They can be described as the amount your non-dependants are expected to contribute towards your rent.

6.10   A non-dependant is usually an adult son, daughter, other relative or friend who lives with you on a non-commercial basis: for details see paras 4.26-32.

When a deduction is made

6.11   Unless any of the exceptions in table 6.3 applies:

(a)   one deduction is made for each non-dependant you have;

(b)   but if two non-dependants are a couple, one deduction is made between them (para 6.18).

There are further rules if you are a joint tenant (para 6.19) or aged over 65 (para 6.20).

The amount of the deduction

6.12   The amounts of the deductions are in table 6.4. These vary depending on whether your non-dependant is working at least 16 hours per week and (if they are) on their gross income (paras 6.14-17).

Assuming the amount of the deduction

6.13   If you don't provide evidence of your non-dependant's circumstances, the council could make an assumption about which deduction applies. It mustn't make an assumption that is unlikely to reflect the non-dependant's actual circumstances (CH/48/2006), but otherwise it could make the highest deduction if they are working at least 16 hours per week. If you then provide evidence showing a lower deduction applies, the council must award you arrears of HB (but see paras 17.11-15 if you delay doing this).

6.10   HB 3; HB60+ 3; NIHB 3; NIHB60+ 3

6.11   HB 74(1)-(3); HB60+ 55(1)-(3); NIHB 72(1)-(3); NIHB60+ 53(1)-(3)

6.12-13 HB 74(1),(2); HB60+ 55(1),(2); NIHB 72(1),(2); NIHB60+ 53(1),(2)

Table 6.3 **No non-dependant deductions**

Your circumstances:

No deductions are made for any non-dependants you have if you or your partner are:

(a) getting the daily living component of personal independence payment;

(b) getting the care component of disability living allowance;

(c) getting attendance allowance, or constant attendance allowance paid with an industrial injury or war disablement pension;

(d) getting an armed forces independence payment; or

(e) severely sight-impaired, blind or have recently regained sight (paras 12.50-51).

But (a)-(c) don't apply if the benefits mentioned cease – e.g. when you/your partner have been in hospital for four weeks.

Your non-dependant's circumstances:

In any other case, there is no deduction for a non-dependant who is:

(f) aged under 18;

(g) on state pension credit;

(h) aged under 25 and:

- on JSA(IB),

- on the assessment phase of ESA(IR),

- on income support, or

- on universal credit without any earned income;

(i) a full-time student (paras 22.4-8) – but see note;

(j) getting a government training allowance as a youth trainee;

(k) a member of the armed forces (regular or reserve) who is away on operations;

(l) a patient who has been in hospital or similar institution for more than 52 weeks (ignoring breaks of up to four weeks);

(m) a prisoner, whether sentenced, on remand or bail; or

(n) a temporary resident or visitor or anyone whose normal home is elsewhere.

There is also no deduction for anyone who isn't a non-dependant (table 4.4).

Note: Full-time students

The only time there is a deduction for a non-dependant who is a full-time student is when:

- you (the claimant) and your partner are under the age of 65;

- the student is in their summer vacation (para 22.18) and is working at least 16 hours per week (para 6.14); and

- none of the other exceptions in this table apply.

T6.3   HB 2(1), definition: 'attendance allowance', 3(2), 74(7),(8),(10); HB60+ 2(1), 3(2), 55(7)-(9);
         NIHB 2(1), 3(2), 72(7),(8),(10); NIHB60+ 2(1), 3(2), 53(7)-(9)

Table 6.4 **Weekly non-dependant deductions: 2017-18**

HB for rent:

If the non-dependant works at least 16 hours per week and has gross weekly income of:

▪	at least £430	£94.50
▪	at least £346 but under £430	£86.95
▪	at least £259 but under £346	£76.35
▪	at least £200 but under £259	£46.45
▪	at least £136 but under £200	£34.00
▪	under £136	£14.80
	Any other non-dependant (regardless of income level)	£14.80

HB for rates in Northern Ireland:

If the non-dependant is on JSA(IB), ESA(IR), IS or state pension credit (either kind)   Nil

If the non-dependant works at least 16 hours per week and has gross weekly income of:

▪	at least £394	£94.50
▪	at least £316 but under £394	£86.95
▪	at least £183 but under £316	£76.35
▪	under £183	£46.45
	Any other non-dependant (regardless of income level)	£14.80

Note:

For exceptions see table 6.3. For working 16 hours per week and gross income, see paras 6.14-17.

Working at least 16 hours per week

6.14   The rules about working at least 16 hours per week (which the law calls 'remunerative work') apply to non-dependants in the same way as they apply to you (the claimant): for the details see paras 14.69-72. For example, a non-dependant on maternity, paternity, adoption or sick leave doesn't count as working at least 16 hours per week (para 14.72).

Gross income

6.15   When a non-dependant's income is taken into account (table 6.4), the following are wholly disregarded:

(a)   personal independence payment;

(b)   disability living allowance;

(c)   attendance allowance, or constant attendance allowance paid with an industrial injury or war disablement pension; and

---

T6.4   HB 74(1),(2); HB60+ 55(1),(2); NIHB 72(1),(2); NIHB60+ 53(1),(2)

6.15   HB 2(1), definition: 'attendance allowance', 74(9); HB60+ 2(1), 55(10); NIHB 2(1), 72(9); NIHB60+ 2(1), 53(10)

(d) payments from (or originally derived from) the government-sponsored trust funds for people infected by NHS blood products, the Independent Living Funds and the London Bombings Relief Charitable Fund (para 15.42).

6.16   Apart from that, HB law says that the non-dependant's 'normal weekly gross income' is taken into account, without giving a list of what to include. In practice the council is likely to include:

(a) employed earnings (before tax, national insurance, etc have been deducted);

(b) self-employed net profit (after the deduction of reasonable expenses but before tax, national insurance, etc have been deducted);

(c) social security benefits, pensions and credits (except those in para 6.15);

(d) state, occupational and private pensions;

(e) rental income;

(f) maintenance;

(g) charitable and voluntary income; and

(h) interest on savings.

6.17   Because the 'normal' amount of gross weekly income is taken into account, short-term variations are likely to be ignored, but longer-term changes are taken into account. For example, a non-dependant who is a school assistant could count as working at least 16 hours per week throughout the year (see para 14.70(c)) but changes in their income may mean different levels of non-dependant deduction in term-times and holidays.

Non-dependant couples

6.18   If you have non-dependants who are a couple (or a polygamous marriage) only one deduction is made for them. This is the higher (or highest) of the amounts that would have applied if they were single. For the gross income limits in table 6.4, each of them is treated as having the gross income of both (or all) of them.

Example: A non-dependant couple

A claimant in Great Britain has two non-dependants, Nick and Pat, who are a couple. Nick works for 30 hours per week and has gross earnings of £300 per week. Pat works for 12 hours and has gross earnings of £200 per week.

If they were single, there would be two deductions, £76.35 for Nick and £14.80 for Pat (table 6.4).

Because they are a couple, there is only one deduction. Their combined gross income is £500 per week, so the deduction is £94.50 (table 6.4 and para 6.18).

6.16   HB 74(1),(2); HB60+ 55(1),(2); NIHB 72(1),(2); NIHB60+ 53(1),(2)

6.18   HB 74(3),(4); HB60+ 55(3),(4); NIHB 72(3),(4); NIHB60+ 53(3),(4)

Non-dependant of joint tenants

6.19 The following applies if you are a joint tenant of your home (with someone other than your partner), and there is also a non-dependant living there. If the non-dependant normally resides (para 4.29) with:

(a) only you (and your family), the whole non-dependant deduction is made from your HB;

(b) only your joint tenant (or more than one joint tenant), no non-dependant deduction is made from your HB;

(c) both you and your joint tenant (or more than one joint tenant), each of you gets a share of the non-dependant deduction.

The share mentioned in (c) need not be equal: the council should take into account the number of joint tenants concerned and the proportion of rent each of you pays (paras 8.12-13, 9.7-8 and table 10.5).

Delayed non-dependant deductions if you are aged 65 or over

6.20 The following rule applies if:

(a) you or your partner are aged 65 or more; and

(b) a non-dependant moves in, or there is any change in a non-dependant's circumstances which causes an increase in the amount of the deduction.

In these cases the change in your entitlement to HB is not implemented until the day 26 weeks after the change actually occurred. But if that is not a Monday, it is implemented from the following Monday.

The HB benefit cap

6.21 The 'benefit cap' sets a limit on the amount of HB and other welfare benefits working age claimants can receive. This section explains when it applies and how your HB is reduced if it does.

6.22 The benefit cap applies in Great Britain since April 2013 and in Northern Ireland since May 2016 (table 1.2). If your HB is reduced because of it, you may be able to get help from discretionary housing payments (para 25.9) and/or in Northern Ireland from welfare supplementary payments (para 6.33). The benefit cap does not amount to unlawful discrimination: R (SG and others) v SSWP.

When the benefit cap applies

6.23 The benefit cap applies to all working age claims (paras 1.23-25) unless any of the exceptions in table 6.5 apply to you. But the council/NIHE doesn't have to apply the benefit cap or reduce your HB unless and until it receives notice from the DWP/DFC (para 6.31).

6.19   HB 74(5); HB60+ 55(5); NIHB 72(5); NIHB60+ 53(5)

6.20   HB60+ 59(10)-(13); NIHB60+ 57(12)-(15)

6.22-23 WRA 96-97; HB 75A-75H; SI 2012/2994; NIWRO 101; NIHB 73A-73H; NISR 2016/55;
        R (SG and others) v SSWP UKSC (2015) www.bailii.org/uk/cases/UKSC/2015/16.html

Table 6.5 **Exceptions to the benefit cap**

The HB benefit cap doesn't apply in any of the following circumstances:

(a) You, your partner or a child or young person in your family are getting:

- personal independence payment,

- disability living allowance,

- attendance allowance or constant attendance allowance paid with an industrial injury pension (you or your partner only), or

- a war disablement or bereavement pension (para 13.16) (you or your partner only);

or are entitled to them but not receiving them because of being in a hospital or care home.

(b) You, your partner or a child or young person in your family are getting:

- carer's allowance,

- guardian's allowance, or

- working tax credit (you or your partner only);

or are entitled to them but not receiving them (paras 12.45-46).

(c) You or your partner are getting:

- main phase ESA with a support component,

- industrial injuries disablement benefit, or

- universal credit in specified supported accommodation (see para 6.28).

(d) Your claim is a pension age HB claim (table 1.5).

(e) During an extended payment of HB (para 17.46).

(f) During the 39 week 'grace period' after leaving work (para 6.29).

Notes:

- In practice, the DWP's/DFC's Benefit Cap Calculation Team is expected to notify the council/NIHE when these exceptions apply, apart from those relating to war pensions (HB A15/2013 paras 23, and 52).

- The exception relating to carer's allowance and guardian's allowance was introduced on the 7th November 2016, but in some cases it applied before then (Hurley and others v SSWP).

T6.5   HB 2(1), definition: 'attendance allowance', 75A, 75C, 75D, 75G; NIHB 2(1), 73A, 73C, 73D, 73G; SI 2016/909;
        NISR 2016/375; Hurley and others v SSWP EWHC (2015) www.bailii.org/uk/cases/EWHC/Admin/2015/3382.html

The amount of the benefit cap

6.24 The amount of the benefit cap is:

(a) for single claimants (table 4.1):

- £296.35 per week (£15,410 per year) in Greater London,

- £257.69 per week (£13,400 per year) elsewhere in Great Britain and in Northern Ireland;

(b) For lone parents and couples (table 4.1):

- £442.31 per week (£23,000 per year) in Greater London,

- £384.62 per week (£20,000 per year) elsewhere in Great Britain and in Northern Ireland.

6.25 Before 7th November 2016, the benefit cap throughout the UK was:

(a) £350.00 per week for single claimants;

(b) £500.00 per week for lone parents and couples.

These higher amounts continue to apply to you unless and until the council/NIHE receives notice from the DWP/DFC (para 6.31).

6.26 If you are in a polygamous marriage (table 4.1), the benefit cap applies to the two of you who were married earliest as though you were a couple. It doesn't apply to the others in the marriage.

The amount of the HB reduction

6.27 Table 6.6 explains how the reduction in your HB is calculated. As the table shows, the calculation can't reduce your HB to below 50p per week. This is so that you are eligible to claim a discretionary housing payment (para 25.5), but in Northern Ireland see also para 6.33.

Specified supported accommodation

6.28 If you live in specified supported accommodation (para 2.13 and table 2.3) and you aren't on universal credit, the amount of your HB is excluded from the benefit cap calculation (table 6.6) so you are unlikely to be affected by the benefit cap (HB A15/2013 para 6.5). If you are on UC, the HB benefit cap doesn't apply at all (but a benefit cap may apply to your UC instead: see *Help with Housing Costs Volume 1*).

6.24-25 HB 75CA, 75G definition: 'relevant amount'; NIHB 73CA, 73G; SI 2016/909; NISR 2016/375

6.26   HB 75G definition: 'couple'; NIHB 73G

6.27   HB 75D(2); NIHB 73D(2)

6.28   HB 75C(2)(a), 75F(1)(g), 75H; NIHB 73C(2)(a), 73F(1)(g), 73H

Table 6.6 **Calculating HB benefit cap reductions**

For each benefit week (para 5.31):

- (a) Add: together your and your partner's entitlement in that week to:
  - ■ HB, except in specified supported accommodation (para 6.28);
  - ■ JSA, ESA and IS;
  - ■ child benefit, child tax credit and maternity allowance;
  - ■ incapacity benefit and severe disablement allowance;
  - ■ widowed mother's/parent's allowance; and
  - ■ widow's pension and bereavement allowance.
- (b) If the total exceeds the benefit cap (paras 6.24-26), your HB is reduced by the amount of the excess.
- (c) But your HB can't be reduced below 50p per week.

Notes:

- ■ *HB:* Use the weekly amount before any reductions are made for recovering overpayments or administrative penalties. If you qualify for HB on two homes, include both amounts; the DWP advises the reduction in your HB is apportioned pro rata (HB A15/2013 para 50).
- ■ *Other benefits:* Use the weekly amount before any reductions are made for recovering overpayments, third party deductions or sanctions. In practice, the DWP's/DFC's Benefit Cap Calculation Team provides the council/NIHE with the figures (HB A15/2013 paras 12 onwards).

Example: The HB benefit cap

A claimant and her children are renting their home in London (it isn't specified supported accommodation). Before the benefit cap is applied, she qualifies for:

HB	£240.00 per week
Other benefits in table 6.6	£220.00 per week

Because the total of £460.00 per week exceeds the benefit cap of £442.31 per week (para 6.24), her HB is reduced by the difference (£17.69 per week) to £222.31 per week.

The 39 week grace period after leaving work

6.29   The HB benefit cap does not apply during the 39 weeks beginning with the day after you or your partner's last day of work if the following conditions are met (para 6.30). The DWP calls this time limited exception a 'grace period'. If you are a couple, either you or your partner must meet all the conditions; and if you each meet all the conditions from different dates, both grace periods apply.

T6.6   WRA 96(10) definition: 'welfare benefit'; NIWRO 101(7); HB 75A, 75C, 75D, 75G definition: 'reference period'; NIHB 73A, 73C, 73D, 73G

6.30 The conditions are that you/your partner:

(a) have ceased work; and

(b) for at least 50 of the 52 weeks before the last day of work, were engaged in work for which payment was made or expected, and were not entitled to JSA, ESA or IS; and

(c) in the last full week of work, worked for 16 hours or more.

For these purposes, being on maternity, paternity or adoption leave, or getting statutory sick pay, counts as being in work.

Applying and changing benefit cap reductions

6.31 In any particular case, the council need not apply the benefit cap or change the amount of any reduction until it receives notification from the DWP's/DFC's Benefit Cap Calculation Team. The council may however do either of these on its own initiative if it has the relevant information and evidence to do so.

When benefit cap reductions take effect

6.32 A benefit cap reduction can apply from the beginning of your HB claim. It can also start, change or end during your award of HB, and when it:

(a) starts or increases, HB changes from the date the council makes the decision to do so (this prevents overpayments of HB occurring solely as a result of a reduction);

(b) reduces or ends, HB changes from the date entitlement to the relevant welfare benefit (table 6.6) changed (so you get your resulting arrears of HB).

Claims wrongly decided as to a reduction may be corrected at any time.

Welfare supplementary payments in Northern Ireland

6.33 In Northern Ireland if you are responsible for a child you may be entitled to a welfare supplementary payment that covers your benefit cap reduction (paras 25.19-33) (or in any other case, a discretionary housing payment: para 25.9).

Conversion to weekly amounts

Rent, rates and service charges

6.34 Whenever a weekly figure is needed for rent, the following rules apply. The same rules apply to service charges; and in Northern Ireland to any rates payable with the rent:

(a) for rent due in multiples of weeks, divide by the number of weeks it covers;

(b) for rent due calendar monthly, multiply by 12 then divide by 52 to find the weekly figure;

(c) for rent due daily, multiply by seven to find the weekly figure.

6.29-30 HB 72E(1),(3)-(5); NIHB 72E(1),(3)-(5)

6.31 HB 75B; NIHB 73B

6.32 DAR 4(7H), 7(2)(r), 8(14F); NIDAR 4(6E), 7(2)(m), 8(14A)

6.33 NISR 2016/178 regs 2-5, 11-16

6.34 HB 80; HB60+ 61; NIHB 78; NIHB60+ 59

Rent-free periods

6.35   No HB is awarded during rent-free periods, including in Northern Ireland rate-free periods where rates are paid with the rent. HB is awarded only for periods in which rent is due (and if a rent-free or rate-free period begins or ends part way through a benefit week, the eligible rent and rates that week are calculated on a daily basis: para 6.34).

6.36   During the periods in which rent is due, the calculation factors (i.e. applicable amount, income and any non-dependant deductions) are adjusted as follows:

 (a) if rent is expressed on a weekly basis: multiply the calculation factors by 52 or 53, then divide by the number of weeks when rent is due in that year;

 (b) if rent is not expressed on a weekly basis: multiply the calculation factors by 365 or 366, then divide by the number of days when rent is due in that year.

Income

6.37   Whenever a weekly income figure is needed, the following rules apply:

 (a) for an amount relating to a multiple of weeks, divide by the number of weeks it covers;

 (b) for an amount relating to a calendar month, multiply by 12 then divide by 52;

 (c) for an amount relating to a year, there are two rules. For working age claims, divide the annual amount by 365 or 366 then multiply by seven. For pension age claims, simply divide the annual amount by 52;

 (d) for an amount relating to any other period longer than a week, divide the amount by the number of days it covers, then multiply by seven;

 (e) for an amount relating to a period less than a week, that is the weekly amount.

But for income in a self-employed person's assessment period (para 14.30), divide the amount by the number of days in the assessment period to find the daily figure, then multiply the daily figure by seven.

Rounding

6.38   The council may 'if appropriate' round any amount involved in the calculation of HB to the nearest penny, halfpennies being rounded upwards.

6.35   HB 81(1),(2),(3); HB60+ 62(1),(2),(3); NIHB 79(1),(2),(3); NIHB60+ 60(1),(2),(3)

6.37   HB 33; HB60+ 33; NIHB 30; NIHB60+ 31(a)

6.38   HB 80(8); HB60+ 61(7); NIHB 78(8); NIHB60+ 59(7)

Chapter 7 **Eligible rent**

- The payments HB can meet: see paras 7.2-4.
- Landlord and tenant types and which eligible rent rules apply to you: see paras 7.5-23.
- Rent restrictions – protected groups: see paras 7.24-38.

7.1 This chapter explains the general rules about eligible rent and chapters 8-11 give the detailed rules for social renters, private renters and other cases. Your eligible rent is the starting point in the calculation of your HB (para 6.2). So the higher it is, the more HB you get.

The payments HB can meet

Meaning of 'rent'

7.2 For HB purposes all the payments in table 7.1 count as 'rent'. This is different from landlord and tenant law (where rent means only payments under the terms of a tenancy agreement).

'Actual rent' and 'rent'

7.3 Your:

(a) 'actual rent' means the total of all payments in table 7.1 which you are liable to pay on your home (including any charges that HB can't cover);

(b) 'eligible rent' means the (often lower) figure used in calculating your HB (para 7.5).

Payments that don't count as rent

7.4 Table 7.2 lists the payments that don't count as 'rent' for HB purposes (or can't be met by HB for other reasons). You may be able to get help from a passport benefit with some of these (chapter 24).

7.2   HB 2(1) definition: 'rent'; HB60+ 2(1); NIHB 2(1); NIHB60+ 2(1)

7.3   HB 12(1)(a)-(j), Old 12(1)(a)-(j); HB60+ 12(1)(a)-(j), Old 12(1)(a)-(j);
        NIHB 13(1)(a)-(h), Old 13(1)(a)-(h); NIHB60+ 13(1)(a)-(h), Old 13(1)(a)-(h)

7.4   CBA 130(1)(a),(2)(b); NICBA 129(1),(2); HB 7(1),(5), 9(1)(k),(4), 11(2), 12(2); HB60+ 7(1),(5), 9(1)(k),(4), 11(2), 12(2);
        NIHB 7(1),(5), 9(1)(k),(4), 11(2), 13(2); NIHB60+ 7(1),(5), 9(1)(k),(4), 11(2), 13(2)

Table 7.1 **Payments that count as rent for HB purposes**

(a) Rent payable under a tenancy agreement.

(b) Rent payable under a shared ownership (also called equity sharing) tenancy but not mortgage payments.

(c) Board and lodging payments.

(d) Licence fees and payments for 'use and occupation'.

(e) Rent payable to a co-operative ('co-op') if you have no more than a nominal equity share in the co-op (GM A4.170-172).

(f) Payments under a rental purchase scheme – where you pay instalments to purchase your home over a fixed period, but your landlord remains the owner until you make the final payment (GM A4.140).

(g) In Scotland, payments in respect of a croft and the land it is on or relates to.

(h) 'Mesne profits' (in Scotland 'violent profits') payable after your tenancy or right to occupy is terminated.

(i) Site charges for a caravan or mobile home (whether or not you own it) as well as rent (if you don't own it).

(j) Mooring charges and berthing fees for a houseboat (whether or not you own it) as well as rent (if you don't own it) – this includes a narrow boat 'fitted out as a dwelling suitable for permanent residence' (R(H) 9/08).

(k) Service charges you have to pay as a condition of occupying your home (paras 8.43-45).

(l) Contributions towards maintenance and essential services in a charitable almshouse provided by a housing association (para 7.9) in Great Britain.

Notes: For exceptions see table 7.2. For limits on your eligible rent and for when service charges are (or aren't) included in it, see chapters 8-11.

T7.1   HB 12(1)(a)-(j), Old 12(1)(a)-(j); HB60+ 12(1)(a)-(j), Old 12(1)(a)-(j);
         NIHB 13(1)(a)-(h), Old 13(1)(a)-(h); NIHB60+ 13(1)(a)-(h), Old 13(1)(a)-(h)

Table 7.2 **Payments that don't count as rent for HB purposes**

(a) Mortgage and all other payments on a home you and/or your partner own, even if you only have the right to sell it with the consent of other joint owners (but HB can meet rent and service charges or a shared ownership tenancy).

(b) Payments on a long lease ('long tenancy') which was for more than 21 years when it was first granted, and which meets the legal formalities for a lease (R(H) 3/07).

(c) Payments under a co-ownership scheme – where you are entitled to a payment related to the value of your home when your membership of the scheme ends.

(d) Payments under a hire purchase or credit sale agreement (e.g. to buy a mobile home or furniture) or under a conditional sale agreement (unless it is for land).

(e) Payments on many Crown and government department tenancies.

(f) Payments for a tent or its pitch.

(g) Payments on some night shelters (para 3.7).

(h) Payments on bail and probation hostels ('approved premises') – for prisoners on remand and former prisoners.

(i) Payments on care homes and independent hospitals (see notes).

Notes:

In HB law, payments (a) to (e) because they don't count as 'rent', and payments (f) to (i) because you are treated as not being liable to pay rent. For other exclusions from HB, see chapter 2.

'Independent hospital' means a non-NHS hospital that is regulated by the Care Quality Commission in England; Healthcare Improvement Scotland in Scotland; Healthcare Inspectorate Wales in Wales; and the Regulation and Quality Improvement Authority in Northern Ireland.

Different landlord and tenant types and your eligible rent

7.5   The rules that determine how your eligible rent is worked out mainly depend on the type of landlord you have (social, private or other not-for-profit). Table 7.3 explains these differences and summarises which of chapters 8-10 apply to you. Paras 7.6-23 provide detailed definitions of general terms used such as 'landlord' and 'housing association' as well as terms that apply to the less common types of letting mainly covered in chapter 10.

Tenants and joint tenants

7.6   In this guide 'tenant' means any kind of rent-payer (table 7.1). If you are a joint tenant (para 4.42) your HB may be based on your share of the rent (paras 8.12, 9.7, 10.10 and 11.16).

T7.2(a)-(e)   CBA 130(2)(b); NICBA 129,(2); HB 12(2), Old 12(2); HB60+ 12(2), Old 12(2); NIHB 13(2), Old 13(2); NIHB60+ 13(2), Old 13(2)

T7.2(f)   HB 11(2); HB60+ 11(2); NIHB 11(2); NIHN60+ 11(2)

T7.2(g)-(h)   CBA 130(1)(a); NICBA 129(1)(a); HB 7(1),(5); HB60+ 7(1),(5); NIHB 7(1),(5); NIHB60+ 7(1),(5)

T7.2(i)   CBA 130(2); NICBA 129(2); HB 9(1)(k),(4); HB60+ 9(1)(k),(4); NIHB 9(1)(k),(4); NIHB60+ 9(1)(k),(4)

Table 7.3 **Eligible rent: types of landlord and tenant**

Landlords

(a) Social landlords

- Councils in Great Britain that administer HB (para 1.28).
- The Northern Ireland Housing Executive.
- Registered housing associations (para 7.10).

(b) Not for profit landlords

- Housing associations that are not registered with the national regulator (para 7.10).
- Registered charities (para 10.7).
- Not for profit voluntary associations (para 10.8).
- English county councils that don't administer HB.

(c) Private landlords

- Individuals, companies and firms.
- Any landlord not listed in (a).

Tenants

(d) Social renters (chapter 8)

- Tenants of a council in Great Britain that administers HB ('council tenants').
- Tenants of the NIHE.
- Tenants of a registered housing association (unless (e) or (f) apply to you).

(e) Private renters (chapter 9)

- Tenants of a private landlord (unless (f) applies to you).
- Tenants of a registered housing association in England but only if your home isn't social housing (para 7.12).
- Tenants of a not-for-profit landlord (unless (f) applies to you).

(f) Tenants of exempt accommodation or hostels (chapter 10)

- Tenants of a registered housing association only if you are provided with care, support or supervision.
- Tenants of a not-for-profit landlord only if you are provided with care, support or supervision (table 10.1).
- 'Hostel' residents of a private landlord where the building is managed by a not-for-profit body (para 7.23).

Notes: For 'rent referral cases see chapter 10. Other special cases are all given in paras 7.13-23 and in the relevant places in chapters 8-11.

'Hostel' means a building with units of non-self contained accommodation where meals or facilities for preparing food are provided (para 7.23).

Landlords and managing agents

7.7   Your 'landlord' means the person you owe a legal liability to pay rent to. This means your immediate landlord, not someone they are leasing the property from or a managing agent (even if you pay your rent to them). For example:

(a) if you are renting from a housing association, it is your landlord even if it is leasing the property from a private landlord;

(b) if you are renting from a private landlord, they are your landlord even if a housing association manages your tenancy;

(c) if you are renting from a council, it is your landlord even if your council manages its homes through a separate company (typically an 'arms-length management organisation' or 'tenant management organisation': ALMO/TMO).

7.8   It is your 'landlord' type (rather than their managing agent) that usually determines how your eligible rent is worked out, but if you live in a hostel it can be either your landlord or your managing agent (paras 7.21-23).

Housing associations

7.9   A 'housing association' means a society, body of trustees or company:

(a) whose objects or powers include the power to provide, manage, construct or improve housing; and

(b) which doesn't trade for profit or, if it does, is limited by its constitution not to pay a dividend.

7.10   A housing association is 'registered' (para 8.6) if it is registered:

(a) in England, with the Homes and Communities Agency;

(b) in Scotland, with the Scottish Housing Regulator;

(c) in Wales, with the Welsh Government;

(d) in Northern Ireland, with the Department for Communities.

In any other case it is 'unregistered' (paras 8.3 and 10.4).

7.11   In Scotland and Wales, registered housing associations are known as 'registered social landlords'. In England, they are known as 'private registered providers of social housing' (often shortened to 'registered providers'). 'Private' here simply means non-council (because councils are also registered providers).

7.7   HB 2(1) definition: 'hostel', 12(1), Old 12(1); HB60+ 2(1), 12(1), Old 12(1); NIHB 2(1), 13(1), Old 13(1); NIHB60+ 2(1), 13(1), Old 13(1)

7.9   Housing Associations Act 1985 s1(1); Housing (Northern Ireland) Order 1992 art 3; HB 2(1) definition: 'housing association'; HB60+ 2(1); NIHB 2(1); NIHB60+ 2(1)

7.10-11 HB 2(1) definition: 'registered housing association', 13C(5)(a),(6), sch 2 para 3(1),(1A); HB60+ 2(1), 13C(5)(a),(6), sch 2 para 3(1),(1A); NIHB 2(1), 14C(5)(a), sch 3 para 3(b); NIHB60+ 2(1), 14C(5)(a), sch 3 para 3(a),(1A)

7.12   In England only, if a registered housing association is profit-making, its lettings can be either social housing or private rented. A letting is 'social housing' if

(a)   it is a shared ownership tenancy; or

(b)   it is made available for rent 'to people whose needs are not adequately served by the commercial […] market', and 'the rent is below the market rate' (such as part of the Affordable Rent Programme).

In any other case (i.e. let at a market rent) unless paras 7.13-23 or 7.30 apply the eligible rent is worked out under the LHA rules (chapter 9).

Old HB claims

7.13   If you have an 'old HB claim' (para 7.14) your eligible rent is worked out in exactly the same way as if you lived in exempt accommodation (para 10.10).

7.14   You have an 'old HB' claim only if all of the following apply:

(a)   you have been continuously entitled to HB since 1st January 1996 (in Northern Ireland, 1st April 1996), ignoring breaks of four weeks or less;

(b)   you have not moved home since then, or moved only because your home was made uninhabitable by fire, flood or natural disaster; and

(c)   your landlord is not the council/NIHE or a registered housing association.

Protected tenancies

7.15   If you have a 'protected tenancy' (paras 7.16-20) your eligible rent is worked out in the same way as a social renter (chapter 8). The only exception to this rule is if you live in exempt accommodation or have an 'old HB' claim (para 10.2). Protected tenancy status only determines if you are a social renter. It is separate from protected renter status (paras 7.30-36) and neither, one or both could apply at any time.

7.16   In HB law these lettings are called 'excluded tenancies' because they cannot be referred to the rent officer. In landlord and tenant law they are sometimes called Rent Act or 'protected' tenancies but the landlord and tenant definition does not perfectly overlap with the HB one.

7.17   Protected tenancies are usually older kinds of letting agreement that started before January 1989 (in Northern Ireland, June 2006) and/or agreements where you are entitled to ask the rent officer to register your rent (i.e. set the legal maximum rent you can be charged).

7.18   In England and Wales your letting agreement is a protected tenancy if:

(a)   (regardless of the agreement) it was entered into before 15th January 1989; or

(b)   it is a housing association secure tenancy; or

(c)   it is any other type of housing association or private sector letting where the rent officer is entitled to register a rent.

7.12   Housing and Regeneration Act 2008 s68-71 and 77; HB 13C(5)(a), sch 2 para 3(1A); HB60+ 13C(5)(a), sch 2 para 3(1A)

7.13   CPR sch 3 para 4(1)(a); NICPR sch 3 para 4(1)(a)

7.14   CPR sch 3 para 4(2)(aa),(3),(10); NICPR sch 3 para 4(1A)(aa),(2),(9)

7.15   HB 12B(1), 13C(5)(c), 14(2)(b); HB60+ 12B(1), 13C(5)(c), 14(2)(b); NIHB 13A(1), 14C(5)(c), 15(3)(b); NIHB60+ 13A(1), 14C(5)(c), 15(3)(b)

7.18   HB sch 2 paras 4-8; HB60+ sch 2 paras 4-8

7.19   In Scotland your letting is a protected tenancy if:

(a) (regardless of the agreement) it was entered into before 2nd January 1989; or

(b) it is a housing association tenancy or any other kind of private sector letting where the rent officer is entitled to register a rent.

7.20   In Northern Ireland your letting is a protected tenancy if your rent is controlled (tied to a historic rateable value) or is fixed by a rent officer. In broad terms this applies to your tenancy if:

(a) in certain circumstances, it began before 1st October 1978; or

(b) it began on or after 14th June 2006; and

  ▪   your house or flat was built or converted before 6th November 1956; and

  ▪   it does not meet the fitness standard.

Hostels

7.21   If you are a private renter table 7.3 and para 9.2) and live in a 'hostel' your eligible rent is worked out using the rent referral rules (paras 10.35 and 10.38) unless it also qualifies as exempt accommodation in which case the old scheme rules apply instead (paras 10.10-11). But your dwelling only counts as a hostel if it meets the conditions in the next two paragraphs. (Note that if you rent from a social landlord (table 7.3(a)) your eligible rent is worked out using the social renter rules unless your home isn't social housing: para 7.12).

7.22   A hostel means a building which provides domestic accommodation for residents or a class of residents:

(a) that is not separate or self-contained together with either meals or adequate facilities for preparing food; and

(b) which is not a independent hospital or Abbeyfield Home; and

(c) meets one or more of the operating conditions in para 7.23.

7.23   The operating conditions referred to in para 7.22 are that the building is:

(a) managed by a registered charity or not for profit voluntary organisation which provides care, support or supervision to help people be rehabilitated or resettled within the community;

(b) run on a non-commercial basis, and wholly or partly funded by a government department or agency or local authority; or

(c) managed or owned by a registered housing association (para 7.10).

Condition (c) is only relevant if you don't fall under the social renter rules (e.g. if your home isn't social housing or if it is managed, rather than owned by, a registered housing association).

7.19   HB sch 2 paras 4-8; HB60+ sch 2 paras 4-8

7.20   NIHB sch 3 para 4; NIHB60+ sch 3 para 4

7.21-23 HB 2(1) definition: 'hostel', HB60+ 2(1); NIHB 2(1); NIHB60+ 2(1)

Rent restrictions and temporary protection

7.24   This section describes the general rules about how your eligible rent can be restricted (limited) depending on whether you are a social renter, private renter or if you fall within the 'old scheme' or rent referral rules (chapters 8-11). It also describes the common rules that give you time-limited protection from the restrictions described in those chapters.

High rents and over-sized accommodation

7.25   There are a number of rules about how your eligible rent can be reduced (or limited) if your rent is considered to be too high or your home to be too large. These are:

(a)   the social renter size criteria (paras 8.15-26);

(b)   the rules for exempt accommodation and old (pre-1996) HB claims (paras 10.9-20);

(c)   local housing allowance (LHA) rules (paras 9.4-9);

(d)   the rent referral rules (paras 10.28-38);

(e)   the rules for protected and similar tenancies (paras 7.15-20 and 8.8); and

(f)   the default power to restrict rents (paras 7.26-27)

See also chapter 11 for general rules about the size criteria ('the bedroom tax'), and paras 7.28-38 to see if you qualify for time-limited protection.

The default power to restrict the rent

7.26   If your eligible rent 'appears [...] greater than it is reasonable to meet by way of HB', the authority has the power to reduce it to 'such lesser sum as seems [...] to be an appropriate rent'.

7.27   Although the residual power to restrict can apply to council tenants (Burton v Camden LBC) the law is somewhat unclear and disputed as to when and how it can be used. It seems it can't be used if you fall under social renter size criteria or old scheme rules (para 7.25(a)-(b)); has disputed or limited use if you fall under the LHA or rent referral rules ([2011] UKUT 156 (AAC), at para 40); and therefore is only likely to affect you if none of these apply (e.g. you are a social renter unaffected by the size criteria: para 7.25(e) and table 8.2). If the power is used, the authority must take your personal circumstances into account as well as matters that relate to your rent (R v Westminster HBRB ex parte Laali).

Temporary protection from rent restrictions

7.28   If you are a protected renter (para 7.30) you are wholly or partly protected from your eligible rent being reduced (paras 7.25-27) for a period of up to 13 weeks or one year depending on which type of protection you qualify for (paras 7.29-36).

7.26   HB 12B(6); HB60+ 12B(6); NIHB 13A(7); NIHB60+ 13A(7)

7.27   HB 12B(1); HB60+ 12B(1); NIHB 13A(1); NIHB60+ 13A(1)
          Burton v Camden LBC 17/12/97 CA 30 HLR 991;
          R (Laali) v Westminster CC HBRB 08/12/00 QBD www.casetrack.com subscriber site case reference CO/1845/2000)

7.29 The protections apply whether your eligible rent is worked out under:

(a) the rules if you are a social renter (chapter 8);

(b) the LHA rules if you are a private renter (chapter 9);

(c) the rules for exempt accommodation and old (pre-1996) HB claims (chapter 10); or

(d) the rent referral rules if your claim is referred to the rent officer.

The footnotes give separate references for each of these.

Who is a protected renter

7.30 You are a protected renter if you:

(a) could previously afford their rent; or

(b) have had a death in your home; or

(c) are considered vulnerable.

Protections (a) and (b) apply to all kinds of HB (para 7.29), and are described in paras 7.31-36. But protection (c) only applies if you live in exempt accommodation or have an old (pre-1996) HB claim, and is described in paras 10.22-25.

People who could previously afford their home

7.31 This protection applies if you meet the following conditions when you make a claim for HB:

(a) you or any combination of the occupiers of your home (para 7.37) could afford the financial commitments there when your liability for rent was entered into (no matter how long ago that was); and

(b) you have not received HB for any period during the 52 weeks before your award of HB starts, and nor has your partner (if you have one: table 4.1).

7.32 In this case, the protection lasts for the first 13 weeks of your award of HB. This may give you time to move or change your circumstances (e.g. by getting someone else to move in with you or improving your income) without the additional pressure of having insufficient HB. If you stop receiving HB (during or after the 13 weeks) the protection can only apply to a new HB claim if there are at least 52 weeks between the end of your old HB award and the start of the new one.

7.31 Social renter: HB 12BA(6),(7); NIHB 13AA(6),(7)
Private renter: HB 12D(5),(6); HB60+ 12D(5),(6); NIHB 13C(5),(6); NIHB60+ 13C(5),(6)
Old scheme: HB Old 13(7),(8); HB60+ Old 13(7),(8); NIHB Old 14(7),(8); NIHB60+ Old 14(7),(8)
Rent referral: HB 13(8), 13ZA(3),(4); HB60+ 13(8), 13ZA(3),(4); NIHB 14(8), 14A(3),(4); NIHB60+ 14(8), 14A(3),(4)

7.32 Social renter: HB 12BA(8); NIHB 13AA(8)
Private renter: HB 12D(7)(b); HB60+ 12D(7)(b); NIHB 13C(7)(b); NIHB60+ 13C(7)(b)
Old scheme: HB Old 13(7); HB60+ Old 13(7); NIHB Old 14(7); NIHB60+ Old 14(7)
Rent referral: HB 13ZA(3); HB60+ 13ZA(3); NIHB 14A(3); NIHB60+ 14A(3)

7.33   While the protection applies to you, your eligible rent is:

(a) the full actual rent payable on your home (para 7.3);

(b) minus an amount for service charges which are ineligible for HB (worked out as described in paras 8.47-51) and in Northern Ireland an amount for rates unless you are billed separately (para 19.7).

People who have had a death in their home

7.34   This protection applies if you meet the following conditions when you make a claim for HB or during your award of HB:

(a) any of the occupiers of your home (para 7.37) has died within the past 12 months (including occupiers who were temporarily absent); and

(b) you have not moved since the date of that death.

7.35   In this case, the protection lasts for the 12 months following the date of the person's death. This may give you time to move or change your circumstances (e.g. by getting someone else to move in with you or improving your income) without the additional pressure of having insufficient HB. If you stop receiving HB and then make a new claim at the same address within the 12 months, the protection resumes until 12 months after the date of the person's death (in other words, it isn't extended). If you move, the protection ends.

7.36   While the protection applies to you:

(a) if you weren't on HB on the date of the person's death, your eligible rent is worked out in the same way as in para 7.33;

(b) if you were on HB on that date, your eligible rent must not be reduced below whatever it was immediately before that date (but it is increased if any rule requires this).

7.33   Social renter: HB 12BA(6); NIHB 13AA(6)
         Private renter: HB 12D(5); HB60+ 12D(5); NIHB 13C(5); NIHB60+ 13C(5)
         Old scheme: HB Old 13(7); HB60+ Old 13(7); NIHB Old 14(7); NIHB60+ Old 14(7)
         Rent referral: HB 13ZA(3); HB60+ 13ZA(3); NIHB 14A(3); NIHB60+ 14A(3)

7.34-35 Social renter: HB 12BA(3),(4),(5); NIHB 13AA(3),(4),(5)
         Private renter: HB 12D(3),(4),(7)(a); HB60+ 12D(3),(4),(7)(a); NIHB 13C(3),(4),(7)(a); NIHB60+ 13C(3),(4),(7)(a)
         Old scheme: HB Old 13(5),(6); HB60+ Old 13(5),(6); NIHB Old 14(5),(6); NIHB60+ Old 14(5),(6)
         Rent referral: HB 13(8), 13ZA(1),(2); HB60+ 13(8), 13ZA(1),(2); NIHB 14(8), 14A(1),(2); NIHB60+ 14(8), 14A(1),(2)

7.36   Social renter: HB 12BA(3)(a),(b); NIHB 13AA(3)(a),(b)
         Private renter: HB 12D(3)(a),(b); HB60+ 12D(3)(a),(b); NIHB 13C(3)(a),(b); NIHB60+ 13C(3)(a),(b)
         Old scheme: HB Old 13(5); HB60+ Old 13(5); NIHB Old 14(5); NIHB60+ Old 14(5)
         Rent referral: HB 2(1) definition: 'reckonable rent', 13ZA(1); HB60+ 2(1), 13ZA(1); NIHB 2(1), 14A(1); NIHB60+ 2(1), 14A(1)

Occupiers related to a protected renter

7.37   In deciding if you qualify as a protected renter, the only 'occupiers' taken into account are:

(a) you (the claimant) and members of your family (partner, children, young persons: para 4.2); and

(b) any 'relative' of you or your partner (including non-dependants, lodgers and joint occupiers) who has no separate right to occupy the dwelling.

In the law, the term 'linked persons' is also used to refer to these occupiers.

Who is a 'relative'

7.38   A 'relative' is defined for all HB purposes as:

(a) a parent, daughter, son, sister or brother;

(b) a parent-in-law, daughter-in-law, son-in-law, step-daughter or step-son, including equivalent relations arising through civil partnership;

(c) a partner of any of the above (by marriage or civil partnership, or by living together as a married couple or as civil partners); or

(d) a grandparent, grandchild, aunt, uncle, niece or nephew.

7.37   HB 2(1) definition: 'linked person', Old 13(10),(11); HB60+ 2(1), Old 13(10),(11); NIHB 2(1), Old 14(10),(11); NIHB60+ 2(1), Old 14(10),(11)

7.38   HB 2(1) definitions: 'close relative', 'couple', 'relative'; HB60+ 2(1); NIHB 2(1); NIHB60+ 2(1)

Examples: The protected groups

Redundancy

A claimant makes a claim for HB after he is made redundant. His actual rent is high. He moved to this address when he was in a well-paid job and could easily afford the rent and outgoings. He has not been on HB in the last 52 weeks.

Because of the protection for people who could formerly afford their accommodation, his eligible rent must not be restricted in any way for the first 13 weeks of his award of HB. During those weeks, his eligible rent is his actual rent minus amounts for any ineligible services.

Bereavement before claiming HB

A claimant makes a claim for HB after the death of her husband. She has not moved since her husband's death. Her actual rent is high.

Because of the protection for people who have had a bereavement, her eligible rent must not be restricted in any way until the first anniversary of her husband's death. Until then, her eligible rent is her actual rent minus amounts for any ineligible services.

Bereavement while on HB

A claimant is on HB and his mother lives with him as his non-dependant. His eligible rent takes account of the fact that he qualifies for two bedrooms (chapter 11) and is £125 per week. Following the death of his mother he only qualifies for one bedroom.

Because he has been bereaved while on HB he is a protected renter and his eligible rent must not be reduced below £125 per week until the first anniversary of his mother's death.

Chapter 8 **Social renters**

- Who is a social renter: see paras 8.2-8.
- Eligible rent for social renters: see paras 8.9-14.
- How and when your eligible rent is reduced if your home is too large: see paras 8.15-26.
- Service charges general rules: see paras 8.27-51.
- Eligible services: see paras 8.52-66.
- Ineligible services: see paras 8.67-84.
- Other items included in setting rents: see paras 8.85-90.

8.1 This chapter explains how your eligible rent is worked out if you rent your home from a social landlord (you are a 'social renter': para 8.2). It includes the general rules about service charges that also apply if you eligible rent is worked out using the rules in chapter 10.

Who is a social renter

8.2 You are a 'social renter' if:

(a) you live in Great Britain and your landlord is the council you claim HB from (para 8.4);

(b) your landlord is the Northern Ireland Housing Executive (para 8.4);

(c) you are a former council/NIHE ('stock transfer') tenant (para 8.5);

(d) in most cases, your landlord is a registered housing association (paras 8.6-7); or

(e) your letting falls within one of the special cases in table 8.1.

Where any of (a)-(e) apply 'landlord' and 'tenant' includes a shared ownership/equity sharing agreement. For further details and exceptions see paras 8.3-8. For the meaning of 'landlord' and tenant see paras 7.6-8.

Tenants of any other 'social' or not-for-profit landlord

8.3 If you rent your home from any other kind of not-for-profit landlord that is not a registered housing association (such as a charity) you are treated as a private renter unless you live in exempt accommodation (para 10.3) or any of the exceptions in table 9.1 apply.

8.2   AA134(1A), NIAA 126(1)(b); HB 12B(1), A13(1),(2); 13C(5)(a)-(c), 14(2)(b), sch 2; HB60+ 12B(1), 13C(5)(a)-(c), 14(2)(b), sch 2; NIHB 13A(1), A14(1),(2), 14C(5)(a)-(c), 15(3)(b), sch 3; NIHB60+ 13A(1), 14C(5)(a)-(c), 15(3)(b), sch 3

8.3   HB 13C(1),(2),(5); HB60+ 13C(1),(2),(5); NIHB 14C(1),(2),(5); NIHB60+ 14C(1),(2),(5)

Local authority and NIHE tenants

8.4   If your landlord is a local council that administers HB or the NIHE (para 8.2) your HB is paid as a rent rebate (para 16.16) and your eligible rent is worked out as a social renter. (The local housing allowance, rent referral and old scheme rules only apply to rent allowance claims). For the meaning of 'landlord' see para 7.7.

Former local authority / NIHE ('stock transfer') tenants

8.5   Where your tenancy started with the council/NIHE but your home was transferred to a new a new landlord (sometimes called a 'stock transfer') your eligible rent is worked out as follows:

(a)   where your new landlord is a registered housing association (para 7.10) according to the rules for that type of landlord (paras 8.6-7);

(b)   in any other case in the same way as in para 8.7(b) (not living in social housing) except that where your rent is unreasonable you fall under the LHA rules,

but (in either case) if your rent has not been increased since the transfer took place your eligible rent is worked out as a social renter.

Registered housing association tenants

8.6   If your landlord is a registered housing association (paras 7.9-12) your eligible rent is worked out as a social renter unless:

(a)   you live in exempt accommodation (paras 10.3-6);

(b)   if you live in England and your home isn't social housing (para 7.12); or

(c)   the council/NIHE considers your rent to be unreasonable (para 8.7).

Registered housing association tenants who are not social renters

8.7   Where your landlord is a registered housing association and any of the exceptions in para 8.6 apply your eligible rent is worked out:

(a)   using the old scheme rules if you live in exempt accommodation (para 10.3);

(b)   using the rules for a private renter (para 9.3) if your home isn't social housing unless

- you have a stock transfer tenancy and your rent is reasonable,

- you have a protected tenancy (paras 7.15-20),

- you live in a hostel (paras 7.22-23),

- a substantial part of your rent is attributable to board and attendance;

8.4   AA134(1A), NIAA 126(1)(b); HB 12B(1), A13(1),(2); HB60+ 12B(1); NIHB 13A(1), A14(1),(2), NIHB60+ 13A(1)

8.5   HB 12B(1), A13(1),(2); 13C(5)(c), 14(2)(b), sch 2 para 11; HB60+ 12B(1), 13C(5)(c), 14(2)(b), sch 2 para 11;
           NIHB 13A(1), A14(1),(2), 14C(5)(c), 15(3)(b), sch 3 para 5; NIHB60+ 13A(1), 14C(5)(c), 15(3)(b), sch 3 para 5

8.6   HB 12B(1), A13(1),(2); 13C(5)(a),(b), 14(2)(b), sch 2 para 3(1),(1A),(2)(b); HB60+ 12B(1), 13C(5)(a),(b), 14(2)(b), sch 2 para 3(1),(1A),(2);
           NIHB 13A(1), A14(1),(2), 14C(5)(a),(b), 15(3)(b), sch 3 para 3(b); NIHB60+ 13A(1), 14C(5)(a),(b), 15(3)(b), sch 3 para 3

8.7   HB 12B(1), A13(1),(2); 13C(5)(a)-(e), 14(2)(b), sch 2 para 3(1),(1A),(2)(b); HB60+ 12B(1), 13C(5)(a)-(e), 14(2)(b), sch 2 para 3(1),(1A),(2);
           NIHB 13A(1), A14(1),(2), 14C(5)(a)-(e), 15(3)(b), sch 3 para 3(b); NIHB60+ 13A(1), 14C(5)(a)-(e), 15(3)(b), sch 3 para 3

(c)   using the rent referral rules in any other case where the authority considers your rent to be unreasonably high (or your home unreasonably large if you have a pension age claim): see table 10.3 and paras 10.42-44.

If either of the first two exceptions to (b) applies you are a social renter, in any other case the rent referral rules apply.

Social renters: other lettings

8.8   Regardless of whom your landlord is, if your tenancy or letting agreement falls within one of the categories in table 8.1 you are treated as a social renter and your eligible rent is worked out using the rules in this chapter.

Table 8.1 **Who is a social renter: other lettings**

You are a social renter and your eligible rent is assessed under the rules in this chapter if:

(a)   you have a protected or similar tenancy (para 7.15) (regardless of who your landlord is);

(b)   you live in a mobile home, caravan or houseboat; and either

- you pay site fees or mooring charges to a local authority that administers HB (whether or not if you also pay rent for your dwelling and whether or not your rent is paid to the same or a different landlord), or

- you live on a gypsy or traveller site (see note) where the landlord is an English county council;

(c)   you have a shared ownership tenancy (para 8.2); and either

- your landlord is a local authority that administers HB, or

- your landlord is a registered housing association (whether or not the authority considers your rent to be unreasonably high).

Note: A gypsy or traveller site means a site provided for:

- people with a cultural tradition of nomadism or living in a caravan; or

- other people with a nomadic or cultural tradition of travelling regardless of their race or religion including travellers, show people, and those who no longer travel through reasons of health or age.

8.8   See table 8.1

T8.1   HB 13C(5)(a),(c),(d), 14(2)(b), sch 2 paras 4-8, 12; HB60+ 13C(5)(4),(c),(d), 14(2)(b) sch 2 paras 4-8, 12;
         NIHB 13C(5)(a),(c),(d), 15(3)(b) sch 3 para 4; NIHB60+ 13C(5)(a),(c),(d), 15(3)(b) sch 3 para 4

Eligible rent

8.9   This section explains how your eligible rent is worked out if you are a social renter. Paras 8.10-13 are also the starting point for exempt accommodation and rent referral cases (chapter 10).

The general rule

8.10   Your eligible rent is:

(a) your actual weekly rent (para 8.11);

(b) minus an amount for service charges which are ineligible for HB (table 8.4) and in Northern Ireland an amount for rates unless you are billed separately (para 19.7).

8.11   Your actual weekly rent means the full weekly amount you are liable to pay on your home (para 7.3). For items in your rent that are not services (e.g. overheads, management costs, garages, land, business premises and space for a carer) see paras 8.85-90.

Joint tenants

8.12   If you have at least one joint tenant who is not a member of your family (paras 4.42-46):

(a) first, the eligible rent for your dwelling is worked out as described in para 8.10;

(b) then it is apportioned (para 8.13) between you and the other joint tenant(s).

8.13   'Apportioning' means deciding how much is fairly attributable to each of you. To do this the authority takes account of:

(a) the number of joint tenants, including any who are ineligible for HB such as students (Nagshabandi v Camden LBC);

(b) the proportion of rent paid by each of you;

(c) the presence or absence of each of you (CH/3376/2002);

(d) the size and number of rooms each of you occupies;

(e) whether there is any written or other agreement between you; and

(f) any other relevant circumstances.

Eligible rent reductions

8.14   Your eligible rent may be reduced:

(a) under the social renter size criteria if your home is too large (paras 8.15-26);

(b) under the rent referral rules if you rent from a registered housing association, and

■   the authority considers your rent to be unreasonably high (para 8.7); or

■   you or your partner are state pension credit age and the authority considers your home to be too large (para 8.7);

(c) in any other case if your rent is unreasonable under the default power (para 7.26).

8.10   HB 12B(2), B13(2)(a); HB60+ 12B(2); NIHB 13A(2), B14(2)(a); NIHB60+ 13A(2)

8.12   HB 12B(4); HB60+ 12B(4); NIHB 13A(4); NIHB60+ 13A(4)

8.13   Nagshabandi v Camden LBC HBRB 19/07/02 CA [2002] EWCA Civ 1038 www.bailii.org/ew/cases/EWCA/Civ/2002/1038.html

The social renter size criteria

8.15   This section explains how your eligible rent can be reduced if you have more bedrooms in your home than you qualify for. This is often called 'under-occupying' your home. In the law the reduced figure is known as the 'maximum rent social sector'.

8.16   The rules about this have applied in Great Britain since 1st April 2013 and in Northern Ireland from 20th February 2017. In Scotland and Northern Ireland if a reduction applies you are normally fully compensated through other payments (para 25.8).

When a reduction applies

8.17   Your eligible rent is reduced if:

(a) you are a social renter (para 8.2);

(b) you – and also your partner(s) if you are in a couple or polygamous marriage – are under state pension credit age (para 1.24);

(c) you have more bedrooms than you qualify for (para 8.22); and

(d) none of the exceptions in table 8.2 apply to you.

But if a member of your household has died or you could afford the rent before you claimed HB you are a 'protected renter' and the reduction can be delayed for up to 13 weeks/one year (paras 7.28-38).

Table 8.2 **Exceptions to the social renter size criteria**

The social renter size criteria don't apply to you if:

(a) you or your partner have reached state pension credit age (para 1.24) (even if you receive IS/JSA(IB)/ESA(IR));

(b) you have a shared ownership tenancy (table 8.1); or

(c) your landlord is a registered housing association and the rent referral rules apply to you because the authority considers your rent is unreasonably high (para 8.7 and table 10.3);

(d) you rent from a registered housing association and your home is exempt accommodation (paras 10.3-6);

(e) live in temporary accommodation provided by the authority because you were homeless or to prevent you from becoming so (paras 8.18-21).

Note:

In Scotland and Northern Ireland if the social renter size criteria apply and your HB is reduced you are likely to be fully compensated through other payments (paras 25.8 and 25.19).

8.16   NISR 2016/326 reg 1(3); NISR 2016/452 reg 7

8.17   HB A13(1), B13(2); NIHB A14(1), B14(2)

T8.2   HB A13(2)(b)-(c); CPR sch 3 para 4(1)(b); NIHB A14(2)(b)-(c); NICPR sch 3 para 4(1)(b)

What is temporary accommodation

8.18   The same authority you claim HB from is responsible helping you if you are homeless. If you apply for help in certain circumstances the authority must provide you with temporary accommodation (e.g. if permanent housing isn't available) or may do so to prevent you from becoming homeless. Temporary accommodation is often provided housing is often provided by the council/NIHE through an arrangement it has with a housing association or a private landlord (such as private rented housing the council/NIHE holds on a short-term lease). Your home counts as temporary accommodation and the social renter size criteria do not apply to you if it meets both conditions in the next two paragraphs.

8.19   The first condition is that the accommodation must have been made available to you by the authority or by a registered housing association (para 7.10) under an arrangement it has with the authority for the purpose of:

(a)   satisfying a homelessness duty it owes you following your application for assistance; or

(b)   preventing you from becoming homeless (as defined in the homeless persons legislation).

8.20   The second condition is that the accommodation is:

(a)   'board and lodging' (as defined in para 23.33); or

(b)   held by the authority or registered housing association on a short-term lease ('licensed accommodation' as defined in para 23.35); or

(c)   provided by someone else but which the authority or registered housing association has a right to use under an agreement (other than a leasehold agreement: para 23.34).

8.21   If you have been temporarily housed by the authority as homeless in one of its own properties (instead of one it has leased or holds on a licence from another landlord) then you are not counted as living in temporary accommodation and the social renter size criteria apply in the normal way.

The amount of the reduction

8.22   The reduction is calculated as follows:

(a)   if your home has one bedroom more than you qualify for (table 11.1), your eligible rent is reduced by 14%;

(b)   if it has two or more bedrooms more than you qualify for, your eligible rent is reduced by 25%.

No reduction applies if your home has the same number of bedrooms as you qualify for, or fewer bedrooms.

8.19   HB A13(3); NIHB A14(3)

8.20   HB A13(4); NIHB A14(4)

8.21   HB A13(4); NIHB A14(4)

8.22   HB B13(2)(b),(3); NIHB B14(2)(b),(3)

The reduction for joint tenants

8.23   If you have at least one joint tenant who is not a member of your family (paras 4.42-46):

(a)   first, the reduction (of 14% or 25%) is made from the eligible rent for your dwelling;

(b)   then the resulting figure is apportioned (para 8.13) between you and the other joint tenant(s).

Eligible rent after a reduction

8.24   The reduced eligible rent is used in calculating your HB. Deductions for non-dependants (para 6.2) and/or because you have excess income (para 6.6) are made from the reduced eligible rent.

The number of bedrooms you qualify for

8.25   You qualify for the appropriate number of bedrooms for the occupiers of your home: see table 11.1.

Which occupiers are taken into account

8.26   The social sector size criteria take account of the occupiers of your dwelling. This means:

(a)   you (the claimant) and members of your family (partner, children and young persons: para 4.2);

(b)   non-dependants (para 4.26);

(c)   lodgers (para 4.36);

(d)   joint tenants (para 4.42); and

(e)   any other person who occupies your dwelling as their home.

For further details, see paras 11.10-11.

Service charges: general rules

8.27   The remainder of this chapter (paras 8.28-90) deals with service charges (and related charges) and whether they are eligible for HB or not it applies if:

(a)   you are a social renter (para 8.2) (unless, in England, your home is not social housing: para 7.12);

(b)   your rent is assessed under the old scheme or rent referral rules described in chapter 10 (for example, if you live in 'exempt accommodation', or if you are a private tenant who has been on HB since before April 2008).

It does not apply if your eligible rent is assessed as a private renter under the LHA rules in chapter 9.

8.23   HB B13(2)(c); NIHB B14(2)(c)

8.25   HB B13(5); B14(5)

The importance of service charges

8.28   If you are a tenant you may pay for services either as part of your rent (whether or not it is mentioned in the letting agreement) or separately. As illustrated in the examples, there are two main methods of showing service charges in your letting agreement:

(a)   your rent may be shown as so much per week (or month, etc) including certain services; or

(b)   it may be shown as so much per week (or month, etc) with an amount for service charges being due on top of your rent.

8.29   If you are a tenant of a social landlord or your eligible rent is assessed under the old scheme or rent referral rules described in chapter 10, the authority must consider whether the service charges you pay are eligible for HB (para 8.43).

(a)   If a charge is 'eligible for HB', this means that it can be included in your eligible rent. It does not need to be valued; and no deduction is made for it at any stage in deciding the amount of your eligible rent unless the charge for it is excessive (para 8.49).

(b)   If a charge is 'ineligible for HB', this means that it cannot be included in your eligible rent. With certain exceptions, it needs to be valued and deducted at some point in deciding your eligible rent (para 8.47).

8.30   The above points (para 8.29) can be particularly significant if you are not a social renter (para 8.2) but you live in supported housing that qualifies as 'exempt accommodation' (para 10.4). The authority has a strong financial incentive to identify any ineligible services (such as support) to ensure your eligible rent does not exceed the rent officer's valuation (para 23.28). It is therefore essential for your landlord to provide a detailed breakdown of the charge for each service they provide.

Examples: Service charges

1.   A council tenant's weekly rent is expressed as being £100 per week including £20 per week for fuel for their own flat and £10 per week for heating, lighting, cleaning and maintaining communal areas. In this case the eligible rent is £80 per week. The ineligible charge for fuel for the tenant's own flat is deducted.

2.   A housing association tenant's weekly rent is expressed as being £70 per week plus £20 per week for fuel for the claimant's own room and £10 per week for heating, lighting, cleaning and maintaining communal areas. In this case the eligible rent is £80 per week. The eligible charge for the communal areas is added.

Notes

■   The facts in the two examples are the same but are expressed differently.

■   Information about the service charges illustrated is given later in this chapter.

■   The terms 'net rent' and 'gross rent' are sometimes used to distinguish between different methods of expressing a rent figure. But they are used in different ways nationally and are best avoided for HB purposes.

Who deals with your service charges for HB

8.31 If you live in Northern Ireland the NIHE deals with all matters for your HB claim to do with service charges. If you live in England, Scotland or Wales the authority always identifies whether a charge is eligible/ineligible but either the authority or the rent officer is responsible for determining its value as follows:

(a) if your landlord is the authority, the authority values it;

(b) if your landlord is a registered housing association, you live in 'social housing' (paras 7.12) and the authority has not referred your rent to the rent officer (table 8.3, step 4), the authority values it;

(c) if you live in 'exempt accommodation' (paras 10.3-6) or have a protected tenancy (paras 7.15-20), the authority values it;

(d) in any other case, if your rent has been referred to the rent officer (for example, if your rent is unreasonably high, you have a pre-April 2008 award, or you live in a hostel or mobile home and so on: table 9.1), either the authority or the rent officer values it depending on type of service (para 8.32).

See table 8.3 for further details about how service charges are identified and assessed.

8.32 When a claim is referred to the rent officer (para 8.31(d)) service charge valuation is carried out as follows:

(a) the authority values any ineligible charges that are not valued by the rent officer (i.e. items with 'No' in both columns in table 8.4) and deducts them from the actual rent; except any charge for meals (see (e)) the result is the 'referred rent' (para 10.40) (and the rent officer is notified of these deductions when the referral is made);

(b) the rent officer takes the referred rent (which includes eligible services), and if he or she has made a significantly high, size-related or exceptionally high rent determination (paras 10.41-44) caps it at whichever of those determinations is the lowest (and in this case this is the 'claim-related rent');

(c) if none of the determinations in (b) apply, the rent officer values any ineligible service charges that he/she is responsible for (table 8.4) and deducts them from the referred rent (and in this case this is the 'claim-related rent'). See paras 10.51 for how the rent officer values ineligible services;

(d) if the rent officer has made a local reference rent or single room rent determination then that figure is passed back to the authority and used instead of the claim-related rent (being the lower of the two); and

(e) where the rent includes meals the authority deducts the appropriate amount (table 8.6) from the rent officer's lowest figure, but if it is a single room rent determination then that figure is the eligible rent unless the claim-related rent less the amount for meals results in a lower figure.

Ineligible charges in (a) above includes deductions from excessive eligible charges (para 8.49).

8.31 HB 12B(2),(5), B13(2)(a); HB60+ 12B(2),(5); CPR sch 3 para 5(1); NIHB 13A(2),(6), 14(2),(5),(7),(9), 15(1), sch 2 paras 6(2A),(3),7; NIHB60+ 13A(2),(6), 14(2),(5),(7), 15(1), sch 2 paras 6(2A),(3),7; NICPR sch 3 para 5(1)

8.32 HB 12C(2), 13(2)-(5),(7), 114A(3)(d)-(f),(4)(b),(6),(8)(a); HB60+ 12C(2), 13(2)-(5), 95A(3)(d)-(f),(4)(b),(6),(8)(a); ROO sch 1 paras 6(2A),(3), 7

Table 8.3 **How to assess service charges**

Step 1: Does the charge relate to a service performed or facility provided? (para 8.40)

- ■ If yes, it is a service charge (and cannot be rent), go to step 2.
- ■ If no, it is not a service charge but it may (or may not) be 'rent' (para 8.42).

Step 2: Does your right to occupy your home depend on payment of the service charge? (para 8.43)

- ■ If yes, go to step 3.
- ■ If no, it is not eligible for HB.

Step 3: Does the charge relate to an ineligible service? (table 8.4 and paras 8.67-84)

- ■ If no, go to step 4.
- ■ If yes, it is not eligible for HB.

Step 4: Are you a social renter (para 8.2) **where a rent determination is not required** (para 8.7); **or a protected tenant** (para 7.15) **of any other kind of landlord?**

- ■ If yes, the authority decides all issues including whether the service charge is excessive.
- ■ If no, got to step 5.

Step 5: Do you live in 'exempt accommodation' (paras 10.3-6) **(not covered by step 4)?**

- ■ If yes, the authority decides all issues including whether any eligible service charge is excessive. The authority must refer your rent and service charges to the rent officer but the authority is not required to use the rent officer's valuation (but they should consider it with any other evidence) (paras 10.16 and 10.37).

- ■ If no, your rent and service charges are assessed under rent referral rules. The authority decides whether each service is eligible and either the authority or the rent officer values it (para 8.32 and table 8.4). The authority must use the rent officer's valuation.

Notes

See paragraph 8.31 for who is responsible for valuing a service charge once the authority has identified it. For how a charge is valued, see para 8.47 if it is ineligible and para 8.48 if it is eligible.

T8.3   HB 12(1)(e),(8), 12B(2), 12C, B13(2), 13(2),(5),(7), sch 1; CPR sch 3 para 5(1); HB60+ 12(1)(e),(8), 12B(2), 12C, 13(2),(5), sch 1; NIHB 13(1)(e),(8), 13A(2), 13B, 14(2),(5),(7), sch 1; NIHB60+ 13(1)(e),(8), 13A(2), 13B, 14(2),(5), sch 1

8.33   When the rent officer values a service (para 8.32(c)) he or she considers whether the service provided is value for money. The rent officer handbook [www] provides guidance about how this is done:

(a)   evidence of service costs provided in the referral are used as a starting point but the value will only equate to the cost if the landlord is providing the service efficiently;

(b)   if the landlord provides 'solid evidence' of service costs the rent officer does not normally deduct more; unless

(c)   if the service cost is very high or the service is not being provided in a cost efficient way.

Distinguishing 'rent' from service charges

8.34   Decision makers (the authority/tribunals) pay more attention nowadays to the distinction between services (as described above) and other costs included when your landlord sets the rent. For example, your landlord's overheads such as vacant lettings cannot be a service because they do not provide any benefit to the tenant: CH/3528/2006 and para 8.40. For the same reason, rent collection costs including bad debt provision, and passing on costs like council tax, are usually regarded as rent rather than a service.

8.35   If you incur charges for: renting a garage or land, an additional room for a live-in carer, or additional rent to cover your arrears (all of which are 'rent' within its ordinary meaning) then special rules apply: see paragraphs 8.85-90 for details.

8.36   It is not always easy to distinguish between 'rent' and service charges and it is fairly common for landlords to classify charges incorrectly. Neither your landlord's classification nor the tenancy agreement determines whether an item is (or is not) rent or a service charge: it is the law which does so: [2009] UKUT 28 (AAC) (para 8.37). But the mere fact that your landlord classifies something incorrectly should not be held against them: CH/3528/2006.

8.37   If a charge relates to an item that falls within the definition of services (para 8.40) then it is a service charge (and it cannot be rent): CH/3528/2006. And if it is, the authority must next decide if it is eligible: CH/3528/2006. So, for example, if your landlord provides you with support or counselling to help you sustain your tenancy (or to every tenant) as part of its housing management, it is a service and it is ineligible (table 8.4 and para 8.81).
The fact that your landlord has classified it as 'housing management' or 'intensive housing management' does not mean that it is somehow eligible as 'rent' (para 8.36).

8.38   But just because an item is not a service it does not necessarily follow that the charge made for it must be rent (and therefore eligible for HB). It must still relate to a matter that is properly considered in setting the rent: CH/3528/2006.

8.39   A charge for a stair lift once installed, or presumably any other item that is physically attached to your property, is rent because it is an 'enhancement' of the premises: [2011] UKUT 513 (AAC).

8.34   HB 12(1)(e),(8); HB60+ 12(1)(e),(8); CPR sch 3 para 5(1); NIHB 13(1)(e),(8); NIHB60+ 13(1)(e),(8); NICPR sch 3 para 5(1)

Definition of 'services'

8.40   'Services' are defined as 'services performed or facilities… provided for, or rights made available to, the occupier…' and 'service charge' as any periodical charge for any such service. A helpful test is to ask: does the tenant derive any benefit or value from the function, or does the benefit or value wholly lie with the landlord?

8.41   A charge for furniture and/or 'household equipment' (e.g. white goods, TV, etc) is treated as a service charge and is eligible for HB; unless those goods become part of your personal property (para 8.71), e.g. under a hire purchase agreement. It seems likely that 'household equipment' includes computers.

8.42   Any item that is not a service may (or may not) be part of the rent – provided it relates to a matter that is properly considered in setting the rent. In most cases provision for vacant tenancies (voids), bad debts and long-term maintenance are allowed as rent provided that the total charge (rent and eligible services) is not excessive: [2010] UKUT 222 (AAC).

Which service charges are eligible

8.43   A service charge is only eligible for HB if:

(a)   you have to pay it as a condition for the right to occupy your home (whether the condition is part of the original tenancy agreement or a separate contract); and

(b)   it is not listed in the regulations as ineligible (table 8.4, paras 8.67-84); and

(c)   it is not excessive in relation to the service provided (para 8.49).

Details of which kinds of service charge are eligible for HB (subject to the above points) follow, and are summarised in table 8.4. For helpful advice see GM A4.700-950.

8.44   The first condition (para 8.43(a)) need not have applied from the start of your tenancy. It is eligible for HB (subject to the other conditions) from whenever you agreed to pay it, if the alternative would have been to lose your home.

8.45   Some not-for-profit landlords sometimes provide services 'for free' but this is often because the charge is wholly funded from elsewhere. DWP guidance concerning hostel residents (though the point is relevant to all claims) states that 'HB should be based only on items included in the resident's charge. [Authorities] must confirm which services are included in the hostel charge' (GM A4.1950).

Management and administration costs of eligible services

8.46   If a service is eligible (table 8.4), the costs of any management and administrative support required (e.g. staff time) to provide it are also eligible, so long as the costs are reasonable and not excessive (para 8.50): [2010] UKUT 222 (AAC).

8.40   HB 12(8); HB60+ 12(8); CPR sch 3 para 5(1); NIHB 13(8); NIHB60+ 13(8); NICPR sch 3 para 5(1)

8.41   HB 12(8), sch 1 para 1(b); HB60+ 12(8), sch 1 para 1(b); NIHB 13(8), sch 1 para 1(b), NIHB60+ 13(8), sch 1 para 1(b)

8.43   HB 12(1)(e),(8), sch 1 paras 1-5; HB60+ 12(1)(e),(8), sch 1 paras 1-5; CPR sch 3 para 5(1);
         NIHB 13(1)(e),(8), sch 1 paras 1-5; NIHB60+ 13(1)(e),(8), sch 1 paras 1-5; NICPR sch 3 para 5(1)

Table 8.4 **Service charges summary**

As described throughout this chapter, further details apply in many of the following cases.

Type of service charge	Eligible for HB	Valued by rent officer
Provision of a heating system	YES	NO
Fuel for communal areas	YES	NO
Other fuel	NO	YES
Meals	NO	NO
Water charges (personal use)	NO	YES*
Water charges communal areas	YES	NO
Laundry	NO	YES*
Leisure items	NO	YES*
Other day-to-day living expenses not included above	NO	YES*
Furniture/household equipment if the tenant becomes the owner (for example, under hire purchase)	NO	YES*
Any other furniture and household equipment (i.e. the landlord retains ownership)	YES	NO
Communal window cleaning	YES	NO
Other exterior window cleaning which the occupier(s) cannot do	YES	NO
Other window cleaning	NO	NO
Communal cleaning	YES	NO
Other cleaning	NO	NO
Emergency alarm systems	NO	NO
Counselling and support	NO	NO
Medical/nursing/personal care	NO	NO
Most communal services relating to the provision of 'adequate accommodation'	YES	NO
Any other service that is not related to the provision of adequate accommodation	NO	YES*

* The rent officer only makes a valuation when the authority refers a claim to him/her (paras 8.32, 10.32 and table 10.3); in any other case the authority values the charge.

T8.4   HB 114A(3)(d)-(f), sch 1 paras 1,2(1),5; HB60+ 95A(3)(d)-(f), sch 1 paras 1,2(1),5; NIHB 15(1), sch 1 paras 1,2(1),5; NIHB60+ 15(1), sch 1 paras 1,2(1),5

Valuing ineligible service charges

8.47   When the rent officer is responsible for valuing ineligible charges see paras 8.32 and 10.51; when the authority is (para 8.31), this is done as follows:

(a)   if the amount can be identified from your letting agreement or in some other way (e.g. a detailed breakdown provided by your landlord), the authority uses that value;

(b)   but if the amount cannot be identified or is unrealistically low for the service provided, the authority must decide what amount is fairly attributable to the value;

(c)   however, different rules apply if the charge is for water, fuel or meals (paras 8.72-80).

In practice separating out charges is not always straightforward, particularly for not-for-profit landlords whose functions are often provided by staff whose duties include a mix of activities that are legitimately part of the rent (paras 8.34-42) and both eligible and ineligible services.

Valuing eligible service charges

8.48   When the authority is responsible for valuing eligible service charges (para 8.31), it does so as follows:

(a)   if the amount can be identified from the letting agreement or in some other way, it uses the amount so identified as the value;

(b)   but if this identified amount is excessive, or if the amount cannot be identified, the authority decides what amount is fairly attributable to the value.

Excessive eligible service charges

8.49   The authority must consider the cost of comparable services to decide whether the charge is excessive, and if it is the authority must decide how much would be reasonable and disallow the excess. But even if a service charge is reasonable the authority may still restrict the global rent if the total eligible charge (i.e. rent plus service charges) is unreasonable (paras 7.27, 10.15, 10.38).

8.50   The requirement to consider comparable costs does not prevent the authority from concluding that the charge is excessive for other reasons, and in particular it can take account of what is required to provide the service satisfactorily. For example, if the authority considered a concierge service could be adequately provided by using two workers but your landlord employed four, it could still restrict the charge even if your landlord's wage rates were shown to be comparable with others. In such cases the authority is entitled to make a restriction even if it does not have sufficient evidence to put a precise figure on what a proper charge would be: [2010] UKUT 222 (AAC).

8.51   If you are already on HB and you are seeking to get your eligible rent increased (e.g. to reflect a service charge increase or to include a new service), the burden of proof (para 1.45) is on you to show that the increased charge is eligible by providing the necessary evidence. You

---

8.47   HB 12B(2), B13(2)(a); HB60+ 12B(2); CPR sch 3 para 5(1); NIHB 13A(2); NIHB60+ 13A(2); NICPR sch 3 para 5(1)

8.48   HB 12B(2), B13(2)(a), sch 1 paras 3,4; HB60+ 12B(2), sch 1 paras 3,4; CPR sch 3 para 5(1); NIHB 13A(2), sch 1 paras 3,4; NIHB60+ 13A(2), sch 1 paras 3,4

8.49   HB sch 1 para 4; HB60+ sch 1 para 4; NIHB sch 1 para 4; NIHB60+ sch 1 para 4

cannot rely on the fact that the authority has no evidence with which to make a comparison to prevent it from restricting the charge: [2010] UKUT 222 (AAC).

Eligible services

8.52   This section relates to charges that are eligible for HB. Eligible charges often relate to communal areas. As a general rule, a service charge that would be ineligible if provided for your own exclusive use is eligible if it relates to communal areas. (For example, cleaning your own room is ineligible, but cleaning the communal areas is eligible.) In relation to all eligible services in this section see also paragraph 8.46 on the management and administrative costs of providing them.

'Communal areas'

8.53   Certain service charges relating to the cleaning, maintenance and fuel supplied to 'communal areas' are eligible for HB. For these limited purposes (and to determine who is a non-dependant: para 4.30) 'communal areas' means:

(a)   areas of common access in any type of accommodation (halls, corridors and stairways; also probably reception areas that do not count as a 'room'); and

(b)   in 'sheltered accommodation' only (para 8.54), common rooms (such as a lounge, dining room, or communal laundry facilities).

In all other situations communal areas are not defined and have their ordinary English meaning.

'Sheltered accommodation'

8.54   'Sheltered accommodation' is not defined in the regulations. The term is wide enough to include 'extra care', 'very sheltered' housing and 'supported housing' or indeed any accommodation that is 'more than ordinary accommodation [and is] for people who are in some way (and probably for some defined reason) more vulnerable than most people are, or are vulnerable in a particular kind of way'. If resident staff are at hand, there need not be a warden/manager or an alarm system: [2011] AACR 38, approving [2011] UKUT 136 (AAC) and [2016] AACR 19.

Cleaning communal areas and other window cleaning

8.55   Except where the cost is met by the local authority as part of its Supporting People (para 8.81) programme the following charges are eligible for HB:

(a)   cleaning rooms and windows in 'communal areas' (para 8.53); and

(b)   cleaning the outside of windows which no-one in your household can do (for example, your windows if you live on one of the upper floors in a block of flats).

Any other cleaning charges (such as cleaning your own room) are not eligible (paras 8.70 and 8.81).

8.53   HB sch 1 para 8; HB60+ sch 1 para 8; NIHB sch 1 para 8; NIHB60+ sch 1 para 8;

8.55   HB sch 1 para 1(a)(iv); HB60+ sch 1 para 1(a)(iv); NIHB sch 1 para 1(a)(iv), NIHB60+ sch 1 para 1(a)(iv)

Fuel and water in communal areas

8.56   A charge for fuel used in communal areas (para 8.53) is eligible for HB, but only if it is separate from the fuel charge for your own accommodation.

8.57   Charges for water used by your landlord in communal areas (para 8.53), provided they can be separately identified, are eligible for HB because they relate to the provision of adequate accommodation (para 8.61): [2016] AACR 19. However, communal water charges that relate to an ineligible use such as community entertainment or personal laundry (para 8.69) must be deducted. So for example, water used by the landlord in sheltered housing for cleaning communal laundry facilities is eligible but any water used that relates to personal laundry would not: [2016] AACR 19.

Provision and maintenance of a heating system

8.58   A charge for providing a heating system (both in the common parts and in your own home) is eligible for HB, but only if it is separate from any charge for fuel.

Communal facilities

8.59   Charges for the following communal services are eligible for HB:

  (a)   children's play areas;

  (b)   equipment for receiving radio or 'Freeview' TV channels (e.g. an aerial for a block of flats) and their relay into your home through the communal areas, including any charges for the installation, upgrade and maintenance of that equipment (less any element included for subscription channels: paragraph 8.69). A similar argument seems likely to apply to charges for access to the internet (and see para 8.41);

  (c)   communal laundry facilities (but not personal laundry service: paragraph 8.69);

  (d)   any charge not otherwise specified as being eligible or ineligible by the HB rules, in respect of any part of the premises beyond those exclusive to you but which you have the right to use, for services related to the adequacy of those premises: CIS/1460/1995 and [2016] AACR 19. The authority should not determine the question of 'adequacy' in terms of whether you have a personal need for the facilities but rather by having regard to the characteristics of residents in general for type of accommodation you occupy (for example, for residents with disabilities or vulnerable young people: [2016] AACR 19.

8.60   Any other charge for leisure facilities (including sports facilities or television rental, licence and subscription fees) that is not covered above (para 8.59) is not eligible for HB.

All other eligible services (security, grounds maintenance, etc)

8.61   Except for any ineligible item (paras 8.69 and 8.81) any other charge for a service that is 'related to the provision of adequate accommodation' is eligible for HB. Items that fall under this heading are not restricted to services in respect of the common areas (although more often than not they will be).

8.56   HB sch 1 para 5; HB60+ sch 1 para 5; NIHB sch 1 para 5; NIHB60+ sch 1 para 5

8.58   HB sch 1 para 8; HB60+ sch 1 para 8; NIHB sch 1 para 8; NIHB60+ sch 1 para 8

8.59-60 HB sch 1 para 1(a)(ii),(iii); HB60+ sch 1 para 1(a)(ii),(iii); NIHB sch 1 para 1(a)(ii),(iii); NIHB60+ sch 1 para 1(a)(ii),(iii)

8.61   HB sch 1 para 1(g); HB60+ sch 1 para 1(g); NIHB sch 1 para 1(g); NIHB60+ sch 1 para 1(g)

8.62 The DWP advises (GM A4.730, and A4 Annex D) that this includes charges for:

(a) portering and refuse removal;

(b) the security of the dwelling (para 8.65);

(c) lifts, communal telephones and entry phones; and

(d) the time a scheme manager or similar person spends on eligible services (para 8.46).

8.63 What is meant by the 'provision of adequate accommodation' is fairly narrow and is restricted to only those services that are necessary for the enjoyment of your home (for example, a lift in a block of flats and costs associated with maintaining it): R v Swansea HBRB ex p. Littler/R v St Edmundsbury HBRB ex p Sandys.

8.64 In deciding what is necessary for the enjoyment of the dwelling, no account can be taken of your personal needs. It is only the adequacy of the accommodation that counts, not your ability to take advantage of it or any services you may need in order to do so (Littler/ Sandys and GM A4 Annex).

8.65 A charge for a concierge service (including any management and administrative support costs: para 8.46) is eligible so far as it relates to the safety and security of the dwelling: [2010] UKUT 222 (AAC). Note that while a charge for services that relate to the security of your home itself (such as a door entry system) is eligible, a service connected with you or your family's personal safety (such as a call out service for harassment) is not (para 8.84).

8.66 Charges for maintenance of communal areas are also eligible. This includes a charge for maintaining a communal garden provided that your landlord has an obligation to provide it and you merely have a right of access to it (rather than exclusive use): [2011] UKUT 22 (AAC). However, a charge for maintaining a garden (where you have exclusive use of it) is not eligible, even where your landlord has agreed to it: CH/755/2008 and [2011] UKUT 22 (AAC).

Ineligible services

Day-to-day living expenses: the general rule

8.67 Charges for items that relate to you or your other household members' general living expenses are not eligible for HB so any charges included in your rent must be deducted from it. Examples of items that count as daily living expenses under this rule are in para 8.69 (but this list is not exhaustive).

8.68 For certain items (e.g. fuel, meals) the law sets out how the ineligible charge should be calculated and these rules are described in the following paragraphs. In any other case the authority or the rent officer (as appropriate: paragraphs 8.31-32 and table 8.4) must decide the value.

8.63   R v Swansea HBRB ex parte Littler 15/07/98 CA 48 BMLR 24; R v St Edmondsbury HBRB ex parte Sandys 24/07/97 QBD 30 HLR 800

8.66   HB sch 1 paras 1(g), 8; HB60+ sch 1 paras 1(g), 8; NIHB sch 1 paras 1(g), 8; NIHB60+ sch 1 paras 1(g), 8

8.67   HB sch 1 paras 1(a),(e), 2(1), 5; HB60+ sch 1 para 1(a),(e), 2(1), 5; NIHB sch 1 para 1(a),(e), 2(1), 5; NIHB60+ sch 1 para 1(a),(e), 2(1), 5

8.68   HB sch 1 paras 2,5,6; HB60+ sch 1 paras 2,5,6; NIHB sch 1 paras 2,5,6; NIHB60+ sch 1 paras 2,5,6

8.69   All the following count as daily living expenses, and are ineligible for HB:

(a)   fuel;

(b)   water (other than that used in communal areas);

(c)   meals;

(d)   personal laundry (but see para 8.70);

(e)   medical expenses or other expenses relating to personal hygiene;

(f)   cleaning of rooms and window cleaning (but see para 8.55);

(g)   transport;

(h)   TV (and radio) rental, licence and subscription fees and any other charges for providing equipment to the individual home (e.g. a TV, individual satellite dish, set-top box) or any other leisure items.

8.70   Charges relating to fuel and water for heating and cleaning communal areas are eligible for HB (paras 8.56-57), as are charges for cleaning the outside of windows so long as no-one in your household can do them and the cost is not met by your council through its Supporting People programme. Although personal laundry is not eligible, charges for equipment (such as a washing machine) and premises to enable you to do your own laundry are.

8.71   Note also that charges for renting household furniture and fittings are eligible for HB, but charges for acquiring them are not (para 8.41 and table 8.4).

Water charges

8.72   In Great Britain, water charges that relate to personal use (as opposed to water used in communal areas: para 8.57) are not eligible for HB so any charges included in the rent must be deducted. (But no deduction is made if you are billed by the water company and pay the bill yourself, since they are not then part of the rent.) The same applies in Northern Ireland, though for the time being, until a separate system for water charging is in place, water charges remain eligible for HB in respect of rates (although the rates element is deducted from your rent).

8.73   The authority decides the value of water charges, unless your claim is referred to the rent officer (para 8.31) in which case he or she does (para 8.32). If your dwelling is self-contained and the charge you pay relates solely to your personal use (as opposed to personal use and water used in other parts of the building) then the amount is calculated as follows:

(a)   if you pay a flat rate charge, that amount;

(b)   if the charge varies according to the amount of water used overall, typically where there is a water meter in use in a building which contains a number of self contained units or dwellings ([2016] AACR 19), the charge the authority considers can be fairly put down to your actual personal use or an estimate of it;

(c)   otherwise, a proportion of the water charge for the self-contained unit you share equal to the floor area of your accommodation divided by the floor area of the self-contained unit as a whole (but in practice authorities sometimes use simpler methods).

8.69   HB sch 1 paras 1(a),(e),2(1),5; HB60+ sch 1 para 1(a),(e),2(1),5; NIHB sch 1 para 1(a),(e),2(1),5; NIHB60+ sch 1 para 1(a),(e),2(1),5

8.72   HB 2(1) – 'water charges',12B(2),(5), B13(2)(a), 13(2); HB60+ 2(1),12B(2),(5), 13(2); ROO sch 1 paras 6A(2)(d),(3), 7;
          NIHB 2(1), 13A(2),(6),14(2), sch 2 paras 6(2A)(d),(3),7; NIHB60+ 2(1), 13A(2),(6),14(2), sch 2 paras 6(2A)(d),(3),7

8.73   HB 12B(2),(5), B13(2)(a); HB60+ 12B(2),(5); CPR sch 3 para 5(1); NIHB 13A(2),(6); NIHB60+ 13A(2),(6); NICPR sch 3 para 5(1)

8.74   In situations where your charge includes an amount for both personal and communal water use then the amount that relates to solely to personal use is deducted first (using the appropriate method above). Then any part of the remaining overall eligible rent (that includes an element for communal water) that relates to ineligible water charges is deducted from that figure: [2016] AACR 19. So for example, water used for cleaning the communal laundry facilities is eligible but any amount put down to personal laundry would not be.

Fuel

8.75   Charges for fuel used in your home (such as gas, electricity, etc, and also any standing charges or other supply costs) are not eligible for HB so any charges included in your rent must be deducted. (No deduction is made if you are billed by your energy company and pay the fuel bill yourself, since the fuel charges are not then part of your rent.) For charges for fuel used in the communal areas (e.g. heating and lighting) and providing a heating system, see paragraphs 8.56-58.

Table 8.5 **Standard weekly fuel deductions**

If the claimant and any family occupy more than one room

Fuel for heating	£28.80
Fuel for hot water	£3.35
Fuel for lighting	£2.30
Fuel for cooking	£3.35
Fuel for any other purpose	NIL
Fuel for all the above	£37.80

If the claimant and any family occupy one room only

Fuel for heating and any hot water and/or lighting	£17.23
Fuel for cooking	£3.35
Fuel for any other purpose	NIL
Fuel for all the above	£20.58

8.76   When the authority is responsible for valuing any fuel charges (para 8.31), the rules depend on whether the amount of the charge is known (paras 8.77-78). If your claim is referred to the rent officer he or she is responsible for valuing fuel charges (para 8.32 and table 8.4).

8.77   If the charge is identifiable, the authority uses this figure as the fuel charge. However, if this is unrealistically low or includes an element for communal areas which cannot be separated out, the charge is treated as unidentifiable.

8.75   HB sch 1 para 5; HB60+ sch 1 para 5; NIHB sch 1 para 5; NIHB60+ sch 1 para 5

T8.5   HB sch 1 para 6(2)-(4); HB60+ sch 1 para 6(2)-(4); NIHB sch 1 para 6(2)-(4); NIHB60+ sch 1 para 6(2)-(4)

8.76-77 HB sch 1 para 6(1); HB60+ sch 1 para 6(1); NIHB sch 1 para 6(1); NIHB60+ sch 1 para 6(1)

8.78   If the charge is not identified, the authority deducts the standard amounts, as shown in table 8.5 (a lower deduction applies if you only occupy one room). If the standard amounts are applied, the authority must invite you to provide evidence from which the 'actual or approximate' charge can be estimated; and, if the evidence is reasonable, the authority must use the estimated amount instead.

Meals

8.79   Charges for meals are not eligible for HB so if they are included in your rent a deduction must be made. For these purposes, 'a meal' includes preparation (e.g. where it is prepared somewhere else and then delivered) and also the provision of unprepared food (e.g. cereal, bread still in its wrappings).

8.80   The authority (not the rent officer) makes the deduction for meals. The standard amounts for meals shown in table 8.6 are always deducted, never the actual amount your landlord charges. A deduction is made for each person in your household whose meals are included in your rent (whether this is for you, a member of your family or some other person in your household such as a non-dependant). No deduction is made for anyone whose meals are not included (for example, a baby). When appropriate, deductions are calculated separately (for example fewer meals may be provided for someone who goes out to work than for someone who does not).

Table 8.6 **Standard weekly meals deductions**

A separate amount is assessed and deducted for each person whose meals are provided.

If at least three meals are provided every day

For the claimant, and each other person from the first Monday in September following his or her 16th birthday	£27.10
For each child	£13.75

If breakfast only is provided

For the claimant, and each other person of any age	£3.35

All other cases

For the claimant, and each other person from the first Monday in September following his or her 16th birthday	£9.10
For each child	£18.05

8.78   HB sch 1 para 6(2)-(4); HB60+ sch 1 para 6(2)-(4); NIHB sch 1 para 6(2)-(4); NIHB60+ sch 1 para 6(2)-(4)

8.79   HB sch 1 para 2; HB60+ sch 1 para 2; NIHB sch 1 para 2; NIHB60+ sch 1 para 2

8.80   HB 12B(2)(b), 12C(2), B13(2)(a), 13(5),(7), sch 1 para 2; HB60+ 12B(2), 12C(2), 13(5), sch 1 para 2; NIHB 13A(2)(b), 12B(2) 14(5),(7), sch 1 para 2; NIHB60+ 14(5),(7), sch 1 para 2

T8.6   HB sch 1 para 2; HB60+ sch 1 para 2; NIHB sch 1 para 2; NIHB60+ sch 1 para 2

Personal care and support charges

8.81   Support charges are never eligible for HB. This includes charges for:

(a)   cleaning and window cleaning over and above that mentioned in paras 8.55 and 8.70;

(b)   emergency alarm systems (to summon assistance in the event of a fall, an accident, etc, but see para 8.39 for other disability adaptations);

(c)   counselling and support; and

(d)   medical, nursing and personal care.

If you need any of these services you may be able to have the cost met by Supporting People, a government programme for funding support services administered by local authorities (in Northern Ireland by the NIHE) and independent of HB. For a detailed explanation of care, support and supervision in 'exempt accommodation' see table 10.1.

8.82   In theory the law is straightforward: support is not eligible for HB. In practice, separating any support charge from other eligible charges your landlord provides is more difficult because the member of staff who provides your support will also provide services that are eligible as part of the same job. The task of separating ineligible services from eligible is further complicated by the fact that some staff duties are rent (and so are not services at all) and some duties are services but contain both eligible and ineligible elements.

8.83   Whether a particular activity is a landlord function (and so eligible as part of the rent) or whether it constitutes a service is not determined by how the tenancy agreement describes it nor by the landlord's classification – it is the law that does so (para 8.36). The mere fact that the landlord classifies a charge as 'intensive housing management' does not mean a service that the law says is support is somehow eligible for HB (para 8.37).

8.84   In separating rent, eligible and ineligible service charges the two key tests are:

(a)   does the activity constitute a service (paras 8.37 and 8.40): in broad terms does it provide something that has value to you (as the tenant) rather than the landlord?; and

(b)   if it is a service (and not an excluded item: paras 8.69 and 8.81), is it concerned with the 'provision of adequate accommodation' (paras 8.63-64), or is it provided to help you maintain your tenancy so that you can make use of the facilities (in which case it is support)?

So as a general rule any activity undertaken by your landlord that varies in intensity according to your personal needs is more likely to be considered support (and so not eligible for HB).

Other items included in setting rents

8.85   The distinction between services and other items that should be included as 'rent' are set out in paragraphs 8.34-42. Your landlord's overheads and management costs are usually rent (para 8.34) regardless of how your landlord has classified it (para 8.36).

8.86   If an item is 'rent' then it is eligible for HB without the further conditions that apply to services (para 8.43). In particular, if your landlord is liable for council tax (e.g. if you are a

---

8.81   HB sch 1 para 1(a),(c)-(f); HB60+ sch 1 para 1(a),(c)-(f); sch 1 para 1(a),(c)-(f); NIHB sch 1 para 1(a),(c)-(f)

8.82   HB sch 1 para 1(f); HB60+ sch 1 para 1(f); sch 1 para 1(f); NIHB sch 1 para 1(f)

lodger or live in a house made up of bedsits) then the equivalent amount of your total charge is 'rent' (GM A4.160-161). Special rules apply to rent for garages, land and business premises (paras 8.88 and 8.90).

Increases to cover arrears of rent

8.87 If your rent has been increased to recover any arrears you owe, that part of the rent is not eligible for HB. This rule applies only to cover arrears you have personally incurred for rent on your current or former home. It does not apply if your landlord has increased the rent for all of his or her tenants as a result of arrears generally.

Garages, land, etc

8.88 The rent on a garage, mobility scooter shed, or any other buildings, gardens or land included in your letting agreement, is eligible for HB if:

(a) the facility provided is used for occupying the dwelling as your home; and

(b) you acquired them at the same time as the dwelling; and

(c) you had no option but to rent them at the same time.

Alternatively these facilities are also eligible for HB if you have made or are making reasonable efforts to end your liability for them.

Space for a carer

8.89 If you are a council/NIHE tenant, housing association tenant where referral to the rent officer is not required (paras 8.6-7), or if you live in 'exempt accommodation' (para 10.3), a room for a live-in carer is included in your eligible rent in the normal way, even if your carer occupies a room down the corridor from you: [2009] UKUT 28 (AAC) and [2009] UKUT 116 (AAC). If the room is separated from your own (as in the second case) it is still counted as part of your accommodation because 'functionally and purposively, [you need two rooms to live – one for you and one for your] carer. Common sense dictates that it should not matter whether there is a connecting door between the two.' The situation is different if the carer does not live in your home (for example where you have a rota of carers); or if you want your parents to stay and care for you, but they live elsewhere: [2009] UKUT 79 (AAC). See also paragraphs 11.18-34.

Business premises

8.90 Rent on any part of your home which is used for business, commercial or other non-residential purposes is not eligible for HB. For example, if you rent both a shop and the flat above it, only the part of the rent relating to the flat is eligible for HB. If the rent on the business premises is not separately identified from the rent on the home, the authority decides how much relates to each. If you are self-employed and work from home, see paragraphs 14.43-44.

8.87   HB 11(3); HB60+ 11(2); NIHB 11(3); NIHB60+ 11(2)

8.88   HB 2(4)(a); HB60+ 2(4)(a); NIHB 2(4)(a); NIHB60+ 2(4)(a)

8.90   HB 12B(3),12C(2), B13(2)(a); HB60+ 12B(3),12C(2); NIHB 13A(3),13B(2), B14(2)(a); NIHB60+ 13A(3),13B(2)

Chapter 9 **Private renters (LHAs)**

- Who the local housing allowance (LHA) rules apply to: see paras 9.1-3.
- Eligible rent: the LHA rules: see paras 9.4-9.
- The LHA figures and size of accommodation you qualify for: see paras 9.10-20.
- How LHAs are set: see paras 9.21-29.
- Boarders: see paras 9.30-34.

9.1   This chapter explains how your eligible rent is worked out if you are a private tenant and the local housing allowance (LHA) rules apply to you.

Who is a private renter

9.2   You are a 'private renter' if:

(a) you rent from a private landlord (table 7.3); or

(b) you rent from a registered housing association and your home isn't social housing (para 7.12); or

(c) you rent from a not-for-profit landlord (table 7.3 and paras 10.7-8) and your home isn't exempt accommodation (para 10.3); or

(d) you are a lodger (i.e. you pay rent to live in someone else's home, whether they are the owner or a tenant or someone else with a superior right to occupy).

Private renter includes here if your home is let on a shared ownership tenancy provided that your landlord isn't the authority or a registered housing association (in which case see para 8.8 and table 8.1). For the meaning of 'rent' see paras 7.3-4.

Who falls within the LHA rules

9.3   The LHA rules apply to you if:

(a) you are a private renter (para 9.2); and

(b) you don't fall within any of the exclusions in table 9.1.

If your rent includes a charge for meals see paras 9.30-34.

9.2   HB 11(1), 13C(2),(5)(a); HB60+ 11(1), 13C(2),(5)(a); NIHB 11(1), 14C(2),(5)(a); NIHB60+ 11(1), 14C(2),(5)(a)

9.3   HB 13C(2),(5)(a)-(e); HB60+ 13C(2),(5)(a)-(e); NIHB 14C(2),(5)(a)(e); NIHB60+ 14C(2),(5)(a)-(e)

Table 9.1 **Private renters: exclusions from the LHA rules**

The LHA rules don't apply to you if:

(a) you are a boarder and your rent includes substantial board and attendance (para 9.32);

(b) you live in a hostel (para 7.22);

(c) you live in a caravan, mobile home or houseboat;

(d) you have been receiving HB for your current home since before 7th April 2008;

(e) you rent from a not-for-profit landlord and your home is exempt accommodation (paras 10.3-6);

(f) you have an old (pre-1996) HB claim (paras 7.13-14); or

(g) you have a protected or similar tenancy (paras 7.15-20).

Note:

If (a)-(d) apply to you, your eligible rent is worked out using the rent referral rules (paras 10.37-38). For (e) and (f), see para 10.9 and for (g) see para 8.8 and table 8.1.

Eligible rent: LHA rules

9.4　　This section explains how your eligible rent is worked out under the LHA rules.

The general rule

9.5　　Your eligible rent is the lower of:

(a) the LHA figure that applies to you (para 9.10); and

(b) your actual weekly rent (para 7.3).

But if there has been a recent death in your home, or you could previously afford the rent (without HB) you are a 'protected renter', and the LHA rules can be delayed for up to 13 weeks/one year (paras 7.28-36).

9.6　　Your actual weekly rent means the full weekly rent you are liable to pay on your home (para 7.3). This includes all service charges you are liable to pay, whether or not they would be eligible for HB in other types of HB case (table 8.4).

T9.1　　HB 13C(2),(5)(a)-(e); HB60+ 13C(2),(5)(a)-(e); NIHB 14C(2),(5)(a)(e); NIHB60+ 14C(2),(5)(a)-(e)

9.5　　HB 12D(3),(5), 13D(4),(5); HB60+ 12D(3),(5), 13D(4),(5); NIHB 13D(3),(5), 14D(4),(5); NIHB60+ 13D(3),(5), 14D(4),(5)

9.6　　HB 13D(12); HB60+ 13D(12); NIHB 14D(10); NIHB60+ 14D(10)

Joint tenants

9.7   If there is at least one joint tenant who is part of your household but not your family (paras 4.42-46):

   (a) first, the eligible rent for your dwelling is the lower of:

   - the actual rent for your dwelling, and

   - the LHA figure that applies to you (the joint tenant(s), their family members and non-dependants are included in deciding this: para 9.17);

   (b) then the resulting figure is apportioned (para 8.13) between you and the other joint tenant(s).

9.8   But if you have at least one joint tenant who maintains a separate household from you (paras 4.42-46):

   (a) first, the actual weekly rent for your dwelling is apportioned (para 8.13) between you and the other joint tenant(s);

   (b) then your eligible rent is the lower of:

   - your share of the actual rent, and

   - the LHA figure that applies to you (the joint tenant(s), their family members, non-dependants and others in their household aren't included in deciding this: para 9.17).

9.10   This section explains which LHA figure applies to you and what size of accommodation you qualify for.

The LHA figures

9.11   LHA figures are set by the rent officer in Great Britain and the NIHE in Northern Ireland (para 9.21). Each year the rent officer/NIHE sets weekly figures for the sizes of accommodation in table 9.2, and all the figures are available online [www]. They vary from area to area but can never be greater than the maximum amounts in the table.

9.12   Each year's LHA figures apply from the first Monday in April (3rd April in 2017) if your rent is due weekly or in multiples of a week; or 1st April in other cases (e.g. if your rent is due monthly or daily).

9.7-8   HB 12B(4), 13D(12); HB60+ 12B(4), 13D(12); NIHB 13A(4), 14D(10); NIHB60+ 13A(4), 14D(10)

9.9   HB 13C(2),(3); HB60+ 13C(2),(3); NIHB 14C(2),(3); NIHB60+ 14C(2),(3)

9.11   ROO 4B(2A),(2B),(3A),(3B), sch 3B para 2(3); NIED 3(2),(2A),(3),(3A)
        Great Britain: https://lha-direct.voa.gov.uk/search.aspx
        Northern Ireland: www.nihe.gov.uk/index/benefits/lha/current_lha_rates.htm

9.12   HB 12D(1),(2), 13C(2)(d),(3); HB60+ 12D(1),(2), 14C(2)(d),(3); NIHB 13D(1),(2), 14C(2)(d),(3); NIHB60+ 13D(1),(2), 14C(2)(d),(3)

Table 9.2 **LHA figures: sizes of accommodation and maximum amounts**

Sizes of accommodation	National weekly maximums
(a) One-bedroom shared accommodation	£260.64
(b) One-bedroom self-contained accommodation	£260.64
(c) Two-bedroom dwellings	£302.33
(d) Three-bedroom dwellings	£354.46
(e) Four-bedroom dwellings	£417.02

In practice, actual LHAs are usually lower, and the figures for (a) are lower than those for (b). For which size of accommodation applies to you, see paras 9.16-20.

Which LHA figure applies to you

9.13   The LHA figure that applies to you is the one for:

(a) the size of accommodation you qualify for (para 9.16); and

(b) the area your home is in (para 9.27).

When you claim HB

9.14   When you make a claim for HB, your LHA figure is the one that applies on your date of claim (para 5.32).

When your LHA figure changes

9.15   When your LHA figure changes because:

(a) you qualify for a different size of accommodation (e.g. if someone moves in or out), your HB changes from the date the change in circumstances takes effect (para 17.18);

(b) you move home, your HB changes from the date the move takes effect (table 17.3);

(c) the new figures apply in April, your HB changes from the date in para 9.12;

(d) the rent officer/NIHE corrects a wrongly calculated LHA figure (in practice this is rare), your HB changes from:

■   the date in para 9.12, if the new figure is higher, or

■   the Monday following the date of the correction, if the new figure is lower.

But if the size you qualify for has changed because a person who lives with you has died, see para 7.34.

T9.2   ROO sch 3B para 2(2B)(a); NIED sch para 2(3)(a)

9.13   HB 13D(1)(a),(b); HB60+ 13D(1)(a),(b); NIHB 14D(1)(a),(b); NIHB60+ 14D(1)(a),(b)

9.14   HB 13D(1); HB60+ 13D(1); NIHB 143D(1); NIHB60+ 14D(1)

9.15   HB 13C(2)(d); DAR 7A, 8(15); NIHB 14C(2)(d); NIDAR 7A

The size of the accommodation you qualify for

9.16 This is worked out as follows:

(a) you qualify for accommodation with the appropriate number of bedrooms for the occupiers of your home: see table 11.1;

(b) but the maximum number of bedrooms is always four;

(c) and if you are the only occupier of your home, or you and your partner are, see para 9.18.

Which occupiers are taken into account

9.17 The LHA size criteria take account of the occupiers of your home. This means:

(a) you (the claimant) and members of your family (partner, children and young persons: para 4.2);

(b) non-dependants (para 4.26);

(c) lodgers (para 4.36);

(d) joint tenants who share your household (para 9.7): [2011] UKUT 156 (AAC); and

(e) any other person who occupies your dwelling as their home (except joint tenants who maintain a separate household: para 9.8).

For further details see chapter 11.

One bedroom LHA figures

9.18 You qualify for one bedroom if:

(a) you are a single claimant or couple without children;

(b) there are no other occupiers in your home (para 9.17); and

(c) you don't qualify for an additional bedroom for any of the reasons in paras 11.18-33 .

But there are two LHA figures for one-bedroom accommodation, one for self-contained and one for shared accommodation. See table 9.3 for which of these applies to you.

When your home counts as self-contained

9.19 For the rules in table 9.3, your home counts as self-contained only if you have exclusive use of:

(a) one room plus a bathroom and toilet (in the bathroom or separately) and a kitchen or cooking facilities; or

(b) at least two rooms (counting only bedrooms and living rooms, but regardless of whether you share other facilities).

'Exclusive use' means the right to exclude others; and this must be a legal right, not just what happens in practice: [2011] UKUT 156 (AAC) and [2014] UKUT 36 (AAC). For example, it is unlikely to apply to joint tenants who maintain separate households (para 9.8).

9.16   HB 13D(2); HB60+ 13D(2); NIHB 14D(2); NIHB60+ 14D(2)

9.17   HB 13D(3),(12); HB60+ 13D(3),(12); NIHB 14D(3),(10); NIHB60+ 14D(3),(10)

9.18   HB 13D(2)(a),(b); HB60+ 13D(2)(a),(b); NIHB 14D(2)(a),(b); NIHB60+ 14D(2)(a),(b)

9.19   HB 13D(2)(b); HB60+ 13D(2)(b); NIHB 14D(2)(b); NIHB60+ 14D(2)(b)

Table 9.3 **The LHA one-bedroom categories**

Your circumstances   **Your LHA category**

Single claimants aged 35 or over

- If your home counts as self-contained   One-bedroom self-contained
  (para 9.19)   accommodation
- Otherwise   One-bedroom shared accommodation

Single claimants aged under 35

- If you are in any of excepted groups   One-bedroom self-contained
  (a) to (d) in para 9.20   accommodation
- Otherwise   One-bedroom shared accommodation

Couples of any age

- If your home counts as self-contained   One-bedroom self-contained
  (para 9.19)   accommodation
- If you or your partner are in excepted   One-bedroom self-contained
  groups (a) or (b) in para 9.20   accommodation
- Otherwise   One-bedroom shared accommodation

Notes:

- This table applies when you qualify for only one bedroom (para 9.18).
- Single claimants under 35 who qualify for one-bedroom shared accommodation
  are called 'young individuals' in HB law.

T9.3   HB 13D(2)(a),(b); HB60+ 13D(2)(a),(b); NIHB 14D(2)(a),(b); NIHB60+ 14D(2)(a),(b)

Excepted groups for one-bedroom accommodation

9.20   For the rules in table 9.3 (and also the rules in para 10.47), you are in an excepted group if:

(a) you or your partner meet the conditions for a severe disability premium (para 12.38);

(b) you or your partner are aged under 22, and were previously:

■ in social services care under a court order at any time after the age of 16, or

■ provided with accommodation by social services;

(c) you are aged 25 or over but under 35, and are an ex-offender managed under a level 2 or 3 multi-agency public protection agreement (MAPPA); or

(d) you are aged 25 or over but under 35, and:

■ you have occupied (or at any time formerly occupied) one or more hostels for homeless people for one or more periods totalling at least three months, and

■ while you were there, you were offered and you accepted support with rehabilitation or resettlement within the community.

A 'hostel for homeless people' means a hostel (para 7.22) whose main purpose is to provide accommodation together with care, support or supervision, in order to assist homeless people to be rehabilitated or resettled in the community.

How LHAs are set

9.21   This section explains how the rent officer (in Great Britain) or the NIHE (in Northern Ireland) sets the LHA figures and areas.

9.22   Rent officers are independent of the authority. They are government employees in the Rent Service (in England), the Rent Officer Service (in Wales) or the Rent Registration Service (in Scotland).

Setting the LHA figures

9.23   LHA figures apply from the beginning of April (para 9.12), but are set at the end of January using the data for the year ending on the preceeding 30th September.

9.24   Each year, each LHA figure is the lower of:

(a) the rent at the 30th percentile (para 9.25) for that year; and

(b) the rent at the 30th percentile for the year beginning in April 2015.

The government intends that LHAs won't increase above April 2015's figures before April 2020.

9.25   The 'rent at the 30th percentile' means the highest rent within the bottom 30% of rents in the rent officer's/NIHE's data. In broad terms this means that people on HB can afford rents in the lowest third of the rental market.

9.20   HB 2(1),(1A),(1B) definition: 'young individual', 13D(2)(a); NIHB 2(1),(1A),(1B), 14D(2)(a)

9.23-24 ROO 4B(2A),(2B),(3B), sch 3B para 2(3A),(3),(4); NIED 3(2)(2A),(3A)

9.25   ROO sch 3B para 2(3)(b),(8); NIED sch para 2(3)(b),(8)

The data used to set the LHA figures

9.26   When setting LHA figures, the rent officer/NIHE:

(a) takes account of the range of rents payable (during the year ending on the preceding 30th September) on accommodation which:

■ is the correct size and in the correct area or (if that area doesn't have enough accommodation of that size) in a comparable area or areas,

■ is in a reasonable state of repair, and

■ is let on an assured tenancy;

(b) excludes the value of all services that would be ineligible for HB in other types of HB case (para 8.10 and table 8.4);

(c) excludes rents which a landlord couldn't 'reasonably have been expected to obtain' (in practice this means very low or high rents); and

(d) assumes that 'no-one who would have been entitled to HB had sought or is seeking the tenancy' (in practice this means excluding rents paid by people on HB).

The LHA areas

9.27   LHA areas are called 'broad rental market areas' (BRMAs) and are normally defined by postcodes. They are drawn up by the rent officer/NIHE so that:

(a) a person 'could reasonably be expected to live [there] having regard to facilities and services for the purposes of health, education, recreation, personal banking and shopping, taking account of the distance of travel, by public and private transport, to and from those facilities and services';

(b) they contain 'residential premises of a variety of types' held as a 'variety of tenancies'; and

(c) they contain 'sufficient privately rented premises' to ensure that the LHA figures 'are representative of the rents that a landlord might reasonably be expected to obtain in that area'.

They can only be changed with the DWP's consent.

9.28   BRMAs in Great Britain are on average twice the size of council areas (following changes in the law since large areas were criticised in R (Heffernan) v the Rent Service). Their boundaries don't usually match council boundaries, so some councils are completely within one BRMA and others contain parts of more than one BRMA.

9.26   ROO sch 3B para 2(4),(5),(7); NIED sch para 2(4),(5),(7)

9.27   ROO 4B(1A), sch 3B paras 4,5; NIED sch paras 4,5
        R (Heffernan) v the Rent Service [2008] UKHL 58 www.bailii.org/uk/cases/UKHL/2008/58.html

Appeals about LHA figures and areas

9.29   You can appeal to a tribunal (para) about:

(a)   whether the LHA rules apply to you (para 9.3); or

(b)   whether the authority has correctly decided the size or category of accommodation you qualify for (paras 9.16-20) and therefore whether it has allowed you the correct LHA figure.

You can't appeal to a tribunal or a rent officer about the amount of your LHA figure or about how a BRMA was drawn up, but it may be possible to challenge these by judicial review (para 1.54).

Boarders

9.30   This section explains the eligible rent rules for private tenants who are boarders. (See paras 8.4, 8.6 and 8.10 for boarders who are social tenants, and para 4.38 and table 13.7 for boarders who are lodgers in your home.)

Who is a boarder

9.31   A 'boarder' means someone whose rent includes meals. But for private tenants the following additional rules apply.

Eligible rent

9.32   If you are a private renter (para 9.2) who is a boarder:

(a)   you fall within the rent referral rules (paras 10.28-52) if your rent includes substantial board and attendance (para 9.33);

(b)   otherwise you fall within the LHA rules (unless any of the exclusions in table 9.1(b)-(g) apply to you).

Substantial board and attendance

9.33   Your rent includes substantial board and attendance if:

(a)   it includes 'board and attendance' – this means meals plus some further service such as serving the meals; and

(b)   a 'substantial' amount of it is attributable to this – for example breakfast by itself isn't usually considered to be 'substantial'.

This is decided by making a board and attendance determination (para 9.34).

9.29   CPSA sch 7 para 6(2)(c); NICPSA sch 7 para 6(2)(c)

9.32-33   HB 13C(5)(e), 13D(10); HB60+ 13C(5)(e), 13D(10); NIHB 14C(5)(e), 14D(8); NIHB60+ 14C(5)(e), 14D(8)

Board and attendance determinations

9.34   A 'board and attendance determination' is made by the rent officer in Great Britain or by the NIHE in Northern Ireland. It is only required if:

(a) you are a private tenant who is a boarder; and

(b) you are not excluded from the LHA rules for any of the reasons in table 9.1(b)-(g).

In Great Britain, the authority applies to the rent officer for this determination. If the rent officer decides your rent includes substantial board and attendance, the authority then makes a referral to the rent officer as described in para 10.31 and your eligible rent is worked out as in para 10.38 and table 10.5.

9.34   HB 13D(10), 114A(3),(4); HB60+ 13D(10), 95A(3),(4); NIHB 14D(10); NIHB60+ 14D(10)

Chapter 10 **Old scheme and rent referrals**

- Old scheme and exempt accommodation: see paras 10.1-8.
- Eligible rent in exempt accommodation: see paras 10.9-27.
- Rent referral cases: see paras 10.28-36.
- Eligible rent in rent referral cases: see paras 10.37-53.

What is the old scheme

10.1   This and the next section explain when and how your eligible rent is worked out under the old scheme rules. There are only two ways you can qualify for the old scheme rules:

(a) your landlord is a registered housing association or other not-for-profit landlord (table 7.3) and you live in exempt accommodation; or

(b) you rent from private rent landlord (table 7.3) and you have an 'old HB' claim (broadly you have been on HB at the same address since 1996: para 7.13-14).

10.2   Local councils often refer to these claims as the 'old rules or 'old scheme' because your eligible rent is based on the HB rules in force prior to 1996. These rules are now in 'old' HB regulations 12, 13 and 13ZA which are found in the HB Consequential Provisions Regulations (see footnote) and if you live in exempt accommodation they apply whether you have a new or an existing claim. Exempt accommodation is so called because it is exempt from many of the rules that reduce your eligible rent in other types of HB case (para 7.25) (even if your rent is referred to the rent officer for subsidy purposes: paras 10.26-27 and 10.37).

What is exempt accommodation

10.3   Your home is 'exempt accommodation' if you meet both the conditions in paras 10.4-5. (All exempt accommodation also counts as 'supported accommodation': see table 2.3 and para 6.28.)

10.4   The first condition is that your home must be 'provided' by:

(a) a registered housing association (paras 7.9-10); or

(b) a not-for-profit landlord – this means:

- an unregistered housing association (paras 7.9-10),
- a registered charity (para 10.7),
- a not-for-profit voluntary organisation (para 10.8), or
- an English county council that doesn't administer HB.

They must be your immediate landlord (CH/3900/2005 and [2009] UKUT 12 (AAC)), not someone your landlord is leasing the property from, nor a managing agent (para 7.7). (Your

10.2   HB old 12,13,13ZA in CPR/NICPR sch 3 para 5

10.3-6   CPR sch 3 para 4(1)(b),(10); NICPR sch 3 para 4(1)(b),(9)

home does not qualify as 'exempt accommodation' if your landlord is the authority you claim HB from.)

10.5 The second condition is that your landlord, or someone on their behalf, must be providing you with 'care, support or supervision'. There have been many appeals about this and the main cases are summarised in table 10.1.

Table 10.1 **Care, support and supervision: case law**

(a) Meaning of 'care, support or supervision' (CSS)

This part of the table applies to exempt accommodation (paras 10.3-6), and also to other kinds of specified supported accommodation (paras 2.13 and table 2.3).

- *Meaning of CSS:* the phrase 'care, support or supervision' has its ordinary English meaning (R(S) v Walsall MBC, confirming R(H) 2/07).

- *Availability of CSS:* The CSS must be available in reality to the tenant, and there must be a real prospect that they will find the service of use (R(H) 4/09 and [2009] UKUT 109 (AAC) para 44).

- *Meaning of 'support':* 'Support' might well be characterised as 'the giving of advice and assistance to a claimant in coping with the practicalities of [their] life, and in particular [their] occupation of the property' ([2010] AACR 2 para 129). It is more than ordinary housing management ([2009] UKUT 107 (AAC) para 71).

- *Continuity of support:* The support provided must be on-going (R(H) 4/09). For example, help with gaining exemption from council tax because the tenant is severely mentally impaired is more like a setting up cost and is not enough ([2010] AACR 2 para 120).

- *Need for and provision of 'support':* 'What matters is simply whether support is provided to more than a minimal extent, and it is… implicit that support is not "provided" unless there is in fact some need for it' ([2009] UKUT 150 (AAC) para 73).

- *Dwellings that form part of a group:* A dwelling that forms part of a group (such as sheltered accommodation) doesn't qualify as exempt accommodation just because other dwellings in the group do (e.g. if CSS in provided to only some of the residents): CSS must be provided to that particular dwelling (CH/1289/2007).

- *Amount of CSS:* To count as CSS what is provided must be more than minimal. On the facts of the cases in question an average of ten minutes per tenant per week was not enough (R(H) 7/07), but three hours per tenant per week might be enough (CH/1289/2007). In another case, just helping with HB claims and reviews, and carrying out safety and security inspections, was not enough to be more than minimal; but 'proactively considering what physical improvements or alterations to the properties could usefully be made' in the case of adaptations desirable in the light of the tenant's disability, could be enough ([2010] AACR 2 para 188).

T10.1   R(S) v Walsall MBC [2008] EWHC 3097 and [2009] EWHC 2221
        www.bailii.org/ew/cases/EWHC/2008/3097.html
        www.bailii.org/ew/cases/EWHC/2009/2221.html

- *When there is no relevant history:* Where there is no history of the support being provided (because it is a new development), it is necessary to look at what is contemplated ([2009] UKUT 109 (AAC)).

(b) Provision of CSS in exempt accommodation

This part of the table applies only to exempt accommodation (paras 10.3-6).

- *CSS provided by the landlord:* A landlord can provide CSS by making arrangements for it, or by paying for someone to do it ([2009] UKUT 107 (AAC) para 71).

- *CSS provided on behalf of the landlord:* For CSS to be provided 'on behalf of' the landlord, there must be 'a sense of agency between the [CSS provider and the landlord], or to put it another way, a contract, or something akin to it'. An arrangement that is merely a joint venture is not enough; nor is it enough that there is a contract between the CSS provider and e.g. social services (R(S) v Walsall MBC, confirming R(H) 2/07).

- *CSS provided by landlord as well as care provider:* The landlord may provide CSS without being the principal provider of it to that particular tenant ([2010] AACR 2 para 188).

- *Availability of CSS from elsewhere:* 'The likely nature, extent and frequency of [the CSS], and the extent of support available to the claimant from elsewhere' are to be taken into account in considering whether the CSS provided by a landlord is more than minimal ([2009] UKUT 107 (AAC) para 71).

- *Who pays for the CSS?* It is irrelevant that the landlord is (or is not) paid to provide the CSS by someone else ([2009] UKUT 107 (AAC) para 71).

- *Support vs housing management:* 'Support' means that the landlord does more than an ordinary landlord would do (R(H) 4/09). It is more than ordinary housing management; and carrying out repairs and maintenance do not generally amount to support. But if the tenancy agreement 'imposes unusually onerous repairing and maintenance obligations on the landlord', this can amount to support; as can the fact that a claimant's disabilities impose a 'materially greater burden on the landlord' ([2009] UKUT 107 (AAC) para 71).

- *Live-in carers:* While the presence of a live-in carer may or may not amount to CSS (depending on who provides the carer), the case law on carers in exempt accommodation is more relevant to whether the size of the accommodation is reasonable (paras 10.13 and 11.10).

10.6 In Great Britain, your home is also exempt accommodation if your landlord has received funding for resettlement from the DWP under section 30 of the Jobseekers Act 1995. This mainly applies to hostels and similar kinds of accommodation.

Registered charities

10.7 A 'registered charity' is a charity that is registered with the Charity Commission, the Charity Commission for Northern Ireland or the Scottish Charity Regulator [www].

10.7   www. gov.uk/government/organisations/charity-commission
www.oscr.org.uk/
www.charitycommissionni.org.uk/

Not-for-profit voluntary organisations

10.8 A 'voluntary organisation' is a 'body, other than a public or local authority, the activities of which are carried on otherwise than for profit'. Whether a landlord meets this description can involve looking at all the circumstances (not just the landlord's written constitution), and it is a 'commercial reality' that a voluntary organisation is likely to have contracts with profit-making third parties ([2013] UKUT 291 (AAC)).

Eligible rent in exempt accommodation

10.9 This section explains how your eligible rent is worked out if you live in exempt accommodation (paras 10.3-6). It also applies if you have an old (pre-1996) HB claim (para 7.13). If you have a protected or similar tenancy, see also para 7.15.

Eligible rent

10.10 Your eligible rent is worked out using the general rule for a social renter in paras 8.10-13 but the rules about how your eligible rent can be reduced are different (para 10.11). The social renter size criteria and LHA rules (paras 8.15-26 and chapter 9) don't apply to you.

Eligible rent reductions

10.11 Paras 10.12-20 explain when your eligible rent can be reduced. But if you are a 'protected renter', you are wholly or partly protected against these reductions (paras 10.21-27).

Unreasonably high rents

10.12 Your eligible rent may be reduced if your rent is 'unreasonably high'. This is decided by comparing the actual rent on your home with the rent payable on suitable alternative accommodation. See paras 10.15-16.

Unreasonably large dwellings

10.13 Your eligible rent may be reduced if your home is 'larger than reasonably required'. This is decided by comparing the size of your home with the size of suitable alternative accommodation for all the occupiers of your home. See paras 10.15-16.

Unreasonable rent increases

10.14 Your eligible rent may be reduced if you have a rent increase that:

(a) is 'unreasonably high' compared with the level of increases for suitable alternative accommodation; or

10.8   HB 2(1) – definition 'voluntary organisation'; HB60+ 2(1); NIHB 2(1); NIHB60+ 2(1)

10.10   HB 11(1)(d); HB60+ 11(1)(d); NIHB 11(1)(d); NIHB60+ 11(1)(d); old 12(3)-(5) in CPR/NICPR sch 3 para 5

10.11   HB old 13,13ZA; HB60+ old 13,13ZA; NIHB old 13,13ZA; NIHB60+ old 13,13ZA; (in CPR/NICPR sch 3 para 5

10.12   HB old 13(3)(a); HB60+ old 13(3)(a); NIHB old 13(3)(a); NIHB60+ old 13(3)(a) in CPR/NICPR sch 3 para 5

10.13   HB old 13(3)(b); HB60+ old 13(3)(b); NIHB old 13(3)(b); NIHB60+ old 13(3)(b) in CPR/NICPR sch 3 para 5

10.14   HB old 13ZA(1)(a); HB60+ old 13ZA(1)(a); NIHB old 13ZA(1)(a); NIHB60+ old 13ZA(1)(a) in CPR/NICPR sch 3 para 5

(b) is less than 12 months after the previous increase and is 'unreasonable having regard to the length of time since that previous increase'.

See paras 10.15-16.

The amount of the reduction

10.15   When any of the rules in paras 10.12-14 apply to you the authority can:

(a) reduce your eligible rent to the level of rent for suitable alternative accommodation (paras 10.17-18); or

(b) make a smaller reduction.

Unless you are in a protected group (para 10.21); the authority must make some reduction, but it could be a small amount, or a small amount for the time being.

Decisions about reductions

10.16   When it makes a decision about whether to reduce your eligible rent or about the protected groups, the authority:

(a) must take account of your individual circumstances and of suitable alternative accommodation (paras 10.17-18);

(b) may take account of rent determinations made by the rent officer/NIHE (para 10.28), but must not automatically use these to reduce your eligible rent (para 10.37);

(c) must not apply rigid rules that automatically treat every case the same way (GM A4.962);

(d) must not allow subsidy considerations (paras 10.26-27) to override the HB rules and case law.

Table 10.2 summarises the case law about reductions and protections.

Table 10.2 **Exempt accommodation eligible rent reductions: case law**

These cases apply equally to exempt accommodation (paras 10.3-6) and old (pre-1996) HB claims (para 7.13).

Decisions about unreasonably high rents: The authority must decide:

(a) the actual rent you pay for your home (including all eligible and ineligible service charges);

(b) what would be suitable alternative accommodation (paras 10.17-18) including what services are needed to make it suitable and what other factors need to be taken into account;

10.15   HB old 13(1),(9)(a) 13ZA(1),(9)(a); HB60+ old 13(1),(9)(a) 13ZA(1),(9)(a); NIHB old 13(1),(9)(a) 13ZA(1),(9)(a); NIHB60+ old 13(1),(9)(a) 13ZA(1),(9)(a) in CPR/NICPR sch 3 para 5

(c)   what the rent is for such accommodation; and

(d)   whether (a) is 'unreasonably high' compared with (c).

(R v Beverley BC ex parte Hare.)

'Unreasonably high': This means more than just 'higher' (Malcolm v Tweeddale DC HBRB).

Suitability of alternative accommodation: The authority must have 'sufficient information to ensure that like is being compared with like […] Unless that can be done, no safe assessment can be made of the reasonableness of the rent in question or the proper level of value' (Malcom v Tweeddale DC HBRB). In general terms, your home should be compared with 'more suitable' rather than 'less suitable' accommodation ([2009] UKUT 162 (AAC)).

Decisions about past periods: A decision about a past period should be made as if it was being made then. If evidence about that period is unavailable or unclear, findings of fact must be made about what was likely to have been the case ([2009] UKUT 162 (AAC)).

Decisions about the amount of a reduction: The authority should:

(a)   consider whether there are any circumstances that may make a small reduction appropriate;

(b)   decide the appropriate level of a reduction; and

(c)   be able to say how it arrived at (b).

(Mehanne v Westminster CC HBRB and R v Beverley BC ex parte Hare).

Limits to reductions: Your eligible rent must not be reduced below the cost of suitable alternative accommodation (R v Brent LBC ex parte Connery).

People considered 'vulnerable': availability of suitable alternative accommodation: Although suitable alternative accommodation must be available if you are considered 'vulnerable' (para 10.24), this doesn't mean the authority is expected to find a home for you. It is 'quite sufficient if an active market is shown to exist in houses in an appropriate place at the appropriate level' (the level your eligible rent is reduced to). So long as the authority has evidence of this, it is sufficient 'to point to a range of properties, or a bloc of property, which is available without specific identification of particular dwelling houses' (R v East Devon DC HBRB ex parte Gibson). If the authority doesn't have this evidence, it shouldn't reduce your eligible rent (CH/4306/2003).

People considered 'vulnerable': reasonableness of being expected to move: If you are considered 'vulnerable', the authority should have evidence that it has taken into account the effect a move would have (para 10.25) on employment and schooling (R v Sefton MBC ex parte Cunningham).

T10.2   R v Beverley DC HBRB ex parte Hare 21/02/95 QBD HLR 637
         Malcolm v Tweeddale DC HBRB 06/08/91 CS 1994 SLT 1212
         R v Brent LBC ex parte Connery 20/10/89 QBD 22 HLR 40
         R v East Devon DC HBRB ex parte Gibson 10/03/93 CA 25 HLR 487
         R v Sefton MBC ex parte Cunningham 22/05/91 QBD 23 HLR 534

Suitable alternative accommodation

10.17   When deciding what is 'suitable alternative accommodation' (paras 10.12-16), the authority must take into account:

(a) the nature of the alternative accommodation including any exclusive and shared facilities, having regard to the age and state of health of the occupiers of your home (paras 10.19-20). 'For example, if you are disabled or elderly you might have special needs and require expensive or larger accommodation' (GM para A4.1171);

(b) only alternative accommodation with security of tenure which is reasonably equivalent to what you have.

The alternative accommodation can be either occupied or unoccupied (but at least some of it must be unoccupied if the protection in para 10.22 applies to you).

10.18   The authority normally only looks at alternative accommodation in its own area. If there is nothing comparable there it can look outside, but not at 'other parts of the country where accommodation costs differ widely from those which apply locally' (GM para A4.1172).

Which occupiers are taken into account

10.19   When the authority is deciding the nature and facilities of suitable alternative accommodation (para 10.17) or the rules about protected renters (para 10.21), only the following occupiers of your home are taken into account:

(a) you (the claimant) and members of your family (partner, children and young persons: para 4.2); and

(b) any 'relative' (para 7.38) of you or your partner (including non-dependants, lodgers and joint tenants) who has no separate right to occupy your home.

10.20   But when the authority is deciding the size of suitable alternative accommodation (para 10.13), all the occupiers of your home are taken into account. This means everyone in para 10.19, and also anyone else (e.g. non-dependants, lodgers, joint tenants, foster children and carers) whether they are related to you or not. (Unlike all the other HB rules about accommodation size there are no exceptions.)

Protected renters

10.21   You may be protected against a reduction in your eligible rent if:

(a) you could previously afford the rent without help from HB: see paras 7.31-33; or

(b) an occupier of your home has died within the past year: see paras 7.34-36; or

(c) you or another occupier of your home is considered vulnerable: see paras 10.22-27.

All of these protections apply when your rent is too high or your home is too large (paras 10.12-13) but only (b) applies when you have an unreasonable rent increase (para 10.14).

10.17   HB old 13(1),(9)(a); HB60+ old 13(1),(9)(a); NIHB old 13(1),(9)(a); NIHB60+ old 13(1),(9)(a); in CPR/NICPR sch 3 para 5

10.19   HB old 13(10),(11); HB60+ old 13(10),(11); NIHB old 13(10),(11); NIHB60+ old 13(10),(11); in CPR/NICPR sch 3 para 5

10.21   HB old 13(5)-(8); HB60+ old 13(5)-(8); NIHB old 13(5)-(8); NIHB60+ old 13(5)-(8); in CPR/NICPR sch 3 para 5

Protection for people considered vulnerable

10.22　If you or another occupier of your home are considered to be 'vulnerable' (para 10.23), the authority must not reduce your eligible rent unless:

(a)　there is cheaper suitable alternative accommodation available (para 10.24); and

(b)　it is reasonable to expect you to move (para 10.25).

For this protection, only the occupiers in para 10.19 are taken into account. For case law see table 10.2.

10.23　Someone is considered to be 'vulnerable' only if they:

(a)　have reached state pension credit age (para 1.24); or

(b)　are responsible for a child or young person in your household (paras 4.4-19); or

(c)　have limited capability for work for ESA purposes (para 12.25); or

(d)　count as long-term sick under the 'old' fitness for work test (incapacity benefit).

The authority decides (a) and (b), but (c) and (d) are decided by the DWP (CH/4424/2004).

10.24　Suitable alternative accommodation is described in paras 10.17-20. The point here is that it must be available – and available more cheaply. For example, accommodation you have recently left, or an offer of accommodation you have refused, may be available – but only while it actually remains available to you, not after it has been let to someone else. The DWP advises that the authority 'should regard accommodation as not available if, in practice, there is a little or no possibility of [you] being able to obtain it, for example because it could only be obtained on payment of a large deposit which [you do] not have' (GM para A4.1222).

10.25　When deciding whether it is reasonable to expect you to move, the authority must take into account:

(a)　your prospects of retaining employment; and

(b)　the effect on the education of any children or young persons mentioned in para 10.23 who would have to change school.

The impact of subsidy

10.26　In exempt accommodation cases, a council in Great Britain can get less government subsidy (paras 23.28-31).

10.27　The authority must not take subsidy into account when it decides:

(a)　whether your rent, accommodation size or rent increase is unreasonable; or

(b)　any matter relating to the protected groups.

It may take subsidy into account when deciding the amount of a reduction (R v Brent LBC ex p Connery), but it must exercise its judgment and discretion (paras 1.52-53) and the DWP's advice is that it can't reduce your eligible rent 'on financial grounds alone' (GM para A4.1173).

10.22-23　HB old 13(4),(9)(b); HB60+ old 13(4),(9)(b); NIHB old 13(4),(9)(b); NIHB60+ old 13(4),(9)(b); in CPR/NICPR sch 3 para 5

10.24　HB old 13(4); HB60+ old 13(4); NIHB old 13(4); NIHB60+ old 13(4); in CPR/NICPR sch 3 para 5

10.25　HB old 13(4),(9)(b); HB60+ old 13(4),(9)(b); NIHB old 13(4),(9)(b); NIHB60+ old 13(4),(9)(b); in CPR/NICPR sch 3 para 5

10.27　R v Brent LBC ex p Connery 20/10/89 QBD 22 HLR 40

Rent referral cases

10.28   This and the following section explain who falls within the 'rent referral' rules (also called the rent decision rules in Northern Ireland) and how your eligible rent is affected by the 'rent determinations' that are made in these cases.

Who falls within the rent referral rules

10.29   The rent referral rules only apply in the specific circumstances in table 10.3. If you are a private renter and you pay board, see also paras 9.30-34. The rent referral rules never apply if your landlord is the authority you claim HB from.

Table 10.3 **Who the rent referral rules apply to**

The rent referral rules apply to you if category (a) to (d) apply to you and none of the exceptions in (e) apply.

(a) You are a private renter (table 7.3)

You only fall with the rent referral rules if:

- you are a boarder and your rent includes substantial board and attendance (paras 9.33-34);

- you live in a hostel (paras 7.22-23);

- you live in a caravan, mobile home or houseboat (table 7.1); or

- you have been receiving HB for your current home since before 7th April 2008.

If none of the above apply you fall under the LHA rules (chapter 9).

(b) Your landlord is a registered housing association (paras 7.9-11)

You only fall within the rent referral rules if:

- the authority considers your rent is unreasonably high; or

- you have a pension age HB claim (para 1.23-25) and the authority considers your home is unreasonably large.

But if your home isn't social housing (para 7.12), the rules in (a) apply. See also (c) below if you are a former local authority ('stock transfer') tenant.

(c) You are a former local authority/NIHE ('stock transfer') tenant

If ownership of your home was transferred from the authority, new town or the NIHE to another landlord, you only fall within the rent referral rules if:

- the rent on your home has increased since the date of the transfer; and either

- the authority considers your rent is unreasonably high; or

- the transfer took place before 7th October 2002 and the authority considers your home unreasonably large.

T10.3   HB 2(1) definitions: 'hostel' 'housing association' 'voluntary organisation', 75H

T10.3   HB 12C(1), 13(1), 13C(5),(6), 14(1)(a)-(h), sch 2 paras 3, 11(2)(a); HB60+ 12C(1), 13(1), 13C(5),(6), 14(1)(a)-(h), sch 2 paras 3, 11(2)(a); NIHB 13B(1), 14(1), 14C(5),(6), 15(1),(4), sch 3 paras 3, 5(2)(a); NIHB60+ 13B(1), 14(1), 14C(5),(6), 15(1),(4), sch 3 paras 3, 5(2)(a)

But if your new landlord is a registered housing association the rules in both (b) and (c) must be true.

(d) Additional rules if you live in a caravan, mobile home or houseboat

Your eligible rent is assessed under the rent referral rules if you pay site fees or mooring charges for your caravan, mobile home or houseboat except if:

- ▪ you live in England, Scotland or Wales and pay your site fees or mooring charges to the authority you claim HB from; or

- ▪ you live in England on a gypsy or traveller site (see notes) owned by a county council.

If either of these exceptions apply see para 8.8 and table 8.1.

(e) Exceptions

The rent referral rules do not apply to you if:

- ▪ you have an old (pre-1996) HB claim (para 7.13);

- ▪ you have a protected or similar tenancy (para 7.15); or

- ▪ you have a shared ownership tenancy (table 8.1 and para 9.2).

Note:

A gypsy or traveller site means a site provided for:

- ▪ people with a cultural tradition of nomadism or living in a caravan; or

- ▪ other people with a nomadic or cultural tradition of travelling regardless of their race or religion, including travellers, show people, and those who no longer travel through reasons of health or age .

Rent determinations

10.30   In rent referral cases, one or more rental valuations called 'rent determinations' are made, including a claim-related rent determination in all cases and a local reference and/or single room rent determination in some cases. A 'rent determination' means any of these individually, and also the overall decision about which of them apply to you. For the details, see paras 10.39-52.

Who makes rent determinations

10.31   In Great Britain, rent determinations are made by the rent officer as follows:

- (a) the authority refers details of your rent, accommodation and household composition to the rent officer – it should do this within three working days of a rent determination becoming required (para 10.32);

- (b) the rent officer then provides the authority with the rent determinations that apply to you – they should do this within five working days of receiving the referral or any further information they need (26 working days if they intend to visit your home).

10.30   HB 13(1),(5),(9); HB60+ 13(1),(5),(9); ROO sch 1; NIHB 14(1),(5),(9), sch 3; NIHB60+ 14(1),(5),(9), sch 3

10.31   AA 134(1); HB 14(1),(5),(9); HB60+ 14(1); ROO sch 1; NIAA 129(1); NIHB 15(1), sch 3; NIHB60+ 15(1), sch 3

In Northern Ireland, rent determinations are made by the NIHE itself – it should do this within three working days of a rent determination becoming required.

When rent determinations are required

10.32   A rent determination is required on each of the following occasions:

(a) when you claim HB;

(b) when you move home;

(c) whenever there is a 'relevant change' in your circumstances: see table 10.4; and

(d) whenever 52 weeks have passed since the most recent rent determination was made for your home.

But in cases (a) and (b), if there is already a valid rent determination for your home (para 10.33) this is used instead. For hostels, see also para 10.35.

10.33   For this purpose, a rent determination for your home is valid if:

(a) it was made less than 52 weeks ago for you or another person (because you or they previously claimed or received HB there, or requested a pre-tenancy determination there: para 10.36); and

(b) there is no difference that amounts to a 'relevant change' (table 10.4) between your current circumstances and your/their circumstances then.

Table 10.4 **'Relevant changes' in rent referral cases**

Rent determinations are required in all these situations (paras 10.32 and 10.35):

Changes that could affect the size of accommodation you qualify for

(a) There is a change in the number of occupiers in your home – but this doesn't apply if you live in a hostel (para 10.35) or to the beginning or end of an armed forces absence (para 11.15).

(b) A child in your home reaches the age of 10 or 16 – but only if your most recent rent determination included a size-related rent determination (para 10.43).

(c) There is a change in the household composition of the occupiers of your home (e.g. two people start or stop being a couple) – but only if your most recent rent determination included a size-related rent determination (para 10.43).

(d) You start or stop qualifying for an additional bedroom for any of the reasons in para 11.18 (foster parents, overnight carers, and disabled children who need their own bedroom).

(e) You start to meet the conditions for a single room rent determination (which applies to certain single claimants under the age of 35: para 10.47) – e.g. because you are a care-leaver and have reached the age of 22 (para 9.20).

10.32   HB 14(1)-(3),(6),(8), sch 2 para 2; HB60+ 14(1), sch 2 para 2; ROO sch 1; NIHB 15(1), sch 3 para 2; NIHB60+ 15(1), sch 3 para 2

10.33   DAR 7A(3), 8(6A),(6B); NIDAR 7A(3), 8(6A),(6B)

T10.4   HB 14(1),(8), sch 2 para 2; HB60+ 14(1),(8), sch 2 para 2; NIHB 15(1), sch 3 para 2; NIHB60+ 15(1), sch 3 para 2

Other changes

(f)   There is a substantial change in the terms of your letting agreement or the condition of your home (e.g. your landlord has made improvements) – this applies whether or not your rent changes (but not if the only change is in your rent).

(g)   Your rent increases – but this only applies if:

- the increase is under a term of your letting agreement (which needn't be in writing but must be a term of your letting, not just a provision of law: CH/3590/2007);

- that term is the same (or substantially the same) as when your most recent rent determination was made; and

- in your most recent rent determination, your actual rent was used as your claim related rent (para 10.41).

Note:

Other increases in your rent don't count as a 'relevant change'. For reductions in your rent, see para 10.38. For moves, see paras 10.32-33.

When rent determinations take effect

10.34   A rent determination relating to a claim takes effect when your HB starts (para 5.45). One relating to a move or relevant change takes effect when the move or change takes effect (para 17.18). One made because 52 weeks have passed takes effect as follows:

(a)   if it means you qualify for more HB (or the same amount), it takes effect on:

- the day after the 52 weeks run out, but

- if that isn't a Monday and your rent is due weekly or in multiples of weeks, on the preceding Monday;

(b)   if it means you qualify for less HB, it takes effect on the Monday following:

- the day the authority receives the determination from the rent officer (Great Britain), or

- the day the NIHE makes the determination (Northern Ireland).

Rent determinations for hostels

10.35   Once one rent determination has been made for a hostel (para 7.22), it applies for 12 months for all other lettings there that provide sleeping accommodation for the same number of people. If the hostel has lettings that provide sleeping accommodation for different numbers of people (e.g. single rooms and shared rooms) this applies separately for each kind. But rent determinations are required for 'relevant changes' (table 10.4) and when the 12 months run out.

10.34   DAR 7A, 8(6A),(6B); NIDAR 7A, 8(6A),(6B)

10.35   HB 14(2)(a),(7); HB60+ 14(2)(a),(7); NIHB 15; NIHB60+ 15

Pre-tenancy determinations

10.36   If your landlord agrees, you can ask the authority to provide you with a 'pre-tenancy' rent determination (PTD) before you:

(a)   move into a new home; or

(b)   renew your letting agreement – so long as it is at least 11 months since your last agreement began.

This may help you decide whether you can afford the new home or new letting agreement. Advice to authorities on PTDs is in GM A4.2050-70.

Eligible rent

10.37   Rent determinations are advisory when your home is exempt accommodation (paras 10.3-6) or when you have an old (pre-1996) HB claim (para 7.13). In these cases, your eligible rent is worked out as described in paras 10.10-27.

10.38   Rent determinations are binding in all other rent referral cases. In these cases:

(a)   your eligible rent is worked out as described in table 10.5;

(b)   if this results in a lower figure than your actual rent then your eligible rent can't exceed:

- your actual rent,

- minus an amount for ineligible service charges calculated as described in paras 8.27-84.

In HB law this final eligible rent figure is known as your 'maximum rent'.

But if there has been a recent death in your home or you could previously afford the full rent you are a 'protected renter', and the rent determinations are not used to calculate your eligible rent for up to 13 weeks/one year (paras 7.28-38).

Which rent determinations apply to you

10.39   This section is about rent referral cases (para 10.29). It explains which rent determinations apply to you and how the rent officer/NIHE makes them. For appeals about rent determinations see paras 16.91-96.

The referred rent and your actual rent

10.40   Rent determinations are made by reference to your 'referred rent' (i.e. the figure the authority passes to the rent officer). This means the full actual rent you are liable to pay your landlord including all eligible service charges together with most ineligible service charges except those, other than meals, which the authority values (see table 8.4). In Great Britain, the authority has to provide the rent officer with details of these and say which service charges are ineligible to be met by HB (table 8.4).

10.36   HB 14(4)(8); HB60+ 14(4),(8); ROO 3(1); NIHB 16, sch 1 para 3(1); NIHB60+ 16, sch 1 para 3(1)

10.38   HB 13(1)-(3),(5),(7); HB60+ 13(1)-(3),(5),(7); NIHB 14(1)-(3),(5),(7); NIHB60+ 14(1)-(3),(5),(7)

10.40   HB 114A(3)(d),(4),(8)(a); HB60+ 95A(3)(d),(4),(8)(a); NIHB 16(a); NIHB60+ 16(a)

Table 10.5 **Eligible rent in rent referral cases**

Steps 1 and 2 apply to all rent referral cases. Steps 3 and 4 apply when rent determinations are binding (para 10.38).

Step 1: Rent determinations

The rent officer/NIHE may determine one or more (or none) of the following:

    (a)   a significantly high rent determination (para 10.42);

    (b)   a size-related rent determination (para 10.43);

    (c)   an exceptionally high rent determination (para 10.44);

    (d)   a local reference rent (paras 10.45-46);

    (e)   a single room rent (paras 10.47-48);

    (f)   a service charge determination (para 10.51).

Step 2: Your claim-related rent

The rent officer/NIHE always determines this. It is:

- the lowest of determinations (a) to (c); or
- if none of those apply to you, your actual rent (para 10.40).

Step 3: Adjustments to the figures

The authority then makes adjustments in the following order:

- if your actual rent is used as your claim-related rent, any service charge determination is deducted from it;
- if you have one or more joint tenants who are not a member of your family (para 4.43), the claim-related rent and any local reference rent are apportioned (para 8.12) between you;
- if necessary, convert all the figures to a weekly amount (para 6.34);
- if your actual rent includes meals, the standard amount (table 8.6) is deducted from the claim-related rent (in all cases) and any local reference rent (only if it includes board and attendance) – or from your share of these if you are a joint tenant.

Step 4: Your eligible rent

The authority decides this. It is the lowest of the following (after the above adjustments):

- your claim-related rent;
- the local reference rent (if any);
- the single room rent (if any).

But see para 10.38 for exceptions and protections.

T10.5   HB 2(1) – definition 'hostel', 12C, 13(1)-(3),(5),(7), 14(1),(2)(a),(3),(7),(8); HB60+ 2(1), 12C, 13(1)-(3),(5),(7), 14(1),(2)(a),(3),(7),(8);
       ROO 3(1), 6(2),(3),(7), sch 1 paras 6,7,9, sch 4 paras 1,2;
       NIHB 2(1), 13B, 14(1)-(3),(5),(7), 15(1), sch 2 paras xx; NIHB60+ 2(1), 13B, 14(1)-(3),(5),(7), 15(1), sch 2 paras xx

Claim-related rent determinations

10.41   The rent officer/NIHE always determines a 'claim-related rent'. This is the lowest of the following:

(a)   a significantly high rent determination (para 10.42);

(b)   a size-related rent determination (para 10.43);

(c)   an exceptionally high rent determination (para 10.44);

or your actual rent if none of (a) to (c) apply to you.

10.42   A 'significantly high rent determination' is a valuation of the reasonable market rent for your dwelling as it is (regardless of its size, etc). It only applies if your actual rent is 'significantly higher' than this.

10.43   A 'size-related rent determination' is a valuation of the highest reasonable market rent for a dwelling that is as similar as possible to yours but is of the size you qualify for (table 11.1). It only applies if your dwelling is larger than this. It doesn't apply if you live in a caravan, mobile home or houseboat (table 7.1).

10.44   An 'exceptionally high rent determination' is a valuation of the highest reasonable market rent for a dwelling that is of the size you qualify for that isn't 'exceptionally high' (in other words, the highest rent that isn't at the luxury end of the market: see also para 10.46). It only applies if your actual rent and/or the determination(s) in paras 10.42-43 are higher than this.

Local reference rent determinations

10.45   The rent officer/NIHE determines a 'local reference rent' (para 10.46) if this is lower than your claim-related rent (para 10.41). It doesn't apply if you live in a hostel (para 7.22).

10.46   The local reference rent is a valuation of the mid-point of market rents (ignoring exceptionally high or low ones: see Heffernan (No 2) v the Rent Service for how these are determined) for an appropriate dwelling. If you live in one room, this means a dwelling in the same category as yours. The categories are:

(a)   one-room dwellings where your rent includes 'board and attendance' (meals plus some further service such as serving the meals);

(b)   other one-room dwellings where you share a kitchen, living room, bathroom and toilet with someone who is not a member of your household; and

(c)   other one-room dwellings.

In any other case, it means a dwelling of the size you qualify for (table 11.1), or of the same size as yours if this is smaller.

10.41   HB 13(9); HB60+ 13(9); ROO sch 1 para 6; NIHB 14(9), sch 2 para 6; NIHB60+ 14(9), sch 2 para 6

10.42   ROO sch 1 para 1; NIHB sch 2 para 1; NIHB60+ sch 2 para 1

10.43   ROO 7, sch 1 para 2; NIHB 16(a), sch 2 para 2; NIHB60+ 16(a), sch 2 para 2

10.44   ROO 6(2), sch 1 para 3; NIHB 16(a), sch 2 para 3; NIHB60+ 16(a), sch 2 para 3

10.45   ROO 6(2), sch 1 para 4; NIHB 16(a), sch 2 para 4; NIHB60+ 16(a), sch 2 para 4

10.46   Heffernan (No 2) v the Rent Service [2009] EWHC (Admin) 3539 www.bailii.org/ew/cases/EWHC/Admin/2009/3539.html

Single room rent determinations

10.47   The rent officer/NIHE determines a 'single room rent' (para 10.48) if this is lower than your claim-related rent (para 10.41) and:

(a)   you are a single claimant aged under 35;

(b)   you aren't in any of the excepted groups in para 9.20 (ignoring references there to a partner) – in broad terms these are seriously disabled people, care-leavers, ex-offenders and former occupiers of hostels for homeless people;

(c)   there are no other occupiers in your home (para 10.53); and

(d)   you don't qualify for an additional bedroom for any of the reasons in para 11.19.

It doesn't apply if you live in a hostel (para 7.22) or rent from a registered housing association (paras 7.9-11).

10.48   The single room rent is a valuation of the mid-point of market rents (ignoring exceptionally high or low ones) for a dwelling that:

(a)   has exclusive use of (only) one bedroom;

(b)   has shared use of a kitchen, living room, bathroom and toilet;

(c)   has no exclusive use of facilities for cooking or preparing food; and

(d)   does not provide 'board and attendance'.

General rules about rent determinations

10.49   When making rent determinations (paras 10.42-48) the rent officer/NIHE:

(a)   takes account of the range of rents payable on accommodation which is in the correct area, is in a reasonable state of repair, and is let on an assured tenancy (in Northern Ireland, an uncontrolled tenancy);

(b)   excludes rents payable to housing associations and charities; and

(c)   excludes the value of all ineligible service charges apart from meals (and also excludes meals in the case of single room rent determinations: see para 8.32).

10.50   Rent determinations (paras 10.42-48) are set using rental data from the appropriate area in which your dwelling is located which is:

(a)   the 'broad rental market area' for local reference and single room rent determinations (paras 9.27-28);

(b)   the 'area immediately surrounding the dwelling' (the 'vicinity') for significantly high and size-related rent determinations;

(c)   'a distinct area of residential accommodation' (the 'neighbourhood') for exceptionally high rent determinations;

(d)   in Northern Ireland only, the 'locality' is used in place of all the above.

10.47   ROO 6(2), sch 1 para 5; NIHB 16(a), sch 2 para 5; NIHB60+ 16(a), sch 2 para 5

10.49-50   ROO sch 1 paras 1-5,7,8; NIHB sch 2 paras 1-5,7,8; NIHB60+ sch 2 paras 1-5,7,8

Service charge determinations

10.51   The rent officer/NIHE determines the value of any ineligible service charges included in your rent apart from meals (paras 8.79-80). Because these are already excluded from all rent determinations (para 10.49) this valuation is only needed when the authority uses your actual rent as your claim-related rent (see table 10.5, which also explains the rules about meals). The rent officer manual provides useful guidance [www] on how rent officers value service charges.

The size of accommodation you qualify for

10.52   You qualify for the appropriate number of rooms (bedrooms/living rooms) for the occupiers of your home: see table 11.1.

Which occupiers are taken into account

10.53   The size criteria for rent referral cases take account of the occupiers of your dwelling. This means:

(a) you (the claimant) and members of your family (partner, children and young persons: para 4.2);

(b) non-dependants (para 4.26);

(c) lodgers (para 4.36);

(d) joint tenants (para 4.42); and

(e) any other person who occupies your dwelling as their home.

The authority, not the rent officer, decides which occupiers are included: R v Swale BC HBRB ex parte Marchant. For further details see paras 11.22.

10.51   ROO sch 1 paras 6(3),7; NIHB sch 2 paras 6(3),7; NIHB60+ sch 2 paras 6(3),7
http://manuals.voa.gov.uk/corporate/publications/Manuals/RentOfficerHandbook/
HousingBenefitReferral/Determination/i-roh-ineligible-charges.html#P76_808

10.52   ROO 2(1), sch 2 paras 1,1A,2,3; NIHB 2(1), sch 2 para 10; NIHB60+ 2(1) sch 2 para 10

10.53   R v Swale BC HBRB ex p Marchant 09/11/99 CA, 32 HLR 856 www.casetrack.com case reference QBCOF 1999/0071/C

Chapter 11 **The size criteria**

- The size criteria and eligible rent: see paras 11.1-9
- Which occupiers are included: see paras 11.10-16
- How many bedrooms you qualify for: see paras 11.17-34
- What counts as a bedroom: see paras 11.35-38

The size criteria and eligible rent

11.1   This chapter explains the rules about the HB size criteria. Opponents of the rules say they are a 'bedroom tax'; supporters claim they prevent a 'spare room subsidy'.

11.2   The size criteria for social renters and private renters are summarised in paras 11.3-8. The size criteria depend how your eligible rent is assessed: whether as an ordinary social renter, a private renter under the local housing allowance rules, or either kind of renter if your claim has been referred to the rent officer. Footnotes for each of these are given separately. See also para 25.9 for discretionary housing payments if you are affected by the size criteria.

Social renters and the size criteria

11.3   The social renter size criteria apply if you are a social renter (para 8.2) and you (and your partner) are under state pension credit age (para 1.24). For exceptions see table 8.2.

11.4   If you are a social renter:

 (a) you qualify for the number of bedrooms in table 11.1 (with no upper limit);

 (b) your eligible rent is normally reduced if you have more bedrooms than this is your home (paras 8.15-26).

The LHA size criteria

11.5   The LHA size criteria apply if you are a private renter (para 9.2) and you fall within the LHA rules (para 9.3). For exceptions, see table 9.1 and para 9.5.

The LHA size criteria

11.6   When the LHA size criteria apply:

 (a) you qualify for the number of bedrooms in table 11.1, but only up to a maximum of four bedrooms;

 (b) if this is one bedroom, there are further rules about what category of accommodation you qualify for (para 9.18);

 (c) your eligible rent is normally limited to the LHA figure for the size (or category) of accommodation you qualify for (paras 9.4-20).

11.4   HB B13(2)(b),(3),(5); NIHB B14(2)(b),(3),(5)

11.6   HB 13D(2),(3); HB60+ 13D(2),(3); NIHB 14D(2),(3); NIHB60+ 14D(2),(3)

The rent referral size criteria

11.7   The rent referral size criteria apply to certain social and private renters: see table 10.3.

11.8   When the rent referral rules apply:

(a) you qualify for the number of bedrooms (with no upper limit) and living rooms in table 11.1;

(b) if you live in one room, or are single and under 35, there are further rules about the category of accommodation you qualify for (paras 10.45-48);

(c) your eligible rent is normally limited to the rent officer's or NIHE's rent determination for the size (or category) of accommodation you qualify for (para 10.3 and table 10.5).

But different rules apply if you live in exempt accommodation or have an old (pre-1996) HB claim (paras 10.1-27).

The size criteria and unlawful discrimination

11.9   On 9th November 2016, the Supreme Court decided (R (Daly and others) v SSWP [2016]) that the size criteria unlawfully discriminated between adults and children who require overnight care or can't share a bedroom, and the regulations were amended from the 1st April 2017 to take account of this (paras 11.19-20). The Supreme Court also decided that the size criteria don't unlawfully discriminate against other people with disabilities or against women living in sanctuary schemes as a result of domestic violence, and that it wasn't unreasonable for them to request discretionary housing payments (para 25.4). An earlier case decided that the size criteria don't unlawfully discriminate against separated parents with shared care of a child (R (Cotton and others) v SSWP [2014]).

Which occupiers are included

11.10   The size criteria take account of the occupiers of your dwelling. This means:

(a) you (the claimant) and the members of your family (partner, children and young persons: para 4.2);

(b) non-dependants (para 4.26);

(c) lodgers (para 4.36);

(d) joint tenants (para 11.16); and

(e) any other person who occupies your dwelling as their home – for example family members of people in (b)-(d), resident carers (para 4.33) and employees (para 4.50).

See paras 11.11-34 for further details and exceptions

11.8   ROO sch 1 para 2(1), sch 2 paras 1, 2; NIHB sch 2 paras 2(1), 10, 11; NIHB60+ sch 2 paras 2(1), 10, 11

11.9   R (Daly and others) v SSWP [2016] UKSC Civ 58
www.bailii.org/uk/cases/UKSC/2016/58.html
R (Cotton and others) v SSWP [2014] EWHC Admin 3437 www.bailii.org/ew/cases/EWHC/Admin/2014/3437.html

11.10   Social renter: HB B13(5); NIHB B14(5)
LHA: HB 13D(3),(12); HB60+ 13D(3),(12); NIHB 14D(3),(10); NIHB60+ 14D(3),(10)
Rent referral: ROO sch 2 para 1; NIHB sch 2 para 10; NIHB60+ sch 2 para 10

11.11   The authority decides who is an occupier (not, for example, the rent officer: R v Swale BC HBRB ex p Marchant). In doing so it should have regard to the general HB rules about this (chapter 3); and even though some of the law was written to apply to claimants and partners, it should be adapted to apply to non-dependants (for example): [2010] UKUT 129 (AAC). A decision about which occupiers are included is appealable to a tribunal: [2010] UKUT 79 (AAC).

Children and young persons

11.12   The size criteria take into account children and young persons for whom you, your partner or someone else in your household is responsible (para 4.18), including those who are temporarily absent (para 4.24).

11.13   The following are not included:

(a) children and young persons who are foster children or are placed for adoption (table 4.3(a) and (b)) – but in these cases see paras 11.21-24;

(b) children and young persons who don't live with you, or don't normally live with you (table 4.3(c) and (e)).

Students and others gradually leaving home

11.14   When a student starts at a university and lives in a hall of residence, coming home frequently, it is correct to include them as an occupier of the parent's home: [2009] UKUT 67 (AAC), [2010] UKUT 129 (AAC). By perhaps the second year, especially if the student has taken on the rent of a flat or house, this is less likely to be the case. There is no fixed rule, each case depending on its facts.

Armed forces absences

11.15   If your or your partner's son, daughter, step-son or step-daughter is in the armed forces (regular or reserve), he or she continues to count as an occupier of your home during an absence on operations, so long as he or she:

(a) was a non-dependant (paras 4.26-32) before that absence (regardless of whether a non-dependant deduction then applied); and

(b) intends to return to reside in your dwelling when that absence ends.

11.11   R v Swale BC HBRB ex p Marchant 09/11/99 CA 32 HLR 856
         www.casetrack.com case reference QBCOF 1999/071/C

11.12-13 All: HB 2(1) definitions: 'child' etc; HB60+ 2(1); NIHB 2(1); NIHB60+ 2(1)
         Social renter: HB B13(5)(ba)-(e); NIHB B14(5)(b)-(f)
         LHA: HB 13D(3)(ba)-(e); HB60+ 13D(3)(ba)-(e); NIHB 14D(3)(ba)-(e); NIHB60+ 14D(3)(ba)-(e)
         Rent referral: ROO sch 2 para 1(ba)-(e); NIHB sch 2 para 10(ba)-(e); NIHB60+ sch 2 para 10(ba)-(e)

11.15   All: HB 2(1) definition: 'member of armed forces away on operations'; HB60+ 2(1); NIHB 2(1); NIHB60+ 2(1)
         Social renter: HB B13(8); NIHB B14(8)
         LHA: HB 13D(12); HB60+ 13D(12); NIHB 14D(10); NIHB60+ 14D(10)
         Rent referral: ROO sch 2 para 2(4); NIHB sch 3 para 2(4); NIHB60+ sch 3 para 2(4)

Joint tenants

11.16　　The size criteria take into account the following joint tenants (paras 4.42-46):

(a) if the social renter or rent referral size criteria apply to you (paras 11.3-8), all joint tenants;

(b) if LHA size criteria apply to you, joint tenants who share your household but not joint tenants who maintain a separate household.

Table 11.1 **The HB size criteria**

The social renter, LHA and rent referral size criteria (paras 11.3-8) are based on the occupiers of your dwelling (paras 11.10-16).

Bedrooms (all size criteria)

You qualify for one bedroom for each of the following occupiers:

- each couple (para 4.5);
- each other person aged 16 or over;
- two children under 16 of the same sex;
- two children under 10 of the same or opposite sex;
- each other child under 16.

Additional bedrooms (all size criteria)

You may qualify for an additional bedroom for each of the following occupiers:

You may qualify for one or more additional bedrooms for:

- a foster parent (para 11.21);
- an overnight carer (para 11.23);
- a disabled person who can't share a bedroom (para 11.30).

Living rooms (rent referral size criteria only)

When the social renter or LHA rules apply, living rooms are ignored But when the rent referral rules apply, you qualify for living rooms as follows:

- one if there are one to three occupiers;
- two if there are four to six occupiers;
- three if there are seven or more occupiers.

This applies regardless of the age of the occupiers.

Notes:

- When the LHA rules apply, the maximum number of bedrooms you can qualify for (including additional bedrooms) is four.
- When the LHA or rent referral rules apply, there are further rules about one-bedroom accommodation (paras 9.18 and 10.46-48).

T11.1　Social renter: HB B13(5)-(9); NIHB B14(5)-(9)
　　　　LHA: HB 13D(2)-(3B),(12); HB60+ 13D(2)-(3B),(12); NIHB 14D(2)-(3B),(10); NIHB60+ 14D(2)-(3B),(10)
　　　　Rent referral: ROO sch 2 paras 1, 1A, 1B, 2, 3; NIHB sch 2 paras 10, 10A, 10B, 11, 15; NIHB60+ sch 2 para 10, 10A, 10B, 11, 15

How many bedrooms you qualify for

General rules

11.17   The general rules about how many bedrooms you qualify for are given in table 11.1. They take account of all the occupiers in your dwelling (paras 11.10-16).

Sharing a bedroom

11.18   The only occupiers who can be counted as sharing a bedroom (table 11.1) are:

(a) couples (para 4.5) – and for the size criteria this appears to include (only) two members of a polygamous marriage (table 4.1);

(b) children (para 4.15) – and if children could share bedrooms in different ways, you qualify for the smaller number of bedrooms (example 2);

but not young persons (para 4.16) or anyone else aged 16 or over. If a couple or a child can't share a bedroom, see paras 11.30-34.

Examples: bedrooms – general rules

1. A lone parent has two children: a boy aged 7 and a girl aged 12.

Three bedrooms are allowed: one for the lone parent, and one each for the children (because they are not counted as sharing a bedroom: table 11.1).

2. A couple have four children: girls aged 8 and 12 and boys aged 5 and 14.

Three bedrooms are allowed: one for the couple, one for the two girls and one for the two boys (because this is fewer than if the two younger children shared a bedroom and the two old children had a bedroom each: para 11.18).

3. A lone parent has two young persons daughters aged 17 and 19.

Three bedrooms are allowed: one for the claimant, and one each for the young persons (table 11.1).

4. A single claimant has two non-dependants: sons aged 21 and 25.

Three bedrooms are allowed: one for the claimant, and one each for the non-dependants (table 11.1).

5. A couple have a child of their own, a foster child, and two non-dependants who are themselves a couple.

Under the general rules, three bedrooms are allowed: one for the couple, one for their own child, and one for the non-dependent couple. But an additional bedroom is allowed because they are foster parents (para 11.21).

11.18   All: HB 2(1) definitions: 'child', 'couple'; HB60+ 2(1); NIHB 2(1); NIHB60+ 2(1)
           Social renter: HB B13(5); NIHB B14(5)
           LHA: HB 13D(3); HB60+ 13D(3); NIHB 14D(3); NIHB60+ 14D(3)
           Rent referral: ROO sch 2 para 1; NIHB sch 2 para 10; NIHB60+ sch 2 para 10

Additional bedrooms: carers and disability

11.19   You may qualify for an additional bedroom for an occupier of your dwelling (paras 11.10-16) who:

(a)   is a foster parent, or has a child placed with them for adoption (paras 11.21-22); or

(b)   requires overnight care from a non-resident carer (paras 11.23-29); or

(c)   can't share a bedroom due to their disability (paras 11.30-34).

You could qualify for one or more additional bedrooms under each of (a), (b), and (c). But if you fall under the LHA rules, the maximum number of bedrooms (under the general rules and these rules) is always four.

Periods before 1st April 2017

11.20   Before 1st April 2017, the regulations relating to para 11.19(b) and (c) were different. They only allowed an extra bedroom for adults who require overnight care (not children) and children who can't share a bedroom (not adults). But on 27th January 2016 the Court of Appeal decided that children who require overnight care qualify (R (Rutherford and others) v SSWP [2016]); and on 9th November 2016 the Supreme Court confirmed this and decided that adult couples who can't share a bedroom qualify (R (Daly and others) v SSWP [2016]). Both cases were decided on the basis of unlawful discrimination (para 11.9). The following applies if you should have qualified for additional HB (or were refused HB but should have been awarded it) as a result of these cases:

(a)   if you had already asked the council to reconsider its decision, or appealed against it, you should normally be paid arrears of HB (this is confirmed in [2017] UKUT 174 (AAC));

(b)   but it is now normally too late to request arrears of HB for these reasons (for periods before 1st April 2017).

For further information see paras 16.80 and 17.43. Guidance to authorities is given in HB U1/2016, HB U3/2016 and HB U1/2017.

Fostering and pre-adoption

11.21   One additional bedroom is allowed if you (the claimant) or your partner:

(a)   have a child or young person placed with you as their foster parent (or kinship carer) or prior to adoption; or

(b)   have been approved as a foster parent (kinship carer) and are waiting for a placement or between placements – but this only applies for up to 52 weeks in each period in which you don't have a placement.

Only one additional bedroom is allowed, even if you have more than one child or young person placed with you. But if any of them require overnight care, see paras 11.23-24.

11.19   See footnotes to paras 11.21-22 and 11.23-29

11.20   SI 2017/213; NISR 2016/70; R (Rutherford and others) v SSWP [2016] EWCA Civ 29 www.bailii.org/ew/cases/EWCA/Civ/2016/29.html
R(Daly and others) v SSWP [2016] UKSC 58 www.bailii.org/ew/cases/UKSC/58.html

11.21-22   All: HB 2(1) definition: 'qualifying parent or carer'; HB60+ 2(1); NIHB 2(1); NIHB60+ 2(1)
Social renter: HB B13(6)(b),(9); NIHB B14(6)(b),(9)
LHA: HB 13D(3A)(b); HB60+ 13D(3A)(b); NIHB 14D(3A)(b); NIHB60+ 14D(3A)(b)
Rent referral: ROO sch 2 paras 1A(b), 1B, 3; NIHB sch 2 paras 10, 10A(b), 10B, 15; NIHB60+ sch 2 paras 10, 10A(b), 10B, 15

11.22   If you fall under the social renter rules (chapter 8) or rent referral rules (chapter 10) (but not the local housing allowance rules) one additional bedroom is allowed for each single joint tenant couple who meets the conditions in para 11.21. Apart from that, no additional bedroom is allowed for any other occupier of your dwelling who is a foster parent etc.

People who require overnight care

11.23   One additional bedroom is allowed for each occupier of your dwelling who:

(a)   requires overnight care: see para 11.25; and

(b)   has arrangements in place for it to be provided by a non-resident carer or carers: see paras 11.26-28.

One additional bedroom is allowed for each couple, whether one or both of them meet the conditions. And one additional bedroom is allowed for each other person who meets them, whether as an adult, child or young person. But for each additional bedroom allowed, your dwelling must have an actual bedroom (paras 11.28 and 11.35) that is in addition to those allowed for anyone else.

11.24   For this rule, the occupiers of your dwelling are:

(a)   anyone in para 11.10 (you, your family, non-dependants, lodgers, joint tenants except under the LHA rules, and others); and

(b)   any child or young person who placed with you (the claimant) or your partner as their foster parent (or kinship carer) or prior to adoption.

The need for overnight care

11.25   An occupier of your dwelling 'requires overnight care' (para 11.23) if they:

(a)   are in receipt of:

- the daily living component of personal independence payment,
- attendance allowance, or constant attendance allowance paid with an industrial injury pension,
- the highest or middle rate of the care component of disability living allowance, or
- an armed forces independence payment; or

(b)   don't receive any of the above, but have sufficient evidence to show that they require overnight care.

For example, someone who gets the lower rate of the care component of disability living allowance doesn't meet (a), but could meet (b), and the fact of getting the lower rate can be used as evidence of this ([2014] UKUT 325 (AAC)). Or someone who hasn't claimed any of the benefits in (a) could meet (b).

11.23-29   All: HB 2(1) definitions: 'attendance allowance', 'child who cannot share a bedroom', 'member of a couple who cannot share a bedroom';
HB60+ 2(1); NIHB 2(1); NIHB60+ 2(1)
Social renter: HB B13(5)(ba)-(e); NIHB B14(5)(b)-(f)
LHA: HB 13D(3); HB60+ 13D(3); NIHB 14D(3); NIHB60+ 14D(3)
Rent referral: ROO sch 2 paras 1A(a), 1B, 3; NIHB sch 2 paras 10, 10A(a), 10B, 15; NIHB60+ sch 2 paras 10, 10A(a), 10B, 15

The arrangements for overnight care

11.26   For an additional bedroom to be allowed (para 11.23), the person requiring overnight care (or someone on their behalf) must reasonably require, and have in fact arranged, that one or more people who don't occupy your dwelling as their home:

(a)   are engaged in providing the overnight care;

(b)   regularly stay overnight in your dwelling for that purpose (para 11.27); and

(c)   are provided with an additional bedroom for that purpose (para 11.28).

11.27   The carer could be the same person on each night a carer is required, or there could be a rota of carers. It is not enough to require a carer only by day. The carer(s) must stay overnight regularly. 'Regularly' does not mean normally, ordinarily or at reasonably even intervals, but is closer to habitually, customarily or commonly; so the question is whether the need for overnight care 'arises steadily and often enough to require a bedroom to be kept for the purpose', and a minority of nights can be enough: [2014] UKUT 325 (AAC).

11.28   There must be an actual bedroom provided for the carer(s), and it must be additional to those used by you, your family and the other occupiers of your dwelling. In this context, the Upper Tribunal has held that a bedroom means a room which has a bed in or is used for sleeping in: [2014] UKUT 48 (AAC). In that case, the claimant rented a two bedroom bungalow. He qualified for one bedroom for himself and his wife (table 11.1), but on medical advice they slept apart – one in each bedroom. Their daughter was an overnight carer, and she slept in a portable bed or sofa in the lounge. This met the condition for an additional bedroom. This is the same as if the daughter had slept in one of the two bedrooms and the husband or wife had slept in the lounge. For further considerations about what is a bedroom, see paras 11.35-38 and table 11.2.

Overnight care: waiting to move in and temporary absence

11.29   An additional bedroom is also allowed if:

(a)   the person requiring overnight care (paras 11.24-25) is waiting to move in or temporarily absent; and

(b)   there is an additional bedroom now, and the other arrangements in para 11.26 will be in place when they move in or return.

'Waiting to move in' and 'temporarily absent' have the same meanings as in paras 3.29-66 (adapting these as described in para 11.11).

Disabled people who can't share a bedroom

11.30   An additional bedroom is also allowed for each occupier of your dwelling (para 11.31) who:

(a)   is in a couple and meets the conditions in para 11.32; or

(b)   is a child under 16 who meets the conditions in para 11.33.

11.30   Social sector: HB B13(5)(za),(ba); NIHB B14(5)(za),(c);
         LHA: HB 13D(3)(za),(ba); HB60+ 13D(3)(za),(ba); NIHB 14D(3)(za),(ba); NIHB60+ 14D(3)(za),(ba)

One additional bedroom is allowed for each couple, whether one or both of them meet the conditions. And one additional bedroom is allowed for each child who meets them. But if you fall under the LHA or rent referral rules (but not if you are a social renter), for each additional bedroom allowed, your dwelling must have an actual bedroom (paras 11.35) that is in addition to those allowed for anyone else.

11.31   For this rule, the occupiers of your dwelling are:

(a) any couple or child in para 11.10 (you, your family, non-dependants, joint tenants except under the LHA rules, and others);

(b) but not a foster child or child placed for adoption (table 4.3(a) and (b)).

Young persons aren't included, because they qualify for their own bedroom under the general rules (table 11.1).

Couple who can't share a bedroom

11.32   An additional bedroom is also allowed for a couple if one partner is (or both partners are):

(a) due to their disability, not reasonably able to share a bedroom (para 11.34) with their partner; and

(b) entitled to

- the daily living component of personal independence payment,
- the higher rate of attendance allowance,
- the highest or middle rate of the care component of disability living allowance, or
- armed forces independence payment.

Children who can't share a bedroom

11.33   An additional bedroom is also allowed for a child (under the age of 16) who is:

(a) due to their disability, not reasonably able to share a bedroom (para 11.34) with another child; and

(b) entitled to the highest or middle rate of the care component of disability living allowance.

This can only apply if there are at least two children in your dwelling (because a single child would qualify for their own bedroom under the general rules: Table 11.1). So first a bedroom is allowed for each child who can't share a bedroom, then a bedroom or bedrooms are allowed for the other child(ren) under the general rules.

11.31   HB B13(5) 13D(3); HB60+ 13D(3); NIHB B14(5),14D(5); NIHB60+ 14D(5)

11.32   HB 2(1) definition: 'couple who cannot share a bedroom'; HB60+ 2(1); NIHB 2(1)

11.33   Social sector: HB definition: 'child who cannot share a bedroom' B13(5)(ba)-(e); NIHB B14(5)(c)-(f)
LHA: HB 2(1) definition: 'child who cannot share a bedroom' 13D(3)(ba)-(e); HB60+ 2(1) 13D(3)(ba)-(e);
NIHB 2(1), 14D(3)(c)-(f); NIHB60+ 2(1),14D(3)(c)-(f)

'Not reasonably able to share a bedroom'

11.34   DWP advice in relation to children is in circular HB 21/2013. This focuses on whether the child requires overnight care and advises authorities to 'keep in mind the policy intention which is to safeguard the wellbeing of children and prevent them being put at risk of physical harm or having their sleep frequently and significantly disrupted by... sharing a bedroom when it is inappropriate to do so because of severe disability' (HB A21/2013 paras 10-11).

What counts as a bedroom

11.35   If you are a social renter (or in some cases if the rent referral rules apply)whether a particular room in your dwelling is or isn't a bedroom can be important in deciding in deciding whether, or by how much your eligible rent is reduced (para 8.22); or whether you qualify for an additional bedroom (paras 11.23 and 11.30).

11.36   There is no definition in the HB regulations of what counts as a bedroom, but Upper Tribunals have given a number of decisions relating to this. The leading case (at the time of writing) is [2014] UKUT 525 (AAC) (SSWP v Nelson), which was decided by a panel of three judges. It and other decisions are summarised in table 11.2.

11.37   The council is entitled to use its judgment in deciding whether a room is or is not a bedroom (para 1.52). Initially it is likely to base this decision on how your landlord has categorised the rooms in your home (circular HB/CTB A4/2012), but it is not bound by this and should consider each case on its individual details.

11.38   Possible considerations about whether a room is a bedroom include:

(a)   the potential or actual use of the room;

(b)   how the room was described by the landlord when the accommodation was let, or on the building's plans;

(c)   practical considerations including the room's size;

(d)   in limited cases, issues relating to overcrowding.

For further details see table 11.2.

Table 11.2 **What counts as a bedroom: case law**

All the cases in this table are about the social renter size criteria (paras 8.15-26 and 11.3-4).

Applying the undefined term 'bedroom'. The word 'bedroom' has its ordinary or familiar English meaning. It should not be paraphrased, but should be understood and applied 'having regard to the underlying purpose of the legislation' which is 'to limit the HB entitlement of those under-occupying accommodation'. Like an 'elephant', a 'bedroom' is capable of description rather than definition. And in an individual case, the authority's understanding of what is a bedroom 'is best provided by the reasons given for [its] decision'. ([2014] UKUT 525 (AAC) paras 19-24.) The description of a bedroom required by an overnight carer (see para 11.28) as a room with a bed or beds in and/or a room suitable for sleeping in ([2014] UKUT 48 (AAC)) is unlikely to be a conclusive general definition.

Actual, potential and changed use of the room. The council should consider the potential use of the room by any of the adults or children referred to in the regulations (the occupiers and overnight carers: see paras 11.10-34). In general, actual, former or planned occupation is less likely to be relevant, as the assessment of the room is 'essentially of a property when vacant'. ([2014] UKUT 525 (AAC) paras 27-28; CH/2512/2015.) But a bedroom can stop counting as a bedroom if exceptional circumstances relating to physical or mental disability mean it is now used as a living room ([2015] UKUT 282 (AAC)).

The description of the room by the landlord or in the building's plans. The council can take account of the description of the room by the original or current landlord (for example in the letting agreement or marketing materials) or in the plans or designs for the building. But this is 'a starting point' and is not conclusive. ([2014] UKUT 525 (AAC) para 30.)

Relevant practical considerations. The council should consider practical factors including '(a) size, configuration and overall dimensions, (b) access, (c) natural and electronic lighting, (d) ventilation, and (e) privacy'. For example, it should not be necessary to 'jump from a passage through an outward opening door in order to get into bed'. It should be possible to get into bed from within the room, and there should be somewhere to put clothes and a glass of water. These factors are 'case sensitive' (in other words, based on the individual circumstances) and take account of the adults and children referred to in the regulations (see paras 11.10-34). ([2014] UKUT 525 (AAC) paras 31-44; [2016] UKUT 164 (AAC))

Underoccupation and overcrowding. Underoccupation is not 'the flip side of overcrowding'. The two sets of rules are different, and overcrowding law takes account of living rooms as well as bedrooms (Housing Act 1985 s326, Housing (Scotland) Act 1987 s137). But overcrowding rules (for example if a room has very small dimensions) can sound 'warning bells' that a room may not be a bedroom. ([2014] UKUT 525 (AAC) paras 53-55;[2016] UKUT 164 (AAC)) In practice, direct conflict between overcrowding law and the HB size criteria is rare.

Chapter 12 **Applicable amounts**

- ■ Basic rules: see paras 12.1-7.
- ■ Amounts for you and your family: see paras 12.8-19.
- ■ Working age components and the disability premium: see paras 12.20-32.
- ■ Other premiums for disability and caring: see paras 12.33-48.
- ■ Further definitions and special cases: see paras 12.49-54.

Basic rules

12.1   Your 'applicable amount' represents your family's basic living expenses. It is compared to your income when calculating how much HB you are entitled to (paras 6.4-6). It is also sometimes used for other HB matters (e.g. in the rules about student eligibility: table 22.1).

Definitions

12.2   In this chapter the following terms all have the specific HB meanings given in chapter 4 and summarised in table 4.1: 'family', 'single claimant', 'lone parent', 'couple', 'partner', 'child' and 'young person'. For 'pension age' and 'working age' see paras 1.23-25 and table 1.5.

How much is your applicable amount?

12.3   Your applicable amount is the total of:

- (a) a personal allowance for you, or for you and your partner (paras 12.9-10);
- (b) up to two (or sometimes more) personal allowances for children and young persons in your family (paras 12.11-18); and
- (c) any additional amounts (known as premiums and components) you qualify for (paras 12.19-48).

The figures for 2017-18 are given in table 12.1. For working age claimants, the personal allowances have remained the same since April 2015, and the government does not plan to increase them before April 2020.

How many premiums and components at once

12.4   Except as described in the remainder of this chapter, there are no limitations on how many premiums and components can be awarded at a time.

12.2   CBA 137; NICBA 133; HB 2(1) definitions: 'child', 'claimant', 'family', 'partner', 'young person', 22; HB60+ 2(1), 22; NIHB 2(1), 20, NIHB60+ 2(1), 20

12.3   CBA 135; NICBA 131; HB 22, sch 3; HB60+ 22, sch 3; NIHB 20, sch 4; NIHB60+ 20, sch 4

12.4   HB sch 3 paras 4-5, 6(1); HB60+ sch 3 para 4; NIHB sch 4 para 4; NIHB60+ sch 3 para 4

How to be better off if you are a couple on ESA

12.5   If you are a couple and one or both of you receives ESA (or national insurance credits instead of ESA) your applicable amount can be higher or lower depending on which one of you makes the claim for HB (para 5.4). If this applies to you and you are worse off because the wrong member has claimed HB your council should advise you that you would be better off if you swapped roles (GM BW3.143 and BW3.305). To ensure that you are better off through the right member making the HB claim, see the next two paragraphs.

12.6   If both you and your partner receive ESA (or credits) but you receive different components, you are better off if the member who gets the support component claims HB.

12.7   If only one of you receives ESA the member who claims HB should be as follows:

(a) if you are both aged under 18, the member who gets ESA;

(b) if one of you receives the support component, that member;

(c) if one of you qualifies for a disability premium and the other a work-related activity component, the member who qualifies for the disability premium;

(d) if neither of you qualify for a disability premium, the member who receives the work-related activity component.

'ESA', 'support component' and 'work-related activity component' means receiving ESA with that component or national insurance credits (para 12.23) instead of ESA.

Example: A 'better off' problem for couples

Information

A working age couple meet the condition for a disability premium which relates to being disabled or long-term sick (e.g. one of them is on DLA or is registered blind), but one partner in the couple is on ESA(C).

Entitlement to additions in the HB applicable amount

This depends on which partner is the HB claimant.

(a) If the HB claimant is on ESA(C):

their HB applicable amount does not include a disability premium (at any point), but it does include a work-related activity or support component from the claimant's 14th week on ESA(C).

(b) If the HB partner is on ESA(C):

their HB applicable amount includes a couple-rate disability premium (from the beginning), but it never includes a work-related activity or support component.

Conclusion

So they are better off if (b) applies to them – by about £30 per week HB during the first 13 weeks on ESA(C) (and by a lower amount after that).

12.6   HB sch 3 paras 23-26; NIHB sch 4 paras 23-26

12.7   HB sch 3 paras 1(3)(a),(c), 13(9), 22-26; NIHB sch 4 paras 1(3)(a),(c), 13(9), 22-26

Amounts for you and your family

12.8   This section explains the basic amounts that take account of your family size. These are 'personal allowances' and (for some claimants) a family premium.

Personal allowances: you and your partner

12.9   A personal allowance is always awarded for you if you are a single claimant or a lone parent, or for you and your partner if you are a couple. (For polygamous marriages see para 12.52.)

12.10   Your personal allowance increases (table 12.1) when:

(a)   you start to get main phase ESA or main phase ESA credits (paras 12.23 and 12.26), if this happens before (b);

(b)   you reach 25 (single claimants) or 18 (lone parents and couples), if (a) didn't apply to you;

(c)   you reach state pension credit age (para 1.24);

(d)   you reach 65.

For couples, (b) to (d) apply when the first of you reaches that age, but (a) only applies to you (the claimant) get ESA or ESA credits: see para 12.7 to ensure you get this increase.

Personal allowances: children and young persons

12.11   Personal allowances are awarded for children and young persons in your family (paras 4.14-19 and 4.23-25) as follows:

(a)   in Great Britain, for periods before 6th April 2017 you qualify for a personal allowance for each child/young person in your family ;

(b)   in Great Britain, for periods from 6th April 2017 there can be a two child/young person limit: see paras 12.12-18 for the details;

(c)   in Northern Ireland, you qualify for a personal allowance for each child/young person in your family, but the two child/young person limit is likely to be introduced later in 2017-18.

The two child limit

12.12   In Great Britain from 6th April 2017, you qualify for a personal allowance for:

(a)   one child/young person if there is just one in your family; or

(b)   two children/ young persons if there are two or more in your family.

But you may qualify for personal allowances for more children/young persons if the following exceptions apply.

12.9-10   HB 22(1)(a), sch 3 paras 1, 1A; HB60+ 22(1)(a), sch 3 paras 1, 1A; NIHB 20(1)(a), sch 4 paras 1, 1A; NIHB60+ 20(1)(a), sch 4 paras 1, 1A

12.11   HB 22(1)(b), sch 3 para 2(1); HB60+ 22(1)(b), sch 3 para 2(1); NIHB 20(1)(b), sch 4 para 2(1); NIHB60+ 20(1)(b), sch 4 para 2(1)

12.12   HB 22(1)(b),(2); HB60+ 22(1)(b),(2)

Exceptions to the two child limit

12.13   There are exceptions to the two child/young person limit if:

(a)   you were entitled to HB on the 5th April 2017 (paras 12.14-15); or

(b)   you have made a claim for child tax credit (paras 12.16-18).

These only apply when they result in personal allowances for more children/young persons in your family. If they both apply, you qualify for whichever results in the largest number of personal allowances.

If you were entitled to HB on 5th April 2017

12.14   This exception to the two child/young person limit applies if:

(a)   you were entitled to HB (including backdated HB: para 5.50) on 5th April 2017 and had at least one child/young person in your family then; and:

(b)   you haven't made a new claim for HB since then (e.g. following a break in your entitlement or a move to a new local authority area).

12.15   In this case:

(a)   you qualify for a personal allowance for each 'protected' child/young/person –this means each one who:

  ■   was in your family on 5th April 2017, and

  ■   is in your family now (even if they haven't been in your family continuously since then);

(b)   and if there are one or more other children/young persons in your family now, you qualify for a personal allowance for:

  ■   two of them if you don't have any protected children/young persons, or

  ■   one of them if you have one protected child/young person, or

  ■   none of them if you have two or more protected children/young persons.

If you have claimed child tax credit

12.16   This exception to the two child/young person limit applies if:

(a)   you have made a claim for CTC – whether or not you qualify for CTC as a result; and:

(b)   the assessment of your CTC included one or more child elements for children/young persons – the council can ask you to provide your CTC decision notice as evidence of this.

12.17   In this case, you qualify for an HB personal allowance for each child/young person who:

(a)   you get a CTC child element for (para 12.18); or

(b)   you would get a CTC child element for, except that you don't qualify for CTC (e.g. because of the level of your income).

12.13   HB 22(1)(b),(2),(3); HB60+ 22(1)(b),(2),(3); NIHB 20(1)(b),(2),(3); NIHB60+ 20(1)(b),(2),(3); reg 9 of SI 2017/376

12.14-15   Reg 9 of SI 2017/376

12.16-17   HB 22(3)-(5); HB60+ 22(3)-(5)

So if you qualify for more HB personal allowances under this rule (and aren't already on CTC), you should claim CTC even if you know you won't qualify for it. If this results in an increase in your HB, the law about when this takes effect is unclear, but it seems likely councils will apply (or adapt) the rules in paras 17.33 and table 17.5.

12.18   CTC also has a two child/young person limit from 6th April 2017. But certain children/young persons don't count towards the CTC limit, and this means you can get an HB personal allowance (para 12.17) as well as CTC for them. In general terms, these are children/young persons who:

(a)   were born before 6th April 2017; or

(b)   are part of a multiple birth (twins, triplets and so on) – in this case, one child counts towards the CTC limit and the other or others don't; or

(c)   were conceived as a result of rape or controlling or coercive behaviour; or

(d)   are born to a child aged under 16, and are included in your family rather than hers; or

(e)   are not your own child, and who:

- you have adopted, or

- you receive guardians allowance for, or

- live with you under formal arrangements made by social services or a court, or

- live with you under informal arrangements (made by you) and would otherwise be likely to enter local authority care.

The full details are available online, including changes to the rules expected to take effect from 31st October 2018 at the earliest [www].

Family premium

12.19   The family premium was abolished for new HB claims on 1st May 2016 (in Northern Ireland, 5th September 2016). You only qualify for a family premium now if:

(a)   you were entitled to HB (including backdated HB: para 5.50) on 30th April 2016 (in Northern Ireland, 4th September 2016) and had at least one child or young person in your family then; and:

(b)   you have had at least one child or young person in your family continuously since then (not necessarily the same child/young person); and

(c)   you haven't made a new claim for HB since then (e.g. following a break in your entitlement or a move to a new local authority area).

12.18   https://www.gov.uk/government/uploads/system/uploads/attachment_data/file/584802/government-response-to-universal-credit-and-child-tax-credit-exceptions-to-the-2-child-limit-consultation.pdf

12.19   HB 22(1)(c), sch 3 para 3; HB60+ 22(1)(c), sch 3 para 3; NIHB 20(1)(c), sch 4 para 3; NIHB60+ 20(1)(c), sch 4 para 3; regs 2,4 of SI 2015/1857; regs 3,5 of NISR 2016/310

Table 12.1 **Weekly HB applicable amounts: 2016-17**

Personal allowances

Single claimant	aged under 25 – on main phase ESA	£73.10	
	aged under 25 – other	£57.90	
	aged 25+ but under pension age	£73.10	
	over pension age but under 65	£159.35	
	aged 65+	£172.55	
Lone parent	aged under 18 – on main phase ESA	£73.10	
	aged under 18 – other	£57.90	
	aged 18+ but under pension age	£73.10	
	over pension age but under 65	£159.35	
	aged 65+	£172.55	
Couple	both under 18 – claimant on main phase ESA	£114.85	
	both under 18 – other	£87.50	
	at least one aged 18+ both under pension age	£114.85	
	at least one pension age, both under 65	£243.25	
	at least one aged 65+	£258.15	
Plus for each child/ young person		£66.90	

Additional amounts

Family premium	at least one child/young person (but see para 12.19)	£17.45	
Disability premium	single claimant/lone parent	£32.55	*
	couple (one/both qualifying)	£46.40	*
Disabled child premium	each child/young person	£60.90	
Enhanced disability premium	single claimant/lone parent	£15.90	*
	couple (one/both qualifying)	£22.85	*
	each child/young person	£24.78	
Work-related activity component	single claimant/lone parent/couple	£29.05	*
Support component	single claimant/lone parent/couple	£36.55	*
Carer premium	claimant or partner or each	£34.95	
Severe disability premium	single rate	£62.45	
	double rate	£124.90	

* Only awarded with working age claims (para 1.24)

Examples: The two-child limit

1. A couple have four children. They claim HB in March 2017.

    From March 2017, they qualify for four HB personal allowances for the children. This continues from 6th April 2017, because all the children were included in their HB before that date (para 12.15(a)).

2. A lone parent has one child. She claims HB in May 2017. In June 2017 she has a baby.

    From May 2017, she qualifies for an HB personal allowance for the child. From June 2017, she also qualifies for an HB personal allowance for the baby, because she has just two children (para 12.15(b)).

3. A couple have two children. They claim HB in July 2017. In August 2017 they have a baby.

    From July 2017, they qualify for two HB personal allowances for the children. From August 2017, they don't qualify for an HB personal allowance for the baby unless they make a claim for child tax credit (paras 12.15(b) and 12.17). When they do claim CTC the baby is included in their CTC award, and so they qualify for an HB personal allowance for the baby as well (para 12.18).

4. A couple have one child and are on CTC. They claim HB in September 2017. In October 2017 they have baby twins.

    From September 2107, they qualify for an HB personal allowance for the child. From October 2017, both the twins are included in their CTC award, and so they qualify for an HB personal allowance for both the twins as well (para 12.18).

5. A lone parent has three children and is on CTC, which includes all three children. In November he claims HB. In December 2017 his oldest daughter has a baby when she is 15.

    From November 2017, he qualifies for three HB personal allowances for the children. From December 2017, the daughter's baby is also included in his CTC award, and so he qualifies for an HB personal allowance for the baby as well (para 12.18).

Note: Examples 1 to 4 would be the same if all the children referred to were young persons (para 4.16).

Working age components and the disability premium

12.20   The components, disability premium and transitional addition described in this section can only apply to you if you have a working age claim (paras 1.23-25 and table 1.5).

12.21   If you or your partner have a sickness or disability that affects your fitness to work then you may be entitled to either:

(a)   a work-related activity component: see paras 12.23-28;

(b)   a support component: see paras 12.23-27; or

(c)   a disability premium: see paras 12.31-32.

You can only receive one of these at any one time. You do not necessarily receive the one that is the highest value – that is determined by the DWP's assessment of your (or your partner's) fitness for work and, if you are a couple, which one of you makes the claim. See paras 12.5-7 to ensure you are better off.

12.22   If you qualify for a component, and your period of sickness or disability began before 27th October 2008, you may also be entitled to a transitional addition: see paras 12.29-30.

The components and the ESA fitness for work test

12.23   The general rule is that you are awarded a work-related activity component or support component in your HB if:

(a)   you have claimed employment and support allowance (ESA); and

(b)   the DWP has decided you qualify for that particular component (see paras 12.25-27), and

- ▪   has awarded it in your ESA, or

- ▪   would have done so except that you qualify for national insurance credits instead of ESA. This can only happen if you don't meet the national insurance contribution conditions for ESA, or were receiving ESA(C) but your award has expired because it was paid for the maximum period of one year.

But from 3rd April 2017 you can only get a work-related activity component in limited circumstances (see para 12.28).

12.24   The rules are more complex if you are a couple. If only one of you qualifies for an ESA component, or you both qualify for the same ESA component, you get that component in your HB. But if you qualify for one ESA component and your partner qualifies for the other ESA component, you get the component you (the HB claimant) qualify for. This means you can be 'better off' depending on which one of you claims HB (see paras 12.5-7).

12.25   In your ESA, you qualify for the work-related activity component if the DWP decides you have 'limited capability for work' and you meet one of the conditions in para 12.28. But you qualify for the support component (which is worth more) if the DWP decides your disability is so serious that you have 'limited capability for work-related activity'. In other words, the type of activities the DWP expects you to undertake are more limited than if you were awarded the work-related activity component.

12.21   HB sch 3 paras 13(9), 22(1); NIHB sch 4 paras 13(9), 22(1)

12.23-24   HB sch 3 paras 21,21A,23,24; NIHB sch 4 paras 21,21A,23,24

12.25   HB 2(1) 'limited capability for work', 'limited capability for work-related activity', sch 3 para 21(1)(b); NIHB 2(1), sch 4 para 21(1)(b)

12.26   The DWP's decision about this is called a 'work capability assessment'. The DWP:

(a)   makes this decision during the 'assessment phase' of your ESA;

(b)   awards your component during the 'main phase' of your ESA.

Your assessment phase runs for the first 13 weeks of your ESA claim, and your main phase runs from week 14 onwards (see also para 12.27).

12.27   Your ESA is 'linked' to a previous ESA award if the start of your current period of limited capability for work is within 12 weeks of your previous award ending. 'Linked' ESA awards form a continuous period, so your 'assessment phase' starts from the first day of your previous ESA award, and means some or all of the 13 weeks are already served in your current award.

The work-related activity component from 3rd April 2017

12.28   From 3rd April 2017 you can't get the work-related activity component in your ESA unless:

(a)   you claimed ESA, or your ESA began, before 3rd April 2017; or

(b)   you claim ESA later and your claim is 'linked' (para 12.27) to a previous ESA claim described in (a); or

(c)   you were on ESA before 3rd April 2017, then transferred onto maternity allowance, then reclaim ESA within 12 weeks of your maternity allowance ending; or

(d)   you transfer from IB to ESA.

This means you can't get a work-related activity component in your HB unless you meet one of these conditions (para 12.23).

Transitional addition after transferring to ESA

12.29   You qualify for a transitional addition in your HB if your disability premium stops because you transfer:

(a)   from long-term IB, SDA, or national insurance credits instead of these;

(b)   to contributory ESA, or national insurance credits instead of this (see paras 12.25-27).

But you do not qualify for a transitional addition if you transfer to income-related ESA; or you are a couple and you qualify for a disability premium under the rules in paras 12.31-32. In each case, this is because you can't be worse off (but if (b) applies to you, see paras 12.5-7 to ensure this).

12.30   A transitional addition prevents you from being worse off as a result of transferring to contributory ESA or national insurance credits by restoring your applicable amount to the value it had immediately before you transferred. After that:

(a)   any subsequent increase in your applicable amount due to a change in your circumstances or the annual up-rating is deducted from your transitional addition until it is eroded to nil;

(b)   your transitional addition ends before it is eroded to nil if your contributory ESA ends or your HB ends;

12.28   SI 2017/204 sch 2 paras 1-7

12.29   HB sch 3 para 27(1); NIHB sch 4 para 27(1)

12.30   HB sch 3 paras 27(2),28(1)(b),30,31; NIHB sch 4 paras 27(2),29(1)(c),30, 31

(c)   but if you start back on HB within 12 weeks of your previous award, your transitional addition is restored.

Disability premium: general rules

12.31   You are awarded a disability premium if you have a working age claim (see paras 1.23-25), and are not on ESA or national insurance credits instead of ESA, and

(a)   you are severely sight impaired, blind or have recently regained your sight (paras 12.50-51); or

(b)   you receive one of the following qualifying disability benefits:

- personal independence payment or disability living allowance (either component at any rate),

- the disability element or severe disability element of working tax credit,

- attendance allowance, or constant attendance allowance paid with an industrial injury or war disablement pension,

- an armed forces independence payment, or

- war pensioner's mobility supplement; or

(c)   you have an invalid vehicle supplied by the NHS or get DWP payments for car running costs.

12.32   The rules are more complex if you are a couple. You get a disability premium at the couple rate if:

(a)   either of you meets the conditions in paragraph 12.31, and neither of you are on ESA or national insurance credits instead of ESA; or

(b)   you (the HB claimant) meet the conditions in paragraph 12.31, and your partner is on ESA or national insurance credits instead of ESA.

This means you can be 'better off' depending on which of you claims HB (see paras 12.5-7).

Example: Transitional addition

A single man aged 37 transfers from long-term IB to the work-related activity component of ESA(C). Before he transfers, his applicable amount is:

■ personal allowance	£73.10
■ disability premium	£32.55
■ total	£105.65

After he transfers, his HB applicable amount is:

■ personal allowance	£73.10
■ work-related activity component	£29.05
■ total	£102.15
His transitional addition is the difference between the two totals	£3.50
This restores his applicable amount to	£105.65

12.31-32   HB 2(1) definition: 'attendance allowance', sch 3 paras 12, 13(9); NIHB 2(1), sch 4 paras 12, 13(9)

Other premiums for disability and caring

12.33 The premiums described in this section can apply to you whether you have a working age or pension age claim (except as described in para 12.36).

Disabled child premium

12.34 You qualify for this premium if there is a child or young person in your family who:

(a) is severely sight impaired, blind or has recently regained their sight (paras 12.50-51); or

(b) receives personal independence payment or disability living allowance (either component at any rate).

The premium is awarded for each child or young person who qualifies (regardless of the two child limit). If your child/young person dies the premium continues for eight weeks following their death. If a young person aged 18 or more loses their qualifying benefit because they are in hospital special rules apply – see para 12.54 and table 12.2 for details.

Enhanced disability premium

12.35 You are awarded the enhanced disability premium:

(a) if you or your partner qualify (para 12.36); and/or

(b) for each child or young person in your family who qualifies (para 12.37).

Two or more of these premiums are awarded if appropriate – for example, if you or your partner qualifies and also one or more children qualify. If you lose your qualifying benefit as a result of a stay in hospital special rules apply (para 12.54 and table 12.2).

12.36 An enhanced disability premium for you or your partner is awarded if:

(a) you have a working age claim (para 1.24);

(b) you (or if you are a couple either you or your partner) receive the enhanced rate of the daily living component of personal independence payment, the highest rate of the care component of disability living allowance or an armed forces independence payment; or

(c) you qualify for an ESA(C) support component (but not if only your partner does).

If you are a couple, the couple rate is awarded even if only one of you meets the conditions: so if only one of you qualifies for an ESA support component you are better off if they are the HB claimant (paras 12.5-7).

12.37 An enhanced disability premium is awarded for each child or young person in your family who receives the enhanced rate of the daily living component of personal independence payment, highest rate of the care component of disability living allowance, or (if they are a young person) an armed forces independence payment. If your child/young person dies the premium continues for eight weeks following their death.

12.33   HB sch 3 para 13(1)(a)(i),(9); NIHB sch 4 para 13(1)(a)(i),(9)

12.34   HB sch 3 paras 16(a)-(e), 20(7); HB60+ sch 3 para 8(a)-(e), 12(3);
NIHB sch 4 paras 16(za),(a)-(c), 20(7); NIHB60+ sch 4 para 8(za),(a)-(c), 12(3)

12.35   HB sch 3 para 20(9); HB60+ sch 3 para 12(2); NIHB sch 4 para 20(9); NIHB60+ sch 4 para 12(2)

12.36   HB sch 3 para 15(1)(a)-(d); NIHB sch 4 para 15(1)(a),(aa),(b)

12.37   HB sch 3 para 15(1)(b)-(d),(1A); HB60+ sch 3 para 7; NIHB sch 4 para 15(1)(a),(aa),(b),(1A); NIHB60+ sch 4 para 7

Severe disability premium

12.38   There are three conditions for this premium:

(a) you must be receiving one of the following qualifying benefits:

- the daily living component of personal independence payment,
- the middle or highest rate care component of disability living allowance,
- attendance allowance, or constant attendance allowance paid with an industrial injury or war disablement pension, or
- an armed forces independence payment; and

(b) you must have no non-dependants living with you (but see para 12.40 below for exceptions); and

(c) no-one must be receiving carer's allowance or the UC carer element to care for you (but see para 12.42 for circumstances where either of these is awarded but treated as not being paid).

If you are a couple, except where one of you is severely sight impaired or blind (paras 12.50-51), both of you must be receiving a qualifying benefit. Special rules apply if you lose your qualifying benefit during a stay in hospital (paras 12.39, 12.41, 12.54 and table 12.2).

12.39   If you are single or a lone parent and you satisfy all the conditions in para 12.38 you get the single rate of severe disability premium. If you are in a couple a severe disability premium is awarded as follows:

(a) if you both satisfy all three conditions, you get the double rate;

(b) if you both satisfy the first two conditions but only one of you satisfies the third condition, you get the single rate;

(c) if you are the claimant and you satisfy all three conditions, and your partner is severely sight impaired, blind or has recently regained their sight (paras 12.50-51), you get the single rate. In this case, the member who satisfies all the conditions must be the claimant to qualify for the premium. If the 'wrong' partner makes the claim, you should be advised to 'swap the claimant role' (para 5.4);

(d) if you have been getting the double rate, but one of you loses your qualifying benefit as a result of being in hospital for four weeks, then you get the single rate from that point.

12.40   When assessing the second condition in para 12.38 (non-dependants that live with you) your council must ignore any person in your household who:

(a) is a member of your family (para 4.2);

(b) is aged under 18 or who is excluded from the definition of a non-dependant (table 4.4);

(c) is severely sight impaired, blind or who has recently regained their sight (paras 12.50-51);

(d) receives any of the qualifying benefits in para 12.38(a) (for example, attendance allowance); or

---

12.38   HB 2(1) definition: 'attendance allowance', sch 3 para 14(2); HB60+ 2(1), sch 3 para 6(2); NIHB 2(1), sch 4 para 14(2); NIHB60+ 2(1), sch 4 para 6(2)

12.39   HB sch 3 paras 14(3), 20(6); HB60+ sch 3 paras 6(3), 12(1); NIHB sch 4 paras 14(3), 20(6); NIHB60+ sch 4 paras 6(3), 12(1)

12.40   HB sch 3 para 14(4); HB60+ sch 3 para 6(6); NIHB sch 4 para 14(4); NIHB60+ sch 4 para 6(6)

(e) is jointly liable with you or your partner for rent – unless they were a non-dependant in the previous eight weeks or they are a close relative (para 2.43) and your council believes their liability was created to take advantage of the HB scheme.

12.41   When assessing the third condition in para 12.38 (whether a carer receives carer's allowance or the UC carer element) your council must treat your (or your partner's) carer as receiving carer's allowance during any period when:

(a) you are a member of a couple and carer's allowance or the UC carer element has stopped as a result of you losing your qualifying benefit because you have been in hospital for four weeks or more. (This ensures that if you receive the premium at the single rate you continue to receive it at that rate while you (or your partner) are in hospital); or

(b) your carer has stopped receiving carer's allowance as a penalty for a benefit fraud conviction.

12.42   When assessing the third condition in para 12.38 (whether a carer receives carer's allowance) your council must ignore any period when your (or your partner's) carer:

(a) receives an award of carer's allowance but it is not in payment because it is overlapped by other benefits (para 12.45); or

(b) receives arrears of carer's allowance or the UC carer element, in other words any backdated part of either of these does not cause an overpayment of the severe disability premium.

Example: Severe disability premium, etc

A husband and wife are both under pension age and both receive the standard rate of the daily living component of personal independence payment. Their daughter of 17 is in full-time employment and lives with them. Their son lives elsewhere and receives carer's allowance for caring for the husband. No-one receives carer's allowance or the UC carer element for the wife.

Disability premium: Because of receiving personal independence payment, they are awarded the couple rate of disability premium.

Enhanced disability premium: Because they get the standard (not the enhanced) rate of the daily living component of personal independence payment, this cannot be awarded.

Severe disability premium:

■   Both receive the appropriate type of personal independence payment.

■   Although their daughter is a non-dependant, she is under 18.

■   Their son receives carer's allowance for caring for one of them.

So they are awarded the single rate of severe disability premium (for the second reason in para 12.39).

12.41   HB sch 3 para 14(5)(b),(7); HB60+ sch 3 para 6(7)(b),(8)(b); NIHB sch 4 para 14(5)(b),(7); NIHB60+ sch 4 para 6(7)(b),(8)(b)

12.42   HB sch 3 paras 14(6), 19; HB60+ sch 3 paras 6(8)(a), 11; NIHB sch 4 paras 14(6), 19; NIHB60+ sch 4 paras 6(8)(a), 11

Carer premium

12.43   You qualify for this premium if you or your partner:

(a)   are 'entitled to' carer's allowance (para 12.45); or

(b)   were 'entitled to' carer's allowance (para 12.45) within the past eight weeks (including if the reason you are no longer entitled to the allowance is that the person you cared for has died).

12.44   If you are a couple you can get one or two carer premiums, one if only one of you satisfies the condition, two if you both do. If you are in a polygamous marriage you get one premium for each partner who satisfies the condition.

12.45   You only have to be 'entitled to' carer's allowance: it does not necessarily have to be in payment. This means that if an award has been made but it cannot be paid because it is overlapped by another benefit (typically retirement pension, ESA(C), JSA(C) or widowed parent's allowance) then that is sufficient. But if your carer's allowance is overlapped by retirement pension you only receive a carer premium if the person you are caring for continues to receive attendance allowance (or equivalent benefit).

12.46   You cannot be entitled to carer's allowance until you have made a claim for it – but once you have done so and entitlement has been confirmed (with or without payment) it continues indefinitely until such time as you no longer satisfy the conditions for it (e.g. the person being cared for dies). It does not matter that your original claim for carer's allowance was made before your HB claim: you continue to be 'entitled' to carer's allowance without the need to make a further claim for it (CIS/367/2003).

12.47   If you are awarded carer's allowance but later lose it as a result of taking part in a government training scheme you continue to be treated as entitled to it.

Interaction of carer and severe disability premium

12.48   Although carer's allowance qualifies you for a carer premium, the person you care for may lose their severe disability premium (but not during any period your carer's allowance is backdated: para 12.42(a)). However this happens only if your carer's allowance (or part of it) is actually in payment and not if it is overlapped (para 12.45) – see second example. If you are a couple it is therefore possible to qualify for a severe disability premium (at the single or double rate) and two carer premiums if you care for each other.

12.43   HB sch 3 para 17; HB60+ sch 3 para 9; NIHB sch 4 para 17; NIHB60+ sch 4 para 9

12.44   HB sch 3 para 20(8); HB60+ sch 3 para 12(4); NIHB sch 4 para 20(8); NIHB60+ sch 4 para 12(4)

12.45   HB sch 3 paras 7(1)(a),(2), 17(1); HB60+ sch 3 paras 5(2), 9(1); NIHB sch 4 paras 7(1)(a),(2), 17(1); NIHB60+ sch 4 paras 5(2), 9(1)

12.46   AA 1(1); NIAA 1(1)

12.47   HB sch 3 para 7(1)(b); HB60+ sch 3 para 5(1)(b); NIHB sch 4 para 7(1)(b); NIHB60+ sch 4 para 5(1)(b)

12.48   HB sch 3 paras 14(1)(a),(b), 19; HB60+ 6(1)(a),(b), 11; NIHB sch 4 paras 14(1)(a),(b), 19; NIHB60+ sch 4 paras 6(1)(a),(b), 11

Examples: Carer premium and overlapping benefits

Claimant over 65

A claimant and her partner are both aged over 80 and in receipt of retirement pension. She looks after her partner who has been in receipt of attendance allowance since 7th February 2017. On 10th February 2017 she made a claim for carer's allowance and was notified by the DWP that she was entitled to carer's allowance from 13th February 2017 but it could not be paid because it was overlapped by her retirement pension (in other words, payment of the latter prevents payment of the former).

On 8th May 2016 she makes a claim for HB for the first time and is awarded HB from 13th February 2017 (para 5.52). The award includes the carer premium. If her partner subsequently dies, she would lose the premium after a further eight weeks.

Claimant under 65

A claimant aged 49 is in receipt of bereavement allowance. He cares for his severely disabled sister who receives the daily living component of personal independence payment. He lives alone in his own flat. He claims carer's allowance and is entitled to it but it cannot be paid because it is overlapped by his bereavement allowance. Once having claimed carer's allowance he remains 'entitled' to it indefinitely until such time as he no longer meets the conditions for it (e.g. he starts work, becomes a student or his sister dies or no longer receives the daily living component of personal independence payment).

While he remains entitled to carer's allowance he should be awarded the carer premium in his HB without the need for a further claim for carer's allowance even if there are breaks in his HB award. One year after his bereavement, his bereavement allowance ends and his carer's allowance is put into payment. His sister is also entitled to the severe disability premium during the period while his bereavement allowance is in payment (because although he is 'entitled' to carer's allowance it is not in payment: para 12.45). But once his carer's allowance is in payment she will lose her severe disability premium.

Special cases

DWP concessionary payments

12.49   For the purpose of entitlement to any premium, if you receive a DWP concessionary payment compensating for non-payment of any qualifying benefit it is treated as if it were that benefit.

Meaning of severely sight impaired, blind or recently regained sight

12.50   For the purpose of determining whether a non-dependant deduction applies (table 6.3) or entitlement to certain premiums in this chapter (paras 12.31, 12.34, 12.39-40) you are 'severely sight impaired' or 'blind' if you have been certified as such by a consultant ophthalmologist.

12.49   HB sch 3 para 18; HB60+ sch 3 para 10; NIHB sch 4 para 18; NIHB60+ sch 4 para 10

12.51   If you were previously certified as 'severely sight impaired' or blind you are treated as still being so for a further 28 weeks from the date you regained your sight (i.e. from the date when your certification was revoked).

Polygamous marriages

12.52   If you are in a polygamous marriage (table 4.1) your personal allowance is the appropriate amount in table 12.1 for a couple according to the age of the oldest member in the marriage plus (during 2017-18) the appropriate amount for each additional spouse as follows:

(a)   if you and every partner in the marriage are all under pension age (para 1.24):   £41.75;

(b)   if at least one of you is pension age but none of you are aged 65 or over: £83.90;

(c)   if at least one of you is aged 65 or over: £85.60.

Personal allowances for children and young persons are awarded as in paras 12.11-18.

12.53   Premiums and components are awarded in a similar way as for a couple. But in the case of the severe disability premium, you get the double rate if all members of the marriage satisfy all three conditions in para 12.38; the single rate if all members of the marriage satisfy the first two of those conditions but one member has a carer who gets a carer's allowance or the UC carer element in respect of caring for one of them; and the single rate if you are the claimant and you satisfy all three conditions and all the other members of the marriage are severely sight impaired, blind or have recently regained their sight (paras 12.50-51).

If you or your family are in hospital

12.54   Certain premiums may be lost if you (or your partner) lose your qualifying benefit as a result of you spending four weeks or more in hospital – see table 12.2 for details. In addition, your right to HB is lost if you are single/a lone parent after you have been in hospital for 52 weeks; or, if it is your partner or child, they are unlikely to be treated as a member of your family: in either case this overrides any special rules in table 12.2 (paras 3.2, 3.30, 4.23).

12.50   SI 2014/2888; NISR 2014/275; HB sch 3 para 13(1)(a)(v); HB60+ sch 3 para 6(4); NIHB sch 4 para 13(1)(a)(v); NIHB60+ sch 4 para 6(4)

12.51   HB sch 3 para 13(2); HB60+ sch 3 para 6(5); NIHB sch 4 para 13(2); NIHB60+ sch 4 para 6(5)

12.52   HB 23; HB60+ sch 3 para 1(3),(4); NIHB 21; NIHB60+ sch 4 para 1(3),(4)

Table 12.2 **Premiums after a period in hospital**

(a) Disability premium (para 12.31)

- If you or your partner lose your personal independence payment, disability living allowance or constant attendance allowance solely because of being in hospital for four weeks or more, the disability premium is still awarded.

(b) Enhanced disability premium (para 12.35)

- If you, your partner or a young person aged 18 or more lose your personal independence payment or disability living allowance solely because of being in hospital for four weeks or more, the enhanced disability premium is still awarded.

(c) Disabled child premium (para 12.34)

- If a young person aged 18 or more loses their personal independence payment or disability living allowance solely because of being in hospital for four weeks or more, the disabled child premium is still awarded.

(d) Severe disability premium (para 12.38)

- If you are single or a lone parent and you lose your personal independence payment or disability living allowance because you have been in hospital for four weeks or more, you lose your severe disability premium.

- If you are a couple and you or your partner lose your personal independence payment or disability living allowance solely because of being in hospital for four weeks or more, the severe disability premium is still awarded.

(e) Carer premium (para 12.43)

- Your or your partner's carer's allowance continues until you have spent over 12 weeks in hospital, and your carer premium continues for a further eight weeks after that (making 20 in total).

- If the person you or your partner care for is aged 18 or more and is in hospital you will lose your carer's allowance after they have been in hospital for four weeks and your carer premium continues for a further eight weeks after that (making 12 in total).

Notes:

- The four week period does not have to be continuous but can be made up of two or more separate periods which are less than 29 days apart.

- Children or young persons aged under 18 can no longer lose DLA or PIP due to being in hospital.

T12.2(a) HB sch 3 para 13(1)(a)(iii),(iiia); NIHB sch 4 para 13(1)(a)(iii)

T12.2(b) HB sch 3 para 15(1)(b),(c); NIHB sch 4; para 15(1)(b)

T12.2(c) HB sch 3 para 16(a),(d); HB60+ sch 3 para 8(a),(d); NIHB sch 4; para 16(a); NIHB60+ sch 4 para 8(a)

T12.2(d) HB sch 3 para 14(2)(a),(b),(5)(a),(c); HB60+ sch 3 para 6(2)(a),(b),(7)(a),(c);
NIHB sch 4; para 14(2)(a),(b),(5)(a); NIHB60+ sch 4 para 6(2)(a),(b),(7)(a)

T12.2(e) HB sch 3 para 17(2),(4); HB60+ sch 3 para 9(2); NIHB sch 4; para 17(2),(4); NIHB60+ sch 4 para 9(2)

Chapter 13 **Income**

- General rules about assessing income: see paras 13.1-8.
- State benefits, pensions and payments: see paras 13.9-22.
- Council benefits and payments: see paras 13.23-25.
- Private pensions, maintenance, rent and other income: see paras 13.26-40.
- Additional rules about income disregards: see paras 13.41-45.
- Notional income: see paras 13.46-57.

General rules

13.1 This chapter and chapter 14 explain how your income is assessed for HB purposes, including:

(a) unearned income (see paras 13.9-40);

(b) earned income (see chapter 14);

(c) notional income (see paras 13.46-57); and

(d) assumed income from your capital (see para 15.5).

This section gives rules relating to all types of income.

'Your' income

13.2 If you are single, your own income is taken into account. If you are in a couple, the income of your partner is taken into account as well as yours. If you are in a polygamous marriage, the income of all your partners is included. In this chapter and chapter 14, 'your' income always includes the income of your partner (or partners). But if a child or young person in your family has income of their own, this is never included and nor is the income of a non-dependant (but see para 13.57).

How your income affects your HB

13.3 If you are on a passport benefit (see para 13.5), all your income is disregarded (ignored) and you qualify for maximum HB: see para 6.2-3.

13.4 If you are not on a passport benefit, some kinds of income are counted and some are wholly or partly disregarded. The details are in this chapter and chapter 14. The more income you have (apart from disregarded income) the less HB you qualify for: see para 6.4-6. (See also para 13.15 if you are on the savings credit of SPC.)

13.1   HB 27(1)(a),(b),(4); HB60+ 25, 29(1),(2); NIHB 24(1)(a),(b),(4); NIHB60+ 23, 27(1),(2)

13.2   CBA 136(1); HB 25; HB60+ 23; NICBA 132(1); NIHB 22; NIHB60+ 21

13.3   CBA 130(1)(c)(i),(3)(a); HB sch 4 para 12, sch 5 paras 4,5; HB60+ 26; NICBA 129(1)(c)(i),(3)(a); NIHB sch 5 para 12, sch 6 paras 4,5; NIHB60+ 24

13.4   CBA 130(1)(c),(3); HB 36(2), 38(2), 40(2), sch 4, sch 5; HB60+ 33(8),(9), sch 4, sch 5; NICBA 129(1)(c),(3); NIHB 33(2), 35(2), 37(2), sch 5, sch 6; NIHB60+ 31(8),(9), sch 5, sch 6

The passport benefits

13.5   The passport benefits are:

(a) income-based JSA;

(b) income-related ESA;

(c) income support;

(d) the guarantee credit of SPC; and

(e) universal credit if you live in specified supported accommodation (see paras 2.13 and 6.3).

Current income

13.6   Your current income is taken into account for the period it covers (apart from the amounts which are disregarded). In the case of a state benefit this means the period for which it is payable.

Arrears of income

13.7   The rules in para 13.6 also apply to arrears of income. So income paid for a past period counts as income in that past period (apart from the amounts which are disregarded). Para 15.13 explains when arrears of income turn into capital.

Weekly income

13.8   HB is a weekly benefit, so your income is assessed as a weekly figure. The law says this is done by accurately calculating or estimating the likely amount of your average weekly income. In practice this means:

(a) the actual weekly amount if your income is paid weekly; or

(b) the weekly equivalent if your income is paid on a non-weekly basis (see para 6.37).

In working age HB claims, unearned income must not be averaged over a period longer than 52 weeks. In pension age HB claims, it is not in practice averaged over a period longer than one year. For earned income see paras 14.8-10 and 14.29-31.

Examples: Assessing income

1. A working age HB claim

A couple in their 30s have two children at school. One partner works full time. The other receives child maintenance from the children's father, child benefit, and child tax credit. They have £3,000 in a savings account.

When they claim HB, their income is assessed as follows:

- the child benefit and the child maintenance are disregarded (see tables 13.1 and 13.6)

13.5   HB sch 4 para 12, sch 5 paras 4,5, sch 6 paras 5,6; HB60+ 26; NIHB sch 5 para 12, sch 6 paras 4,5, sch 7 paras 5,6; NIHB60+ 24V

13.6   HB 27(1), 31(1),(2); HB60+ 30(1), 33(1),(6); NIHB 24(1), 28(1),(2); NIHB60+ 28(1), 31(1),(6)

13.7   HB 27(1), 31(1),(2); HB60+ 30(1), 33(1),(6); NIHB 24(1), 28(1),(2); NIHB60+ 28(1), 31(1),(6)

13.8   CBA 136(4); HB 27(1), 29-31; HB60+ 30(1), 33(1); NICBA 132(3); NIHB 24(1), 26-28; NIHB60+ 28(1), 31(1)

- the child tax credit is counted as income (see para 13.12):
  it works out as   £101.84 pw
- the earnings are counted as their income, after all the appropriate
  deductions and disregards have been made (see chapter 14):
  they work out as   £285.49 pw
- they do not have assumed income from their capital (see para 15.5)

This figure is used in calculating their HB. So their total income is   £387.33 pw

2. A pension age HB claim

A single woman in her 70s receives a state pension, a private pension, and a war widow's pension. She has £12,000 in a savings account.

When she claims HB, her income is assessed as follows:

- her council runs a local scheme which disregards the whole of the
  war widow's pension (see paras 13.16-18)
- the state pension and the private pension are counted as her
  income (see paras 13.13 and 13.27): they work out as   £130.95 pw
- she has assumed income from her capital (see para 15.5) of   £4.00 pw

This figure is used in calculating her HB. So her total income is   £134.95 pw

State benefits, pensions and payments

13.9   This section gives the rules for state benefits and pensions, tax credits and war pensions.

13.10   Table 13.1 lists which state benefits, pensions and other payments are disregarded. Table 13.2 lists the ones which are taken into account, and summarises the other rules which apply.

Table 13.1 **Disregarded state benefits, pension, etc**

Income from all the following is wholly disregarded. For the first five 'passport benefits' see also para 13.3.

   (a)   income-based JSA (JSA(IB))

   (b)   income-related ESA (ESA(IR))

   (c)   income support

   (d)   the guarantee credit of SPC

   (e)   universal credit

   (f)   disability living allowance (DLA)

   (g)   personal independence payment (PIP)

T13.1   HB 40(2), sch 5; HB60+ 29(1), 33(9), sch 5; NIHB 37(2), sch 6; NIHB60+ 27(1), 31(9), sch 6

T13.1(a)-(e)   HB sch 5 para 4; HB60+ 26; NIHB sch 6 para 4; NIHB60+ 24

T13.1(f)-(g)   HB sch 5 para 6; HB60+ 29(1)(j)(i),(ia); NIHB sch 6 para 7; NIHB60+ 27(1)(h)(i)

(h) attendance allowance, or constant attendance allowance paid with an industrial injury or war disablement pension

(i) bereavement support payments (paid for deaths occurring after 5th April 2017) other than the initial lump sum (see para 15.51)

(j) child tax credit (CTC) in pension age HB claims (see para 13.12)

(k) child benefit

(l) guardian's allowance

(m) Christmas bonus

(n) social fund payments (see also para 15.50)

(o) government and related payments to disabled people to help with obtaining or retaining work (for example by buying special equipment)

(p) payments from government work programme training schemes. There are rare exceptions in working age claims (see GM paras BW 2.597-611), but even in these cases expenses for travel etc are always disregarded

(q) payments compensating for non-payment of:
- (a) to (i) in working age HB claims
- all the above in pension age HB claims.

Note: Payments (n) to (p) and in most cases (q) are also disregarded as capital. See paras 15.50-52 for details about this and about arrears of benefits.

Table 13.2 **Counted state benefits, pensions etc**

Income from the following is counted in full.

(a) contribution-based JSA (JSA(C)) (see para 13.11)

(b) contributory ESA (ESA(C)) (see para 13.11)

(c) working tax credit (WTC) (see para 13.12)

(d) child tax credit (CTC) in working age HB claims (see para 13.12)

T13.1(h)   HB 2(1) definition: 'attendance allowance', sch 5 para 9; HB60+ 2(1), 29(1)(j) (ii)-(v);
           NIHB 2(1), sch 6 para 10; NIHB60+ 2(1), 27(1)(h) (ii)-(iv)

T13.1(i)   HB sch 5 para 67; HB60+ 29(1)(j)(xiii); SI 2017/422; NIHB sch 6 para 65; NIHB60+ 27(1)(h)(xi); NISR 2017/66

T13.1(j)   HB60+ 29(1); NIHB60+ 27(1)

T13.1(k)   HB sch 5 para 65; HB60+ 29(1)(j)(vi); NIHB sch 6 para 64; NIHB60+ 27(1)(h)(v)

T13.1(l)   HB sch 5 para 50; HB60+ 29(1)(j)(vii); NIHB sch 6 para 52; NIHB60+ 27(1)(h)(vi)

T13.1(m)   HB sch 5 para 32; HB60+ 29(1)(j)(x); NIHB sch 6 para 33; NIHB60+ 27(1)(h)(ix)

T13.1(n)   HB sch 5 para 31, sch 6 para 20; HB60+ 29(1)(j)(ix); NIHB sch 6 para 32, sch 7 para 21; NIHB60+ 27(1)(h)(viii)

T13.1(o)   HB sch 5 para 49, sch 6 paras 43,44; HB60+ 29(1); NIHB sch 6 para 51, sch 7 para 44; NIHB60+ 27(1)

T13.1(p)   HB 2(1) definitions, sch 5 paras A2,A3,13,15,58,60,61; HB60+ 29(1); NIHB 2(1), sch 6 paras 13,15,60; NIHB60+ 27(1)

T13.1(q)   HB 2(1) definition: 'concessionary payment', sch 5 para 9; HB60+ 2(1), 29(1)(ii)-(v); NIHB 2(1), sch 6 para 10; NIHB60+ 2(1), 27(1)

(e) state retirement pension (see para 13.13)

(f) the savings credit of SPC (see para 13.14)

(g) carer's allowance

(h) maternity allowance

(i) bereavement allowance (for deaths occurring before 6th April 2017)

(j) incapacity benefit (IB)

(k) severe disablement allowance (SDA)

(l) widow's pension

(m) industrial death benefit

The following have individual rules.

(n) widowed mother's allowance and widowed parent's allowance: disregard £15 per week and count the rest as income (for deaths occurring before 6th April 2017)

(o) industrial injuries disablement benefit: disregard any increase for attendance and count the rest as income

(p) bereavement payment: this counts as capital (not income)

(q) war pensions: see paras 13.16-18

(r) increases in benefits for dependants: see para 13.20

(s) reductions in benefits: see para 13.21

(t) statutory sick, maternity, paternity and adoption pay: count as earned income (see table 14.1(c) and paras 14.15-16)

Note: See paras 15.50-52 for arrears of payments (c), (d) and (f).

JSA(C) and ESA(C)

13.11   Contribution-based JSA and contributory ESA are counted in full as your income: see para 13.22 if payments are reduced due to sanctions. In the longer term they will become known as just JSA and ESA once JSA(IB) and ESA(IR) are replaced by UC: see para 1.15.

WTC and CTC

13.12   Working tax credit is counted in full as your income (in working age and pension age HB claims). Child tax credit is counted in full as your income in working age HB claims, but is wholly disregarded in pension age HB claims. Table 17.5 shows what period a payment of WTC or CTC covers. In some uncommon cases, part of the earned income disregards can be deducted from your WTC or CTC: see para 14.61(c) and (d).

T13.2(a)-(m) HB 31(1),(3), 40(1); HB60+ 29(1)(b),(c),(j); NIHB 28(1),(3), 37(1); NIHB60+ 27(1)(b),(c),(h)

T13.2(n)   HB sch 5 para 16; HB60+ sch 5 paras 7,8; NIHB sch 6 para 17; NIHB60+ sch 6 paras 8,9

T13.2(o)   HB 2(1) definition: 'attendance allowance', sch 5 para 9; HB60+ 2(1), 29(1)(j)(iii),(n); NIHB 2(1), sch 6 para 10; NIHB60+ 2(1), 27(1)(h)(iii),(l)

T13.2(p)   HB 44(1); HB60+ 29(1)(j)(xiii); NIHB 41(1); NIHB60+ 27(1)(h)(xi)

13.11   HB 31(1),(2), 40(1); HB60+ 31(1)(a), 33(6); NIHB 28(1),(2), 37(1); NIHB60+ 29(1)(a), 31(6)

13.12   HB 27(1)(c),(2)(b), 31(1), 32, 40(1); HB60+ 30(1)(a),(c),(2)(b), 32; NIHB 24(1)(c),(2)(b), 28(1), 29, 37(1); NIHB60+ 28(1)(a),(c),(2)(b), 30

State retirement pension

13.13   State retirement pension is counted in full as your income. If you defer your state pension:

(a)   it is not included as your income until you begin receiving it. Any increase you receive (because you deferred it) is then included;

(b)   any lump sum you receive (because you deferred your state pension) is disregarded as your capital until your state pension begins.

Savings credit

13.14   The savings credit of state pension credit (SPC) is counted in full as your income. But if you are also on the guarantee credit of SPC, see para 13.3.

Other rules if you are on savings credit

13.15   The following rules apply if you are on savings credit (but not guarantee credit):

(a)   the DWP assesses your income and capital as part of your savings credit claim;

(b)   the DWP tells the council these income and capital figures (when you first claim HB or savings credit, and then whenever your circumstances change);

(c)   the council adjusts these figures as shown in table 13.3;

(d)   the council uses the adjusted figures to calculate your HB.

Table 13.3 **People on savings credit:**
         adjusting the DWP's figures

If you are on savings credit, the following adjustments are made whenever the DWP tells the council your income and capital (see para 13.15).

Your income

The DWP tells the council:

■   the amount of your savings credit; and

■   your 'assessed income figure' (AIF). This is the DWP's assessment of your income (apart from savings credit).

The council adds these together, and then deducts the following amounts:

If you receive:	**The amount is:**
(a) maintenance from a current or former husband, wife or civil partner	the full HB disregard (see table 13.6)
(b) a war disablement or bereavement pension	any amount disregarded under a local scheme (in other words, any amount over £10: see para 13.18)

13.13   HB60+ sch 6 para 26A as implied by CPR 2; SI 2005/2677 regs 11,12; NIHB60+ sch 7 para 28

13.14   HB 31(1),(2), 40(1); HB60+ 31(1)(a), 33(6); NIHB 28(1),(2), 37(1); NIHB60+ 29(1)(a), 31(6)

13.15   HB60+ 27(1)-(3); NIHB60+ 25(1)-(3)

(c)	earned income and you are a lone parent	£5
(d)	earned income from 'permitted work'	£120 or £20 (as shown in table 14.5)
(e)	earned income and you qualify for the HB child care disregard	the full HB disregard (see para 14.63)
(f)	Earned income and you qualify for the HB additional earnings disregard	£17.10 (see para 14.68)

If you have a partner who was excluded from your savings credit claim but is included in your HB claim, the council assesses their income and adds it.

Your capital

The DWP tells the council the amount of your capital. The council changes this only if your capital increases to more than £16,000, in which case your HB stops.

War disablement and bereavement pensions

13.16   Table 13.4 gives the rules for assessing income from:

(a) pensions under the Armed Forces Pensions and Compensation schemes (and similar payments) for:

- war disablement;
- war widows;
- war widowers; and
- war bereaved civil partners;

(b) payments compensating for non-payment of the above;

(c) equivalent payments from governments outside the UK; and

(d) pensions paid by any (non-UK) government to the victims of Nazi persecution.

The payments in (a) include both 'service attributable pensions' for service before 5th April 2005 and 'guaranteed income payments' for service on or after that date.

13.17   War pensions not included in para 13.16 are assessed in the same way as private pensions: see para 13.27.

Local schemes for war disablement and bereavement pensions

13.18   Councils in Great Britain can run a 'local scheme' to disregard more than £10 per week of the war disablement and bereavement pensions in para 13.16 (apart from those which are always wholly disregarded: see table 13.4).

13.19   Most councils do this, and some disregard the whole amount. The government pays councils up to 75% of the cost of running a local scheme (see para 23.4), but decisions about local schemes are not appealable to a tribunal (see table 16.4).

T13.3   HB60+ 27(3)-(8); NIHB60+ 25(3)-(8)

13.16   HB sch 5 para 15; HB60+ 29(1)(e)-(h),(l)-(m), sch 5 para 1; NIHB sch 6 para 15; NIHB60+ 27(1)(e)-(f),(j)-(k), sch 6 para 1; SI 2017/174; NISR 2017/62

13.18   AA 134(8)-(10); SI 2007 No. 1619

Table 13.4 **War disablement and bereavement pensions**

This table applies to the pensions etc in para 13.16.

Assessment in Great Britain

(a) Disregard the whole amount of:

- 'pre-1973' special payments to war widows, war widowers and war bereaved civil partners (currently £91.31 per week: HB circular A1/2017);

- a mobility supplement paid with any war disablement or bereavement pension; and

- an increase for constant attendance paid with any war disablement pension (including war injured civilians) or an Armed Forces independence payment.

(b) Disregard £10 per week from the total of any other war disablement or bereavement pension. But see paras 13.18-19 (local schemes).

Assessment in Northern Ireland

(c) Disregard the whole amount of all war disablement and bereavement pensions.

Increases in benefits for dependants

13.20   The following applies if you receive an increase for a dependant in any of the state benefits which count as income (see table 13.2):

(a) if the increase is for your partner, it is included as your income;

(b) if the increase is for a child or young person in your family, it is included as your income in working age HB claims, but disregarded in pension age HB claims;

(c) if the increase is for someone not in your family, it is disregarded.

Reductions in benefits

13.21   If you receive a reduced amount of any of the state benefits which count as income (see table 13.2) only the reduced amount is counted as your income if the reduction is:

(a) because of the rules about overlapping state benefits;

(b) because your WTC or CTC is reduced to recover an earlier year's overpayment;

(c) because your incapacity benefit is reduced when you have an occupational pension (CH/51/2008); or

(d) in pension age HB claims, because a state benefit is reduced when you are in hospital.

T13.4   HB 2(1) definitions: 'attendance allowance', 'guaranteed income payment', 'war pension' etc, 31(1), 40(1), sch 5 paras 8,9,15,53-55; HB60+ 2(1), 29(1)(e)-(h),(l),(m), 30(1)(a), sch 5 paras 1-6; NIHB 2(1), 28(1), 37(1), sch 6 paras 9,10,15,55-57; NIHB60+ 2(1), 27(1)(f),(j),(k), 28(1)(a), sch 6 paras 1-7

13.20   HB 40(1), sch 5 para 52; HB60+ 29(1)(j)(viii), 30(1)(a), sch 5 para 13; NIHB 37(1), sch 6 para 54; NIHB60+ 27(1)(h)(vii), 28(1)(a), sch 6 para 14

13.21   HB 40(1),(5),(5A),(6); HB60+ 29(3)-(5), 30(1)(a); NIHB 37(1),(3),(3A),(4); NIHB60+ 27(3)-(5), 28(1)(a)

13.22 But the gross amount (the amount before the reduction is made) is counted as your income in any other circumstances, for example if a state benefit (but not WTC or CTC) is reduced:

(a) to recover an overpayment; or

(b) to pay your rent, fuel, water or other priority debts; or

(c) as a result of a work-related sanction in JSA(C) or ESA(C) (and in the case of ESA(C) the law expressly says so).

Council benefits and payments

13.23 This section gives the rules for benefits, allowances and other payments from local councils.

13.24 Table 13.5 lists which council allowances and payments are disregarded.

Social services and similar payments for care and support

13.25 The payments in table 13.5 (a)-(h) are disregarded if they are paid by:

(a) a social services department in Great Britain;

(b) the Health and Social Services Board, a Health and Social Services Trust or a Juvenile Justice Centre in Northern Ireland;

(c) a voluntary organisation on behalf of the above; or

(d) in the case of respite care payments, a Primary Care Trust.

Table 13.5 **Disregarded council payments**

Income from the following is wholly disregarded. For payments (a) to (h) see also para 13.25.

(a) foster care payments, also called kinship care payments in Scotland;

(b) adoption allowances;

(c) special guardianship payments;

(d) payments to avoid taking children into care;

(e) payments to care leavers, including payments passed on to you by a care leaver aged 18 or more who lives with you;

(f) boarding out and respite care payments, including contributions you receive from the person you are caring for;

13.22   HB 40(1),(5A); HB60+ 29(3),(5); NIHB 37(1),(3A); NIHB60+ 27(3),(5)

13.25   HB 2(1), sch 5 paras 25-28A,57; HB60+ 29(1); NIHB 2(1), sch 6 paras 26-29A,59; NIHB60+ 27(1)

T13.5(a)-(f)   HB 2(1) definition – 'voluntary organisation', sch 5 paras 25-28A; HB60+ 29(1); NIHB 2(1), sch 6 paras 26-29A; NIHB60+ 27(1)

(g) community care payments;

(h) direct care payments;

(i) supporting people payments, for housing-related support to help you maintain your tenancy;

(j) 'local welfare assistance' (para 25.38);

(k) discretionary housing payments (para 25.1) and in Northern Ireland welfare supplementary payments (para 6.33);

(l) council tax rebates, other council tax reductions, and HB itself.

Note: In some cases these are also disregarded as capital. See paras 15.50-52 for details about this and about arrears of benefits.

Other unearned income

13.26   This section gives the rules for private pensions, maintenance, charitable and voluntary payments, rent, and other kinds of income. For assumed income from capital see para 15.5, and for student income see chapter 22.

Private pensions

13.27   Income from a private pension is counted in full, after any deductions have been made for tax paid on it. This applies to any kind of:

(a) occupational pension;

(b) personal pension; or

(c) pension from the Pension Protection Fund.

But if a court has ordered part of your pension to be paid to someone else (for example your former partner), that part is disregarded (CH/1672/2007). See also paras 13.50-51 and 13.56.

Maintenance

13.28   Table 13.6 gives the rules for assessing maintenance you receive from a former partner or anyone else (other than your current partner).

13.29   If you pay maintenance for a child or anyone else, the amount you pay cannot be deducted when your income is assessed. But if it is for a student son or daughter, see para 13.43.

T13.5(g)-(h)   HB sch 5 para 57; HB60+ 29(1); NIHB sch 6 para 59; NIHB60+ 27(1)

T13.5(i)   HB sch 5 para 63; HB60+ 29(1); NIHB sch 6 para 63; NIHB60+ 27(1)

T13.5(j)   HB 2(1) definition – 'local welfare provision', sch 5 para 31A; HB60+ 29(1)

T13.5(k)   HB sch 5 para 62; HB60+ 29(1); NIHB sch 6 para 62; NIHB60+ 27(1); NISR 2016/178 reg 12

T13.5(l)   HB sch 5 para 41; HB60+ 29(1); NIHB sch 6 para 43; NIHB60+ 27(1)

13.27   HB 2(1), definition – 'occupational pension' 31(1), 35(2), sch 5 para 1; HB60+ 2(1), 29(1)(c),(d),(t),(x), 30(1)(a), 33(12), 35(2); NIHB 2(1), 28(1), 32(2), sch 6 para 1; NIHB60+ 2(1), 27(1)(c),(d),(r),(v), 28(1)(a), 31(12), 33(2)

13.29   HB 31(1); HB60+ 30(1); NIHB 28(1); NIHB60+ 28(1)

Table 13.6 **Income from maintenance**

	Assessment
Maintenance for a child or young person	
Working age HB claims	
(a) if it is paid by:	
■ a husband, wife or civil partner you or your partner are separated from, or	
■ a parent or step-parent of the child/young person, or	
■ someone whose payments of maintenance mean they can reasonably be treated as the father of the child or young person	Disregard in full
(b) if it is paid by someone else	Count in full
Pension age HB claims	
(c) whoever it is paid by	Disregard in full
Maintenance for you or your partner, if you have a child or young person	
Working age HB claims	
(d) if it is paid by your or your partner's former partner	Disregard £15 pw
(e) if it is paid by someone else	Count in full
Pension age HB claims	
(f) if it is paid by your or your partner's current or former husband, wife or civil partner	Disregard £15 pw
(g) if it is paid by someone else	Disregard in full
Maintenance for you or your partner, if you do not have a child or young person	
Working age HB claims	
(h) whoever it is paid by	Count in full
Pension age HB claims	
(i) if it is paid by your or your partner's current or former husband, wife or civil partner	Count in full
(j) if it is paid by someone else	Disregard in full
Maintenance for a non-dependant	
(k) working age HB claims	Same as (d), (e) or (h)
(l) pension age HB claims	Disregard in full

Note: 'Partner', 'child', 'young person', and 'non-dependant' have the same meanings as in chapter 4. But 'husband', 'wife' and 'civil partner' have their ordinary English meanings.

T13.6   HB 31(1), sch 5 paras 47,47A; HB60+ 29(1)(o), sch 5 para 20; NIHB 28(1), sch 6 para 49,49A; NIHB60+ 27(1)(m), sch 6 para 21

Charitable and voluntary payments

13.30   Payments of income you receive which are charitable and/or voluntary are wholly disregarded. For example, these could be from a charity, family, friends, etc (but for maintenance see table 13.6). For payments of capital see para 15.53. If the only money you have is charitable or voluntary income, you qualify for maximum HB (see paras 5.20 and 6.5).

Rent

13.31   Table 13.7 gives the rules for assessing rent you receive from people living in your home. Table 13.8 gives the rules for rent you receive on other property. But if you are self-employed and you receive rent as part of your business, see para 15.33.

Examples: Letting out a room

1. A lodger whose rent does not include meals

A couple on HB have a spare room. They let it out to a lodger for £80 per week inclusive of fuel and water, but not meals.

Their income from this lodger (see table 13.7(c)) is £80 minus £20, which is £60 per week.

2. A lodger whose rent includes meals

The couple increase the lodger's rent to £90 per week because they now provide him with meals.

Their income from the lodger (see table 13.7(b)) is now £90 minus £20, which is £70, the result being divided by two, which is £35 per week.

Table 13.7 **Rent from people in your home**

(a) Household members

Rent (or 'keep') you receive from a child, young person or non-dependant in your home is wholly disregarded.

(b) Lodgers whose rent includes meals (boarders)

If you receive rent from one or more lodgers in your home and their rent includes meals (see para 4.38):

- ■ start with the total amount your lodger(s) pay you each week (for rent, meals and any other services);
- ■ deduct £20 for each lodger you charge for (counting adults and children);
- ■ divide the result by two;
- ■ this gives your weekly income.

13.30   HB sch 5 para 14(1)(a),(b),(2); HB60+ 29(1); NIHB sch 6 para 14(1)(a),(b),(2); NIHB60+ 27(1)

T13.7(a) HB sch 5 para 21; HB60+ 29(1); NIHB sch 6 para 22; NIHB60+ 27(1)

T13.7(b) HB sch 5 para 42; HB60+ 2(1) definition: 'board and lodging acommodation', 2(1), 29(1)(p), sch 5 para 9;
          NIHB sch 6 para 44; NIHB60+ 27(1)(n), sch 6 para 10

T13.7(c) HB sch 5 para 22; HB60+ 29(1)(v), sch 5 para 10; NIHB sch 6 para 23; NIHB60+ 27(1)(t), sch 6 para 11

(c) Lodgers whose rent does not include meals

If you receive rent from one or more lodgers in your home and their rent does not include meals:

- start with the total amount your lodger(s) pay you each week (for rent and any other services);
- deduct £20 for each separate letting;
- this gives your weekly income.

Table 13.8 **Rent from property other than your home**

(a) When the rent counts as income

The rent you receive counts as unearned income:

- only in working age HB claims; and
- only if the property's capital value is disregarded for any of the reasons in table 15.1(b) to (g).

In these cases your unearned income equals the rent you receive on the property, minus outgoings you pay on the property (during the period the rent covers) for:

- mortgage payments (both interest and capital);
- council tax (rates in Northern Ireland);
- water charges; and
- tax paid on the resulting income.

No other outgoings can be deducted.

(b) When the rent counts as capital

The rent you receive counts as capital (not income):

- in working age HB claims other than those described in (a); and
- in all pension age HB claims.

In these cases, your capital:

- increases when you receive the rent;
- but decreases when you pay for outgoings on the property, for example agent's fees, repairs, cleaning, etc, as well as those listed in (a).

Annuities

13.32   If you have an annuity, you get payments from an insurance or similar company in return for investing an initial capital sum with them. Payments from an annuity are counted in full as unearned income (not capital), after any deductions have been made for tax paid on them.

T13.8(a) HB sch 5 paras 1, 17(2),(3); NIHB sch 6 paras 1, 18(2),(3)

T13.8(b) HB 46(4), sch 5 paras 1, 17(1); HB60+ 29(1), sch 5 para 22; NIHB 43(4), sch 6 paras 1, 18(1); NIHB60+ 27(1), sch 6 para 23

13.32   HB 41(2), sch 5 para 1; HB60+ 29(1)(d), 33(12); NIHB 38(2), sch 6 para 1; NIHB60+ 27(1)(d), 31(11)

Home income plans

13.33   A home income plan is an annuity in which the invested capital sum is a loan secured against your home. The payments you receive are assessed as unearned income (see para 13.32). But if you were aged 65 or more when you began the home income plan, the following amounts are disregarded from the payments:

- tax paid on them;
- mortgage repayments made using them; and
- repayments on the loan.

Equity release schemes

13.34   If you are in an equity release scheme, the payments you receive are a form of loan secured against your home. In pension age HB claims, payments from an equity release scheme count in full as unearned income. This also seems likely to be the case in working age HB claims (because of the way loans are treated in HB: see para 15.54), but the law does not specifically say so.

Mortgage and loan protection policies

13.35   If you have insurance against being unable to pay your mortgage or another loan (because of unemployment, sickness, etc), payments you receive from that policy are assessed as follows:

(a) in pension age HB claims, the payments are wholly disregarded;

(b) in working age HB claims, payments for the following are disregarded:

- the mortgage or loan repayments;
- the payments due on the policy;
- in the case of a mortgage protection policy, the payments due on another policy you were required to have to insure against loss or damage to your home,

and the rest (if any) counts as your income.

Income from trusts

13.36   Income you receive from a trust is counted as your unearned income, with the following exceptions:

(a) income from some government supported trust funds is wholly disregarded (see para 13.37);

(b) income from personal injury trusts is wholly disregarded (see para 13.38);

(c) in pension age HB claims, if you receive discretionary income from a trust:

- £20 per week is disregarded if it is for your rent (other than any part of the rent which is not met by HB because of a non-dependant deduction), mortgage

13.33   HB 41(2), sch 5 para 1; HB60+ 29(1)(d), 33(12), sch 5 para 11; NIHB 38(2), sch 6 para 1; NIHB60+ 27(1)(d), 31(11), sch 6 para 12

13.34   HB60+ 29(1)(w),(8); NIHB60+ 27(1)(u),(8)

13.35   HB sch 5 para 29; HB60+ 29(1); NIHB sch 6 para 30; NIHB60+ 27(1)

13.36   HB 31(1), sch 5 para 14(1)(c); HB60+ 29(1)(i), sch 5 para 12; NIHB 28(1), sch 6 para 14(1)(c); NIHB60+ 27(1)(g), sch 6 para 13

interest or other housing costs that could be met by the guarantee credit of SPC, council tax (in Northern Ireland rates), water charges, household fuel, food, or ordinary clothing or footwear;

■ the whole amount is disregarded if it is for anything else.

For further details about trusts see paras 15.37-41.

Government supported trust funds

13.37 Income from the following government-supported trust funds: Independent Living Fund, the Macfarlane Trust and other trusts for people infected by NHS products, the VCJD Trust, the London Bombings Charitable Relief Fund, is disregarded. For the details see para 15.42.

Income for a personal injury

13.38 Income you receive for a personal injury is wholly disregarded. For the details see paras 15.43-45.

Other sources of unearned income

13.39 Table 13.9 lists other kinds of unearned income which are disregarded, along with the exceptions which apply in working age HB claims. For grants, loans, EMAs, and other student payments see chapter 22.

13.40 Apart from that, if you have any other source of unearned income it is:

(a) counted as income in working age HB claims, apart from any tax paid on it;

(b) disregarded in pension age HB claims.

Table 13.9 **Other unearned income disregards**

The following kinds of income are wholly disregarded (except as shown in (k) to (n)):

(a) expenses you receive as a volunteer or for charitable or voluntary work;

(b) expenses you receive as a member of a service user group (for example when these are run by local councils, social landlords or health authorities);

(c) expenses you receive from your employer (for exceptions see table 14.1(n));

(d) payments you receive as a teacher under the Student Loans Repayment Scheme;

(e) payments for travel for hospital visits;

13.37   HB 2(1) definition: 'Macfarlane Trust' etc, sch 5 para 35; HB60+ 29(1); NIHB 2(1), sch 6 para 37; NIHB60+ 29(1)

13.38   HB sch 5 para 14; HB60+ sch 5 paras 14,15; NIHB sch 6 para 14; NIHB60+ sch 6 paras 15,16

13.40   HB 31(1), sch 5 para 1; HB60+ 29(1); NIHB 28(1), sch 5 para 1; NIHB60+ 27(1)

T13.9(a)   HB sch 5 para 2; HB60+ 29(1); NIHB sch 6 para 2; NIHB60+ 27(1)

T13.9(b)   HB 2(1) definition: 'service user group', 35(2)(d), sch 5 para 2A; HB60+ 29(1), 35(2)(f);
         NIHB 2(1), 32(2)(d), sch 6 para 2A; NIHB60+ 27(1), 33(2)(e)

T13.9(c)   HB 35(2)(b), sch 5 para 3; HB60+ 29(1), 35(2)(b); NIHB 32(2)(b), sch 6 para 3; NIHB60+ 27(1), 33(2)(b)

T13.9(d)   HB sch 5 para 12; HB60+ 29(1); NIHB60+ 27(1)

T13.9(e),(f)   HB sch 5 para 44; HB60+ 29(1); NIHB sch 6 para 46; NIHB60+ 27(1)

(f)   payments for health service supplies;

(g)   payments replacing free milk and vitamins;

(h)   payments replacing healthy start vouchers;

(i)   payments for travel for prison visits;

(j)   payments you receive as a holder of the Victoria Cross or George Cross, and similar payments (see para 15.48);

(k)   payments in kind (in other words, in goods rather than money or vouchers)

-   but in working age HB claims, goods bought for you by someone who receives income an your behalf can count as notional income: see para 13.50;

(l)   concessionary coal

-   but in working age HB claims, cash in lieu of it is counted as unearned income (R v Doncaster MBC and another ex parte Bolton);

(m) juror's allowance

-   but in working age HB claims, compensation for loss of earnings or state benefits is counted as unearned income;

(n)   career development loans paid by banks in Great Britain under arrangements in s2 of the Employment and Training Act 1973 [www];

-   but in working age HB claims, loans for living expenses are counted as unearned income until the course you are on ends.

Note: In working age HB claims, payments (e) to (i) are also disregarded as capital for 52 weeks.

Additional rules about income disregards

13.41   The rules about disregards for each kind of unearned income are given earlier in this chapter. Those for earned income are in chapter 14. This section gives further rules about disregards which can apply to more than one kind of unearned or earned income.

Income tax

13.42   Income tax paid on any kind of unearned income is always disregarded in the assessment of that income. For earned income see paras 14.19-21 and 14.53-55.

T13.9(g),(h)   HB sch 5 para 45; HB60+ 29(1); NIHB sch 6 para 47; NIHB60+ 27(1)

T13.9(i)   HB sch 5 para 46; HB60+ 29(1); NIHB sch 6 para 48; NIHB60+ 27(1)

T13.9(j)   HB sch 5 para 10; HB60+ 29(1); NIHB sch 6 para 11; NIHB60+ 27(1)

T13.9(k)   HB 35(2)(a), sch 5 para 23; HB60+ 29(1); NIHB 32(2)(a), sch 6 para 24; NIHB60+ 27(1)

T13.9(l)   HB60+ 29(1); NIHB60+ 27(1); R v Doncaster MBC & Another ex p Boulton 11/12/92 QBD 25 HLR 195

T13.9(m)   HB sch 5 para 39; HB60+ 29(1); NIHB sch 6 para 41; NIHB60+ 27(1)

T13.9(n)   HB 41(4); HB60+ 29(1)

13.42   HB sch 5 para 1; HB60+ 33(12); NIHB sch 6 para 1; NIHB60+ 31(11)

Parental contributions to a student

13.43   If you make a parental contribution to a son or daughter who is a UK student, the following amount is disregarded from the total of your unearned and earned income:

(a)   if you were assessed as having to make a contribution towards their student loan or grant, the whole of that contribution;

(b)   if (a) does not apply, and they are under 25, any amount you contribute up to:

- £57.90 per week,

- minus the weekly amount of any discretionary grant they receive.

Income outside the UK

13.44   Unearned or earned income you receive outside the UK is assessed in the normal way (as described in this chapter and chapter 14), and any commission for converting it to sterling is then disregarded. But if you are prohibited (by the country you receive the income in) from bringing it to the UK, the whole amount is disregarded.

The over-riding limit on certain disregards

13.45   If you qualify for more than one of the following unearned income disregards, the disregard from all of them is limited to £20 per week:

(a)   the £15 disregard from widowed mother's allowance or widowed parent's allowance (see table 13.2(n));

(b)   in England, Scotland and Wales, the £10 disregard from war pensions for disablement or bereavement (see table 13.4(b)), but this does not stop your council running a local scheme (see para 13.18);

(c)   in pension age HB claims, the £20 disregard from discretionary trust income (see para 13.36(c));

(d)   in working age HB claims, the £10 disregard from income from student loans (see table 22.2(d));

(e)   in working age HB claims, the £20 disregard from income from student access funds (see para 22.30).

Apart from that, you get the full amount of any disregard you qualify for.

13.43   HB sch 4 para 11, sch 5 paras 19,20; HB60+ sch 4 para 6, sch 5 paras 18,19; NIHB sch 6 paras 20,21; NIHB60+ sch 5 para 6, sch 6 paras 19,20

13.44   HB sch 4 paras 13,14, sch 5 paras 24,33; HB60+ 29(1)(k), 33(7), sch 4 para 10, sch 5 paras 16,17; NIHB sch 5 paras 13,14, sch 6 paras 25,34; NIHB60+ 27(1)(i), 31(7), sch 5 para 10, sch 6 paras 17,18

13.45   HB sch 5 para 34; HB60+ sch 5 para 12(3)(b),(c); NIHB sch 6 para 35; NIHB60+ sch 6 para 13(3)(b),(c)

Notional income

13.46   This section explains when you are counted as having unearned or earned income you do not in fact have. This is called 'notional' income.

13.47   For working age HB claims, this section also includes rules about notional capital when these are similar. The main rules about notional capital are in paras 15.56-59.

Types of notional income

13.48   You can be counted as having notional income when:

(a)   there is income available to you (paras 13.50-52);

(b)   in working age HB claims, you are paid income on behalf of someone else (paras 13.53 and 13.55);

(c)   someone else is paid income on your behalf (paras 13.54-55);

(d)   you have deprived yourself of income (see para 13.56);

(e)   a non-dependant has more income and capital than you (para 13.57); or

(f)   in working age HB claims, you are paid less than the going rate for a job (see para 14.24).

Assessing notional income

13.49   If you are counted as having notional income, it is assessed in the same way as actual income and all the disregards given earlier in this chapter and in chapter 14 apply. This means this section does not apply if you are on a passport benefit.

Money which is available to you

13.50   If income is available to you and you could get it by applying for it, it is counted as your notional income (but only from when you would get it if you did apply). In working age HB claims, this rule also applies to capital. For further details see paras 13.51-52.

13.51   In pension age HB claims, the rule in para 13.50 applies only to income from:

(a)   a private pension (see para 13.27); or

(b)   a state pension unless you have deferred it (see para 13.13).

For DWP guidance, see GM paras BP2.680-750.

13.52   In working age HB claims, the rule in para 13.50 applies to any kind of income or capital except for:

(a)   income/capital from a private pension (see para 13.27);

(b)   income/capital from a personal injury payment (paras 15.43-44);

(c)   income/capital from a discretionary trust;

(d)   income/capital from WTC or CTC;

13.49   HB 42(11),(12); HB60+ 25; NIHB 39(11),(12); NIHB60+ 23

13.50   HB 42(2), 49(2); HB60+ 41(1),(4); NIHB 39(2), 46(2); NIHB60+ 39(1),(4)

13.51   HB60+ 41(1)-(7); NIHB60+ 39(1)-(7)

13.52   HB 42(2),(12A), 49(2); NIHB 39(2),(12A), 46(2)

(e) income from expenses or earnings as a service user group member;

(f) income from a DWP rehabilitation allowance; or

(g) capital from a loan you could raise against disregarded property or against other disregarded capital.

The DWP says this rule should not be used in the case of any state benefit if there is a doubt about whether you would qualify or how much you would get (see GM para BW2.682). See also paras 13.49 and 15.59.

Payments received by one person on behalf of another

13.53   In working age HB claims, if you receive payments of income on behalf of someone else, they are counted as your notional income if you keep or use them for yourself or your family. This rule also applies to payments of capital. For exceptions see para 13.55.

13.54   If someone else receives payments of income on your behalf, they are counted as your notional income if they are from:

(a) a private pension (paras 13.27 and 13.55(a)); or

(b) some other source, but in this case only if the payment is used for your or your family's:

■ rent (other than any part of the rent which is not eligible for HB, or not met by HB because of a non-dependant deduction);

■ council tax (rates in Northern Ireland); or

■ water charges, household fuel, food or ordinary clothing or footwear (apart from school uniform/sportswear).

In working age HB claims, this rule also applies to payments of capital. For exceptions see para 13.55.

13.55   The rules in paras 13.53-54 do not apply to

(a) income/capital from a private pension (see para 13.27) if:

■ the person whose pension it is, is bankrupt (or sequestered in Scotland) and has no other income; and

■ the person it is paid to is their trustee in bankruptcy or someone else acting on behalf of their creditors;

(b) income/capital from the government-sponsored trusts and funds in paras 15.42(a) to (d);

(c) income/capital from government work programme training schemes;

(d) income from expenses or earnings as a service user group member; or

(e) income from cash in lieu of concessionary coal.

See also paras 13.49 and 15.59.

13.53   HB 42(6)(c), 49(3)(c); NIHB 39(6)(c), 46(3)(c)

13.54   HB 2(1) definition: 'ordinary clothing and footwear', 42(6)(a),(b),(13), 49(3)(a),(b),(8), sch 5 para 23(2); HB60+ 42(1); NIHB 2(1), 39(6)(a),(b),(14), 46(3)(a),(b),(8), sch 6 para 24(2); NIHB60+ 40(1)

13.55   HB 42(7),(12A), 49(4); HB60+ 29(1), 42(2),(3); NIHB 39(7),(12A), 46(4); NIHB60+ 27(1), 40(2),(3)

Income you have deprived yourself of

13.56 If you have deprived yourself of income, it is counted as your notional income. To 'deprive' yourself of income means:

(a) you have disposed of it (for example by stopping it being paid); and

(b) your purpose in doing so was to make yourself entitled to HB or to more HB.

This rule is likely to be interpreted in a similar way to the rule about deprivation of capital (see table 15.3(a) to (e)). In practice it is rare, but could in some cases apply if you sell your right to receive income from a private pension by 'assigning' your pension annuity (HB G8/2016). It does not apply to income from expenses or earnings as a service user group member, or to income from a state pension you have deferred (see para 13.13). See also para 13.49.

If your non-dependant has more income and capital than you

13.57 You are counted as having your non-dependant's income and capital (instead of yours) if:

(a) they have more income and capital than you; and

(b) you and they arranged to 'take advantage of' (abuse) the HB scheme, for example by deliberately making them your non-dependant rather than making you their non-dependant.

This rule is in practice rare. It does not apply if you are on a passport benefit.

13.56   HB 42(1),(12A); HB60+ 41(8)-(8C),(11),(12); NIHB 39(1),(12A); NIHB60+ 39(8)-(10A),(13),(14)

13.57   HB 26; HB60+ 24, 27(4)(f); NIHB 23; NIHB60+ 22, 25(4)(f)

Chapter 14 **Earned income**

- General rules: see paras 14.1-4.
- Employed earnings and how they are assessed: see paras 14.5-16.
- Calculating net earnings: see paras 14.17-25.
- Self-employed earnings and how they are assessed: see paras 14.26-35.
- Calculating net profit: see paras 14.36-59.
- Earnings disregards: see paras 14.60-73.

General rules

14.1　This chapter explains how your earned income is assessed for HB purposes.

14.2　In this chapter, 'your' earned income always includes the earned income of your partner. See paras 13.1-8 for details about this and for other general rules.

14.3　The rules in this chapter apply to income from employment or self-employment in the UK (England, Wales, Scotland and Northern Ireland). If you are claiming HB in Northern Ireland they also apply to income from employment or self-employment in the Republic of Ireland. For other countries see para 13.44.

The amount of your earned income

14.4　For HB purposes, the amount of your earned income is:

(a) the weekly amount of your (and your partner's):
- net earnings from employment (see para 14.17), and/or
- net profit from self-employment (see para 14.36);

(b) minus the earned income disregards which apply to you (see para 14.60).

It can also include notional earnings (see para 14.24).

Example: Earned income

One partner in a couple is employed and has net earnings of £230 per week. The other is self-employed and has a net profit of £150 per week. They qualify for a standard earned income disregard of £20 per week.

Their combined earned income after the disregard has been made is £360 per week. This figure is used in calculating their HB.

14.4　HB 2(1) definition: 'earnings', 36(1),(2), 38(1),(2); HB60+ 2(1), 33(8)(a), 36(1), 39(1);
　　　NIHB 2(1), 33(1),(2), 35(1),(2); NIHB60+ 2(1), 31(8)(a), 34(1), 37(1)

Employed earnings

14.5   This section explains what employed earnings are and the information used to assess them. This information is needed to calculate your 'net earnings', which is the figure used in HB. (The calculation is in paras 14.17-32.)

What are employed earnings

14.6   Your employed earnings are your earnings from employment 'under a contract of service' (an employment contract) or 'in an office'. An 'office' means the kind of job that may not have an employment contract. People employed in an office include directors of limited companies, local authority councillors and clergy.

14.7   Table 14.1 explains which payments count as employed earnings and which do not. Payments which count as employed earnings are usually shown on your pay slip. For arrears of earnings see para 13.7.

Table 14.1 **Employed earnings**

The following count as employed earnings:

   (a) Employed earnings generally (see para 14.6).

   (b) Employed earnings paid in a lump sum.

   (c) Sick, maternity, paternity, shared parental and adoption pay from your employer.

   (d) Statutory sick, maternity, paternity, shared parental and adoption pay.

   (e) Holiday pay.

   (f) Retainers.

   (g) Bonuses and commission.

   (h) Tips.

   (i) Payments in lieu of notice.

   (j) Payments in lieu of earnings (but for redundancy payments see (q) below).

14.6   CBA 2(1)(a); NICBA 2(1)(b); HB 2(1) definition: employed earner; HB60+ 2(1), 29(1)(a); CBA 2(1)(a); NIHB 2(1) ; NIHB60+ 2(1), 27(1)(a)

14.7   HB 35; HB60+ 35; NIHB 32; NIHB60+ 33

T14.1(a)   HB 35(1); HB60+ 35(1); NIHB 32(1); NIHB60+ 33(1)

T14.1(b)   HB 41(3); HB60+ 26; NIHB 38(3); NIHB60+ 24

T14.1(c)   HB 35(1)(j); HB60+ 35(1)(k); NIHB 32(1)(k); NIHB60+ 33(1)(k)

T14.1(d)   HB 35(1)(i); HB60+ 35(1)(h)-(j); NIHB 32(1)(i); NIHB60+ 33(1)(h)-(j)

T14.1(e)   HB 35(1)(d); HB60+ 35(1)(d); NIHB 32(1)(d); NIHB60+ 33(1)(d)

T14.1(f)   HB 35(1)(e); HB60+ 35(1)(e); NIHB 32(1)(e); NIHB60+ 33(1)(e)

T14.1(g)   HB 35(1)(a); HB60+ 35(1)(a); NIHB 32(1)(a); NIHB60+ 33(1)(a)

T14.1(h)   HB 35(1); HB60+ 35(1); NIHB 32(1); NIHB60+ 33(1)

T14.1(i)   HB 35(1)(c); HB60+ 35(1)(c); NIHB 32(1)(c); NIHB60+ 33(1)(c)

T14.1(j)   HB 35(1)(b); HB60+ 35(1)(b); NIHB 32(1)(b); NIHB60+ 33(1)(b)

(k) Non-cash vouchers which are earnings for national insurance purposes.

(l) Councillor's allowances, but for expenses see (n) below (R(IS) 6/92). For detailed guidance see GM paras BW2.83-95.

(m) Company director's income (see para 14.6).

The following have individual rules:

(n) Expenses paid by your employer:

- these are disregarded if they are 'wholly, exclusively and necessarily incurred' in carrying out your employment. For example, for travel between workplaces (R(IS) 16/93, CIS 507/94), or all travel if you don't have a fixed workplace and can be asked to work anywhere in your area (CH/1330/2008, in which the claimant was a care worker);

- apart from that, they count as your employed earnings. For example, for travel between your home and workplace, or for caring for a member of your family.

(o) Expenses you receive as a member of a service user group are disregarded (for example when these are run by councils, social landlords or health authorities).

(p) Compensation payments for unfair dismissal or under laws about equal pay etc, whether made by an employment tribunal or in an out of court settlement:

- count as your employed earnings in working age HB claims;

- do not count as your employed earnings in pension age HB claims (but are likely to be included as your capital).

(q) Redundancy payments count as your capital, not earnings (but for payments in lieu of notice see (j) above).

(r) Payments in kind (in other words, in goods rather than money or vouchers) are disregarded (see also table 13.9(k)). But payments in private currencies count as your employed earnings, for example in local exchange trading schemes (see GM paras BW2.99-101) or in internet currencies.

(s) Bounty payments you receive as a part-time firefighter, a part-time lifeboat worker, an auxiliary coastguard or a member of the Territorial Army or similar reserve forces – all these count as your capital, not earnings, if they are paid to you annually or at longer intervals (see also table 14.5(f)).

T14.1(k)   HB 35(1)(k); HB60+ 35(1)(g); NIHB 32(1)(l); NIHB60+ 33(1)(g)

T14.1(l)   HB 35(1); HB60+ 35(1); NIHB 32(1); NIHB60+ 33(1)

T14.1(m)   HB 35(1); HB60+ 35(1); NIHB 32(1); NIHB60+ 33(1)

T14.1(n)   HB 35(1)(f),(2)(b); HB60+ 35(1)(f),(2)(b); NIHB 32(1)(f),(2)(b); NIHB60+ 33(1)(f),(2)(b)

T14.1(o)   HB 2(5) definition: 'participating as a service user' 35(2)(d); HB60+ 2(6) 35(2)(f); NIHB 2(4A), 32(2)(d); NIHB60+ 2(5A), 33(2)(e)

T14.1(p)   HB 35(1)(g),(gg),(h), 41(3); HB60+ 35(2)(e); NIHB 32(1)(g),(gg),(h), 38(3); NIHB60+ 33(2)(d)

T14.1(q)   HB 35(1)(b), 44(1); HB60+ 35(1)(b), 44(1); NIHB 32(1)(b), 41(1); NIHB60+ 33(1)(b), 44(1)

T14.1(r)   HB 35(2)(a),(3); HB60+ 35(2)(a),(3); NIHB 32(2)(a),(3); NIHB60+ 33(2)(a),(3)

T14.1(s)   HB 46(1); NIHB 43(1)

(t)   Advances of earnings and loans from your employer count as your capital, not earnings.

(u)   Tax refunds on your earnings count as your capital, not earnings.

(v)   Occupational pensions count as your unearned income (see para 13.27).

(w)   Strike pay counts as your unearned income in working age HB claims, but is disregarded in pension age HB claims.

(x)   Self-employed earnings are assessed separately (see paras 14.26-35, and for royalties and similar payments see paras 14.58-59).

Notes

- The rules in (b), (s), (t) and (u) are given in the law for working age HB claims. They are also likely to apply for pension age HB claims.

- See also paras 14.13-16 if you are absent from work or your job ends.

Assessing employed earnings

14.8   When your employed earnings are assessed, the purpose is to estimate 'the amount which is likely to be' your average weekly net earnings (for net earnings see para 14.17). This is done using information from an assessment period or employer's estimate (see paras 14.9-11), but other relevant information should also be taken into account in order to obtain a fair and accurate result. For these purposes, your earnings count as belonging to the period they cover, whether they are paid at the beginning or end of that period or part way through it.

Assessment periods

14.9   In working age HB claims, when you make your claim your assessment period is usually:

(a)   the two months before you claimed if you are paid monthly; or

(b)   the five weeks before you claimed if you are paid weekly; or

(c)   if you have not been working long enough for the above to apply:

- the period you have been working if what you have been paid is representative;

- if what you have been paid is not representative, or you haven't yet been paid, an employer's estimate is used (see para 14.11);

(d)   but if your earnings vary, whatever period gives a more accurate result.

If your earnings change while you are on HB, your assessment period is whatever period gives an accurate result. But it must not be longer than 52 weeks, and must not include periods before the change occurred ([2015] UKUT 237 (AAC)).

T14.1(t)   HB 46(5); NIHB 43(5)

T14.1(u)   HB 46(2); NIHB 43(2)

T14.1(v)   HB 35(2)(c); HB60+ 35(2)(c); NIHB 32(2)(c); NIHB60+ 33(2)(c)

T14.1(w)   HB 35(1); HB60+ 29(1); NIHB 32(1); NIHB60+ 27(1)

14.8   HB 27(1)(a), 29(1)-(3), 29A; HB60+ 30(1)(a), 33(2),(2A),(3),(3A); NIHB 24(1)(a), 26(1)-(3), 26A; NIHB60+ 28(1)(a), 31(2),(2A),(3),(3A)

14.9   HB 2(1) definition: 'assessment period', 29(1)-(3); NIHB 2(1), 26(1)-(3);

14.10   In pension age HB claims, when you make your claim your assessment period usually uses the following information:

(a)   your most recent two payments if they are one month or more apart; or

(b)   your most recent four payments in other cases; or

(c)   whatever payments give a more accurate result;

(d)   but if your hours vary over a recognisable cycle (for example you work a regular pattern of shifts, or you work in term-times but not school holidays), information about the whole of that cycle.

If your earnings change while you are on HB, the rules in (c) or (d) usually apply.

Employer's estimates

14.11   Your council can ask your employer to provide information about your earnings (see also para 5.13), or can ask you to obtain this information from your employer. Many councils have a 'certificate of earnings' form which can be used for this.

Examples: Assessing employed earnings

1.   A claimant's weekly earnings have been the same over the five weeks before she claimed HB.

    ▪   Her weekly net earnings are calculated from this weekly amount.

2.   A claimant's monthly earnings have varied over the two months before he claimed HB. Evidence about his earlier earnings shows that an average can fairly be taken over the past six months.

    ▪   His weekly net earnings are calculated from the past six months' figures.

3.   A claimant has moved to the area for a new job. She claims HB a few days after starting work.

    ▪   She is asked to provide an employer's estimate, and her weekly net earnings are calculated from that.

Starting a job

14.12   When you start a job, your earnings can be estimated to begin with (see paras 14.9(c) and 14.11). They are taken into account from the Monday following the first day you are paid for (see para 17.21), even if your first pay day is later on. But if you have been out of work for 26 weeks or more, you may qualify for an 'extended payment' of HB (see para 17.46).

Leaving a job

14.13   When you leave a job, your earnings are taken into account until the Sunday following the last day you are paid for (see para 17.21). But in working age HB claims, holiday pay counts as your capital, not earnings, if it is payable more than four weeks after you left.

14.10   HB60+ 2(1) definition: 'assessment period', 33(2),(3); NIHB60+ 2(1),31(2),(3)

14.12   HB 29A(b); HB60+ 33 (2A)(b),(3A)(b); NIHB 26A(b); NIHB60+ 31(2A)(b),(3A)(b)

14.13   HB 35(1)(d), 46(3); NIHB 32(1)(d), 43(3)

14.14   And if your job ended before your first day of entitlement to HB:

(a)   in working age HB claims, all your earnings from that job are disregarded except for compensation (see table 14.1(p)) and retainers;

(b)   in pension age HB claims, all your earnings from that job are disregarded.

Absences from work

14.15   When you are absent from work, your earnings are reassessed if they change (see para 17.21). This applies to all absences, whether they are:

(a)   due to sickness (with or without leave);

(b)   due to maternity, paternity, shared parental or adoption leave;

(c)   'with good cause' (for example you are laid off);

(d)   on holiday;

(e)   on strike; or

(f)   for any other reason (including absences 'without good cause').

But in working age HB claims, holiday pay counts as your capital, not earnings, if it is payable more than four weeks after your absence began.

14.16   And in working age HB claims, if your absence:

(a)   began before your first day of entitlement to HB; and

(b)   is for one of the reasons in para 14.15(a), (b) or (c),

all your earnings from that job are disregarded except for employer's and statutory sick, maternity, paternity, shared parental or adoption pay, compensation (see table 14.1(p)) and retainers.

Calculating net earnings

14.17   It is your 'net earnings' which are used in assessing your HB. They are calculated as follows, using the information described in paras 14.8-16:

(a)   start with your gross earnings: see para 14.18;

(b)   deduct amounts for tax and national insurance: see paras 14.19-21;

(c)   deduct half of your pension contributions: see para 14.22;

(d)   convert the result to a weekly figure: see para 6.37;

(e)   this gives your weekly net earnings: see para 14.23.

See also paras 14.60-73 for the earned income disregards.

14.14   HB sch 4 paras 1(a),(b), 2(a),(b),(i), 16; HB60+ sch 4 para 8; NIHB sch 5 paras 1(a),(b), 2(a),(b),(i), 16; NIHB60+ sch 4 para 8

14.15   HB 35(1)(d), 46(3); NIHB 32(1)(d), 43(3)

14.16   HB sch 4 paras 1(c), 2(a),(b),(ii), 16; NIHB sch 5 paras 1(c), 2(a),(b),(ii), 16;

14.17   HB 2(1) definition: 'net earnings', 29(4), 36; HB60+ 2(1), 28, 36; NIHB 2(1), 26(4), 33; NIHB60+ 2(1), 26, 34

Example: Calculation of net earnings

A single claimant is employed and her gross earnings are £1,450 per month. From this, her employer deducts £98.67 each month for tax, £93.40 each month for class 1 national insurance contributions (NICs), and £40 each month towards a pension scheme. Her net earnings are calculated as follows.

From her gross earnings	£1,450 pcm
deduct:	
■ tax	£98.67 pcm
■ NICs	£93.40 pcm
■ half her pension contributions	£20.00 pcm
This gives her net earnings	£1,237.93 pcm
They are converted to a weekly figure:	
■ £1,237.93 x 12 ÷ 52	£285.68 pw

The earned income disregards which apply to her are then deducted (see para 14.60).

Gross earnings

14.18   Your 'gross earnings' are the total of your employed earnings: see paras 14.5-16 and table 14.1.

Deductions for tax and national insurance

14.19   Deductions are made from your gross earnings for:

(a)   income tax; and

(b)   class 1 national insurance contributions (NICs).

The deductions equal the amounts deducted by your employer for these. The amounts should be shown on your pay slip. The exceptions to this are in paras 14.20-21.

14.20   If your gross earnings were assessed using an employer's estimate (see para 14.11) or you have notional earnings (see para 14.24), the deductions are calculated by the council. They equal what would be deducted (if they were actual earnings) for:

(a)   income tax, using only the specific personal reliefs that you are entitled to (i.e. the personal allowance, the blind person's allowance, the tax deduction for married couples and civil partners where one was born before 6th April 1935 and the transferable tax allowance for married couples and civil partners) [www]; and using the basic rate of tax, or for a Scottish taxpayer, the Scottish basic rate; and

(b)   class 1 NICs.

14.18   HB 35; HB60+ 35; NIHB 32; NIHB60+ 33

14.19   HB 36(3),(a),(d); HB60+ 36(2),(a),(d); NIHB 33(3),(a),(d); NIHB60+ 34(2),(a),(d)

14.20   HB 2(1) definitions: 'basic rate', 'Scottish basic rate', 'Scottish taxpayer', 36(6),(a),(b), 42(12)(a),(b); HB60+ 2(1),36(5),(a),(b); NIHB 2(1),33(6),(a),(b),39(12)(a),(b); NIHB60+ 2(1),34(5),(a),(b)
www.gov.uk/income-tax-rates

14.21   If you are claiming HB in Northern Ireland and work in the Republic of Ireland, the deductions are calculated by the NIHE. They equal what would be deducted for tax and class 1 NICs if you worked in Northern Ireland.

Deductions for pension contributions

14.22   If you make contributions towards an occupational or personal pension, one half of the amount you contribute is deducted from your gross earnings. If your gross earnings were assessed using an employer's estimate (see para 14.11) or you have notional earnings (see para 14.24), the deduction is calculated by the council. It equals one half of what you would contribute (if they were actual earnings).

Net earnings

14.23   The above calculation (see paras 14.18-22) gives your net earnings. They are converted to a weekly figure (see para 6.37). No other amounts can be deducted from them, even if you have to pay work expenses which are not met by your employer. Your weekly net earnings are used in calculating your HB (but only after the earned income disregards have been made: see paras 14.60-73).

Notional earnings

14.24   In working age HB claims, you are counted as having 'notional' earnings (see para 13.48(f)) if:

(a)   you work or provide a service for someone;

(b)   they pay you less than the rate for comparable employment in the area, or do not pay you; and

(c)   none of the exceptions in para 14.25 apply.

Your notional earnings equal the amount (if any) which would be reasonable for the comparable employment. Apart from that, notional earnings are assessed in the same way as actual earnings (but see para 14.20 and 14.22).

14.25   The rule in para 14.24 does not apply to work you do or a service you provide:

(a)   for someone whose means are insufficient to pay you, or to pay you more; or

(b)   for a charitable or voluntary organisation or as a volunteer, if it is reasonable for you to work without being paid; or

(c)   in a government work programme training scheme or work placement.

14.21   NIHB 33(7); NIHB60+ 34(6)

14.22   HB 36(3)(b),(c),(4),(5),(6)(c), 42(12)(c); HB60+ 36(2)(b),(c),(3),(4),(5)(c);
         NIHB 33(3)(b),(c),(4),(5),(6)(c), 39(12)(c); NIHB60+ 34(2)(b),(c),(3),(4),(5)(c)

14.23   HB 2(1) definition: 'net earnings', 29(4), 36; HB60+ 2(1), 28, 36; NIHB 2(1), 26(4), 33; NIHB60+ 2(1), 26, 34

14.24   HB 27(4), 42(9),(12); NIHB 24(4), 39(9),(12)

14.25   HB 42(9),(10),(10A),(12A); NIHB 39(9),(10),(10A),(12A)

Self-employed earnings

14.26 This section explains what self-employed earnings are, and the information used to assess them. This information is needed to calculate your 'net profit', which is the figure used in HB. (The calculation is in paras 14.36-57.)

What are self-employed earnings

14.27 Your self-employed earnings are your earnings which:

(a) are from 'gainful employment'; but

(b) are not employed earner's earnings (see para 14.6).

This applies whether you are a sole trader or in a partnership. Royalties and similar payments also usually count as self-employed earnings (see paras 14.58-59).

14.28 Your self-employed earnings only include payments which:

(a) are income (not capital); and

(b) are 'derived from' your self-employment.

Table 14.2 lists payments which (for those reasons) do not count as self-employed earnings. Apart from that, self-employed earnings include payments in money, in kind (in other words, in goods) and in any other form (for example barter).

Table 14.2 **Self-employed earnings: exclusions**

The following do not count as self-employed earnings:

(a) Your business assets. These are capital (not income) and are disregarded (see para 15.33).

(b) Grants and loans to your business. These are usually capital and (if so) are disregarded as part of your business assets.

(c) New enterprise allowance. This can help you start up in business if you are on JSA, ESA or IS [www]. It can pay you:

- a weekly allowance for up to 26 weeks: this is unearned income and is disregarded (circular A11/2011);

- a low cost loan: this is disregarded as part of your business assets (circular A8/2011).

(d) Access to work. This can help you start up in business if you have a disability [www]. It is unearned income and is disregarded (see table 13.1(p)).

(e) Other government work programme training schemes. Payments from these are usually disregarded (see table 13.1(p)).

(f) Sports Council awards. These are usually disregarded (see para 22.32).

14.27   CBA 2(1)(b); NICBA 2(1)(b); HB 2(1) definition: 'self-employed earner', 37(1); HB60+ 2(1), 38(1); NIHB 2(1), 34(1); NIHB60+ 2(1), 36(1)

14.28   HB 37(1); HB60+ 38(1); NIHB 34(1); NIHB60+ 36(1)

T14.2   HB 37(2); HB60+ 38(2); NIHB 34(2); NIHB60+ 36(2); www.gov.uk/new-enterprise-allowance; www.gov.uk/access-to-work

(g) Foster care and kinship care payments. These are disregarded (see table 13.5(a)).

(h) Boarding out and respite care payments. These are disregarded (see table 13.5(f)).

(i) Rent you receive on your home (see table 13.7).

(j) Rent you receive on other property: R(FC) 2/92 (see table 13.8). But if you rent out property as a business this counts as self-employed earnings (see para 15.33).

(k) Employed earnings are assessed separately (see paras 14.5-16).

(l) Income you receive as a director of a limited company counts as employed earnings (not self-employed earnings).

Assessing self-employed earnings

14.29 When your self-employed earnings are assessed, the purpose is to estimate 'the amount which is likely to be' your average weekly net profit (for net profit see para 14.36). This is done using information from an assessment period, but other information should be taken into account to obtain a fair and accurate result.

Assessment periods

14.30 Your assessment period is whatever period is appropriate to enable the most accurate estimation of your weekly net profit (CH/329/2003, [2003] UKUT 104 (AAC)). In working age HB claims it must not be longer than one year, and in pension age HB claims it is a year unless this would not be appropriate.

14.31 When you make your claim for HB your assessment period is usually:

(a) the most recent full year for which you have accounts or other records; or

(b) the period you have been self-employed if this is less than a year; or

(c) in either case, a shorter or different period if this would be more representative;

(d) but if you are just starting self-employment, an estimated future period (see para 14.33).

If your self-employed earnings change while you are on HB (see para 14.35), your assessment period should usually be from the date the change occurred to the most recent date you have figures for (CH/329/2003, [2003] UKUT 104 (AAC)). For DWP guidance on assessment periods see GM paras BW2.330, BW2.333.

Providing accounts or other records

14.32 You are expected to provide information about your income and expenses in your assessment period. You can draw up accounts or other records yourself, or get someone else to do this for you. They can be drawn up on:

(a)   a cash basis, counting income when it comes in, and expenses when you pay them; or

(b)   an accrual basis, counting income when you issue a bill and expenses when you get a bill,

so long as you are reasonable, consistent, and fairly reflect your income and expenses.

Example: Self-employed earnings and net profit

Dennie Wroclaw is a self-employed window-cleaner. The records of his most recent year's trading show he had gross income of £10,268, and spent £354 on telephone, postage and stationery, £3,534 on petrol and other costs for his van, £187 on overalls and disposable equipment, £507 on advertising, and £613 to pay someone to cover his round while he was on holiday. His mileage records show that two-thirds of his use of the van is for his business (see para 14.41).

The council decides that year is appropriate as his assessment period (see para 14.31), as the figures are likely to represent his current income and expenses. His pre-tax profit (see para 14.36) is calculated as follows.

From his gross income	£10,268 pa
Deduct his allowable expenses (see table 14.3):	
telephone, postage and stationery	£354 pa
business use of van (⅔ of £3,534)	£2,356 pa
overalls and disposable equipment	£187 pa
advertising	£507 pa
holiday cover payments	£613 pa
This gives his pre-tax profit	£6,251 pa

This is used to calculate his weekly net profit (see para 14.36). The earned income disregards which apply to him are then deducted (see para 14.60).

Starting self-employment

14.33   When you start self-employment, your self-employed earnings can be estimated to begin with (see para 14.31(d)). The estimate usually covers the first 13 weeks you will be self-employed. Most councils have a form you can use to give your estimated income and expenses for this period, and expect you to provide records of your actual income and expenses after that. If you have been out of work for 26 weeks or more, you may qualify for an 'extended payment' of HB: see para 17.46.

Leaving self-employment

14.34   When you leave self-employment, all your self-employed earnings are disregarded from the date you stopped being self-employed, except for royalties etc (see para 14.58-59).

14.34   HB sch 4 para 4A; HB60+ sch 4 para 8; NIHB sch 5 para 4A; NIHB60+ sch 5 para 8

Changes in your self-employed earnings

14.35   Your self-employed earnings can change in different ways. Generally speaking:

(a)   short-term variations in your cash flow (for example from month to month) are a normal part of being self-employed, and do not mean your HB should be reassessed; but

(b)   significant changes in your trading pattern mean your HB should be reassessed. For example, this could be because you change from full-time to part-time or from part-time to full-time, or gain or lose a major customer, or have a break from trading because you are sick or are caring for someone.

Calculating net profit

14.36   It is your 'net profit' which the council uses to calculate your HB. It is calculated as follows using the information described in paras 14.29-35:

(a)   start with your gross income: see para 14.37;

(b)   deduct your allowable expenses: see paras 14.38-45 (or if you are a childminder see para 14.52);

(c)   this gives your pre-tax profit (or if you are in a partnership your share is your pre-tax profit): see paras 14.46-52;

(d)   deduct amounts for tax and national insurance: see paras 14.53-55;

(e)   deduct half your pension contributions: see para 14.56;

(f)   convert the result to a weekly figure: see para 6.37;

(g)   this gives your weekly net profit: see para 14.57.

See also paras 14.60-73 for the earned income disregards.

Gross income

14.37   Your gross income is the total of your self-employed earnings before any deductions have been made from them: see paras 14.26-35.

Allowable expenses

14.38   Your allowable expenses are deducted from your gross income. There are two main conditions about this:

(a)   expenses are only allowable if they are 'wholly and exclusively incurred' for the purposes of the business: see paras 14.40-44;

(b)   but expenses are not allowable if they are not 'reasonably incurred': see para 14.45.

Some types of expenses also have special rules, and these are all included in table 14.3.

14.39   Table 14.3 summarises which expenses are allowable and which are not, and further details are in paras 14.40-45. Different rules apply if you are a childminder: see para 14.52.

14.36   HB 2(1) definition: 'net profit', 30(2), 38; HB60+ 2(1), 28,39; NIHB 2(1), 27(2), 32; NIHB60+ 2(1), 26,37

14.37   HB 37(1); HB60+ 38(1); NIHB 34(1); NIHB60+ 36(1)

14.38   HB 38(3)(a),(4),(7); HB60+ 39(2)(a),(3),(6); NIHB 35(3)(a),(4),(7); NIHB60+ 37(2)(a),(3),(6)

Table 14.3 **Self-employed expenses**

This table is about which expenses are allowable if you are self-employed (see paras 14.38-39).

Allowable expenses

(a) Expenditure (from your income) on repairing an existing business asset, apart from costs covered by an insurance policy.

(b) Capital repayments on a loan used for repairing an existing business asset, apart from costs covered by an insurance policy.

(c) Capital repayments on a loan used for replacing business equipment or machinery (this includes a loan for replacing a car: R(H) 5/07).

(d) Interest payments on any business loan.

(e) Any VAT you pay (minus any VAT you receive).

(f) Any other expenditure which meets the conditions in para 14.38. For example, the following expenses are likely to meet those conditions:

- telephone, postage, stationery and delivery costs,
- transport and vehicle costs,
- materials, supplies, stock and protective clothing,
- advertising and subscriptions to trade and professional bodies,
- bank charges, insurance costs, and accountancy and legal fees,
- hire and leasing charges,
- staff costs and payments to subcontractors,
- premises costs such as rent, rates, cleaning and fuel.

Non-allowable expenses

(g) Capital expenditure, such as buying a vehicle, equipment of a lasting nature, or business premises.

(h) Capital repayments on a loan, unless (b) or (c) above applies.

(i) Depreciation of capital assets (even if you claim a capital allowance in your tax return).

(j) Expenditure on setting up or expanding your business (but interest on loans for this is allowable: see (d) above).

(k) Losses you have incurred before your assessment period (see paras 14.30-31).

(l) Expenditure on business entertainment.

T14.3(a)-(e) HB 38(6),(8)(b); HB60+ 39(5),(7)(b); NIHB 35(6),(8)(b); NIHB60+ 37(5),(7)(b)

T14.3(f)   HB 38(3)(a),(4),(7); HB60+ 39(2)(a),(3),(6); NIHB 35(3)(a),(4),(7); NIHB60+ 37(2)(a),(3),(6)

T14.3(g)-(n) HB 38(5),(8)(a); HB60+ 39(4),(7)(a); NIHB 35(5),(8)(a); NIHB60+ 37(4),(7)(a)

(m) Debts you are owed, but proven bad debts are allowable and so are costs you incur in recovering debts. (This rule is given in the law for working age HB claims. It is also likely to apply for pension age HB claims.)

(n) Expenditure for domestic or private purposes (see also paras 14.41-44).

(o) Any other expenditure which does not meet the conditions in para 14.38.

'Wholly and exclusively incurred' expenses

14.40   An expense is wholly and exclusively incurred for your business if all of it is for your business and no part of it is for anything else. For example, if you use a van only for your business (and do not use it for domestic, private or other purposes), your vehicle costs for the van are allowable expenses. See also paras 14.41-44.

Expenses for mixed purposes

14.41   If an expense is partly for your business and partly for another purpose, you can separate it out to find the business part. This is also called 'apportioning' expenses. For example, if you use a car for both business and personal purposes, you can keep records of your mileage and then separate the costs on that basis. The business part is then allowable. But the calculation does not have to be that detailed, so long as the method you use is fair and reasonable.

14.42   Even expenses you would incur anyway can be apportioned. For example you would have to pay for insurance and a vehicle licence on a car (and perhaps repay a car loan) even if you did not use it for your business, but you can apportion these expenses in the same way as the petrol you use (R(H) 5/07, which followed R(FC) 1/91).

Expenses if you work from home

14.43   If you work from home, part of your accommodation costs are an allowable expense. For example, this can include part of your fuel for heating and lighting, standing charges, and rent (see also para 14.44). The business part of these should be calculated in a fair and reasonable way, taking into account the size of your working area compared with the size of the rest of your home, and the amount of time you use it for business rather than domestic purposes. In one case a self-employed claimant used the second bedroom in their home only for business purposes. The difference between the total rent on their home and the rent officer's valuation of the rent for a one-bedroom flat was accepted as an appropriate allowable expense (para 12 of R(H) 5/07).

14.44   But when part of your rent is allowed as a business expense, that part cannot be included in your eligible rent: see para 8.90. This affects you if your eligible rent is based on your actual rent (see chapters 8 and 10), but not if it is based on a local housing allowance (see chapter 9).

14.40   HB 38(3)(a),(4); HB60+ 39(2)(a),(3); NIHB 35(3)(a),(4); NIHB60+ 37(2)(a),(3)

'Reasonably incurred' expenses

14.45 Whether an expense is reasonably incurred depends on the circumstances of the individual case (R(P) 2/54), including how much you earn from your business (R(G) 1/56). If an expense is appropriate and necessary, it should always be considered reasonably incurred unless it is excessive (R(G) 7/62). If an expense is excessive only the part which is reasonable is allowable.

Pre-tax profit (chargeable income)

14.46 Deducting your allowable expenses from your gross income gives your pre-tax profit. In the law it is called your 'chargeable income'. Further rules about pre-tax profit are in paras 14.47-52. See also paras 14.53-56 for deductions for tax etc.

Pre-tax profit for business partnerships

14.47 If you are self-employed in a partnership, your pre-tax profit is worked out for your business and then divided between you. The same applies if you are a share fisherman. The division is made in the same way as you actually share the net profit derived from the business. For example if you are one of two business partners and you get one-third of the net profit (perhaps reflecting the different hours you work in the business or the terms of a partnership agreement), then this is the proportion of the pre-tax profit of the business that the council should use in the calculation of your HB.

Pre-tax profit and couples

14.48 If you are a couple and are also business partners, your pre-tax profit is divided between you (see para 14.47). If one of you is self-employed and employs the other one, the wages or salary are:

(a) allowable expenses for the self-employed one; and

(b) employed earnings for the other one.

If you make a loss

14.49 If your allowable expenses are greater than (or equal to) your gross income, your pre-tax profit is nil, so your self-employed earnings are nil (R(H) 5/08).

14.50 Your losses cannot be deducted from any other employed or self-employed earnings you have, or your partner or any other family member has (R(H) 5/08).

Pre-tax profit and drawings

14.51 If you take drawings from your business (for example as a kind of wage or salary you pay yourself), this has no effect on the calculation of your pre-tax profit. Drawings are not part of your gross income (R(H) 6/09) and are not an allowable business expense (GM paras BW2.390-396).

14.45   HB 38(7); HB60+ 39(6); NIHB 35(7); NIHB60+ 37(6)

14.46   HB 38(3)(a); HB60+ 39(3)(a); NIHB 35(3)(a); NIHB60+ 37(3)(a)

14.47   HB 38(1)(b); HB60+ 39(1)(b); NIHB 35(1)(b); NIHB60+ 37(1)(b)

14.50   HB 38(10); HB60+ 39(9); NIHB 35(10); NIHB60+ 37(9)

Pre-tax profit if you are a childminder

14.52   If you are a self-employed childminder:

(a)   your expenses are not deducted from your gross income;

(b)   instead, your pre-tax profit always equals one-third of your gross income.

This is intended to make the calculation easier.

Example: A self-employed childminder

Hendl Drimic is a self-employed childminder. She gets gross income from her child-minding which averages £240 per week. She works from her home and it would be difficult to assess her expenses, but she does not have to do this because her pre-tax profit is calculated as follows.

Her gross income is	£240
Of this only one-third is counted as her pre-tax profit	£80
This is too low for deductions for tax and national insurance.	
So her net profit is also	£80

The earned income disregards which apply to her are then deducted (see para 14.60).

Deductions for tax and national insurance

14.53   Deductions are made from your pre-tax profit for:

(a)   income tax; and

(b)   classes 2 and 4 national insurance contributions (NICs).

The deductions are calculated by the council and are called 'notional tax' and 'notional NICs'. They are unlikely to be the same as the amounts you actually pay HMRC, for a number of reasons, e.g. different assessment periods and differences in what expenses are treated as allowable for income tax and for HB.

14.54   Table 14.4 shows how the deductions are calculated. It gives the figures for the tax year from 6th April 2016 to 5th April 2017 (this tax year contains 365 days). The calculation:

(a)   uses annual figures. So if your pre-tax profit is not an annual amount it is converted to an annual figure;

(b)   uses the tax and NICs figures for the tax year which is 'applicable to' your assessment period (see paras 14.30-31). If your assessment period spanned two tax years, councils interpret this in different ways. Many use the most straightforward method of using the figures for the tax year containing your date of claim for HB (or the date your HB is reassessed).

When making the calculation, councils can ignore national changes in the tax and NICs rates and allowances for up to 30 weeks.

14.52   HB 39(3)(b); HB60+ 40(3)(b); NIHB 36(3)(b); NIHB60+ 38(3)(b)

14.53   HB 38(1)(b)(i),(3)(b),(9)(a), 39; HB60+ 39(1)(b)(i),(2)(b),(8)(a), 40; NIHB 35(1)(b)(i),(3)(b),(9)(a), 36; NIHB60+ 37(1)(b)(i),(2)(b),(8)(a), 38

14.54   HB 2(1) definitions: 'basic rate', 'tax year', 'Scottish basic rate', 'Scottish taxpayer', 34, 39(1),(2);
             HB60+ 2(1), 34, 40(1),(2); NIHB 2(1), 31, 36(1),(2); NIHB60+ 2(1), 32, 38(1),(2)

14.55   The calculations in table 14.4 apply in Northern Ireland even if your self-employment is based in the Republic of Ireland.

Table 14.4 **Notional tax and NICs: 2017-18 tax year**

This table shows how your notional tax and national insurance contributions (NICs) are calculated if you are self-employed. All three calculations are made (though one or more of them may give a figure of nil).

(a) **Income tax**

- start with your annual pre-tax profit

- subtract the personal relief(s) which apply to you, e.g. the £11,500 personal allowance

- if there is a remainder, multiply it by the basic rate of tax (20%) or in the case of a Scottish taxpayer, the Scottish basic rate

- the result is the annual amount of your notional tax.

(b) **Class 2 NICs**

- if your annual pre-tax profit is £6,025 or more, the annual amount of your notional class 2 NICs is £148.20.

(c) **Class 4 NICs**

- start with your annual pre-tax profit (but if it is greater than £45,000, start with £45,000)

- subtract £8,164

- if there is a remainder, multiply it by 9%

- the result is the annual amount of your notional class 4 NICs.

Notes

(a) The personal reliefs that may be applicable dependent upon your circumstances are: the personal allowance, the blind person's allowance, the tax deduction for married couples and civil partners where one was born before 6th April 1935 and the transferable tax allowance for married couples and civil partners [www];

(b) £148.20 is 52 times the weekly class 2 NICs of £2.85, there being 52 Sundays in the 2017-18 tax year. If your pre-tax profit is below £6,025, your notional class 2 NICs are nil (even if you have not applied to HMRC for exemption).

(c) The 2% class 4 NICs rate for income over £45,000 is not used. (This appears to be the intention of HB law, even though it has not been amended to keep it up to date with NICs law.)

14.55   NIHB 35(12); NIHB60+ 37(11)

T14.4   HB 2(1) definitions: 'basic rate', 'tax year', 'Scottish basic rate', 'Scottish taxpayer' 39; HB60+ 2(1), 40; NIHB 2(1), 36; NIHB60+ 2(1), 38
         www.gov.uk/income-tax-rates

Example: Notional tax and NICs

A self-employed book-keeper lives in England. She claims HB in December 2017 and provides her most recent accounts, which are for the year to 31st October 2017. The council decides that year is appropriate as her assessment period (see para 14.31). In that year she had gross income of £14,500 and allowable expenses of £1,400, so her pre-tax profit is £13,100. She doesn't contribute to a pension scheme. Her notional tax and national insurance contributions (NICs) are calculated as follows (see table 14.4).

(a) **Notional tax**

- from her pre-tax profit   £13,100.00 pa
- subtract the personal allowance   £11,500.00 pa
                                                                                       = £1,600.00 pa
- and multiply this by the basic rate (20%)
  to give her notional tax   £320.00 pa

(b) **Notional class 2 NICs**

- her pre-tax profit is greater than £6,025
  so her notional class 2 NICs are   £148.20 pa

(c) **Notional class 4 NICs**

- from her pre-tax profit   £13,100.00 pa
- subtract the lower earnings threshold   £8,164.00 pa
                                                                                       = £4,936.00 pa
- and multiply this by 9% to give her notional class 4 NICs   £444.24 pa

(d) **Net profit**

- from her pre-tax profit deduct: £13,100.00 pa
  - her notional tax   £320.00 pa
  - her notional class 2 NICs   £148.20 pa
  - her notional class 4 NICs   £444.24 pa
- this gives her annual net profit   £12,187.56 pa
- it is converted to a weekly figure:
  - £11,725.80 ÷ 365 x 7   £233.73 pw

The earned income disregards which apply to her are then deducted (see para 14.60).

Deductions for pension contributions

14.56   If you make regular contributions towards a qualifying personal pension scheme half of the amount you contribute is deducted from your pre-tax profit. If your contributions change (or you start or stop making contributions) your HB is reassessed.

14.56   HB 2(1) definition: 'personal pension scheme', 38(1)(b)(ii),(3)(c),(9)(b),(11),(12); HB60+ 2(1),39(1)(b)(ii),(2)(c),(8)(b),(10),(11); NIHB 2(1),35(1)(b)(ii),(3)(c),(9)(b),(11),(13); NIHB60+ 2(1),37(1)(b)(ii),(2)(c),(8)(b),(10),(12)

Example: Pension contributions

The self-employed book-keeper in the previous example begins making pension contributions of £40 per month in February 2018. Her HB is reassessed to take account of this as follows. (Her trading pattern has not changed so her income and expenses do not need to be reassessed: see para 14.35.)

Her weekly net profit was	£233.73 pw
From this, deduct the weekly equivalent of half of her qualifying pension contributions (see para 6.44):	
■ £20 x 12 ÷ 365 x 7	£4.60 pw
This gives her new weekly net profit	£229.13 pw

The earned income disregards which apply to her are then deducted (see para 14.60).

Net profit

14.57   The above calculation (see paras 14.37-56) gives your net profit. This is converted to a weekly figure (see para 6.37). The council uses your weekly net profit to calculate your HB (but only after the earned income disregards have been made: see paras 14.60-73).

Royalties and similar payments

14.58   The following payments count as earned income. In working age HB claims they are assessed as self-employed earnings (see para 14.36), and in practice this is also done in pension age HB claims:

(a)   royalties or other payments you receive for the use of, or right to use, a copyright, design, patent or trademark;

(b)   payments you receive as an author under the Public Lending Right scheme or a similar international scheme; and

(c)   in pension age HB claims, any other 'occasional' payment you earn.

The rules in (a) and (b) only apply if you are the first owner of the copyright etc or an original contributor to the book etc. If you have inherited the right to receive royalties etc, this is unearned income (see para 13.40).

14.59   Because these payments are often annual, six monthly or irregular, there are special rules saying what period they cover:

(a)   in pension age HB claims, they are averaged over the year beginning with the date of payment. For example, a payment of £364 is gross income of £7 per week over that year (see para 6.37);

14.57   HB 2(1) definition: 'net profit', 30(2), 38; HB60+ 2(1), 28,39; NIHB 2(1), 27(2), 35; NIHB60+ 2(1), 26,37

14.58   HB 37(3); HB60+ 29(1)(q),(r), 33(5),(8)(b),(8A); NIHB 34(3); NIHB60+ 27(1)(o),(p), 31(5),(8)(b),(8A)

14.59   HB 37(4); HB60+ 33(4); NIHB 34(4); NIHB60+ 31(4)

(b) in working age HB claims, work through the following steps:

- start with the weekly amount of your HB (calculated as though you did not receive the royalties etc);

- add to that all the earned income disregards which apply to you (see para 14.60);

- the result is your gross income for each week until payment is used up. For example, if your HB is £90 per week and you qualify for only the £10 per week earned income disregard, a payment of £364 is gross income of £100 per week for three weeks, then £64 in the fourth week.

Earned income disregards

14.60   This section describes the amounts which are disregarded from your earned income. You may qualify for one, two, or all three of the following:

(a) a standard earned income disregard (see para 14.62);

(b) a child care disregard (see paras 14.63-67);

(c) an additional earned income disregard (see para 14.68).

They can be described as the amounts you are allowed to 'keep' before your earned income affects the amount of your HB.

How the disregards work

14.61   The earned income disregards work as follows:

(a) first add together all your (and your partner's):

- weekly net earnings from employment (see para 14.17), and

- weekly net profit from self-employment (see para 14.36);

(b) then (from that total) deduct the standard earned income disregard;

(c) then deduct the child care disregard if you qualify for it. But if:

- the result of (b) is not enough to deduct the whole of the child care disregard, and

- you are on working tax credit or child tax credit,

    the balance of the child care disregard is deducted from your WTC and/or CTC;

(d) then deduct the additional earned income disregard if you qualify for it. But if:

- the result of (c) is not enough to deduct the whole of the additional earned income disregard, and

- you are on working tax credit,

    the whole of the additional earned income disregard (not just the balance) is instead deducted from your WTC.

Except as described in (c) and (d), no part of the earned income disregards can be deducted from your unearned income. (See para 13.43 if you make parental contributions to a student.)

14.61   HB 2(1) definition: 'earnings' 27(1)(c),(2), 36(2), 38(2), sch 4 paras 3-10A, sch 5 para 56;
           HB60+ 2(1), 30(1)(c),(2), 33(8), sch 4 paras 1-5A, 7, 9(1),(3), sch 5 para 21;
           NIHB 2(1), 24(1)(c),(2), 33(2), 35(2), sch 5 paras 3-10A, sch 6 para 58;
           NIHB60+ 2(1), 28(1)(c),(2), 31(8), sch 5 paras 1-5A, 7, 9(1),(3), sch 6 para 22

Examples: Earned income disregards

1. A couple without children

A couple in their 40s are both employed for 35 hours a week. Their combined net earnings are £500 per week. They do not have children.

From their weekly net earnings:	£500.00

Deduct:

■ the standard earned income disregard for a couple (see table 14.5 (g))	£10.00
■ the additional earned income disregard (see para 14.68 and table 14.7(b))	£17.10
This gives the figure used in calculating their HB	£472.90

2. A lone parent with child care costs

A lone parent aged 30 is self-employed for 20 hours a week, and his net earnings are £250 per week. He pays child care charges of £70 per week for his daughter aged 9.

From his weekly earnings:	£250.00

Deduct:

■ the standard earned income disregard for a lone parent (see table 14.5(b))	£25.00
■ the child care disregard (see paras 14.63-64)	£70.00
■ the additional earned income disregard (see para 14.68 and table 14.7(c))	£17.10
This gives the figure used in calculating his HB	£137.90

The standard earned income disregard

14.62   Everyone who has earned income qualifies for a standard earned income disregard. The disregard has different amounts, but whether you are a single claimant, a lone parent, or a couple, you qualify for only one amount. Table 14.5 explains the conditions for each amount, and which one you qualify for.

14.62   HB sch 4 paras 3-10A; HB60+ sch 4 paras 1-5A, 7; NIHB sch 5 paras 3-10A; NIHB60+ sch 5 paras 1-5A, 7

Table 14.5 **The standard earned income disregard**

The standard earned income disregard has different amounts (see para 14.62), all given in this table. You qualify for the first amount you meet the conditions for.

(a) **'Permitted work' approved by the DWP: £120.00 per week**

The disregard is £120.00 per week if you are in 'permitted work'. This means work the DWP has agreed you can do while you are receiving:

- ESA(C);
- incapacity benefit;
- severe disablement allowance; or
- national insurance credits instead of those benefits.

If you are a couple and only one of you is in permitted work, it is disregarded from that one's earned income. But if that is less than £120.00 per week, the balance up to £20 per week is disregarded from the other one's earned income.

The disregard is set at 16 times the national living wage, so when that goes up the £120.00 per week increases (DWP HB G9/2015 (para 18) and A13/2015 Revised, p11).

(b) **Lone parents: £25 per week**

Unless (a) applies to you, the disregard is £25 per week if you are a lone parent.

(c) **Sickness or disability: £20 per week: working age HB claims**

In working age HB claims, unless (a) or (b) apply to you, the disregard is £20 per week if your applicable amount includes:

- a work-related activity component (see para 12.28);
- a support component (see paras 12.23-25);
- a disability premium (see para 12.31); or
- a severe disability premium (see para 12.38).

(d) **Sickness or disability: £20 per week: pension age HB claims**

In pension age HB claims, unless (a) or (b) apply to you, the disregard is £20 per week if you or your partner:

- receive attendance allowance or an equivalent benefit (see para 13.22);
- receive personal independence payment or disability living allowance;

T14.5(a)   HB sch 4 para 10A; HB60+ sch 4 para 5A; NIHB sch 5 para 10A; NIHB60+ sch 5 para 5A

T14.5(b)   HB sch 4 para 4; HB60+ sch 4 paras 1(a),2; NIHB sch 5 para 4; NIHB60+ sch 5 paras 1(a),2

T14.5(c)   HB sch 4 para 3; ; NIHB sch 5 para 3;

T14.5(d)   HB60+ 2(1) definition: 'attendance allowance', sch 4 para 5; NIHB60+ 2(1), sch 5 para 5

- receive the disability element or severe disability element of working tax credit;

- receive an armed forces independence payment;

- receive war pensioner's mobility supplement;

- receive main phase ESA, or national insurance contributions instead of it (see para 12.26);

- meet the old work fitness test (incapacity benefit). But in the case of national insurance credits the qualifying period is 28 weeks (not one year). And unlike the rules for the disability premium it can be you or your partner who meets this condition; or

- qualified for the £20 per week disregard (as described in (c) above) at any time in the eight weeks before you reached pension age (see paras 1.23-25), and there have been no breaks in either your entitlement to HB or your employment since you reached that age.

(e) Carers: £20 per week

Unless (a) to (d) apply to you, the disregard is £20 per week if your applicable amount includes a carer premium (see para 12.43)

If you are a couple and only one of you is a carer, it is disregarded from the carer's earned income. But if that is less than £20 per week, the balance up to £10 per week is disregarded from the other one's earned income.

(f) Special occupations: £20 per week

Unless (a) to (e) apply to you, the disregard is £20 per week if you or your partner are:

- a part-time fire-fighter;

- a part-time lifeboat worker;

- an auxiliary coastguard; or

- a member of the Territorial Army or similar reserve forces.

(See also table 14.1(s).)

(g) Couples: £10 per week

For all other couples, the disregard is £10 per week.

(h) Single claimants: £5 per week

For all other single claimants, the disregard is £5 per week.

T14.5(e)   HB sch 4 paras 5,6; HB60+ sch 4 paras 1(b),4; NIHB sch 5 paras 5,6; NIHB60+ sch 5 paras 1(b),4

T14.5(f)   HB sch 4 paras 8,9; HB60+ sch 4 paras 1(b),3; NIHB sch 5 paras 8,9; NIHB60+ sch 5 paras 1(b),3

T14.5(g)   HB sch 4 para 7; HB60+ sch 4 para 7(b); NIHB sch 5 para 7; NIHB60+ sch 5 para 7(b)

T14.5(h)   HB sch 4 para 10; HB60+ sch 4 para 7(a); NIHB sch 5 para 10; NIHB60+ sch 5 para 7(a)

The child care disregard

14.63   You qualify for the child care disregard if:

(a) you pay child care charges to one or more of the providers in table 14.6;

(b) you pay them for one or more children who meet the age condition (see para 14.66); and

(c) you are:

  ■   a lone parent and you work at least 16 hours per week, or

  ■   a couple and you both work at least 16 hours per week, or

  ■   a couple and one of you works at least 16 hours per week and the other one meets one or more of the conditions in para 14.67.

Paragraphs 14.69-72 explain when you count as working at least 16 hours per week.

14.64   The disregard equals the weekly amount of child care charges you pay (see para 14.65), up to:

(a) £175 per week if the charges are for one child;

(b) £300 per week if the charges are for two or more children.

See para 14.61(c) for further information about how the disregard works.

14.65   Table 14.6 explains which child care charges are taken into account. The weekly amount is found by averaging them over whatever period, up to one year, gives an accurate figure. The council can ask the person providing the care for the information about this.

Table 14.6 **Child care providers**

Charges you pay to the following are taken into account for the child care disregard (see paras 14.63-66):

(a) A registered child minder, nursery or play scheme.

(b) A child minding scheme that does not have to be registered, for example, one run by a school or local authority or in Northern Ireland on Crown property.

(c) Any child care provider if the child care has been approved for working tax credit purposes.

(d) An out-of-school-hours scheme provided by a school on school premises, by a local authority, or in Northern Ireland by an education and library board or HSS trust. But in this case only, the child must be aged 8 or more.

(e) A foster parent or kinship carer (apart from the child's own foster parent or kinship carer) under the Fostering Services Regulations 2002, or equivalent provisions in Wales, or the Looked After Children (Scotland) Regulations 2009.

14.63   HB 28(1) ; HB60+ 31(1); NIHB 25(1) ; NIHB60+ 29(1)

14.64   HB 27(3); HB60+ 30(3); NIHB 24(3); NIHB60+ 28(3)

14.65   HB 28(5),(10); HB60+ 31(5),(10); NIHB 25(5),(10); NIHB60+ 29(5),(10)

(f) A domiciliary care worker under the Domiciliary Care Agencies Regulations 2002, or equivalent provisions in Wales.

(g) Anyone else who provides care wholly or mainly in the child's home, for example, a friend who comes in to provide care for the child. But this does not apply if they are your partner or a relative of the child. See para 7.38 for who counts as a 'relative'.

But payments you make in respect of compulsory education do not count towards the child care disregard.

14.66   A child meets the age condition for the child care disregard from birth until:

(a) the first Monday in September following their 15th birthday; or

(b) if they meet the conditions for a disabled child premium (see para 12.34), the first Monday in September following their 16th birthday.

14.67   The conditions listed in this paragraph are about the child care disregard for couples: see para 14.63(c). If you are a couple and one of you works at least 16 hours per week, the other one does not have to do so if they:

(a) meet the conditions for:

- a work-related activity component (see para 12.28),

- a support component (see paras 12.23-25), or

- a disability premium;

(b) are receiving:

- disability living allowance (DLA),

- personal independence payment (PIP),

- attendance allowance, or constant attendance allowance paid with an industrial injury or war disablement pension,

or would do so except that they are in hospital (see para 12.54 and table 12.2);

(c) are receiving:

- main phase ESA (see para 12.26),

- incapacity benefit at the short-term higher rate or the long-term rate, or

- severe disablement allowance;

(d) have been accepted by the DWP as having limited capability for work (see para 12.25) or as being incapable of work (i.e. for incapacity benefit) for a continuous period of 28 weeks (ignoring breaks of up to 12 or 8 weeks respectively);

T14.6   HB 28(5),(7)-(9); HB60+ 31(5),(7)-(9); NIHB 25(5),(7)-(9); NIHB60+ 29(5),(7)-(9)

14.66   HB 28(6),(9),(13); HB60+ 31(6),(9),(13); NIHB 25(6),(9),(13); NIHB60+ 29(6),(9),(13)

14.67   HB 28(1)(c),(11); HB60+ 31(1)(c),(11) ; NIHB 25(1)(c),(11); NIHB60+ 29(1)(c),(11)

14.67(a)   HB 28(11)(a),(b),(ba); HB60+ 31(11),(b),(ba); NIHB 25(11)(a),(b),(ba); NIHB60+ 29(11),(b),(ba)

14.67(b),(c) HB 28(11)(d)-(f); HB60+ 31(11),(d)-(f); NIHB 25(11)(d)-(f); NIHB60+ 29(11),(d)-(f)

14.67(d)   HB 28(11)(c),(ca),(12),(12A); HB60+ 31(11)(c),(ca),(12),(12A); NIHB 25(11)(c),(ca),(12),(12A); NIHB60+ 29(11)(c),(ca),(12),(12A)

(e)   have an invalid carriage or similar vehicle;

(f)   are aged 80 or more;

(g)   are in hospital; or

(h)   are in prison (serving a sentence or on remand).

But condition (d) only applies to the HB claimant. (See para 5.4 for how to change which partner in a couple is the claimant.)

The additional earned income disregard

14.68   You qualify for the additional earned income disregard if you meet one or more of the conditions in table 14.7. The amount of the disregard is £17.10 per week. See para 14.61(d) for further information about how the disregard works.

Working at least 16 hours per week

14.69   You count as working at least 16 hours per week if:

(a)   you are employed or self-employed in work for which payment is made or expected; and

(b)   you work at least 16 hours per week every week, or on average (see para 14.70).

The law calls this 'remunerative work'.

14.70   If your hours vary, they are averaged as follows:

(a)   if there is no recognisable cycle to your work, over five weeks or whatever period would give a more accurate figure;

(b)   if your work has a recognisable cycle (for example you work a regular pattern of shifts), over the whole of that cycle. In this case, the averaging includes periods you don't work;

(c)   but if your work has a recognisable cycle of a year (for example you work in term-times but not school holidays) over the whole year. In this case, the averaging excludes periods you don't work but the result applies throughout the year. (So if you work at least 16 hours every week in term-times, you count as working at least 16 hours per week throughout the year.)

14.67(e)   HB 2(1) definition: 'invalid carriage', 28(11)(g); HB60+ 2(1), 31(11)(g) ; NIHB 2(1), 25(11)(g); NIHB60+ 2(1), 29(11)(g)

14.67(f)   HB60+ 31(11)(a); ; NIHB60+ 29(11)(a)

14.67(g),(h) HB 28(1)(c); HB60+ 31(1)(c); NIHB 25(1)(c); NIHB60+ 29(1)(c)

14.68   HB sch 4 para 17; HB60+ sch 4 para 9; NIHB sch 5 para 17; NIHB60+ sch 5 para 9

14.69   HB 2(1) definition: 'remunerative work'; HB60+ 2(1), 6(1); NIHB 2(1), 6(1); NIHB60+ 2(1), 6(1)

14.70   HB 6(2)-(4); HB60+ 6(2)-(4); NIHB 6(2)-(4); NIHB60+ 6(2)-(4)

Table 14.7 **The additional earned income disregard**

You qualify for the additional earned income disregard (see para 14.68) if you meet one or more of the conditions (a) to (e). Paras 14.69-73 explain when you count as working at least 16 or 30 hours per week. The examples illustrate how the conditions work for couples.

(a) You receive working tax credit and it includes the WTC '30 hour element'.

If you are a couple, at least one of you has to qualify for the WTC 30 hour element. See example 1.

(b) You:

- ■   are aged 25 or more; and

- ■   work at least 30 hours per week.

If you are a couple, at least one of you has to meet both halves of this condition. See example 2.

(c) You:

- ■   are responsible for one or more children or young persons; and

- ■   work at least 16 hours per week.

If you are a couple, only one of you has to work at least 16 hours per week. See example 3.

(d) In working age HB claims, you:

- ■   qualify for a work-related activity component, a support component, or a disability premium (see paras 12.20-27 and 12.31); and

- ■   work at least 16 hours per week.

If you are a couple, at least one of you has to meet each half of this condition (but it need not be the same one who meets both halves). See example 4.

(e) In pension age HB claims, you:

- ■   qualify for the £20 disregard for sickness or disability (see table 14.5(d)); and

- ■   work at least 16 hours per week

If you are a couple, at least one of you has to meet both halves of this condition. See example 5.

Note:

For condition (a) you have to be on WTC (and getting the WTC 30 hour element). For conditions (b) to (e) you don't have to be on WTC (but they are the same as the conditions used in WTC for getting the 30 hour element).

T14.7   HB sch 4 para 17(2); HB60+ sch 4 para 9(2); NIHB sch 5 para 17(2); NIHB60+ sch 5 para 9(2)

Examples: The additional earned income disregard for couples

1. A couple on working tax credit

A couple are on WTC. One of them has been awarded the WTC '30 hour element'.

- They qualify for the additional earned income disregard: see table 14.7(a).

2. A couple without children

A couple are aged 22 and 27. The 22-year-old works for 35 hours a week. The 27-year-old does not work.

- They do not qualify for the additional earned income disregard: see table 14.7(b). (They would qualify if the 27-year-old worked at least 30 hours a week.)

3. A couple with a child

A couple with a baby. One of them works for 20 hours a week. The other one does not work.

- They qualify for the additional earned income disregard: see table 14.7(c).

4. A working age couple, one with a disability

A couple are in their 50s. One of them receives personal independence payment (PIP) and does not work. The other one works for 20 hours a week.

- They qualify for the additional earned income disregard: see table 14.7(d). (They would also qualify if the one on PIP worked at least 16 hours a week, or they both did.)

5. A pension age couple, one with a disability

A couple are in their 70s. One of them receives attendance allowance and does not work. The other one works for 20 hours a week.

- They do not qualify for the additional earned income disregard: see table 14.7(e). (They would qualify if the one on attendance allowance worked at least 16 hours a week, or they both did.)

14.71   Once you count as working at least 16 hours per week:

(a)   you continue to do so during the following absences from work:

- while you are on holiday, or
- while you are absent from work 'without good cause';

(b)   for the purposes of the child care disregard (only), you also continue to do so:

- while you are on maternity, paternity, shared parental or adoption leave. This only applies while you are getting statutory maternity, paternity, shared parental or adoption pay, or maternity allowance, or income support because of paternity leave (these can be paid for up to 39 weeks. And if you are getting the child element of WTC when they stop, it continues to apply until the WTC child element stops), or

---

14.71-72   HB 2(1) definitions: 'adoption leave', 'maternity leave', 'paternity leave', 'shared parental', 'sports award', 6(1),(5)-(8), 28(2)-(4),(14),(15); HB60+ 2(1), 6(1),(5)-(8), 31(2)-(4),(14)-(16); NIHB 2(1), 6(1),(5)-(8), 25(2)-(4),(14),(15); NIHB60+ 2(1), 6(1),(5)-(8), 29(2)-(4),(14)-(16)

- while you are on sick leave. This is limited to 28 weeks. And it only applies while you are getting statutory sick pay, incapacity benefit at the short-term lower rate, ESA, income support because of incapacity for work, or national insurance credits instead of these.

14.72   You do not count as working at least 16 hours per week:

(a) while you are absent from work 'with good cause' (for example you are laid off);

(b) while you are doing unpaid work;

(c) while your only income is from a Sports Council award (para 22.32);

(d) in any benefit week in which you are on JSA(IB), ESA(IR) or income support for more than three days;

(e) while you are on maternity, paternity, shared parental or adoption leave, with the right to return to work under your contract or under employment law; or

(f) while you are absent from work due to illness, whether or not you are being paid.

There are exceptions to (e) and (f) in relation to the child care disregard: see para 14.71(b).

Working at least 30 hours per week

14.73   The rules about whether you count as working at least 30 hours per week are the same as in paras 14.69-72, apart from the different number of hours.

14.73   HB sch 4 para 17(4); HB60+ sch 4 para 9(4); NIHB sch 5 para 17(4); NIHB60+ sch 5 para 9(4)

Chapter 15 **Capital**

- General rules about assessing capital: see paras 15.1-13.
- How capital is valued: see paras 15.14-20.
- Savings and investments: see paras 15.21-27.
- Property and possessions: see paras 15.28-35.
- Trust funds, compensation payments and other capital: see paras 15.36-55.
- Notional capital: see paras 15.56-69.

General rules

15.1   This chapter explains how your capital is assessed for HB purposes, including actual capital (see paras 15.21-55) and notional capital (see paras 15.56-69). This section gives rules relating to all types of capital.

'Your' capital

15.2   If you are single, your own capital is taken into account. If you are in a couple, the capital of your partner is taken into account as well as yours. If you are in a polygamous marriage, the capital of all your partners is included. In this chapter, 'your' capital always includes the capital of your partner (or partners). But if a child or young person has capital of their own, this is never included.

How your capital affects your HB

15.3   If you are on a passport benefit (see para 13.5), all your capital is disregarded (ignored) and you qualify for maximum HB: see paras 6.2-3.

15.4   If you are not on a passport benefit, some kinds of capital are counted and some are disregarded. The details are in this chapter. Once the amount of your capital is valued (see paras 15.21-27), it is taken into account as follows:

(a)   if it is more than £16,000 you are not entitled to HB; otherwise

(b)   the first £6,000 is ignored in working age HB claims;

(c)   the first £10,000 is ignored in pension age HB claims;

(d)   the remainder up to £16,000 is counted as providing you with an assumed amount of income (see para 15.5).

(See also para 13.15 if you are on the savings credit of SPC.)

15.1   HB 44(1); HB60+ 44(1); NIHB 41(1); NIHB60+ 42(1)

15.2   CBA 136(1); HB 25, 45; HB60+ 23; NICBA 132(1); NIHB 22, 42; NIHB60+ 21

15.3   HB sch 6 paras 5,6; HB60+ 26; NIHB sch 7 paras 5, 6; NIHB60+ 24

15.4   CBA 134(1); HB 43, 44(2), 52(1), sch 6; HB60+ 28, 29(2), 43, 44(2); NICBA 130(1), NIHB 40, 41(2), 49(1), sch 7; NIHB60+ 26, 27(2), 41, 42(2)

Assumed income from capital (tariff income)

15.5   The assumed income from your capital (apart from disregarded capital) is calculated as follows (in the law it is also called 'tariff income'):

(a) in working age HB claims, deduct £6,000 from your capital and divide the remainder by 250;

(b) in pension age HB claims, deduct £10,000 from your capital and divide the remainder by 500;

(c) if the result of (a) or (b) is not an exact multiple of £1, round the result up to the next £1.

This gives the weekly amount of your assumed income from capital. It is added to your other income: see para 13.1. (For interest and other kinds of actual income from capital see para 15.26.)

Examples: Assessing capital and assumed income from capital

1. A working age HB claim

A single man in his 40s has £14,085 in his bank account when he claims HB. Of this, £2,000 is an insurance payment he received three weeks ago to replace his motorbike after an accident. He has no other capital.

Assessment:

- ▪ The £2,000 is disregarded (see table 15.1(j))
- ▪ So his capital for HB purposes is   £12,085

Assumed income from capital (tariff income):

- ▪ From the £12,085, £6,000 is deducted leaving   £6,085
- ▪ Dividing this by 250 gives   £24.34
- ▪ Rounding up to the next whole pound gives   £25
- ▪ So he has £25 per week of assumed income from capital

2. A pension age HB claim

A couple in their 80s have £15,085 in their bank account when they claim HB. Of this, £3,000 is arrears of disability living allowance they received three months ago after winning an appeal. They have no other capital.

Assessment:

- ▪ The £3,000 is disregarded (see table 15.2)
- ▪ So their capital for HB purposes is   £12,085

Assumed income from capital (tariff income):

- ▪ From the £12,085, £10,000 is deducted leaving   £2,085
- ▪ Dividing this by 500 gives   £4.17
- ▪ Rounding up to the next whole pound gives   £5
- ▪ So they have £5 per week of assumed income from capital

15.5   CBA 136(2); HB 27(1)(b), 52; HB60+ 30(2)(b); NICBA 132(2); NIHB 24(1)(b), 49; NIHB60+ 28(2)(b)

Distinguishing capital from income

15.6 HB law does not give a definition of capital or income. Instead the rules 'operate at a stage after the money has been classified' (CH/1561/2005). But the distinction is usually straightforward: see paras 15.7-13.

Capital you hold

15.7 DWP guidance says 'As a general rule, capital includes all categories of holdings which have a clear monetary value' (GM para BW1.70). The rules for savings, investments, property and other items are given later in this chapter, including when they count as your capital and when they are disregarded.

Capital someone else holds for you

15.8 If someone else holds your capital for you, it counts as yours. For example, this includes money held for you by the Court of Protection ([2011] UKUT 157 (AAC)) or by someone who has power of attorney for you.

Capital you hold for someone else

15.9 If you hold someone else's capital for them, it does not count as yours. For example, you might be looking after your child's savings for them, or someone you are caring for may have put your name on a joint bank account with them so you can deal with their money for them. It is up to you to provide evidence that the money is not yours, but you do not need to be a formally documented trustee for them ([2010] UKUT 437 (AAC)). (If you are a trustee, see para 15.41.)

Payments of income and capital

15.10 A payment you receive can be income (for example earnings or benefits) or capital (for example an inheritance). This is decided by looking at 'the true characteristics of the payment in the hands of the recipient' (in other words, what it is to you), rather than whether the person pays it you periodically or in a lump sum or whether they (or you) call it 'income' or 'capital' (Minter v Hull City Council). DWP guidance says it is more likely to be capital if it is '(i) made without being tied to a period, (ii) made without being tied to any past payment, and (iii) not intended to form part of a series of payments' (GM para BW1.71).

Payments of arrears of income

15.11 A payment of arrears of income is assessed in both the following ways:

(a) it is income for a past period, except when that kind of income is disregarded. This may mean you have been overpaid HB (see chapter 18);

(b) it is capital from when you receive it until when you spend it. But arrears of some benefits are disregarded as capital for 52 weeks or longer (see para 15.52).

The fact that arrears of income can affect your capital does not stop them being income for a past period. For example a large lump sum settlement of an equal pay claim can be income for a past period if it is 'properly characterised as wages' (Minter vs Hull City Council).

15.10-11   Minter v Hull CC 13/10/11 CA [2011] EWCA Civ 1155 www.bailii.org/ew/cases/EWCA/Civ/2011/1155.html

15.11   HB 27(1), 31(1),(2), 44(1); HB60+ 30, 33(1),(6), 44(1); NIHB 24(1), 28(1),(2), 41(1); NIHB60+ 28, 31(1),(6), 42(1)

Payments of capital in instalments

15.12   If capital is payable to you in instalments, outstanding instalments are assessed as follows:

- (a)   in pension age HB claims, they do not count as your capital until you receive them;
- (b)   in working age HB claims, they count as your capital straight away (in other words even before you receive them). But if they would take your capital over £16,000, they count instead as your income.

When payments of income become capital

15.13   Income you do not spend becomes capital. 'A payment of income… remains income for the period in which it is paid. Any surplus at the end of that period metamorphoses into capital' (CH/1561/2005). This applies to counted income (for example earnings) and also to disregarded income (for example fostering allowances: CIS/3101/2007). So if your income is paid monthly, only what is left at the end of the month is capital. Different rules apply to arrears of income (see para 15.11).

Valuing capital

15.14   The value of each item of capital you have (apart from disregarded capital) is assessed by working through the following steps:

- (a)   start with its current market or surrender value (see para 15.15);
- (b)   then deduct 10% if selling it would involve costs (see para 15.16);
- (c)   then deduct any debt or charge secured against it (see para 15.17).

Further rules are in paras 15.18-20. See para 13.15 if you are on the savings credit of state pension credit.

Market or surrender value

15.15   Dwellings, non-residential property, and some other items have a market value. It is what they would fetch if you sold them on the open market. Your council can ask the Valuation Office Agency to assist them in valuing these (forms for this are in GM BW1 annexes D and E, and further DWP guidance is in circular A25/2009). Insurance policies and some other investments have a surrender value. It is what you would be paid if you cashed them in now. For cash in a bank account see para 15.22.

Sales costs

15.16   If selling a capital item would mean you had to pay a fee or other costs, 10% is deducted from its value. For example this applies to property and shares. You do not have to work out what the actual sales costs would be. Instead, the 10% deduction always applies.

15.12   HB 41(1), 44(1), sch 6 para 18; HB60+ 44(1); NIHB 38(1), 41(1), sch 7 para 19; NIHB60+ 42(1)

15.14   HB 47; HB60+ 45; NIHB 44; NIHB60+ 43

15.15   HB 47; HB60+ 45; NIHB 44; NIHB60+ 43

15.16   HB 47(a); HB60+ 45(a); NIHB 44(a); NIHB60+ 43(a)

Secured debts or charges

15.17   Any debt or charge secured against a capital item is deducted from its value. For example this includes the outstanding mortgage on a property. Only secured debts and charges can be deducted (the law calls them 'encumbrances'). Other debts (such as rent arrears) cannot be deducted from your capital (CH/3729/2007).

Jointly owned capital

15.18   If you own a capital item jointly with one or more other people (other than just your partner), only your share of its capital value is taken into account. This means:

(a) your actual share if you own it in known shares (for example if you own a one-third share and another person owns a two-thirds share): R(IS) 4/03;

(b) an equal share in other cases (for example one-half if there are two of you).

Your share is valued as described in paras 15.14-16. The reason your share is valued rather than the whole item, is that the value of a half-share (for example) can be less than half the value of the whole item. In some cases the value of a share of capital can be minimal (CH/1953/2003).

Examples: Valuing capital

1. Shares in a company

A woman owns 1,000 shares. Their sell price is currently £0.78 each.

■ Their market value is 1,000 x £0.78	£780
■ Deduct 10% for sales costs	£78
■ Their value for HB purposes is	£702

2. Jointly owned land

Three brothers jointly own some land in equal shares. It is worth £35,000, but the value of a one-third share is £10,500. One brother claims HB. He took out a loan using his share of the land as security and £5,400 of the loan remains to be paid.

■ The market value of his share is	£10,500
■ Deduct 10% for sales costs	£1,050
■ Deduct the loan	£5,400
■ The value of his share for HB purposes is	£4,050

Capital outside the UK

15.19   If you own capital in a country outside the UK:

(a) its market or surrender value in that country is taken into account (see also para 15.20);

(b) but if you are prohibited (by that country) from bringing the money to the UK, it is valued at what a willing buyer in the UK would give for it.

In each case steps (b) and (c) in para 15.14 then apply.

15.17   HB 47(b); HB60+ 45(b); NIHB 44(b); NIHB60+ 43(b)

15.18   HB 51; HB60+ 49; NIHB 48; NIHB60+ 47

15.19   HB 48; HB60+ 46; NIHB 45; NIHB60+ 44

Capital not in sterling

15.20 If you have capital in a currency other than sterling, any banking charge or commission for converting it to sterling is disregarded.

Savings and investments

15.21 This section gives the rules for savings and various kinds of investment. (For property and possessions, see paras 15.28-35.)

Savings and cash

15.22 Your savings are counted in full as your capital whether you keep them as cash or in a bank, and interest is included as capital from when it is due. But if you have more than one bank account, and the bank has the power to use money in one to pay an overdraft on another, it is the net amount (across those accounts) which is counted: [2011] UKUT 63 (AAC). See also para 15.13 if your income is paid into an account.

Savings certificates

15.23 National Savings and Ulster Savings certificates count in full as your capital. You can find out their current value using an online calculator, and the DWP says your council should use this to value them (GM BW1.440-451).

Shares and similar investments

15.24 Shares, unit trusts, income bonds and similar investments count in full as your capital. Shares and unit trusts are valued at their current 'sell' price. Then 10% is deducted for sales costs in the case of shares (see para 15.16), but not normally for unit trusts because their sell price already allows for this.

Pension schemes, annuities, life insurance and funeral plans

15.25 Capital held in the following is wholly disregarded:

    (a) an occupational or personal pension scheme (see para 13.27);

    (b) an annuity (see paras 13.32-33);

    (c) a life insurance policy, including a bond or similar investment which has a life insurance element (R(IS) 7/98), including compensation paid by the UK government (£5,000) to holders of Equitable Life pre-1992 policies (HB G10/2013);

    (d) in pension age HB claims, a funeral plan contract if its sole purpose is to provide a funeral in the UK for you and/or your partner.

15.20   HB sch 6 para 23; HB60+ sch 6 para 23; NIHB sch 7 para 24; NIHB60+ sch 7 para 23

15.22   HB 44(1); HB60+ 44(1); NIHB 41(1); NIHB60+ 42(1)

15.23   HB 44(1); HB60+ 44(1); NIHB 41(1); NIHB60+ 42(1)

15.24   HB 44(1), 47(a); HB60+ 44(1), 45(a); NIHB 41(1), 44(a); NIHB60+ 42(1), 43(a)

Their surrender value is also disregarded (this means what you would get if you cashed them in), but capital you actually receive from them (if you do cash in part or all) is counted in full.

Interest and other actual income from capital

15.26 Interest you receive on a bank account, and other kinds of actual income you receive on capital, are counted as increasing your capital from when they are due. (They are not counted as income, because instead there are rules about assumed income from capital: see para 15.5.) But see tables 13.7 and 13.8 if you receive rent on property you have let out, and para 15.33 for income you receive on business assets.

The value of your right to receive an asset in the future or future income

15.27 Your right to receive an asset in the future can be sold. And the income from some investments can be sold (the purchaser would receive the income in the future instead of you). So each of these has a capital value. But this capital value is disregarded in the case of reversionary interest (see table 15.1(g)), occupational and personal pensions, annuities, rent, a life interest/life rent (see para 15.31) and any kind of income you cannot bring to the UK (see para 13.44).

Property and possessions

15.28 This section gives the rules for property, money relating to property, personal possessions, and business assets. (For property held in a trust see paras 15.37-40.)

Property

15.29 The rules about property apply to dwellings and non-residential premises. Your home and some other property is disregarded: see the first part of table 15.1. Property which is not disregarded is counted as your capital. Its value is assessed as described in paras 15.14-20. If you have rented it out, this is taken into account in valuing it. For example the presence of a sitting tenant can reduce the value of a dwelling (CH/1953/2003). If ownership of a property is in dispute, it may have no value until the dispute is settled.

Money relating to property

15.30 Money for buying, repairing or improving a home (e.g. including adaptations for people who are elderly or disabled) can be disregarded: see the second part of table 15.1. If you receive rent on a property you have let out, see table 13.8.

15.25   SI 2013/2980 reg 5; HB 2(1) definition: 'policy of life insurance', sch 6 paras 13,17,32; HB60+ 2(1), sch 6 paras 11,12,24,29; NIHB 2(1), sch 7 paras 13,18,31A,33; NIHB60+ 2(1), sch 7 paras 11,12,24,31,31A

15.26   HB 46(4); HB60+ 29(1)(i), sch 5 paras 22,24; NIHB 43(4); NIHB60+ 27(1)(g), sch 6 paras 23,25

15.27   HB sch 6 paras 7,13,15,16,31,33; HB60+ sch 6 paras 5,24,27-29; NIHB sch 7 paras 7,13,16,17,32,34; NIHB60+ sch 7 paras 5,24,29-31

15.29   HB 44, sch 6; HB60+ 44(1),(2), sch 6; NIHB 41, sch 7; NIHB60+ 42(1),(2), sch 7

15.30   HB sch 6; HB60+ sch 6; NIHB sch 7; NIHB60+ sch 7

Table 15.1 **Capital disregards relating to property**

Your home and other property

Working age and pension age HB claims: disregards (a) to (g)

In (a) to (e) only one dwelling can be a person's home at any one time. In (a) to (c) there is no time limit. (if you rent out property as a self-employed business see para 15.33.)

(a) Your home, and any land or buildings (including croft land in Scotland) which are part of it or are impracticable to sell separately. For example, your home is disregarded if you are a shared owner, or an owner claiming HB for rates in Northern Ireland, or are claiming HB temporarily on other accommodation (see paras 3.8, 3.42).

(b) The home of a partner or 'relative' (see para 7.38) of yours or of anyone in your family, if that partner/relative:

  ▪ has reached state pension credit age (see para 1.24); or

  ▪ is 'incapacitated'. This word has its ordinary English meaning. For example it is not limited to people on ESA or similar benefits.

(c) The home of your partner if:

  ▪ you have not divorced, dissolved your civil partnership or become estranged (in other words your relationship has not ended: CH/3777/2007); but

  ▪ you no longer count as a couple (or polygamous marriage) for HB purposes (see para 4.6).

(d) A home you intend to occupy if:

  ▪ you acquired it within the past 26 weeks*; or

  ▪ you are taking steps to obtain possession of it, and first sought legal advice about this or began legal proceedings within the past 26 weeks*; or

  ▪ you are carrying out essential repairs or alterations to make it fit for occupation or re-occupation, and began doing so within the past 26 weeks*.

(e) Your former home, and any land or buildings (including croft land in Scotland) which are part of it or are impracticable to sell separately, if:

  ▪ you ceased to occupy it because you have divorced, dissolved your civil partnership or become estranged from your partner (in other words your relationship has ended: CH/117/2005 and CH/3777/2007); and either

T15.1   HB 44(2), sch 6; HB60+ 44(2), sch 6; NIHB 41(2), sch 7; NIHB60+ 42(2), sch 7

T15.1(a) HB sch 6 para 1; HB60+ sch 6 para 26; NIHB sch 7 para 1; NIHB60+ sch 7 para 26

T15.1(b) HB sch 6 para 4(a); HB60+ sch 6 para 4(a); NIHB sch 7 para 4(a); NIHB60+ sch 7 para 4(a)

T15.1(c) HB sch 6 para 4(b); HB60+ sch 6 para 4(b); NIHB sch 7 para 4(b); NIHB60+ sch 7 para 4(b)

T15.1(d) HB sch 6 paras 2, 27, 28; HB60+ sch 6 paras 1-3; NIHB sch 7 paras 2, 28,29; NIHB60+ sch 7 paras 1-3

T15.1(e) HB sch 6 para 25; HB60+ sch 6 para 6; NIHB sch 7 para 26; NIHB60+ sch 7 para 6

- they are now a lone parent and live in it as their home (in this case there is no time limit); or
- you ceased to occupy it within the past 26 weeks (this time limit cannot be extended).

(f) A home and any other premises you are taking reasonable steps to dispose of, and began doing so within the past 26 weeks*.

(g) Any property you will not own until a future event occurs (for example you reach a particular age). This is called a 'reversionary interest'. (But for a life interest/life rent see para 15.31.)

Money relating to property

Working age HB claims: disregards (h) to (m)

(h) Money which:

- is from the sale of your former home (including compensation for compulsory purchase but not a home loss payment) and which you intend to use to buy a home within 26 weeks* of the date of sale; or
- was deposited with a housing association as a condition of occupying your home and which you intend to use to buy a home within 26 weeks* of the date the deposit was returned (DMG chapter 28 para 295330).

This disregard does not apply if you haven't yet decided what to do with the money (CH/2255/2006).

(i) A local authority grant you received as a council tenant within the past 26 weeks*, for:

- buying a home; or
- carrying out repairs or alterations to make a future home fit for occupation.

(j) Insurance or compensation payments you received within the past 26 weeks* for repairs or replacements following loss or damage to your home or personal possessions.

(k) Any other payments received within the past 26 weeks* solely for essential repairs or improvements to your home.

(l) Money deposited with a housing association as a condition of occupying your home.

(m) Tax refunds for interest on a mortgage, or on a loan for home repairs or improvements.

T15.1(f)   HB sch 6 para 26; HB60+ sch 6 para 7; NIHB sch 7 para 27; NIHB60+ sch 7 para 7

T15.1(g)   HB sch 6 para 7; NIHB sch 7 para 7

T15.1(h)   HB 2(1) definition: 'housing association', sch 6 paras 3, 11(b); NIHB 2(1) definition: 'housing association', sch 7 paras 3, 11(a)

T15.1(i)   HB sch 6 para 38; NIHB sch 7 para 39

T15.1(j)   HB sch 6 para 10(a); NIHB sch 7 para 10(a)

T15.1(k)   HB sch 6 para 10(b);;NIHB sch 7 para 10(b);

T15.1(l)   HB 2(1) definition: 'housing association', sch 6 para 11(a); NIHB 2(1) definition: 'housing association', sch 7 para 11(a)

Pension age HB claims: disregards (n) to (p)

(n) Any money paid to you (or deposited in your name) within the past year for the sole purpose of buying a home. For example this can include money from the sale of your former home, compensation for compulsory purchase, local authority grants, and gifts or loans from relatives or friends.

(o) Insurance or compensation payments you received within the past year for repairs or replacements following loss or damage to your home or personal possessions.

(p) Any other payments you received within the past year solely for essential repairs or improvements to your home or a future home.

Extending the 26-week time limits

* The time limits marked with an asterisk can be extended if it is reasonable to do so in the circumstances. But the time limit in (h) is not extended if your only reason for needing longer is that you are taking a hard line in negotiations about your share of the money from the sale of your home (CH/2255/2006).

Examples: Property

1. The home of a relative

A man owns a house where his mother lives. She is aged 87. He claims HB on the flat he is renting.

■ The value of the house is disregarded: see table 15.1(b).

2. A couple end their relationship

A couple jointly own a house where they live with their school-age children. They decide to end their relationship. The man moves out and rents a flat. He claims HB there. The woman remains in the home with the children.

■ His share of the value of the house is disregarded: see table 15.1(e).

3. A new partner moves in

Nine months after the man moved out (see example 2) the woman's new partner moves in with her and the children.

■ The man's share of the value of the house is no longer disregarded, because the woman is no longer a lone parent and because more than 26 weeks have passed since he moved out: see table 15.1(e).

T15.1(m)   HB sch 6 para 21; NIHB sch 7 para 22

T15.1(n)   HB60+ sch 6 paras 18,20(a); NIHB60+ sch 7 paras 18,20(a)

T15.1(o)   HB60+ sch 6 paras 18,19; NIHB60+ sch 7 paras 18,19

T15.1(p)   HB60+ sch 6 paras 18,20(b); NIHB60+ sch 7 paras 18,20(b)

4. The house is put up for sale

The former partners (see examples 2 and 3) decide to sell the house. They put it on the market.

■ The man's share of the value of the house is disregarded for 26 weeks, or longer if this is reasonable to allow a sale to take place: see table 15.1(f).

5. Money for buying a home

A woman sells her home and moves to a rented flat in a new area while she looks for a new property to buy. She claims HB on the flat. She has £240,000 from the sale, and a further £50,000 which her brother gave her towards a new home.

■ If she is over state pension credit age, both these amounts are disregarded for one year, but no longer: see table 15.1(n).

■ If she is under state pension credit age, only the money from the sale is disregarded, and only for 26 weeks or longer if reasonable: see table 15.1(h).

6. A property which is rented out

A couple own a house which is rented out to a tenant through an agency. The house has a market value of £200,000 and there is an outstanding mortgage on it of £175,000. They claim HB on a flat they are renting.

■ The market value of the house is £200,000.

■ Deduct 10% for sales costs, leaving £180,000.

■ Deduct the outstanding mortgage, leaving £5,000.

■ This £5,000 is their capital for HB purposes.

■ The rent they receive on the house also counts as their capital (not income), after allowing for the mortgage interest, agency fees, and other outgoings they pay on it: see table 13.8(b).

Life interest and life rent

15.31   If you have a life interest (or in Scotland a life rent) in property or any other asset, this means you have the right to use it until you die, or someone else dies. Unless the property or other asset is disregarded (see for example table 15.1), the value of the life interest or life rent (if it has a value) is counted as your capital.

Personal possessions

15.32   The value of your personal possessions is disregarded. This means any physical assets apart from land, property and business assets (R(H)7/08). Payments for loss or damage to your personal possessions are also disregarded (see table 15.1(j) and (o)). But in working age claims, personal possessions you bought with the purpose of gaining HB are counted as your capital (see para 15.63).

15.31   HB 44(1); HB60+ 44(1); NIHB 42(1); NIHB60+ 42(1)

15.32   HB sch 6 para 12; HB60+ sch 6 para 8; NIHB sch 7 para 12; NIHB60+ sch 7 para 8

Self-employed business assets

15.33   If you are self-employed (see para 14.27) your business assets are disregarded:

(a)   while you are self-employed;

(b)   if you are not self-employed because of sickness or disability but intend to return to the self-employment, for 26 weeks, or longer if you reasonably need longer to return;

(c)   if you have ceased to be self-employed, for as long as you reasonably need to dispose of the assets.

'Business assets' means assets held in the course of your self-employment (CH/4258/2004). In some circumstances they can include property you rent out, though this is unlikely if you just rent out one property as a single letting ([2016] UKUT 357 (AAC)). Business capital is disregarded (as a business asset) if it is 'part of the fund employed and risked in the business' (R (SB) 4/85 para 11), which is unlikely to be the case unless you keep it separate from your personal savings. But rent and other income you receive on your business assets counts as part of your self-employed earnings (see para 14.28).

Company ownership

15.34   If you are a company owner the full value of the company is counted as your capital. If you are in a partnership, this means your share of the full value. The value of a company is always at least equal to the value of all its assets minus the sum of all its liabilities. (Your income counts as your employed earnings: see para 14.6.)

15.35   You are counted as having notional capital (see paras 15.56-58) if:

(a)   you are not the owner of a company or a partner in it; and

(b)   you are not engaged in activities in the course of the company's business; but

(c)   your involvement in the company is equivalent to ownership or partnership.

Your notional capital is assessed as in para 15.34, and the value of your actual interest in the company is disregarded.

Trusts and compensation

15.36   This section gives the rules for trusts, personal injury payments, and other compensation and gallantry payments. (For compensation relating to property and possessions see table 15.1.)

Trusts

15.37   Assets held in a trust, such as cash, investments or property are:

(a)   legally owned by the trustees (or trustee) of the trust; and

(b)   beneficially owned by the beneficiary (or beneficiaries) of the trust.

15.33   HB sch 6 para 8(1),(2); HB60+ sch 6 paras 9,10; NIHB sch 7 para 8(1),(2); NIHB60+ sch 7 paras 9,10

15.34   HB 44(1); HB60+ 44(1); NIHB 41(1); NIHB60+ 42(1)

15.35   HB 49(5),(6);HB60+ 47(3),(4);NIHB 46(5),(6);NIHB60+ 45(3),(4)

The trustees have a duty to use the assets under the terms of the trust for the benefit of the beneficiary, for example by making payments to them. Paras 15.38-41 explain how this is assessed.

If you are a beneficiary of a trust

15.38 Capital held in a trust for you counts in full as your capital, but see para 15.39 for exceptions. If you are not the only beneficiary of the trust, it is your share of the capital which is taken into account (see para 15.18).

15.39 Capital held in a trust for you is disregarded:

(a) if you cannot obtain it until a particular event occurs, for example when you reach a certain age (this is called a 'reversionary' trust); or

(b) if it relates to a personal injury (see para 15.43); or

(c) in pension age HB claims if:

■ it is property, and

■ the trustees make payments to you, or could do so.

15.40 If you receive a payment of capital from a trust (whether the capital in the trust itself is counted or disregarded):

(a) it is disregarded if any of the disregards in this chapter apply to it (see for example table 15.1(k), (n) and (p));

(b) otherwise it counts in full as your capital.

For payments of income from a trust see para 13.36.

If you are a trustee of a trust

15.41 Capital you hold as a trustee is wholly disregarded. But to count as a trustee it is not enough just to say that you are holding money (or other assets) for someone else, or plan to give it to them. You must have received it on clearly stated terms requiring you to hold it for them, or you must have clearly and consistently expressed that you hold it for them and have given up all intentions of using it for yourself (R(IS)1/90). If you meet these conditions it is not necessary for the trust to be legally documented ([2012] UKUT 115 (AAC)).

Government sponsored trust funds

15.42 Any payment of capital or income you receive from the following is disregarded:

(a) the Independent Living Funds (which help severely disabled people live independently);

(b) the Caxton Fund, the Eileen Trust, 'the Fund', Macfarlane Trusts, MFET Ltd, Scottish Infected Blood Support Scheme, and the Skipton Fund (for people infected with HIV or hepatitis C from NHS blood and other products);

15.38   HB 44(1); HB60+ 44(1); NIHB 41(1); NIHB60+ 42(1)

15.39   HB sch 6 paras 7,14; HB60+ sch 6 para 30; NIHB sch 7 paras 7,14; NIHB60+ sch 7 para 32

15.40   HB 44; HB60+ 44(1),(2); NIHB 41; NIHB60+ 42(1),(2)

15.42   HB 2(1) definitions: 'Independent Living Fund' etc, sch 5 para 35, sch 6 paras 24, 34, 55; HB60+ 2(1), 29(1), sch 6 paras 14,16,30; NIHB 2(1), sch 6 para 37, sch 7 paras 25,35,52; NIHB60+ 2(1), 27(1), sch 7 paras 14,16,32

(c)   the Variant Creutzfeldt-Jacob Disease Trust (for people with vCJD and their families); and

(d)   the London Bombings Relief Charitable Fund (for victims of the bombings on 7th July 2005 and their families).

The disregards in (a), (b) and (d) have no time limit. The disregard in (c) has no time limit if the payment is to the person with vCJD or their partner or surviving partner, but is limited to two years if it is to a parent or guardian of a child with vCJD. The disregards in (b) to (d) can continue if the payment is passed on to a relative as a gift or inheritance (but the usual HB definition of 'relative' does not always apply here). For further details see GM para BW2.620.

Personal injury payments

15.43   The following payments of capital are disregarded if they relate to a personal injury you or your partner have had:

(a)   damages for personal injury which are:

   ▪ held by a court and administered by it, or

   ▪ held by someone else and can only be used under a court order or direction;

(b)   any payment for personal injury which is held in a trust; and

(c)   any other payment for personal injury except for capital paid to you by a trust (but see para 15.40(a)).

The disregards in (a) and (b) have no time limit. The disregard in (c) has no time limit in pension age HB claims, but in working age HB claims it is limited to 52 weeks from the day you receive the first or only payment. (It does not start again if you receive a further payment for that injury.) The 52 weeks is called a 'grace period' because it should give you time to form a trust to hold the money (see (b) above) or invest it in an annuity (see para 15.25(b)).

15.44   Payments of income you receive for a personal injury to you or your partner are wholly disregarded. For example this includes income paid to you by a trust or from an annuity in which a personal injury payment was invested. In pension age HB claims, payments of income are also disregarded if they are paid to you by order of a court for a personal injury to your child.

Examples: Personal injury payments

1. A working age HB claim

A woman in her 20s is awarded £500,000 for a personal injury. It is paid into her bank account.

   ▪ This is disregarded for 52 weeks (see para 15.43(c)).

Five months later a trust is formed, with her parents and solicitor as the trustees and her as the beneficiary. The whole of the personal injury payment is paid into the trust.

   ▪ This is now disregarded without time limit (see para 15.43(b)).

15.43   HB sch 6 paras 14, 14A, 45, 46; HB60+ sch 6 para 17; NIHB sch 7 paras 14,15,45; NIHB60+ sch 7 para 17

15.44   HB sch 5 para 14(1)(c)-(e); HB60+ sch 5 paras 14,15; NIHB sch 6 para 14(1)(c)-(e); NIHB60+ sch 6 paras 15,16

The trust pays her an income of £70 per week.

- This is disregarded in the assessment of her income (see para 15.44).

The trust later pays her a lump sum of £15,000 for the cost of adapting her home to improve wheelchair access.

- This is disregarded for 26 weeks, or longer if this is reasonable, to allow the work to take place (see para 15.40(a) and table 15.1(k)).

2. A pension age HB claim

A man in his 70s is awarded £500,000 for a personal injury. It is paid into his bank account.

- This is disregarded without time limit (see para 15.43(c)).

Payments compensating for death of a parent

15.45   If you are under 18, compensation you receive for the death of a parent is wholly disregarded if it is held by a court and administered by it, or held by someone else and can only be used under a court order or direction.

Second World War payments

15.46   Payments of compensation are wholly disregarded if they were paid because you, your partner, or your or your partner's deceased husband, wife or civil partner:

(a) were a slave labourer or forced labourer; or

(b) suffered property loss or personal injury; or

(c) were a parent of a child who died; or

(d) were imprisoned or interned by the Japanese

during the Second World War. There is no time limit. The disregard in (d) is always £10,000 (which is the standard amount paid in these cases), and £10,000 is disregarded from the total of your capital without any time limit (so you do not need to keep track of the money).

The families of the disappeared

15.47   In Northern Ireland, compensation paid to the families of the disappeared is disregarded for 52 weeks from the date of payment.

Gallantry payments

15.48   Payments you receive as a holder of the Victoria Cross or George Cross, and similar payments, are wholly disregarded:

(a) in working age HB claims in the assessment of both your income and your capital;

(b) in pension age HB claims in the assessment of your income.

15.45   HB sch 6 para 45, 46; NIHB sch 7 para 45

15.46   HB sch 6 paras 54, 56; HB60+ sch 6 paras 13,15; NIHB sch 7 paras 51,53; NIHB60+ sch 7 paras 13,15

15.47   NIHB sch 7 para 58; NIHB60+ sch 7 para 27

15.48   HB sch 5 para 10, sch 6 para 47; HB60+ 29(1); NIHB sch 6 para 11, sch 7 para 46; NIHB60+ 27(1)

Other capital

15.49   This section gives the rules for benefits which are paid as a lump sum, arrears of benefits, charitable and voluntary payments, loans, and other kinds of capital.

Benefits paid as a lump sum

15.50   Lump sum payments of the following are wholly disregarded:

(a) social fund payments (winter fuel payments, cold weather payments, Sure Start maternity grant and funeral expenses payment);

(b) government and related payments to disabled people to help with obtaining or retaining employment;

(c) payments from government work programme training schemes;

(d) in working age HB claims:

- adoption payments,

- special guardianship payments,

- payments to avoid taking children into care, and

- payments to care leavers;

(e) community care payments;

(f) direct care payments;

(g) supporting people payments;

(h) 'local welfare assistance' (para 25.34); and

(i) discretionary housing payments (para 25.1) and in Northern Ireland welfare supplementary payments (para 25.19).

All are also disregarded as income.

15.51   Bereavement payment is a lump sum paid for deaths occurring before 6th April 2017. It counts in full as capital. The initial lump sum of bereavement support payment (for deaths occurring after 5th April 2017) is disregarded for 52 weeks (HB circular A6/2017).

Arrears of benefits and compensation relating to benefits

15.52   Table 15.2 explains when the capital value of arrears of benefits is disregarded. The same rules apply to payments compensating for non-payment of the benefits. Arrears of benefits not included in the table are taken into account as described in para 15.11.

15.50(a)   HB sch 6 para 20; HB60+ sch 6 paras 18, 21(1),(2)(n); NIHB sch 7 para 21; NIHB60+ sch 7 paras 18, 21(1),(2)(m)

15.50(b)   HB sch 6 paras 43, 44; NIHB sch 7 para 44

15.50(c)   HB 46(7),(8), sch 6 paras A2,A3, 8(3),(4), 35,49,52,55; NIHB 43(7),(8), sch 7 paras 8(3),(4), 36,48,52

15.50(d)   HB sch 6 paras 19,19A,59,60; NIHB sch 7 paras 20,20A,56,57

15.50(e),(f) HB sch 6 para 58; HB60+ sch 6 para 26D; NIHB sch 7 para 55; NIHB60+ sch 7 para 28C

15.50(g)   HB sch 6 para 57; HB60+ sch 6 paras 18,21(1)(e); NIHB sch 7 para 54; NIHB60+ sch 7 paras 18,21(1)(e)

15.50(h)   HB sch 6 para 20A; HB60+ sch 6 paras 18,21(1)(f)

15.50(i)   HB sch 6 para 9(1)(d); HB60+ sch 6 paras 18,21(1),(2)(k); NIHB sch 7 para 9(1)(d); NIHB60+ sch 7 paras 18,21(1),(2)(j)

15.51   HB 44(1), sch 6 para 61; HB60+ 29(1)(j)(xiii), 44(1), sch 6 para 26H; NIHB 41(1), sch 7 para 59; NIHB60+ 27(1)(h)(xi), 42(1), sch 7 para 28D

Table 15.2 **Capital disregards: arrears of benefits**

(a) Disregarded arrears

Arrears of all the following are disregarded when your capital is assessed:

- income-based JSA
- income-related ESA
- income support
- state pension credit (both guarantee credit and savings credit)
- universal credit
- WTC and CTC
- disability living allowance
- personal independence payment
- attendance allowance, or constant attendance allowance paid with an industrial injury or war disablement pension
- HB and the former council tax benefit (but not council tax rebates)
- discretionary housing payments (para 25.1) and in Northern Ireland welfare supplementary payments (para 25.19).

(b) Standard time limit

The disregard lasts for 52 weeks in working age HB claims, and one year in pension age HB claims, in each case beginning with the day you received the arrears.

(c) Extended time limit

If the arrears:

- are £5,000 or more;
- are paid while you are on HB; and
- are because you were underpaid due to official error (see para 17.63),

the disregard continues for as long as you or your partner remain continuously on HB (including periods one of you remains continuously on HB after the other one's death).

(d) Arrears of war disablement and bereavement pensions

Arrears of the war disablement and bereavement pensions in table 13.4(a) are disregarded:

- for 52 weeks in working age HB claims (the extended time limit does not apply);
- without time limit in pension age HB claims.

Note: The rules in (a) to (c) above also apply to payments compensating for non-payment of the benefits.

T15.2   CBA 123 definition: 'income related benefit'; HB 46(9), sch 6 paras 9,37,39; HB60+ 44(3), sch 6 paras 18, 21(1)(a)-(d),(2), 22, 26B;
NICBA 122; NIHB 43(8), sch 7 paras 9,38,40; NIHB60+ 42(3), sch 7 paras 18, 21(1)(a)-(d),(2), 22,28A

Charitable and voluntary payments

15.53   Payments of capital you receive which are charitable and/or voluntary are counted as your capital. But in working age HB claims, payments in kind (in other words in goods not money) are disregarded. For payments of income see para 13.30.

Loans

15.54   Money which was loaned to you (and which you still have) is counted as your capital. But in pension age HB claims, loans for buying a home are disregarded (see table 15.1(n)). And the following count as income, not capital:

(a)   student loans (see para 22.23);

(b)   in working age HB claims, career development loans (see table 13.9(n));

(c)   in pension age HB claims, payments from an equity release scheme (see para 13.34).

Other loans can be counted as income if the council has clear evidence that they should be (R(IS) 6/03, R(H) 8/08). This is likely to mean that (c) above also applies in working age HB claims.

Other kinds of capital

15.55   If you have any other kind of capital, it is counted in full. But for payments you receive as an earner see chapter 14, and for payments you receive as a student see chapter 22.

Notional capital

15.56   This section explains when you are counted as having capital you do not in fact have. This is called 'notional capital'.

Types of notional capital

15.57   In working age HB claims, you can be counted as having notional capital when:

(a)   you have deprived yourself of capital (see paras 15.60-62);

(b)   there is capital available to you (see paras 13.50 and 13.52);

(c)   you are paid capital on behalf of someone else (see paras 13.53 and 13.55);

(d)   someone else is paid capital on your behalf (see paras 13.54-55);

(e)   a non-dependant has more income and capital than you (see para 13.57); or

(f)   you are counted as a company owner or partner (see para 15.35).

15.58   In pension age HB claims, you can be counted as having notional capital when:

(a)   you have deprived yourself of capital (see paras 15.60-62);

(b)   a non-dependant has more income and capital than you (see para 13.57); or

(c)   you are counted as a company owner or partner (see para 15.35).

15.53   HB 44(1), 46(6), sch 6 para 34; HB60+ 44(1); NIHB 41(1), 43(6), sch 7 para 35; NIHB60+ 42(1)

15.55   HB 44(1); HB60+ 44(1); NIHB 41(1); NIHB60+ 42(1)

Assessing notional capital

15.59   If you are counted as having notional capital, it is assessed in the same way as actual capital. All the rules and disregards given earlier in this chapter apply. This means this section does not apply if you are on a passport benefit (except as described in table 15.3(e)).

Capital you have deprived yourself of

15.60   If you have deprived yourself of capital, it is counted as your notional capital. To 'deprive' yourself of capital means:

(a)   you have disposed of it (for example by spending it or giving or lending it to someone); and

(b)   your purpose in doing so was to make yourself entitled to HB, or to more HB (we use 'gain HB' to cover both these).

This is called the 'deprivation of capital rule'.

15.61   Table 15.3 explains how the rule works. See paras 15.62-64 for exceptions and further details. See paras 15.59 and 15.65-69 for how notional capital is assessed and how it reduces.

Table 15.3 **Deprivation of capital: case law**

This table is about the deprivation of capital rule (see paras 15.60-62).

(a)   *The test of purpose:* To count as depriving yourself of capital, 'the test is one of purpose'. Gaining HB must have formed 'a positive part of your planning'. [2011] UKUT 500 (AAC).

(b)   *Thinking about the consequences:* You can only count as depriving yourself if you knew what you were doing. If you did not think about the consequences, you cannot have acted with the purpose of gaining HB. [2011] UKUT 500 (AAC). And if you had no legitimate choice but to spend capital, this cannot count as deprivation: [2015] UKUT 15 (AAC).

(c)   *Your personal circumstances:* Your mental state and capabilities are taken into account. A schizophrenic man without an appointee, who lived in 'an intolerable level of chaos', spent almost all of a big windfall on 'alcohol and high living'. He did not count as depriving himself, because it was not shown that he appreciated what he was doing or what the consequences would be. R(H)1/06.

(d)   *Mixed motives:* If you had some other reason for disposing of capital (which is 'almost always' the case), you count as depriving yourself of it if gaining HB was 'a significant operative purpose' of doing so. This includes looking at 'whether, given [your] knowledge, it was reasonable in all the circumstances' to act as you did, bearing in mind your obligations (for example, to support yourself, and to other people). [2009] UKUT 145 (AAC) para 9, which cited CJSA/1425/2005 para 40.

15.59   HB 49(7); HB60+ 47(5); NIHB 46(7); NIHB60+ 45(5)
15.60   HB 49(1); HB60+ 47(1); NIHB 46(1); NIHB60+ 45(1)

(e) *Passport benefits and HB:* If you deprived yourself of capital to gain a passport benefit, you also count as depriving yourself to gain HB if you plainly expected that getting the passport benefit would lead to getting HB. [2009] UKUT 145 (AAC) para 3.

(f) *Buying an asset whose capital value is disregarded:* Even if what you bought is disregarded, you count as depriving yourself if your purpose was gaining HB (see para 15.63). [2009] UKUT 145 (AAC) para 16, which cited R(SB) 40/85 and R(IS) 8/04.

(g) *Buying personal possessions:* In working age HB claims, if you bought a personal possession with the purpose of gaining HB (in this case, a caravan) its value counts as actual (not notional) capital (see para 15.63). [2009] UKUT 145 (AAC) para 16.

(h) *Providing receipts:* If you are asked to provide receipts for capital you have spent, this 'is primarily to enable [the council] to be satisfied the money has not been retained' (see para 15.63). But it 'can also form the basis as to the reasonableness of the expenditure'. [2009] UKUT 145 (AAC) para 12.

(i) *Seeking to recover the money:* It is irrelevant whether you seek to recover money you deprived yourself of. [2009] UKUT 96 (AAC).

Exceptions

15.62   In pension age HB claims, the deprivation of capital rule does not apply to capital you have used to:

(a)   buy goods or services which are reasonable in your circumstances; or

(b)   repay or reduce a debt you owe.

In working age and pension age HB claims, the rule does not apply if you are on a passport benefit, except as described in table 15.3(e).

Distinguishing notional capital from actual capital

15.63   In general terms, capital you have is your actual capital, and capital you disposed of to gain HB is your notional capital. The Upper Tribunal has summarised the following possibilities ([2009] UKUT 145 (AAC) paras 16, 19):

(a)   if you have spent capital on an item which counts as capital (for example shares), the item is your actual capital;

(b)   if you have spent capital with the purpose of gaining HB (and (a) does not apply), this is your notional capital;

(c)   the exception to (b) is that in working age HB claims, if you bought personal possessions with the purpose of gaining HB, they are counted as your actual capital;

(d)   if you spent capital without the purpose of gaining HB (and (a) does not apply), this is neither actual nor notional capital;

(e)   if you say you have spent capital but in fact you still have it (for example in an undisclosed bank account), this is your actual capital.

For pension age HB claims, see also para 15.62.

15.62   HB60+ 47(2); NIHB60+ 45(2)

15.63   HB 44, 49(1), sch 6 para 12; HB60+ 44(1),(2), 47(1),(2); NIHB 41, 46(1), sch 7 para 12; NIHB60+ 42(1),(2), 45(1),(2)

15.64 There are also differences in other situations. For example:

(a) if one person holds capital on behalf of another, there are rules about whether it is your actual capital (see paras 15.8-9);

(b) the exception is that in working age HB claims, if one person is paid capital on behalf of another, there are rules about whether it is your notional capital (see paras 13.53-55).

How notional capital reduces

15.65 If you have notional capital because of the deprivation of capital rule (see paras 15.60-62), your notional capital reduces each week: see paras 15.66-69. This is called the 'diminishing notional capital rule'. It is illustrated in the example.

The amount of the reduction

15.66 The reduction equals the amount of HB and other benefits you have lost as a result of having notional capital: see paras 15.67-69. But the only benefits taken into account are HB, JSA(IB), ESA(IR), IS, SPC and (for periods before 1st April 2013) council tax benefit. If the figures for these (apart from HB) relate to a part-week, they are converted to a weekly equivalent.

15.67 In weeks in which you qualify for HB, the reduction equals the amount you have lost in that particular week.

15.68 In weeks in which you do not qualify for HB, the reduction is made at a fixed rate. This equals the amount you lost in the most recent of the following weeks:

(a) the week your notional capital was first taken into account; or

(b) the first week you did not qualify for HB; or

(c) any week in which the fixed rate is recalculated (see para 15.69).

15.69 The fixed rate is recalculated only if you make a new unsuccessful claim for HB (in other words you claim but do not qualify for HB) at least 26 weeks after the fixed rate was:

(a) first calculated (see para 15.68(a) or (b)); or

(b) most recently recalculated (as described in this paragraph).

The new fixed rate is then used if it is higher than (or equal to) the old fixed rate. If it is lower, the old fixed rate continues (but this still counts as a recalculation for (b) above). The fixed rate is not recalculated if you make an unsuccessful claim for HB within the 26 weeks (but the old fixed rate continues). If you make a successful claim for HB (at any time) see para 15.67.

15.65   HB 49(1), 50; HB60+ 47(1), 48; NIHB 46(1), 47; NIHB60+ 45(1), 46

15.66   HB 50(1)-(4),(8); HB60+ 48(1)-(4),(8); NIHB 47(1)-(4),(8); NIHB60+ 46(1)-(4),(8)

15.67   HB 50(1)(a),(2),(3),(8); HB60+ 48(1)(a),(2),(3),(8); NIHB 47(1)(a),(2),(3),(8); NIHB60+ 46(1)(a),(2),(3),(8)

15.68   HB 50(1)(b),(4),(8); HB60+ 48(1)(b),(4),(8); NIHB 47(1)(b),(4),(8); NIHB60+ 46(1)(b),(4),(8)

15.69   HB 50(1)(b),(5)-(8); HB60+ 48(1)(b),(5)-(8); NIHB 47(1)(b),(5)-(8); NIHB60+ 46(1)(b),(5)-(8)

Example: Diminishing notional capital

Catalina Pontilo claims HB

Based on her circumstances, including her actual capital of £15,000, she would qualify for HB of £50 pw (but no other benefits). However, she has deprived herself of capital of £5,000.

- Notional capital   £5,000
- Actual capital   £15,000
- Total capital   £20,000

She does not qualify for HB. The notional capital means she has lost £50 per week. This is the fixed rate reduction.

Catalina P. claims HB 20 weeks later

- Notional capital (reduced by 20 x £50 = £1,000)   £4,000
- Actual capital (has reduced to)   £13,000
- Total capital   £17,000

She does not qualify for HB. The fixed rate of reduction is not recalculated (less than 26 weeks have passed).

Catalina claims HB 10 further weeks later

- Notional capital (further reduced by 10 x £50 = £500)   £3,500
- Actual capital (has not changed)   £13,000
- Total capital   £16,500

She does not qualify for HB. The fixed rate of reduction is recalculated (at least 26 weeks have passed). But the new figure turns out to be £40 per week, so the existing £50 per week fixed rate continues.

Cat claims HB 20 further weeks later

- Notional capital (further reduced by 20 x £50 = £1,000)   £2,500
- Actual capital (has reduced to)   £12,000
- Total capital   £14,500

She qualifies for and is awarded HB. Actual rates of reduction are used while she is on HB.

Chapter 16 **Decisions, payments and appeals**

- HB decisions and notices: see paras 16.1-12.
- HB payments: rebates, allowances and payments on account: see paras 16.13-28.
- Paying HB to someone on your behalf: see paras 16.29-33.
- Paying HB to your landlord or agent: see paras 16.34-66.
- HB disputes and appeals: see paras 16.67-98.

Decisions and decision notices

16.1 This section explains how soon the council should make a decision about your claim for HB and about changes to your HB, who decision notices are sent to, and what information the council's notices should contain.

Decisions about claims

16.2 The council must:

(a) decide your claim for HB within 14 days of getting the information and evidence it requires, or as soon as reasonably practicable after that; and

(b) issue a decision notice on the day it makes this decision, or as soon as reasonably practicable after that.

The council must decide your claim and issue a decision notice even if you do not provide the information and evidence (see para 5.26), but does not have to decide a claim you have withdrawn.

Other decisions

16.3 The council must also:

(a) decide about changes to your HB, and about any overpayments that occur; and

(b) issue a decision notice within 14 days of making these decisions, or as soon as reasonably practicable after that.

Decision notices

16.4 Decision notices must:

(a) be in writing;

(b) contain the information described in paras 16.5-7; and

(c) be issued to you and other 'persons affected' by the decision: see paras 16.68-70.

16.2   HB 89, 90(1)(a); HB60+ 70, 71(1)(a); NIHB 85, 86(1)(a); NIHB60+ 66, 67(1)(a)

16.3   HB 89(1), 90(1)(b); HB60+ 70(1), 71(1)(b); NIHB 85(1), 86(1)(b); NIHB60+ 66(1), 67(1)(b)

16.4   HB 90(1); HB60+ 71(1); NIHB 86(1); NIHB60+ 67(1)

Information in decision notices

16.5   A decision notice issued to you (or to someone acting for you: see paras 5.5-7) must contain the following:

(a) if the decision is about your claim for HB, the notices must contain the information in table 16.1;

(b) if the decision notice is about a change to your HB , the notice must say what the change is (and may also contain the information in table 16.1);

(c) if the decision is about an overpayment of HB, the notice must contain the information in paras 18.68-69.

16.6   There are also rules for decision notices issued to:

(a) landlords and agents about paying HB to them: see paras 16.59-60;

(b) landlords, agents and others when the council decides an overpayment is recoverable from them: see paras 18.68-69.

16.7   Every decision notice (whoever it is issued to) must also contain information about the right to:

(a) obtain a statement of reasons (see para 16.72);

(b) ask for a reconsideration (see para 16.75);

(c) appeal, if the right to appeal applies to the decision (see para 16.81);

and how to do these things.

Table 16.1 **Decision notices about claims**

When the council decides your claim for HB, it must issue a decision notice to you containing the following information.

If you are entitled to HB

(a) Your first day of entitlement.

(b) The normal weekly amount of your HB.

(c) If your HB is a rent allowance, when and how often it will be paid (and if it will be paid to your landlord/agent, see paras 16.59-60).

(d) Your duty to notify changes of circumstances, and examples of what these might be (see para 17.3).

If you are not entitled to HB

(e) The reason why you are not entitled.

(f) If your HB is less than 50p a week, the amount and an explanation that this is below the minimum award (see para 6.7).

16.7   HB 90(1), sch 9 paras 1,7,8; HB60+ 71(1), sch 8 paras 1,7,8; DAR 10; NIHB 86(1), sch 10 paras 1,7,8; NIHB60+ 67(1), sch 9 paras 1,7,8; NIDAR 10

T16.1   HB sch 9 paras 1-10, 13,14; HB60+ sch 8 paras 1-10, 13,14; NIHB sch 10 paras 1-10, 13,14; NIHB60+ sch 9 paras 1-10, 13,14

All cases whether or not you are entitled

(g) Your weekly eligible rent, and in Northern Ireland rates.

(h) If standard deductions were made for fuel, how you can get these changed (see para 8.78).

(i) The amount and category of non-dependant deductions.

(j) Your applicable amount and how it was worked out (unless you are on a passport benefit or universal credit).

(k) Your weekly earned income and weekly unearned income (unless you are on a passport benefit, universal credit or savings credit).

(l) If you are on savings credit, the DWP's figures for your income and capital, any adjustments made to them, and the amount of your savings credit (see para 13.15).

(m) Your rights in relation to the decision (see para 16.7).

(n) Any other information the council considers relevant.

Delays in getting a decision or getting a payment

16.8   The DWP expects councils to make decisions about HB claims and changes within time limits (see paras 16.2-3). It collects information about this (see para 1.34) which is available online [www]. Delays are usually only acceptable when councils' workloads are at their heaviest, for example when benefits are uprated in April. The fact that other councils also have delays is not itself sufficient excuse: R v Liverpool CC ex parte Johnson No 1.

16.9   If the council delays making a decision about your HB, you may be able to complain to the Ombudsman (see para 1.35) or apply for judicial review (see para 1.54). If the council has decided you are entitled to HB but delays paying you, you may be able to take action in the county court or sheriff court to enforce payment: Waveney DC v Jones.

Delays and rent arrears

16.10   In England and Wales, the following protections apply if you are a tenant of a council or registered housing association, and have got into rent arrears while waiting for a decision about your HB claim. These are in the civil procedure rules – pre-action protocol for possession claims by social landlords (28th July 2015) [www].

16.11   Your landlord should not begin possession proceedings against you if:

(a) you have provided all the information and evidence needed to decide your claim,

(b) there is a reasonable expectation that you will qualify for HB, and

(c) you have paid any rent which will not be met by HB.

16.9   HB sch 9 paras 2-5; HB60+ sch 8 paras 2-5; NIHB sch 10 paras 2-5; NIHB60+ sch 9 paras 2-5

16.10   www.gov.uk/government/collections/housing-benefit-and-council-tax-benefit-statistics-on-speed-of-processing--2
         R v Liverpool ex p Johnson (No 1) 23/06/94 QBD unreported

16.11   Waveney DC v Jones 01/12/99 CA 33 HLR 3 www.casetrack.com subscriber site case reference CCRTF/1988/1488/B2

16.12   If possession proceedings are begun against you, the court can order the council dealing with your HB claim:

(a) to explain delays and problems with your HB, and

(b) to pay costs if these are shown to have caused the proceedings.

Payments of HB

16.13   This section explains how and when your HB is paid, how soon the first payment should be made, and who your HB is paid to. You can ask the council to reconsider a decision it makes about any of these things (see para 16.75), but only some of them can be appealed to a tribunal (see para 16.82 and table 16.4).

How HB is paid

16.14   Your HB is paid:

(a) as a rent rebate if you are a council or NIHE tenant: see paras 16.16-17;

(b) as a rent allowance in all other cases: see paras 16.18-66.

But in Northern Ireland, HB for rates is usually paid as a rate rebate: see para 19.18. And if your liability for rates is to Land and Property Services your HB can be paid to them if the circumstances in paragraphs 16.50-53 apply.

16.15   In England, Scotland and Wales there are two exceptions:

(a) if you are renting a houseboat, mobile home or caravan (see table 8.1) and you pay:

■   your mooring charges or site charges to the council, but

■   your rent to someone else (for example a private landlord)

your HB for each of these is paid as a rent allowance;

(b) if you pay your rent to the council because your home is subject to a management order or empty dwelling management order (EDMO), your HB is paid as a rent allowance.

Rent rebates

16.16   If your HB is paid as rent rebate (see paras 16.14-15), this means it is paid straight into your rent account. You do not get a payment yourself, but you have less rent to pay (and in some cases no rent to pay).

When rent rebates are paid

16.17   The first payment into your rent account should be within 14 days of your HB claim, or as soon as reasonably practicable after that. Payments are then usually made into your rent account on the days your rent is due.

16.12   https://www.justice.gov.uk/courts/procedure-rules/civil/protocol/pre-action-protocol-for-possession-claims-by-social-landlords

16.14   AA 134(1A),(1B),(2); NIAA 126(1),(2); NIHB 88,93(5); NIHB60+ 69,74(5)

16.15   AA 134(1A); HB 91A; HB60+ 72A

16.16   AA 134(1A); NIAA 126(1)(b),(c)

16.17   HB 91(3); HB60+ 72(3); NIHB 87(3); NIHB60+ 68(3)

Rent allowances

16.18 If your HB is paid as a rent allowance (see paras 16.14-15), this means it is paid:

(a) to you (the HB claimant);

(b) to someone on your behalf (see paras 16.29-33); or

(c) to your landlord or agent (see paras 16.34-66)

The council decides how to make payments, and should take into account your (or the payee's) reasonable needs and convenience. Usually the payments are made by credit transfer straight into a bank account or (increasingly rare) by cheque.

16.19 The council should not insist on paying you by credit transfer if:

(a) you do not have a bank account: R (Spiropoulos) v Brighton and Hove CC (see also GM para A6.120). But the council may be able to tell you which banks in your area offer basic accounts, and may give you a letter confirming your identity to help you open an account; or

(b) your bank is unlikely to let you take the money out because you have an overdraft. Although the 'right of first appropriation' in common law says you have the right to instruct your bank that the money will be used to pay your rent rather than reduce your overdraft, this right can be difficult to insist upon (for example, sometimes banks insist on a fresh instruction for each payment).

When rent allowances are paid

16.20 The first payment of your rent allowance should be within 14 days of your HB claim, or as soon as reasonably practicable after that. If the council cannot do this, it should make a payment on account: see paras 16.23-28.

16.21 The council decides how often payments are made after that, and should take into account how often and on what dates your rent is due. It can make:

(a) payments to you (or someone on your behalf):

- every two weeks – you can insist on this if your HB is more than £2 a week,

- every four weeks,

- every calendar month, or

- every week: see para 16.22;

(b) payments to your landlord or agent:

- every four weeks,

- every calendar month (but only if your rent is due calendar monthly).

The first payment to a landlord or agent can be for a shorter period if they have other tenants on HB. This is to allow all of the HB payments to them to be made on the same dates.

16.18   AA 134(1A),(1B); HB 91(1),94; HB60+ 72(1),75; NIAA 126(1); NIHB 87(1),91; NIHB60+ 68(1),72

16.19   R (Spiropoulos) v Brighton and Hove CC 06/02/07 QBD [2007] EWHC 342 (Admin) www.bailii.org/ew/cases/EWHC/Admin/2007/342.html

16.20   HB 91(3); HB60+ 72(3); NIHB 87(3); NIHB60+ 68(3)

16.21   HB 92; HB60+ 73; NIHB 89; NIHB60+ 70

16.22 The council pays you weekly if:

(a) paying you over a longer period is likely to lead to an overpayment; or

(b) your rent is due weekly and it is in your interests to be paid weekly.

For example, (b) could apply if you have difficulty budgeting. The council is not expected to check whether this is the case, but should take account of information provided by you or by someone on your behalf, including a social worker or key worker (GM para A6.143).

Payments on account

16.23 A 'payment on account' is an estimated amount of HB. The council must make a payment on account if:

(a) your HB will be paid as a rent allowance (see paras 16.14-15);

(b) the council is unable to decide your claim within 14 days of getting it; and

(c) this is not because you have failed to provide information and evidence: see paras 16.24-25.

The rules about who it is paid to, and how it is paid, are the same as for rent allowances (see paras 16.18-19).

16.24 The council does not have to make a payment on account if:

(a) it or the DWP has asked you to provide information or evidence reasonably required to decide your HB claim (see paras 5.13-21; and

(b) you have failed without good cause to provide it.

16.25 But the council does have to make a payment on account if:

(a) it has asked someone other than you for the information and evidence (GM para A6.161). For example it has asked:

- your landlord or agent for confirmation of your rent,

- the rent officer for a determination about your rent,

- the DWP for confirmation of your benefit entitlement, or

- the Home Office for confirmation of your conditions of entry or stay; or

(b) you have not provided information or evidence because :

- you have not been asked for it, or

- you have good cause, for example it does not exist or you cannot get it.

16.26 Payments on account are not discretionary. If you meet the conditions (see paras 16.23 and 16.25), the council:

(a) must make a payment on account within 14 days of getting your claim, and should not wait to be asked: R v Haringey LBC ex parte Ayub (see also GM para A6.158); and

(b) should continue making payments on account until your HB is decided.

16.22   HB 92(6); HB60+ 73(6); NIHB 89(6); NIHB60+ 70(6)

16.23   HB 93(1); HB60+ 74(1); NIHB 90(1); NIHB60+ 71(1)

16.26   R v Haringey LBC ex p Ayub 13/04/92 QBD 25 HLR 566

In practice you may need to remind the council to make a payment on account, or your landlord or agent can do this if your HB is likely to be paid to them.

Payments on account amounts and adjustments

16.27 The amount of your payment on account is whatever the council decides is reasonable, based on the information available to it about your individual circumstances. It must notify you (or the payee) that if this turns out to be greater than your entitlement to HB, the overpayment will be recovered (para 18.12).

16.28 When the council decides your claim, the following rules apply. If your entitlement to HB is:

(a) greater than your payments on account, the council must pay the balance;

(b) less than your payments on account, the council must recover the overpayment by making deductions from your future payments of HB (see para 18.41).

If you are not entitled to HB, the council recovers the overpayment from the person it was paid to (see para 18.37).

Paying HB to someone on your behalf

16.29 This section explains when your HB is paid to someone on your behalf. It only applies if your HB is paid as a rent allowance (see paras 16.14-15).

Attorneys, appointees, etc

16.30 If you are unable to act for yourself, the council can pay your HB to an attorney, appointee etc, who claimed HB on your behalf (see paras 5.5-7).

Nominees

16.31 If you want your council to pay your HB to someone else, the council can do this (but if you are unable to act, see instead para 16.30). They are usually called your nominee. You have to write to the council requesting this, and your nominee must either be:

(a) an individual aged 18 or more (for example an adult relative or friend); or

(b) a corporate body (for example a firm of solicitors).

16.32 The law does not stop your landlord or agent being your nominee. But:

(a) if you fall within the LHA scheme in England Scotland or Wales, the DWP suggests (GLHA paras 5.100-101) that the council should not agree to this if it would undermine the main rules about paying HB to your landlord/agent (see paras 16.36-49);

(b) in all other rent allowance cases, it may be simpler to request payment to your landlord/agent using the main rule about this (see para 16.50).

16.27   HB 93(1),(2); HB60+ 74(1),(2); NIHB 90(1),(2); NIHB60+ 71(1),(2)

16.28   HB 93(3); HB60+ 74(3); NIHB 90(3); NIHB60+ 71(3)

16.30   HB 94(2); HB60+ 75(2); NIHB 91(2); NIHB60+ 68(2)

16.31   HB 94(3); HB60+ 75(3); NIHB 91(3); NIHB60+ 68(3)

Personal representatives and next of kin

16.33   If HB is due to you when you die, the council must pay it to your personal representative (i.e. the person responsible for settling your affairs, such as an executor), or (if you do not have a personal representative) your next of kin. Your next of kin is the first person in the following list who is aged 16 or more:

(a)   your husband, wife or civil partner;

(b)   your children or grandchildren;

(c)   your parents, brothers or sisters, or their children.

This rule only applies if the executor or next of kin writes to the council requesting payment within one year of your death, or longer if the council agrees. But it does not apply to HB the council has to pay your landlord/agent: see para 16.41.

Paying HB to your landlord or their agent

16.34   This section explains when your HB is paid to your landlord or their agent. It only applies if your HB is paid as a rent allowance (see paras 16.14-15).

(a)   The council must pay your HB to your landlord/agent when the rules in paras 16.36-41 apply to you.

(b)   Otherwise, it may pay your HB to your landlord/agent when the rules in paras 16.42-53 apply to you.

(c)   Otherwise, it must pay your HB to you, or to someone on your behalf (see paras 16.29-33).

Table 16.2 summarises these rules. See paras 16.54-56 for exceptions if your landlord/agent is not a 'fit and proper person', and paras 16.57-66 for further general rules.

Table 16.2 **Paying HB to your landlord/agent**

This table summarises when your HB is paid to your landlord or their agent (see paras 16.34-35).

When the council must pay your landlord/agent

All rent allowance cases

In all rent allowance cases (see paras 16.14-15), the council must pay your landlord/agent if:

(a)   you have eight weeks or more rent arrears, unless it is in your overriding interests not to pay your landlord/agent: see paras 16.37-39;

(b)   part of your JSA, ESA, income support or state pension credit is being paid to your landlord/agent: see para 16.40; or

(c)   rent remains due to your landlord/agent when you die: see para 16.41.

16.33   HB 97(1)-(4); HB60+ 78(1)-(4); NIHB 94(1)-(4); NIHB60+ 75(1)-(4)

16.34   HB 94(1),95,96; HB60+ 75(1),76,77; NIHB 91(1),92,93; NIHB60+ 68(1),73,74

T16.2   HB 95,96,97(5); HB60+ 76,77,78(5); NIHB 92,93,94(5); NIHB60+ 73,74,75(5)

When the council may pay your landlord/agent

LHA cases in England, Scotland or Wales

In LHA cases (see para 9.3) in England, Scotland or Wales, the council may pay your landlord/agent if:

(d) your HB has previously been paid to your landlord/agent under the rules in (a) or (b) above: see para 16.45;

(e) paying your landlord/agent would help you secure or retain your tenancy: see para 16.46;

(f) you are likely to have difficulty managing your finances: see para 16.47;

(g) it is improbable that you will pay your rent: see para 16.48; or

(h) the council is considering whether the rules in (f) or (g) apply to you, but in this case only for up to eight weeks: see para 16.49.

See also (k) and (l) below.

Other rent allowance cases

In other rent allowance cases in England, Scotland and Wales which are not LHA cases, and in all rent allowance cases (including LHA cases) in Northern Ireland, the council/NIHE may pay your landlord/agent if:

(i) you have requested this or consented to it: see para 16.50; or

(j) it is in your and your family's interest: see para 16.51.

See also (k) and (l) below.

All rent allowance cases

In all rent allowance cases, the council may pay your landlord/agent if:

(k) you have not paid part or all of your rent, but this only applies to your first payment of HB (or first payment following a change to your HB): see para 16.52; or

(l) you have left your home and rent remains due to your landlord/agent: see para 16.53.

When the council must not pay your landlord/agent

All rent allowance cases

In all rent allowance cases, the council must not pay your landlord/agent if:

(m) your landlord/agent is not a 'fit and proper person', unless paying them is nonetheless in your and your family's best interests: see paras 16.54-56.

Landlord or agent

16.35 When your HB is payable to your landlord or agent, it is payable to:

(a) your landlord if your landlord collects your rent; but

(b) your landlord's agent if the agent collects your rent.

In the following paras, we use 'landlord/agent' to mean whichever of these applies.

16.35   HB 95(1),96(4); HB60+ 76(1),77(4); NIHB 92(1),93(5); NIHB60+ 73(1),74(5)

When HB must be paid to a landlord/agent

16.36   Paras 16.37-41 explain when your HB must be paid to your landlord/agent. The rules about this apply in all rent allowance cases (see paras 16.14-15). See also paras 16.54-66.

HB must be paid to landlord: eight weeks rent arrears

16.37   In all rent allowance cases, the council must pay your HB to your landlord/agent:

(a) if you have eight weeks or more rent arrears, counting arrears of eligible and ineligible service charges as well as arrears of rent: see para 16.38;

(b) unless it is in your overriding interests not to: see para 16.39.

This continues to apply until your rent arrears reduce below eight weeks (but see para 16.45).

16.38   Whether you have rent arrears (including arrears of service charges), and how much they are, are questions of fact (see paras 1.43-46). The council is not expected to check this, but must consider information you or your landlord/agent provide: R v Haringey LBC ex parte Ayub. And it is usually accepted that 'Rent is in arrears once the contractual date for payment has passed irrespective of whether the rent is due in advance or in arrear': Doncaster v Coventry CC. Although this First-tier Tribunal decision is not binding, the DWP considers it is correct (HB/CTB A26/2009 and GLHA 4.061).

Example: Eight weeks rent arrears

A private landlord lets a calendar-monthly tenancy from 1st July 2016. She charges rent in advance on the 1st of each month. The tenant does not pay any rent.

So by 2nd August 2016, there are two calendar months of rent arrears. This is more than eight weeks of arrears, so the landlord is entitled to require the council to pay the tenant's HB to her.

16.39   If you have eight weeks or more rent arrears, it is up to you (or someone on your behalf) to give specific reasons why it is in your 'overriding interests' that your HB should not be paid to your landlord/agent: CH/3244/2007. If this is because your landlord/agent has not done essential repairs, you may be expected to have sent them a solicitor's letter with a schedule of disrepair prepared by a builder or surveyor: CH/3244/2007.

HB must be paid to landlord: deductions from DWP benefits

16.40   In all rent allowance cases, the council must pay your HB to your landlord/agent if the DWP in making direct payments to them towards your rent arrears or hostel charges (see para 25.48). This continues to apply until the DWP stops making direct payments (but see para 16.45). The DWP should inform the council when this rule applies to you (GM para A6.188).

16.37   HB 95(1)(b); HB60+ 76(1)(b); NIHB 92(1)(b); NIHB60+ 73(1)(b)
         R v Haringey ex p Ayub: see footnote to para 16.26; Doncaster v Coventry CC 05/10/09 032/09/00932

16.40   HB 95(1)(a); HB60+ 76(1)(a); NIHB 92(1)(a); NIHB60+ 73(1)(a)

HB must be paid to landlord: rent due following death

16.41   In all rent allowance cases, the council must pay your HB to your landlord/agent if:

(a) HB remains due to you when you die, and rent remains due to your landlord/agent; and

(b) the council has already decided (before your death) to pay your landlord/agent.

But this is limited to the amount of rent remaining due at the date of your death. Any other HB due to you can be paid to your personal representative or next of kin (see para 16.33).

When HB may be paid to a landlord/agent

16.42   Paragraphs 16.45-53 explain when your HB may be paid to your landlord/agent.

(a) The rules in paragraphs 16.45-49 and 16.52-53 apply if you fall within the LHA scheme (see para 9.3) in England, Scotland or Wales.

(b) The rules in paragraphs 16.50-53 apply in:

■   all other rent allowance cases in England, Scotland and Wales (for example housing association, exempt accommodation, rent referral and boarder cases), and

■   all rent allowance cases in Northern Ireland.

See also paragraphs 16.54-66. In England, Scotland and Wales, the overall effect of the rules is that HB is more likely to be paid to the landlord/agent in non-LHA cases than in LHA cases.

16.43   The rules in paragraphs 16.45-53 are discretionary. If their conditions are met, the council may (but does not have to) pay your landlord/agent. The DWP has given councils extensive guidance about applying these rules in LHA cases (GLHA 4.00-6.102). But as with all discretions (see para 1.53), the council must make its own decision. It should not have fixed rules or follow guidance without question: CH/2986/2005.

16.44   Some of the rules require the council to consider quite personal things about you, for example, your ability to manage your finances, the likelihood that you will pay your rent, and what your and your family's interests are (see paras 16.47-48 and 16.51). In these cases, the DWP advises (HB/CTB A26/2009) that the council:

(a) can take account of information it already has, or gets from a home visit; and

(b) should also take account of information provided by you or by someone on your behalf, for example a relative or friend, a social worker or leaving care worker, or your landlord/agent.

Although this guidance is about LHA cases in England, Scotland and Wales, it is equally reasonable in other rent allowance cases.

HB may be paid to landlord: following a period when it must be

16.45   In LHA cases in England, Scotland and Wales, the council may pay your HB to your landlord/agent if it has previously done so under the rules in paragraphs 16.37-40. It can do this as soon as your rent arrears reduce below eight weeks, or as soon as the DWP stops making direct payments, or (in either case) at a later date.

16.41   HB 97(5); HB60+ 78(5); NIHB 94(5); NIHB60+ 75(5)

16.45   HB 96(3A)(b)(iii); HB60+ 77(3A)(b)(iii)

HB may be paid to landlord: to secure or retain your tenancy

16.46   In LHA cases in England, Scotland and Wales, the council may pay your HB to your landlord/agent if this will assist you to secure or retain your tenancy (or other form of letting). This could encourage your landlord/agent to let to you (or continue to do so) while you are on HB. Some councils use this power to encourage the landlord to let at a lower rent (for example, a rent within the LHA figure) than they would have asked for.

HB may be paid to landlord: difficulty managing your finances

16.47   In LHA cases in England, Scotland and Wales, the council may pay your HB to your landlord/agent if you are likely to have difficulty managing your finances. For example, the DWP says (GLHA 5.070-074) this could be because you:

(a)   have difficulty budgeting, debt problems, or an undischarged bankruptcy;

(b)   are illiterate or unable to speak English;

(c)   are fleeing domestic violence;

(d)   are leaving care or prison; or

(e)   are getting Supporting People payments, or help from a charity.

See also paragraphs 16.44 and 16.49.

HB may be paid to landlord: improbable you will pay rent

16.48   In LHA cases in England, Scotland and Wales, the council may pay your HB to your landlord/agent if it is improbable that you will pay your rent. This rule is about whether it is improbable you will pay rent in the future: CH/2986/2005. The DWP says this might be the case if you have regularly failed to pay rent (with no good reason) in the past (GLHA 6.063-064), for example if the council helped you get your tenancy for this reason (HB/CTB A26/2009). See also paragraphs 16.44 and 16.49.

HB may be paid to landlord: while considering who to pay

16.49   In LHA cases in England, Scotland and Wales, the council may pay your HB to your landlord/agent while it is considering whether the rules in paragraphs 16.47-48 apply to you. The council can do this for up to eight weeks. Alternatively, it can pay you during this time. See also paragraph 16.58.

HB may be paid to landlord: at your request or with your consent

16.50   In rent allowance cases in England, Scotland and Wales which are not LHA cases, and in all rent allowance cases in Northern Ireland, the council/NIHE may pay your HB to your landlord/agent if you request this or consent to it. The law does not require you to give a reason, but you can if you wish.

16.46   HB 96(3A)(b)(iv),(4); HB60+ 77(3A)(b)(iv),(4)

16.47   HB 96(3A)(b)(i); HB60+ 77(3A)(b)(i)

16.48   HB 96(3A)(b)(ii); HB60+ 77(3A)(b)(ii)

16.49   HB 96(3B); HB60+ 77(3B)

16.50   HB 96(1)(a),(3A)(a); HB60+ 77(1)(a),(3A)(a)

HB may be paid to landlord: your and your family's interests

16.51 In rent allowance cases in England, Scotland and Wales which are not LHA cases, and in all rent allowance cases in Northern Ireland, the council/NIHE may pay your HB to your landlord/agent if doing so would be in your and your family's interests. Although the rules in paragraphs 16.45-49 do not apply in these cases, in practice the council is likely to take similar considerations into account. See also paragraph 16.44.

HB may be paid to landlord: first payment after a claim or change

16.52 In all rent allowance cases, the council may pay your HB to your landlord/agent if you have not yet paid part or all of your rent for the period HB covers. But this is limited to the first payment following your claim for HB, or following a move or other change affecting your HB. And it only applies when paying your landlord/agent is 'in the interests of the efficient administration' of HB.

HB may be paid to your landlord: when you leave your home

16.53 In all rent allowance cases, the council may pay your HB to your landlord/agent if:

(a) you have left the accommodation the HB is paid for; and

(b) rent remains due to your landlord/agent there.

If your landlord/agent is not a fit and proper person

16.54 In all rent allowance cases, the council must not pay your HB to your landlord/agent:

(a) if your landlord/agent is not a 'fit and proper person' (see paras 16.55-56);

(b) unless paying them is nonetheless in your and your family's 'best interests'.

This rule overrides the rules in paragraphs 16.37-41 and 16.45-53. DWP guidance does not say what your and your family's best interests are, but see paragraph 16.44 for information the council could reasonably take into account.

16.55 DWP guidance (GM A6.198) says the council should only consider whether the landlord/agent is or is not a fit and proper person if it is doubtful about [their] honesty in connection with HB. This could be because they are involved in fraudulent acts relating to HB. The DWP also suggests (GM A6.200) it could be because they have regularly failed to report changes they have a duty to report (see paras 17.3-5), or to repay overpayments which are recoverable from them (see paras 18.34-36).

16.56 The following do not mean a landlord/agent is not a fit and proper person:

(a) their undesirable activity in non-HB matters, for example contravention of the Housing Acts (GM A6.197);

(b) using their right to request a reconsideration, or to appeal, before repaying an overpayment; or

(c) making complaints about maladministration, for example to the Ombudsman.

16.51   HB 96(1)(b),(3A)(a); HB60+ 77(1)(b),(3A)(a)

16.52   HB 96(2); HB60+ 77(2); NIHB 93(2); NIHB60+ 74(2)

16.53   HB 96(1)(c); HB60+ 77(1)(c); NIHB 93(1)(c); NIHB60+ 74(1)(c)

16.54   HB 95(3), 96(3),(4); HB60+ 76(3), 77(3),(4); NIHB 92(3), 93(3),(4); NIHB60+ 73(3), 74(3),(4)

Decisions about paying a landlord/agent

16.57   The council can make a decision about paying your HB to your landlord/agent:

(a)   when you claim HB; and/or

(b)   when there is a change in your or your landlord/agent's circumstances which affects this.

See paragraphs 16.20-21 for when payments to a landlord/agent are made, and paragraphs 16.23 and 16.26-28 about payments on account.

16.58   The council can suspend payments of HB (see para 17.72) while it is deciding who to pay: CH/1821/2006. But the DWP has encouraged councils not to delay payments in this way (GLHA 5.111).

Decision notices about paying a landlord/agent

16.59   The council must issue two decision notices, one to your landlord/agent and one to you, when:

(a)   it decides to pay your HB to them, or changes the amount of the payment (see para 16.60); or

(b)   they have asked the council to pay your HB to them, but the council has refused: CH/180/2006.

These must be in writing, and must be issued within 14 days of when the council makes the decision, or as soon as reasonably practicable after that.

16.60   When the council decides to pay your landlord/agent (or change the amount), the decision notice issued to them must contain:

(a)   the amount of HB they will get for you, and when the payments start (or change);

(b)   their duty to notify changes of circumstances, and examples of what they might be (see para 17.3);

(c)   an explanation about recovering overpaid HB from a blameless tenant (see para 18.46); and

(d)   their rights in relation to the decision (see para 16.61);

but it must not contain other information about your HB (for example personal or financial information about you or your household). The decision notice to you must contain the information in (a) to (c), and your rights in relation to the decision. In practice, this is sometimes instead included in the main decision notice about your HB (see para 16.5).

Reconsiderations and appeals about paying a landlord/agent

16.61   When the council decides to pay, or not pay, your landlord/agent, both you and they are a 'person affected'. So both you and they have the right to obtain a statement of reasons, and to appeal if the right of appeal applies to the decision (see para 16.67): CH/180/2006.

16.57   HB 89(1), 95,96,97(5); HB60+ 70(1), 76,77,78(5); NIHB 85(1), 92,93,94(5); NIHB60+ 66(1), 73,74,75(5)

16.59   HB sch 9 paras 11,12; HB60+ sch 8 paras 11,12; NIHB sch 10 paras 11,12; NIHB60+ sch 9 paras 11,12

16.60   HB sch 9 paras 11,12; HB60+ sch 8 paras 11,12; NIHB sch 10 paras 11,12; NIHB60+ sch 9 paras 11,12

If the council pays the wrong person

16.62   If the council decided it had a duty to pay your landlord/agent (see para 16.34(a)) but paid you instead, the council must pay your landlord/agent: [2008] UKUT 31 (AAC). What it paid you is an overpayment which is likely to be recoverable from you (see para 18.31).

16.63   If the council decided it had a discretion to pay your landlord/agent (see 16.34(b)) but paid you instead, the council cannot pay your landlord/agent but they can seek compensation from the council: R(H) 2/08, [2010] UKUT 254 (AAC).

16.64   It seems reasonable (following the reasoning in [2008] UKUT 31 (AAC)) that if the council decided it had a duty to pay you (see para 16.34(c)) but paid your landlord/agent instead, the council must pay you. What it paid your landlord/agent is an overpayment which is likely to be recoverable from them (see para 18.34).

How paying your landlord/agent affects your rent

16.65   When the council pays your HB to your landlord/agent, this discharges your liability to pay that amount of rent unless the council recovers it as an overpayment from your landlord/agent: see table 18.4.

If your landlord/agent refuses to accept your HB

16.66   A landlord/agent has the right to refuse payments of rent from someone who is not a party to the tenancy agreement: Bessa Plus Plc v Lancaster. Although this is uncommon, it could affect you if:

(a)   you are the HB claimant; but

(b)   your partner is the sole tenant of your home; and

(c)   your landlord/agent refuses to accept payment of your HB (because you are not on the tenancy agreement).

If this happens, you should be able to get the council to pay your HB to you (rather than your landlord/agent), or to your partner as your nominee (see paras 16.31-32).

HB disputes and appeals

16.67   This and the following sections explain your rights to get the reasons for an HB decision, to ask for it to be reconsidered, and to appeal it. These rights belong to you (the claimant) and other 'persons affected'.

Persons affected

16.68   The law uses the term 'persons affected' to mean everyone who:

(a)   must be sent a decision notice (para 16.4); and

(b)   has the rights in para 16.67.

16.65   HB 95(2), 96(4); HB60+ 76(2), 77(4); NIHB 92(2), 93(5); NIHB60+ 73(2), 74(5)

16.66   Bessa Plus plc v Lancaster 17/03/97 CA 30 HLR 48

16.69   All the following are persons affected:

(a) you (the HB claimant);

(b) someone acting for you if you are unable to act on your own behalf (for example an attorney or appointee: see paras 5.5-7);

(c) your landlord or agent if the decision is about whether to pay your HB to them rather than you (see paras 16.34-64);

(d) your landlord or agent or anyone else if the decision is about whether an overpayment is recoverable from them (see paras 18.29-37).

The above are persons affected when their rights, duties or obligations are affected by the decision. So in the situations described in (c) and (d), both you and the landlord, agent or other person are persons affected. A person affected can be either an individual (for example a private landlord) or a corporate body (for example a housing association or a firm of letting agents).

16.70   Others are not persons affected. For example, a landlord providing you with supported accommodation may be very concerned about how the authority decided the amount of your eligible rent, but they aren't a person affected in relation to that decision: Wirral MBC v Salisbury Independent Living Ltd.

Requests and signatures

16.71   The rights in para 16.67 have to be requested in writing. Some councils have forms you can use, otherwise you should put your request in a letter. When a signature is required:

(a) from you (or another individual), it can instead be signed by your (or their) solicitor or authorised representative: [2015] UKUT 28 (AAC);

(b) from a corporate body, it should be signed by someone aged 18 or over acting on its behalf.

Getting a written statement of reasons

16.72   You (or any other person affected) can request a statement of reasons about anything the council didn't explain in its decision notice. Your request should be in writing, signed, and made within one month of the date of the decision notice. The council should provide the statement within 14 days so far as this is practicable.

Reconsideration or appeal

16.73   If you disagree with the authority's HB decision you have two options. You can:

(a) ask the authority to reconsider the decision: this applies to all HB decisions (paras 16.75-80); or

(b) appeal against the decision to an independent tribunal: this applies only to appealable HB decisions (paras 16.81-90).

If you choose the first option, you can go on to the second option next. If you choose the second option, the authority can treat it as a request for a reconsideration (para 16.87).

16.69   HB 2(1) definition – 'person affected'; HB60+ 2(1); DAR 3; NIHB 2(1); NIHB60+ 2(1); NIDAR 3

16.70   Wirral MBC v Salisbury Independent Living Ltd [2012] EWCA Civ 84; [2012] H.L.R. 25; www.bailii.org/ew/cases/EWCA/Civ/2012/84.html

16.71   HB 90(2),(4); HB60+ 71(2),(4); NIHB 86(2),(4); NIHB60+ 67(2),(4); DAR 10(2); NIDAR 10(2)

16.74   Table 16.3 summarises the HB disputes and appeals procedure. The rules are similar to those for universal credit (and other socials security benefits): see *Help with Housing Costs Volume 1*. The main differences in HB are that reconsiderations are dealt with by the council (not the DWP); you don't have to ask for a reconsideration before you appeal; and appeals are sent to the council who forward them to the tribunal (rather than direct to the tribunal).

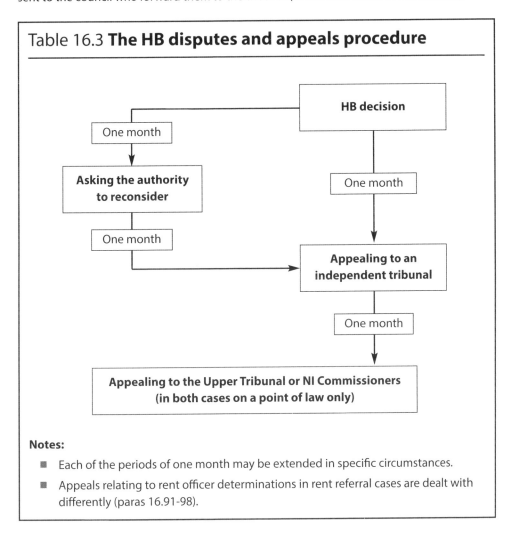

Table 16.3 **The HB disputes and appeals procedure**

Notes:

- Each of the periods of one month may be extended in specific circumstances.
- Appeals relating to rent officer determinations in rent referral cases are dealt with differently (paras 16.91-98).

Asking the council/NIHE to reconsider

16.75   You (or any other person affected) can ask the council/NIHE to reconsider any HB decision it has made. The law calls this asking for a revision or supersession, but you don't have to use these terms, and it is normally called requesting a reconsideration.

How to request a reconsideration

16.76   Your request must be sent to the council/NIHE in writing. It should be within the time limit (paras 16.77-78), otherwise you may get less HB than you might have done (para 16.80).

Time limit for requesting a reconsideration

16.77   Your request for a reconsideration is within the time limit if the council/NIHE receives it within one month of the date of its decision notice (paras 16.2-3). But:

(a) any time is ignored from the date you (or another person affected) requested a statement of reasons (para 16.72) to the date the council/NIHE provided it (both dates included);

(b) any time is ignored before the date the council/NIHE gave notice of the correction of an accidental error (para 17.62);

(c) in special circumstances the time limit can be extended (para 16.78).

16.78   The time limit for requesting a reconsideration is extended if:

(a) the council receives your request within 13 months of the date of its decision notice;

(b) you say you are asking for it to be accepted late and give the reasons for the delay;

(c) your request 'has merit';

(d) there are special circumstances why it wasn't practicable for you to make the request earlier; and

(e) it is reasonable to accept your delay – the longer you delay the more compelling your special circumstances have to be.

When deciding this, the council can't take account of ignorance or misunderstanding of the law or the time limits; or of an Upper Tribunal, the NI Commissioners or a court interpreting the law in a new way.

What happens when you request a reconsideration

16.79   The council must consider your request and decide whether to alter your HB. If it needs further information or evidence it may request this, and must take it into account if you provide it within one month, or longer if reasonable. The council must send you a decision notice saying:

(a) whether it has altered your HB; and

(b) if it has, what it altered.

It must also include information about your rights to appeal etc (para 16.7).

16.77   DAR 4(1),(4),10A(3); NIDAR 4(1),(4),10A(3)

16.78   DAR 4(8),5(1)-(6); NIDAR 4(7),5(1)-(6)

16.79   HB sch 8; HB60+ sch 9; NIHB sch 10; NIHB60+ sch 10; DAR 4(5), 7(5); NIDAR 4(4), 7(5)

16.80   Increases to your HB take effect as follows:

(a)   if your request was within the time limit (paras 16.77-78), the increase takes effect from the date the original decision took effect (or should have) – so you are awarded arrears of HB back to then;

(b)   if your request was outside the time limit, the increase takes effect from the Monday at the beginning of the benefit week in which your request was received – so you aren't awarded arrears before that.

Reductions in your HB (which are rare) take effect as described in para 17.66.

Appealing to a tribunal

16.81   If an HB decision is appealable (paras 16.82-83), you (or any other person affected) can appeal about it to:

(a)   a First-tier Tribunal in Great Britain; or

(b)   an Appeal tribunal in Northern Ireland.

These tribunals are independent of the council/NIHE. You can appeal to them either instead of or after asking the council/NIHE to reconsider its decision.

Which decisions can be appealed

16.82   Table 16.4 show which decisions are appealable to a tribunal and which are not. If a decision is non-appealable, you can ask the council to reconsider it (para 16.75) or may be able to apply for judicial review (para 1.54).

Appeals about overpayments

16.83   In relation to an overpayment appeal you are always a 'person affected'. If the authority decides that the overpayment is recoverable from someone else (e.g. your landlord, their agent or your partner) or both of you, that other person is also always a 'person affected'. So there may be more than one person affected (para 16.69). Each of you has a right of appeal against:

(a)   the existence of the overpayment – i.e. the revised or superseding decision that causes it (R(H) 3/04 para 50); and

(b)   the overpayment determination (Wirral MBC v Salisbury Independent Living Ltd para 13). This includes whether it is recoverable, how much it is, and who it is recoverable from (para 18.39).

16.80   CPSA sch 7 para 3(3); NICPSA sch 7 para 3(3); DAR 6, 7(2)(b), 8(4)-(5); NIDAR 6, 7(2)(b), 8(4)-(5)

16.81   CPSA sch 7 para 6(3); NICPSA sch 7 para 6(3)

16.82   CPSA sch 7 para 6(1),(2),(4)-(6); NICPSA sch 7 para 6(1),(2),(4)-(6); DAR 16(1) and sch; NIDAR 16(1) and sch

16.83   Wirral MBC v Salisbury Independent Living Ltd [2012] EWCA Civ 84; [2012] H.L.R. 25;
        www.bailii.org/ew/cases/EWCA/Civ/2012/84.html

Table 16.4 **Appealable and non-appealable HB decisions**

Decisions about claims

Non-appealable

- Which partner in a couple is to be the claimant (para 5.3)
- Who may claim when someone is unable to act (para 5.5)

Appealable

- When and how a claim is made (paras 5.8-12)
- Whether a claim is incomplete (para 5.23)
- The date of claim and first day of entitlement (paras 5.28-49)
- Backdating (paras 5.50-58)

Decisions about payments

Non-appealable

- When and how HB is paid (paras 16.14-20)
- Making a payment on account (para 16.23)
- The frequency of payment of a rent allowance (paras 16.21-22)
- Making payment to a person entitled (para 16.31-32)
- Paying outstanding HB after a death (para 16.33)
- Suspending or restoring HB (paras 17.71-73)

Appealable

- Adjusting HB to correct a payment on account (para 16.28)
- Who HB is to be paid to (e.g. claimant or landlord/agent) (paras 16.34-53)
- Whether the landlord/agent is a 'fit and proper person' (paras 16.54-56)
- Terminating HB (para 17.75)

Decisions about overpayments

Non-appealable

- What 'an overpayment' means (para 18.1)
- The exercise of discretion to recover or not (paras 18.27-28)
- The method of recovery (paras 18.40-57)

T16.4　　CPSA sch 7 para 6; DAR 16(1) and sch; NICPSA sch 7 para 6; NIDAR 16(1) and sch

　　　　　Beltekian v Westminster CC [2004] EWCA Civ 1784, reported as R(H) 8/05 www.bailii.org/ew/cases/EWCA/Civ/2004/1784.html

Appealable

- The decision which caused the overpayment (para 18.3)
- Whether an overpayment is recoverable (paras 18.11-15)
- The amount of the overpayment (paras 18.16-26)
- Who an overpayment can be recovered from (paras 18.29-39)

Other decisions

Non-appealable

- LHA figures and areas (paras 9.21-28)
- Rent determinations made by the rent officer in Great Britain (but see paras 16.97-98)
- The DWP's assessed income figure or 'AIF' (table 13.3) – though modifications to it are appealable (para 13.15)
- Whether to run a local scheme for pensions for war disablement and war bereavement (paras 13.18)
- A refusal to correct a mistake out-of-time (Beltekian v Westminster CC reported as R(H) 8/05)
- Any figure laid down in the law (e.g. the capital limit or the amount of the HB benefit cap)

Appealable

- All other HB decisions

How to appeal

16.84   Your appeal must:

(a) be sent to the council/NIHE in writing and signed (para 16.71);

(b) say what decision you are appealing about and why you consider it is wrong;

(c) give your name and address, and those of your representative if you have one;

(d) say which address you want documents about your appeal to be sent to; and

(e) be within the time limit (paras 16.85-86).

Time limit for appealing

16.85   Your appeal is within the time limit if the council/NIHE receives it within one month of its decision notice (paras 16.2-3) or, if you requested a reconsideration, within one month of its decision notice about that (para 16.79). But:

(a) if you requested a statement of reasons (para 16.72) within that month, the time limit is 14 days after the end of that month, or after the date the council provides the statement, whichever is later;

16.84   DAR 20(1); NIDAR 20(1); FTPR 23, sch 1

16.85   FTPR 12,23, sch 1; NIDAR 18

(b)   if the time limit runs out on a non-working day it is extended to the next working day;

(c)   if it is in the interests of justice the time limit can be extended (para 16.86).

Disputes about whether your appeal is within the time limit must be referred to the tribunal. And if the council's/NIHE's decision notice is invalid because it didn't meet the relevant legal requirements (paras 16.5-7, 18.68-70 and table 18.6) the time limit doesn't start until the council/NIHE issues a valid notice: CH/1129/2004.

16.86   The time limit for appealing is extended if:

(a)   the council/NIHE receives your appeal within 12 months of the end of the time limit described in para 16.85;

(b)   you say why you are asking for it to be accepted late and give reasons for your delay;

(c)   there are special circumstances why it wasn't practicable to make your appeal earlier – because you, your partner or a dependant have suffered a serious illness or died, or you aren't resident in the UK, or postal services were disrupted, or there were other 'wholly exceptional' special circumstances; and

(d)   it is in the interests of justice to accept your delay – the longer your delay the more compelling your special circumstances have to be.

If the council/NIHE doesn't agree to extend the time limit, it must refer your request for an extension of time to the tribunal, and in some cases the tribunal has wider powers to accept this. But when deciding this, the council/NIHE and the tribunal can't take account of ignorance or misunderstanding of the law or the time limits; or of an Upper Tribunal, the NI Commissioners or a court interpreting the law in a new way.

What happens when you appeal

16.87   When the council/NIHE receives your appeal, it should first consider whether it agrees with it. If the council/NIHE does agree with your appeal (in whole or in part), it must alter its decision, send you a decision notice about this, and award any arrears of HB. This means your appeal 'lapses' and it isn't forwarded to the tribunal, but you can make a fresh appeal if you still consider the council is wrong. In any other case, the council must forward your appeal to the tribunal with a submission saying why it doesn't agree with it and enclosing relevant documents. The council must send a copy of its submission to you and any other person affected.

16.88   The tribunal writes to you asking (among other things) whether you want there to be a hearing or if you want the appeal to be decided without one. The tribunal will keep you informed about what happens next. Once the tribunal has decided your appeal, it notifies its decision to you, the council/NIHE and any other person affected.

16.89   You can then make a further appeal, but only if you consider the tribunal has made a mistake about the law (and not about the facts), and only if you first ask the tribunal for a statement of its reasons within one month of receiving its decision. The council/NIHE can also do this. The further appeal goes to:

16.86   DAR 19(5)-(9), 20(1); FTPR 2(1),(3), 5(3)(a), 7(2), 23(3)-(5),(8); NIDAR 19(3),(5)-(11), 20(1)

16.87   CPSA sch 7 para 3(6); NICPSA sch 7 para 3(6); DAR 4(1),(6), 17(3),(4); NIDAR 4(1),(6), 17(3),(4); FTPR 24

(a) an Upper Tribunal in Great Britain; or

(b) the NI Commissioners in Northern Ireland.

16.90 For more information about appeals and further appeals, see *Help with Housing Costs Volume 1*. You can also get details of tribunal procedures and rules online [www].

Appeals about rent officer/NIHE rent determinations

16.91 This section explains how to appeal against rent determinations made by the rent officer in Great Britain or NIHE in Northern Ireland, and how errors in them are corrected. It applies to:

(a) any of the rent determinations made in rent referral cases (paras 10.28 and 10.40-51); and

(b) board and attendance determinations (paras 9.33-34).

See paras 16.92-97 in Great Britain and para 16.98 in Northern Ireland.

Rent officer re-determinations

16.92 In Great Britain, appeals against rent determinations are dealt with by the council making an application to the rent officer for a 're-determination'. The council:

(a) must make an application within seven days of receiving a valid request from you (para 16.93) – and must include a copy of your request and any information and evidence you provide;

(b) may choose to make an application at any time (with or without a request from you);

(c) can only make a maximum of two applications in the order (a) then (b), or three applications in the order (b) then (a) then (b).

The rules apply each time the rent officer makes a determination (paras 9.34 and 10.32).

16.93 Your request is valid if:

(a) it is sent to the council in writing and signed (para 16.71);

(b) it says you disagree with a rent determination, or raises matters which affect a rent determination; and

(c) you make it within one month of the date of a decision notice about your HB (paras 16.2-3).

16.94 The re-determination is made by the rent officer (known as a re-determination officer) with advice from one or two other rent officers. It covers all rent determinations that apply to you (paras 10.40-51), or if appropriate just the board and attendance determination (paras 9.33-34). The rent officer should send the redetermination to the council within 20 days

---

16.90   www.justice.gov.uk/tribunals/sscs
https://www.gov.uk/administrative-appeals-tribunal
www.gov.uk/government/publications/social-entitlement-chamber-tribunal-procedure-rules
www.courtsni.gov.uk/en-GB/Tribunals/OSSC/Pages/OSSC.aspx
www.communities-ni.gov.uk/services/law-relating-social-security

16.92-93   HB 15,16; HB60+ 15,16; NIHB 15,16; NIHB60+ 15,16

of receiving the application for it or any further information they have requested from the council. They normally include their reasons and send a copy to you [www]. For changes to your HB, see para 16.96.

Correcting errors

16.95   In Great Britain, the rent officer provides a substitute determination (or substitute re-determination) if:

(a)   the council made an error in the information it gave them (e.g. about the occupiers of your home); or

(b)   the rent officer discovers they made an error (e.g. in the data they used).

The council has to request this each time (a) applies, but not normally when (b) applies (DWP circular G5/2005).

Changes to your eligible rent

16.96   If the rent officer's new determination (paras 16.92-95) changes the amount of your eligible rent, the council must send you a decision notice about this (para 16.5). Your HB changes as follows:

(a)   an increase in your eligible rent takes effect from the date the council's original decision took effect (or should have) – so you are awarded arrears of HB back to then; but

(b)   a reduction in your eligible rent takes effect from the Monday following the date of the rent officer's new determination – so you haven't been overpaid HB before then.

Tribunal appeals

16.97   In Great Britain, you can't appeal to a tribunal about the rent officer's determinations or re-determinations, but you may be able to apply for judicial review (para 1.54). You can appeal to a tribunal (para 16.81) about whether you fall within the rent referral rules (table 10.3) and about the information the council provides to the rent officer: [2010] UKUT 79 (AAC), [2010] AACR 40.

Reconsiderations and appeals in Northern Ireland

16.98   In Northern Ireland, you can ask the NIHE to reconsider any rent determinations it has made and appeal to a tribunal about them (paras 16.75-90). If your HB changes as a result:

(a)   an increase in your eligible rent takes effect as described in para 16.80; but

(b)   a reduction in your eligible rent normally takes effect from the Monday following the date of the NIHE's new rent determination.

16.94   ROO 4, sch 3
         www.voa.gov.uk/corporate/publications/Manuals/RentOfficerHandbook/
         HousingBenefitReferral/Determination/r-roh-reasons-for-decision.html

16.95   ROO 4A, 7A; HB 17; HB60+ 17

16.96   DAR 4(3), 7(2)(c) para 6(2)(c)

16.98   NIDAR 4(1), sch para 1

Chapter 17 **Changes**

- Changes of circumstances: see paras 17.2-17.
- When changes take effect: see paras 17.18-45.
- Extended payments and continuing payments: see paras 17.46-55.
- Revisions and supersessions: see paras 17.56-57.
- Reviewing and correcting decisions: see paras 17.58-70.
- Suspending, restoring and terminating awards: see paras 17.71-77.

17.1 This chapter explains how your entitlement to HB can change or end. This could be because:

(a) there is a change in your circumstances, or in the circumstances of someone relevant to your claim (for example a member of your household or your landlord), or in the law: see paras 17.2-55; or

(b) the council reviews and corrects your entitlement: see paras 17.58-70; or

(c) you request a reconsideration or appeal: see paras 16.73-90.

In the law, changes to your HB are also called 'revisions' or 'supersessions': see paras 17.56-57.

Changes of circumstances

17.2 This section describes the duty to tell the council about changes affecting HB and how the council deals with these.

Telling the council about changes

17.3 You have a duty to tell the council about any 'relevant' change of circumstances. The same duty applies to anyone acting for you (paras 5.5-7), and anyone who receives payments (such as a landlord: para 16.34). This means any change which you (or the other person) could reasonably be expected to know might affect:

(a) your entitlement to HB; or

(b) the amount of your HB; or

(c) how your HB is paid or who it is paid to.

17.4 This duty begins on the date your claim is made, and continues for as long as you are receiving HB.

17.3   HB 88(1),(6); HB60+ 69(1),(9); NIHB 84(1); NIHB60+ 65(1)

17.5   The law lists changes that must be notified to the council and changes that need not be notified (summarised in tables 17.1 and 17.2). These are not exhaustive. For example, you should also notify the council of changes in:

(a)   personal details (name, address, etc);

(b)   rent (unless you are a council or NIHE tenant) and in Northern Ireland rates (unless collected by Land and Property Services);

(c)   family and household details (which could affect your applicable amount or non-dependant deductions);

(d)   capital and income; and

(e)   any matter which affects whether HB is payable to your landlord.

Table 17.1 **Changes you must notify**

The following is a list of the items specifically mentioned in the law. Your duty is wider (paras 17.3-5).

Working age claims (para 1.24)

- ■   The end of your (or your partner's) entitlement to JSA(IB), ESA(IR) or IS.
- ■   Changes where a child or young person ceases to be a member of your family: e.g. when child benefit stops or they leave your household.

Pension age claims (para 1.24)

- ■   Changes in the details of your letting (unless you are a council or NIHE tenant).
- ■   Changes affecting the residence or income of any non-dependant.
- ■   Absences exceeding or likely to exceed 13 weeks.

Additional matters for claimants on savings credit

- ■   Changes affecting any child living with you (other than age) which might affect the amount of HB.
- ■   Changes to capital which take it (or may take it) above £16,000.
- ■   Changes to a partner who was ignored in assessing savings credit but is taken into account for HB (table 13.3).
- ■   Changes to a non-dependant if the non-dependant's income and capital was treated as being yours (para 13.57).

T17.1   HB 88; HB60+ 69; NIHB; NIHB60+ 65

Table 17.2 **Changes you need not notify**

- Beginnings or ends of awards of pension credit (either kind) or changes in the amount – because it is the DWP's duty to notify the council.
- Changes which affect your JSA(IB), ESA(IR) or IS but do not affect your HB.
- Changes in rent if you are a council or NIHE tenant.
- Changes in rates in Northern Ireland if collected by the Rating Service.
- Changes in the age of any member of your family or non-dependant.
- Changes in the HB regulations.

How to notify changes

17.6   You must notify changes to the council. Some councils accept notification by telephone or online, though they can require written rather than telephone notifications, or require written or electronic records to be kept by those making online notifications.

17.7   In all other cases, you must notify changes to the council's 'designated office' (para 5.8). However, the council may accept notification by any other method it agrees to in a particular case.

17.8   If you or your partner are on JSA or IS and are starting work, and this will mean that your JSA/IS will stop (or JSA(C) will change), you may notify this by telephone to the DWP. This is part of the DWP's 'in and out of work' process.

Time limits, etc

17.9   There is a one month time limit for notifying changes, which can be extended to 13 months in special circumstances (para 17.14). Rather than placing a duty on you to meet these time limits, HB law spells out the consequences of not doing so (paras 17.10-15) – which in practice amounts to the same thing.

17.10   If you fail to notify a relevant change, or exceed the above time limits, and the change would:

   (a)   reduce or end entitlement to HB – an overpayment has occurred: this may or may not be recoverable (chapter 18);

   (b)   increase entitlement to HB – special rules apply (paras 17.11-15).

T17.2   HB 88(3)(4); HB60+ 69(3),(4); NIHB 84(2),(3); NIHB60+ 65(2),(3)

17.6   HB 88(1),(4),(6), 88A, sch 11; HB60+ 69(1),(4),(9), 69A, sch 10; NIHB 84(1),(3), 84A, sch 11; NIHB60+ 65(1),(2), 65A, sch 10

17.10   DAR 8(2); NIDAR 8(2)

Late notification of advantageous changes

17.11   The following rule (para 17.12) applies when:

(a) you have a duty to notify a relevant change (para 17.3), and the change would increase entitlement to HB (an advantageous change, sometimes called a 'beneficial change'); but

(b) you take longer than one month to do so (or longer in special circumstances: paras 17.14-15).

17.12   In these cases the change is treated (for HB purposes) as occurring on the date the council received the notification. In other words you lose money, as illustrated in the example.

17.13   The rule does not apply to changes in pension credit or in social security benefits (in these cases the rules in paras 17.32 and 17.34-37 apply instead).

Extending the time limit for notifying an advantageous change

17.14   In the case of a change of circumstances which increases entitlement to HB, the one month time limit for notifying it is extended (and you do not lose money) if:

(a) the notification is received by the council within 13 months of the date on which the change occurred; and

(b) you also notify the council of your reasons for failing to notify the change earlier; and

(c) the council is satisfied that there are or were 'special circumstances' as a result of which it was not practicable to notify the change within the one month time limit. The longer the delay (beyond the normal one month), the more compelling those special circumstances need to be; and

(d) the council is satisfied that it is reasonable to allow your late notification of the change. In deciding this, the council may not take account of ignorance of the law (not even ignorance of the time limits) nor of the fact that an Upper Tribunal or court has taken a different view of the law from that previously understood and applied.

17.15   If the authority refuses your late notification, you have the right to ask the authority to reconsider or to appeal (para 16.67).

Example: Late notified advantageous change

A claimant's wages went down four months ago, but the claimant did not inform the council until today. The council asks why she delayed, but she has no special circumstances.

The change is implemented from the Monday following the day the claimant's written notification of the change was received by the council. The claimant does not get her arrears. (However, if the claimant has 'special circumstances', she may get her arrears: para 17.14.)

17.11   DAR 7(2)(a),(3), 8(3),(5); NIDAR 7(2)(a), 8(3),(5)

17.14   DAR 9; NIDAR 9

How the council deals with changes

17.16   The council must make a decision about any change which could affect your HB. For example whether to change the amount, end your award, or change who it is paid to. Paragraphs 17.18-55 give the rules about when changes take effect.

Information, evidence and decision notices

17.17   The council can ask you for information and evidence it reasonably requires in order to make a decision about a change. You are responsible for providing this in the same way as when you made your claim (see para 5.13) and the council must take it into account if you provide it within one month, or longer if reasonable. The council must issue a decision about any change it makes to your HB: see paras 16.3-7.

When changes take effect

17.18   This section describes when a change takes effect in your entitlement to HB. There are two steps involved:

(a)   deciding the date the change actually occurred; and

(b)   working out (from that) what date it takes effect in HB.

The date a change occurs: the general rule

17.19   The starting point is that the date a change actually occurs is the date something new happens (for example, a new baby, a birthday, a change in pay, a rent increase). This is a question of fact (paras 1.43-47).

17.20   Late-notified beneficial changes can be treated as occurring on the date the notification was received (paras 17.11-12). Other special cases are described below (paras 17.22-55).

The date a change takes effect: the general rule

17.21   The date a change takes effect is the Monday after the date the change occurs. Even if the change occurs on a Monday, HB changes on the following Monday. However, there are different rules for moves, changes in rent, and changes in social security benefits and credits. These and other special cases are described below (paras 17.22-55).

17.16   HB 89(1); HB60+ 70(1); NIHB 85(1); NIHB60+ 66(1)

17.17   AA 5(1)(hh); NIAA 5(1)(hh); HB 86(1),90(1)(b), sch 9; HB60+ 67(1),71(1)(b), sch 8;
            NIHB 82(1),86(1)(b), sch 10; NIHB60+ 63(1),67(1)(b), sch 9; DAR 4(5), 7(5); NIDAR 4(4), 7(5)

17.21   HB 79(1); HB60+ 59(1); NIHB 77(1); NIHB60+ 57(1); DAR 7(2)(a)(i), 8(2); NIDAR 7(2)(a)(i), 8(2)

Moving home

17.22   Your HB ends on the date shown in table 17.3 if you:

(a)   move to accommodation where HB can't be paid (chapter 2); or

(b)   move to an area where a different council administers HB – but you can claim HB from the new authority unless the UC rules prevent this (paras 2.9-10); or

(c)   move out of specified supported accommodation while you are on UC (para 17.30).

Otherwise, if you move to an address where the same council administers HB, your HB continues (so long as you remain entitled: table 2.1). But the amount changes to take into account your new eligible rent (or rates) from the date shown in table 17.3.

17.23   The date a move occurs may not be straightforward. However, it is the date you change your normal home, rather than a date on your letting agreement, etc (R(H) 9/05, para 3.17).

Table 17.3 **Moves and changes in rent or rates**

What the change is	When it takes effect in HB
HB for hostels with a daily rent liability (para 5.48)	
All moves and all changes in rent liability	HB changes or ends on the exact day of your move or change in rent/rates
HB in all other cases	
If HB continues after the move or change in rent/rates	HB changes on the exact day of your move or change in rent/rates
If HB ends as a result of the move or change in rent/rates	HB continues until the end of the benefit week containing the day of your move or change in rent/rates

---

Changes in rent and rates

17.24   If your liability for rent or (in Northern Ireland) rates changes, this takes effect in HB from the date shown in table 17.3. For rent- (and rate-) free periods, see paras 6.35-36.

HB on two homes, etc

17.25   The following changes take effect on the exact day: starting or stopping being eligible for HB on a former home, or on two homes, including stopping being eligible because the (four weeks or 52 weeks) time limit runs out (chapter 3).

17.22   HB 79(2),(2A)(a),(8), 80(4)(b),(c),(10); HB60+ 59(2),(2A)(a),(8), 61(4)(b),(c),(11);
         NIHB 77(2),(3)(a),(10), 78(4)(b),(c),(9); NIHB60+ 57(2),(3)(a),(10),59(4)(b),(c),(9); UCTP 6(1),(2)(a)

T17.3   As para 17.22

17.24   NIHB60+ 57(2),(3)(a),(14), 59(4)(b),(c),(9)

17.25   HB 79(2A)(b),(2B), 80(11); HB60+ 59(2A)(b),(2B), 61(12); NIHB 77(3),(4),(11), 78(10); NIHB60+ 57(3),(4),(15), 59(10)

17.26   Whenever you are eligible for HB on two homes, eligible rent in each benefit week is calculated by adding together the daily eligible rent for the two addresses for the appropriate number of days (para 3.15).

Examples: Moves and changes in liability

Moving within a council's area

A woman moves from one address to another within a council's area on Friday 30th June 2017. She is liable for rent at her old address up to and including Thursday 29th June and at her new address from Friday 30th June.

- Her HB changes on and from Friday 30th June (on a daily basis) to take account of her new eligible rent.

Moving out of a council's area

A man moves out of a council's area on Saturday 17th June 2017. He is liable for rent at his old address (which is not a hostel) up to and including Friday 16th June.

- His HB ends at the end of the benefit week containing his last day of liability for rent, in other words his last day of HB is Sunday 19th June.

A rent increase

A woman's rent goes up on Saturday 14th October 2017.

- If her entitlement to HB changes as a result, it changes on and from Saturday 14th October (on a daily basis).

Ending HB when you start to fall within the UC scheme

17.27   Unless you live in specified supported accommodation (para 2.13 and table 2.3), your HB ends when you:

(a)   make a claim for UC; or

(b)   become a couple with someone who is already on UC.

17.28   But the rules in para 17.27 only applies if you are under state pension credit age and meet the UC basic conditions. For further details, and the date of your HB ends, see paras 2.4-14.

Changes to UC in specified supported accommodation

17.29   When you live in specified supported accommodation you can get HB while you are getting (or could get) UC (para 2.13). If your UC starts or ends, the general rules apply (paras 17.19-21) so:

(a)   the date the change occurs is the first day of your new or nil entitlement to UC; and

(b)   the change takes effect in HB on the following Monday.

17.27-28   UCTP 5(2)(b), 7,8

17.29   HB 79(1); HB60+ 59(1); DAR 7(2)(a)(i),(2)

Moving out of specified supported accommodation when you are on UC

17.30   If you are on HB and UC and you move out of specified supported accommodation, your HB ends as described in table 17.3. Your UC normally starts including your housing costs for your new address from the first day of your assessment period (para 2.9) in which you become liable for them. This nearly always means you get both UC for housing costs and HB for a period (see the example) and this does not count as an overpayment of either benefit. For DWP guidance see circular HB A19/2013 paras 15-17.

Moving into specified supported accommodation when you are on UC

17.31   If you are on UC and you move into specified supported accommodation, you need to claim HB (paras 5.10 and 5.41-42). Your UC stops including housing costs for your old address from the first day of your assessment period (para 2.8) in which you stop being liable for them. This nearly always means there is a gap between the end of your UC for housing costs and the start of your HB (see the example). For DWP guidance see circular HB A19/2013 paras 15-17. See also para 25.9 for discretionary housing payments in these cases.

Examples: HB, UC and specified supported accommodation

The hostel in these examples is one of the types of specified supported accommodation (table 2.1). The residents are charged on a daily basis, including the day they arrive but not the day they depart.

Moving out

A resident is on UC and HB. His UC assessment periods begin on the 12th of each month. On Monday 21st August 2017 he moves into a council flat.

- The last day of his HB for the hostel is Sunday 20th August (table 17.3).
- The first day of his UC for housing costs for the council flat is Saturday 12th August (para 17.30).

Moving in

A resident moves in on Monday 21st August 2017. She is on UC and her assessment periods begin on the 5th of each month. She previously lived in a privately rented room.

- The last day of her UC for housing costs for the privately rented room is Thursday 4th August (para 17.31).
- The first day of her HB for the hostel is Monday 21st August (para 5.49).

Changes to pension credit

17.32   If a change in either guarantee credit or savings credit, whether due to a change in your circumstances or due to official error (para 17.61), affects your entitlement to HB, this takes effect from the date shown in table 17.4.

17.30   UCTP 5(2)(a) and as para 17.22

17.31   UCTP 5(2)(a), 6(8)

17.32   HB60+ 41(9), 60; NIHB60+ 39(11), 58; DAR 8(2),(3); NIDAR 8(2),(3)

Changes to tax credits

17.33   When your entitlement to working tax credit or child tax credit starts, changes or ends, the general rule applies (paras 17.19-21). But because of the way tax credits are paid, it can involve counting backwards or forwards from the pay date to work out when the change actually occurs. Table 17.5 explains this and includes examples.

Changes relating to social security benefits (the relevant benefit rule)

17.34   The following rule applies when entitlement to a social security benefit starts, changes, ends or is reinstated. It is sometimes called the 'relevant benefit rule'. It applies to all social security benefits (apart from UC or tax credits) received by you, your partner, or a child or young person.

17.35   The date such a change actually occurs is the first day of that new, different, nil or reinstated entitlement. The date the change takes effect in HB is shown in table 17.6.

17.36   However, if you are on HB and begin receiving JSA, ESA or IS towards your housing costs for the first time (e.g. because you have bought your home: paras 24.32-34), HB continues for a further four weeks.

17.37   When a social security benefit is found to have been awarded from a date in the past, any resulting increase in HB is awarded for the past period (so you get your arrears: see the second example). This is because the 'relevant benefit rule' over-rides the rule about late notification of beneficial changes (para 17.13).

Table 17.4 **When pension credit starts, changes or ends**

What the change is	When it takes effect in HB
Pension credit starts, increasing entitlement to HB	The Monday following the first day of entitlement to pension credit
Pension credit starts, reducing entitlement to HB	The Monday following the date the authority receives notification from the DWP about this (or, if later, the Monday following the first day of entitlement to pension credit)
Pension credit changes or ends, increasing entitlement to HB	The Monday of the benefit week in which pension credit changes or ends

17.34   HB 79(1); HB60+ 59(1); NIHB 77(1); NIHB60+ 57(1);
        DAR 4(7B),(7C), 7(2)(i),(p),(q),(s), 8(14), (14D),(14E),(14G); NIDAR 4(6B),(6C), 7(2)(h), 8(11)

17.36   HB 11(2),(4); NNIHB 11(2),(4)

T17.4   As para 17.32

Pension credit changes or ends,
reducing entitlement to HB:

■ if this is because you delayed   The Monday of the benefit week in
notifying a change in   which pension credit changes or ends
circumstances to the DWP

■ in any other case   The Monday following the date the
authority received notification from the
DWP about this (or, if later, the Monday
following the pension credit change or end)

Note:

If any of the above changes would take effect during your 'continuing payment' period
(para 17.54), the change is instead deferred until afterwards.

Table 17.5 **When a tax credit starts, changes or ends**

Four-weekly instalments

The pay date is the last day of the 28 days covered by the tax credit instalment.

So if a four-weekly instalment is due on the 30th of the month, it covers the period from
3rd to 30th of that month (both dates included).

For example:

■ if that is the first instalment ever of your tax credit, your HB changes on the Monday
following the 3rd of the month;

■ if that is the first instalment of a new rate of your tax credit, your HB changes on
the Monday following the 3rd of the month;

■ if that is the last instalment of your tax credit, the date the change occurs is the 31st
of the month, and your HB changes on the Monday following the 31st of the month.

Weekly instalments

The pay date is the last day of the seven days covered by the tax credit instalment.

So if a weekly instalment is due on the 15th of the month, it covers the period from the
9th to the 15th of that month (both dates included).

For example:

■ if that is the first instalment ever of your tax credit, your HB changes on the Monday
following the 9th of the month;

■ if that is the first instalment of a new rate of your tax credit, your HB changes on the
Monday following the 9th of the month;

■ if that is the last instalment of your tax credit, the date the change occurs is the 16th
of the month, and your HB changes on the Monday following the 16th of the month.

Examples: Changes to social security benefits

Going on to personal independence payment (PIP)

A claimant on HB is awarded PIP from Thursday 13th July 2017. The date of change is Thursday 13th July. So her entitlement to HB goes up on Thursday 13th July.

A claimant is found to have been awarded PIP from a date in the past.

No matter how far the PIP goes back, the council must award the claimant any as-yet-unawarded premium that results from being on PIP (and remove any non-dependant deductions if appropriate) all the way back to the start of his award of PIP (or the start of his award of HB if later).

Table 17.6 **Changes in social security benefits**

What the change is	When it takes effect in HB
A social security benefit reduces or ends:	
All cases (whether HB increases, reduces or ends as a result)	HB changes on the Monday following the change (see also paras 17.46 and 17.54)
A social security benefit starts, increases or is re-instated:	
If HB increases as a result	HB increases on the exact day (or from the start of the HB award if later)
If HB reduces or ends as a result	HB reduces or ends on the Monday following the change
If HB ended as above, but the social security benefit is then reinstated	HB is reinstated on the exact day
Exception for ESA and PIP:	
If you or your partner convert onto ESA (para 12.29) or convert from one ESA component to another or convert from DLA to PIP	HB changes on the exact day (see also para 17.45)
(This table does not apply to UC or tax credits: paras 17.27-33.)	

Changes in income, capital, household membership, etc

17.38   The general rules (paras 17.19-21) apply to all other changes – including changes in income, capital, membership of the family or household, and so on. But see also para 6.20 for when non-dependant deductions are delayed, and paras 13.7 and 15.11 for when arrears of income are (or are not) taken into account.

T17.6   As para 17.34

17.39   The council also has a discretion to disregard, for up to 30 weeks, changes in tax, national insurance and the maximum rate of tax credits when these result from a change in the law (e.g. the Budget). This discretion is rarely used.

Starting work

17.40   The general rules (paras 17.19-21) apply when someone starts work. Their effect is that if you start work on a Monday, you get a whole week of HB as though you had not started work. You may – after that – also qualify for an extended payment (para 17.46).

Changes ending HB

17.41   The general rules (paras 17.19-21) apply to any change of circumstances which means that you no longer satisfy all the basic conditions for HB (table 2.1) – for example if your capital now exceeds the upper limit or income is now too high to qualify. The only exception is when you become entitled to UC (paras 17.27-29).

Death

17.42   There is no provision to award HB following your death (see the reasoning in R(IS) 3/04 para 18). HB must stop at the end of the benefit week containing the date of your death under the normal rule about changes of circumstances (para 17.21). If you have a surviving partner, they may make their own claim. They are not 'covered' by your claim (but see paras 5.35-36). Also, the fact that your estate may be required to pay for a notice period on the property does not mean that you (or the estate) are still entitled to HB.

Changes in the law: case law (the anti-test-case rule)

17.43   The 'anti-test-case rule' applies in HB when an Upper Tribunal or court decides a case (a 'lead case') by interpreting the law in a new way. It requires all similar cases ('look-alike cases') to be amended to follow the new interpretation from the date of the decision on the lead case (not earlier). This does not apply to cases the council should have decided before the decision on the lead case; nor to appeals which a First-tier Tribunal 'stayed' to await the decision on the lead case; nor to decisions by Upper Tribunals: CH/532/2006.

Changes in the law: regulations, upratings, etc

17.44   When regulations relevant to HB are amended, the council alters your entitlement to HB from the date on which the amendment takes effect (unless entitlement reduces to nil, in which case para 17.41 applies). If the April up-rating for social security benefits or tax credits is different from that for HB (para 1.21), they are treated as up-rated on the same day as HB. The same applies if the DWP's 'assessed income figure' (table 13.3) changes at that time, when you convert onto ESA (para 12.29) between 1st and 16th April (both dates included), and when you convert from DLA to PIP in the same benefit week as the up-rating.

More than one change

17.45 If your have more than one change, each is dealt with in turn. But the following rules apply when changes which actually occur in the same benefit week would have an effect (under the earlier rules in this chapter) in different benefit weeks:

(a) If one of the changes is in:

- the annual up-rating (but only in cases when this takes effect on the first Monday in April rather than 1st April);

- the amount of liability for rent on a dwelling;

- moving into a new dwelling; or

- starting or stopping being eligible for HB on a former home or on two homes, including when the (4 weeks or 52 weeks) time limit runs out,

  the other changes in entitlement instead apply when that applies. And for this rule, the first item in the above list takes priority over the other three.

(b) In all other cases, all the changes take effect from the Monday of the benefit week in which the changes actually occur.

Extended payments

17.46 Extended payments (EPs) help long-term unemployed people who find work, by giving them four weeks extra HB. They also help people who increase their hours or earnings. They are also known as HB 'run-on'. They are like the extended payments some people get in JSA or ESA (and people often get both HB and JSA/ESA EPs at the same time).

Entitlement

17.47 You are entitled to an EP if you meet the conditions in table 17.7. As that table shows, there are two routes to qualifying for an EP; either of these is sufficient.

17.48 No claim is required for an EP. All the matters referred to in table 17.7 are for the council to determine (not the DWP), and the council is entitled to information and evidence in the normal way (paras 17.3-8). You must be notified about your entitlement to an EP.

Period and amount

17.49 An EP is awarded from the date the change (getting a job, etc) takes effect, and it lasts for four weeks (as illustrated in the example). In each of those four weeks, the amount of your EP is the greater of:

(a) the amount awarded in your last full benefit week before the EP started. This means the amount that would have been awarded if there was no benefit cap (para 6.21);

(b) the amount which would be your entitlement in that particular week if there were no such thing as EPs.

17.45   HB 42(8),79(4),(5); HB60+ 41(9),(10),59(4),(5); NIHB 39(8),77(6),(7); NIHB60+ 39(11),(12),57(6),(7);
         DAR 7(2)(q), 8(14E); NIDAR 7(2)(h), 8(11)

17.47   HB 2(1),72,73; HB60+ 2(1),53; NIHB 2(1),70,71; NIHB60+ 2(1),51

17.49   HB 72A,72B,72E,73A,73B,73E; HB60+ 53A,53B; NIHB 70A,70B,71A,71B; NIHB60+51A,51B

17.50 Throughout the EP, all changes in your circumstances are ignored. But if your entitlement to HB on two homes ceases during the EP, the amount of EP is reduced by the amount of the eligible rent on the home on which you no longer qualify for HB. And no EP is awarded for rent/rates during any period during which you are not liable for rent/rates.

17.51 If you or your partner reach pension credit age during the EP, the figure used for (b) throughout the EP is whichever would be higher using your entitlement before and after that age.

Table 17.7 **Entitlement to an extended payment**

If you have been on a 'qualifying income-related benefit'

You are entitled to an extended payment if:

- you or your partner start employment or self-employment, or increase your hours or earnings;
- this is expected to last for at least five weeks;
- you or your partner have been entitled to ESA(IR), JSA(IB), JSA(C) or IS continuously for at least 26 weeks (or any combination of those benefits in that period);
- immediately before starting the job, etc, you or your partner were on ESA(IR), JSA(IB) or IS. At this point being on JSA(C) is not enough; and
- entitlement to ESA(IR), JSA(IB) or IS ceases as a result of starting the job, etc.

If you have been on a 'qualifying contributory benefit'

You are entitled to extended payment if:

- you or your partner start employment or self-employment, or increase your hours or earnings;
- this is expected to last for at least five weeks;
- you or your partner have been entitled to ESA(C), IB or SDA continuously for at least 26 weeks (or any combination of those benefits in that period);
- immediately before starting the job, etc, you or your partner were on ESA(C), IB or SDA. And neither of you must be on ESA(IR), JSA(IB) or IS; and
- entitlement to ESA(C), IB or SDA ceases as a result of starting the job, etc.

Example: Extended payments

A claimant who meets all the conditions for an extended payment starts work on Monday 5th June 2017.

His award of HB continues up to and including Sunday 11th June 2017. His extended payment covers the period from Monday 12th June 2017 to Sunday 9th July 2017. If he then continues to qualify for HB after that, the new amount of HB is awarded from Monday 10th July 2017.

17.51   HB60+ 52; NIHB60+ 50

T17.7   As para 17.46

HB after an extended payment

17.52   If you qualify for HB based on your new income (and other circumstances) after the end of the EP, this is awarded in the normal way – and there is no requirement for you to make a fresh claim for this.

Variations for movers

17.53   If you are entitled to an EP, you are entitled to it even if you move home during the EP. In Great Britain, if the move is to another council's area, the determination, notification and award of the EP is done by the council whose area you are moving out of. That council may liaise with the council whose area you are moving into; and may pay the EP to it or to you.

Continuing payments

Entitlement

17.54   Continuing payments are awarded in HB whenever the DWP informs the council that someone on JSA(IB), ESA(IR) or IS has reached pension credit age (para 1.23) (or 65 if they stayed on JSA(IB) beyond that age), or has a partner and the partner has claimed pension credit. Continuing payments enable your award of HB to continue without a break while your entitlement to pension credit (if any) is determined.

Period and amount

17.55   The continuing payment starts immediately after the last day of your entitlement to JSA(IB)/ESA(IR)/IS, and lasts for four weeks plus any extra days to make it end on a Sunday. The amount during that period is calculated by treating you as having no income or capital. And if you move home, your eligible rent or rates are the higher of the amounts at the old and new addresses; and any non-dependant deductions are based on the circumstances at the new address.

Example: Continuing payments

A man is on HB and JSA(IB) when he reaches 65, on Thursday 9th November 2017. The DWP informs the council that his entitlement to pension credit is being considered.

His continuing payment of HB is awarded from Thursday 9th November 2017 to Sunday 10th December 2017 – a total of four weeks and four days.

By then the council knows the claimant's entitlement to HB based on his new circumstances, and awards this from Monday 11th December 2017.

17.52   HB 72D,73D; HB60+ 53D; NIHB 70C,71C; NIHB60+ 51C

17.53   HB 72C,73C,115,116; HB60+ 53C,96,97

17.54   HB60+ 54; NIHB60+ 52

Terminology

Revisions and supersessions

17.56   In HB law, a changed decision is also known as a revision or a supersession:

(a) a 'revision' is required when a decision was wrong from the outset. When a decision is revised, the revision goes back to the beginning (to the date of the decision in question);

(b) a 'supersession' is required when there has been a change of circumstances. When a decision is superseded, the supersession does not go right back: there is always a 'before' and an 'after'.

Some examples are given in table 17.8. Each of the above results in a new decision, which can itself be revised or superseded or appealed.

Table 17.8 **Revisions and supersessions: examples**

Situation	How it is dealt with in HB
Changes of circumstances	
A change notified more than one month after it occurred (this time limit can be extended) if you qualify for more HB	**Supersession:** Typically, from the Monday following the day the council receives the notification (paras 17.11-13)
Any other change of circumstances	**Supersession:** Typically, from the Monday following the day the change occurs (para 17.21)
Overpayments and official errors	
Overpayments, whatever the cause; and underpayments caused by official error	**Revision or supersession:** From when the overpayment or underpayment began
Successful requests for a reconsideration, etc	
Reconsiderations requested within one month (which can be extended)	**Revision:** From the date the decision took effect or should have
Reconsiderations requested outside that time limit (paras 16.75-80 and 17.68-69)	**Supersession:** From the Monday of the week in which the council received the request
Appeals if the council is able to revise in your favour (para 16.87)	**Revision:** From the date the decision took effect or should have

---

17.56   CPSA sch 7; NICPSA sch 7; DAR 4,7,8; NIDAR 4,7,8

Closed period supersessions

17.57   A 'closed period supersession' is done when someone's entitlement to HB is discovered to have reduced to nil for a fixed period in the past (and recommenced at the same or a different rate after that). For example, a claimant has been on JSA(IB) (and HB) for many years but worked last Christmas for a fixed contract of three weeks for a very high income. He did not declare that fact then, but it is discovered now. A 'closed period supersession' means that the council (now) reduces his entitlement to nil for that past period (and recovers the overpayment: chapter 18). The advantage (administratively and to the claimant) is that the claimant remains currently entitled to HB (based on his original claim) without needing to reclaim. There have been doubts about this rule, but it is correct in income support (CIS/2595/2003), and the DWP considers it to be correct in HB (circular HB/CTB A6/2009).

Reviewing and correcting HB

Reviewing decisions

17.58   The council can reconsider any decision it has made about your HB. This is often called 'reviewing' a decision. A review may show that:

(a)   there has been a change of circumstances the council did not know about. In this case the rules in paras 17.9-55 apply;

(b)   a decision was wrong from the outset. In this case the rules in paras 17.60-70 apply.

Information, evidence and decision notices

17.59   The council can ask you for information and evidence it reasonably requires in order to review and correct a decision. You are responsible for providing this in the same way as when you made your claim (para 5.13) and the council must take it into account if you provide it within one month, or longer if reasonable. The council must issue a decision notice about any change it makes to your HB: see paras 16.3-7.

Correcting decisions

17.60   The council can correct mistakes in any HB decision it has made. This applies to mistakes found by the council itself, or which you (or the person your HB is paid to) have brought to its attention. The detailed rules are in paragraphs 17.62-70.

17.61   The law about correcting decisions uses four different terms:

(a)   a 'mistake of fact' means that the decision was based on an incorrect fact (without at this stage saying that it was necessarily anybody's fault);

(b)   an 'error of law' means that the decision was based on an incorrect understanding of the law;

(c)   an 'accidental error' is something on the lines of a slip of the pen – a failure by the authority to put into action (or to record) its true intentions;

17.58   HB 89(1); HB60+ 70(1); NIHB 85(1); NIHB60+ 66(1)

17.59   AA 5(1); NIAA 5(1); HB 86(1),(3); HB60+ 67(1),(3); NIHB 82(1),(3); NIHB60+ 63(1),(3); DAR 4(5), 7(5); NIDAR 4(5), 7(5)

(d) an 'official error' is defined independently (para17.63) and can include one or a combination of the above (CH/943/2003).

'Revisions' and 'supersessions' are explained in paras 17.56-57.

Correcting accidental errors

17.62   The council may correct an accidental error in any decision (including a revised or superseding decision), or the record of any decision, at any time. The correction is deemed to be part of the decision or record, and the council must give written notice of the correction as soon as practicable to you and any other person affected.

Correcting other official errors

17.63   The council may revise (or supersede if it cannot revise) a decision at any time if the decision arose from an 'official error'. An 'official error' means an error by the council, the DWP or HM Revenue and Customs – or someone acting on their behalf (such as a contractor or a housing association which verifies HB claims). However, something does not count as an 'official error' if it was caused wholly or partly by any person or body other than the above, nor if it is an error of law which is shown to have been an error only by a subsequent decision of the Upper Tribunal, the NI Commissioners or a court.

17.64   The effect may be that there has been an underpayment of HB (in which case the arrears must be awarded – no matter how far back they go) or an overpayment (which may or may not be recoverable: chapter 18).

When an appeal decision applies to a case

17.65   The council may revise a decision at any time to take account of an appeal decision in the same case (made by a tribunal, the Upper Tribunal, the NI Commissioners or a court) which the council was not aware of at the time it made the decision.

Mistakes of fact resulting in an overpayment

17.66   The council may revise or supersede a decision at any time if the decision was made in ignorance of, or was based on a mistake as to, some material fact – and the decision was, as a result, more favourable than it would otherwise have been. This creates an overpayment (which may or may not be recoverable: chapter 18).

Mistakes of fact discovered within one month

17.67   The council may revise a decision if, within one month of the date of notifying it, or longer if reasonable, the council has sufficient information to show that it was made in ignorance of, or was based on a mistake as to, some material fact. This can arise only in the case of increases to entitlement (for decreases see para 17.66).

17.62   DAR 10A(1),(2); NIDAR 10A(1),(2)

17.63   DAR 1(2),4(2); NIDAR 1(2),4(2)

17.65   DAR 4(7); NIDAR 4(6)

17.66   DAR 4(2); NIDAR 4(2)

17.67   DAR 4(1),8(4),(5); NIDAR 4(1),8(4),(5)

Other mistakes of fact

17.68   If none of the previous rules in this section apply, the council may supersede a decision at any time if the decision was made in ignorance of, or was based on a mistake as to, some material fact. This can arise only in the case of increases to entitlement (for decreases see para 17.66). For example this rule can be used when you request a reconsideration but are out of time, which is sometimes called an 'any time review'.

17.69   The supersession in such a case takes effect from the Monday at the beginning of the benefit week in which:

(a) the request was received from you or another person affected (if a request was indeed made); or

(b) the council first had information to show that the original decision was made in ignorance or mistake of fact (in any other case).

Other errors of law

17.70   A final rule applies if a decision was based on an error of law but was not due to 'official error' (para 17.63). (This could arise if the Upper Tribunal, NI Commissioners or a court interpret the law in an unexpected way: para 17.43.) The council may supersede the decision at any time. The supersession takes effect from the date on which it is made (or, if earlier, from the date the person's request was received).

Suspending, restoring and terminating HB

17.71   This section describes how the council can suspend, restore and terminate HB. To suspend means stopping making payments for the time being, usually in order to avoid an overpayment or to seek information or evidence. To restore means starting payments again – either at the same amount as before or at a different amount, depending on the circumstances. To terminate means ending an award of HB altogether.

Suspending HB

17.72   The council may suspend HB if any of the following circumstances apply:

(a) the council doubts whether the conditions of entitlement to HB are fulfilled;

(b) the council is considering whether to change a decision about HB;

(c) the council considers there may be a recoverable overpayment of HB;

(d) a First-tier or Upper Tribunal has made a decision (in this or another case) and the council is awaiting the decision or a statement of reasons, or is considering making a further appeal;

17.68   CPSA sch 7 para 4(5),(6); NICPSA sch 7 para 4(4),(5); DAR 7(2)(b),8(4)(5); NIDAR 7(2)(b),8(4),(5)

17.69   DAR 8(4)-(5); NIDAR 8(4)-5)

17.70   CPSA sch 7 para 4(5),(6); NICPSA sch 7 para 4(4),(5); DAR 7(2)(b); NIDAR 7(2)(b)

17.71   DAR 4(5), 7(5); NIDAR 4(4)

(e) an appeal has been made, or leave to appeal has been sought, against a decision of a First-tier or Upper Tribunal or court in the case to be suspended;

(f) an appeal has been made, or leave to appeal has been sought, against a decision of an Upper Tribunal or court in a different HB case, and this may affect the case to be suspended;

(g) you (or another person affected) have failed to provide information or evidence needed by the council to consider changing a decision about HB.

In such cases, HB is usually suspended in full (though the law permits the council to suspend only part).

Restoring HB

17.73   When payments of HB have been suspended, the council must restore them (to the extent that you are still entitled) within 14 days of the following or as soon as reasonably practicable:

■   in cases (a) to (c) (para 17.72), the council is satisfied that HB is properly payable and no outstanding matters remain to be resolved;

■   in case (d), the council decides not to make the further appeal (if it decides to make the further appeal case (e) or (f) then applies);

■   in cases (e) and (f), the appeal or request for leave has been determined;

■   in case (g), the claimant has responded as required (para 17.74).

Information and evidence

17.74   When payments of HB have been suspended for failure to provide information or evidence (para 17.72(g)), the council must notify you of the suspension and of what information and evidence is required. You must then, within one month or such longer period as the council considers necessary:

(a) provide the information or evidence required; or

(b) satisfy the council that the information or evidence does not exist, or is impossible for you to obtain.

Terminating HB

17.75   When payments of HB have been suspended for failure to provide information or evidence (para 17.72(g)) and you have failed to respond as required (para 17.74) your HB entitlement is terminated from the date on which the payments were suspended (i.e. no further payments are made). In some cases, termination should not be done unless a reminder request has been sent: [2008] UKUT 13 (ACC). Terminating benefit under this rule is a kind of supersession: CH/2555/2007. The rule cannot be used to end HB from an earlier date: CH/3736/2006, so if entitlement did end earlier, this is done as an (ordinary) supersession from that earlier date. The second of the examples illustrates this. As may be observed, the two

---

17.72   DAR 10; NIDAR 10; HB sch 9; HB60+ sch 8; NIHB sch 10; NIHB60+ sch 9

17.74   DAR 11,13(1),(2); NIDAR 11,13(1),(2)

17.75   DAR 13(3),(4); NIDAR 13(3),(4)

concepts (termination as a type of supersession, and ordinary supersession at nil) each have the same effect of stopping someone's HB (though the case law generally disapproves of this being described as 'cancelling' HB, because that word does not appear in the law: CH/2555/2007). If in the above or other circumstances HB was wrongly terminated, it must be reinstated: CH/2995/2006.

17.76   A decision to terminate HB must be notified to you and any other person affected.

Appeals

17.77   You have a right of appeal to a First-tier Tribunal (table 16.4) about a decision to terminate HB (CH/402/2007), or to restore HB at a different amount or for a different reason; but not about a determination to suspend HB, or to restore HB at the same amount for the same reasons. A decision to suspend HB may, however, be challenged by judicial review if it is irrational: R (Sanneh) v SSWP.

Examples: Suspending, restoring and terminating HB

A change of circumstances

The council obtains information that a claimant on HB has changed jobs. It suspends his award immediately, and writes to him allowing him one month to respond.

After two weeks, he sends in the necessary information and evidence, and he remains entitled to HB.

The council restores his HB from the date payments were suspended, making any change in his entitlement from the Monday after the day he got the new job.

Another change of circumstances

A claimant has been on HB for some years. On Wednesday 16th August 2017 the council obtains information that he has been doing undeclared work. It suspends his award from the earliest possible date so that the last payment of HB is for week ending Sunday 20th August 2017, and writes to him allowing him one month to respond.

Shortly afterwards he writes in to admit that he has been working since Monday 5th June 2017 and knows that he does not qualify for HB based on those earnings.

The council terminates his HB on Sunday 20th August 2017. It also supersedes his HB (at nil) from Monday 12th June 2017. This creates an overpayment of HB from Monday 12th June to Sunday 20th August inclusive. The overpayment is not due to official error and so is recoverable.

A review

The council decides to review a claimant's award of HB and sends her a short form asking her to confirm her circumstances, allowing her one month to reply. Because the claimant

17.76   CPSA sch 7 para 15; NICPSA sch 7 para 15; DAR 14; NIDAR 14

17.77   R (Sanneh) v SSWP 30/04/12 QBD [2013] EWHC 1840 (Admin) www.bailii.org/ew/cases/EWHC/Admin/2012/1840.html

does not reply within the month, the council suspends her HB and writes to her requesting her to say what her circumstances are, allowing her one further month to respond.

Because the claimant again does not reply within a month, the council terminates her award of HB and notifies her of this.

Two weeks later she returns the original short form, declaring that her circumstances have not changed. The council is satisfied with this and restores her HB from the date payments were suspended.

Chapter 18 **Overpayments**

What is an overpayment?

18.1   An HB 'overpayment' is an amount of HB which has been 'paid' that you had no entitlement to under the HB regulations. The authority may have paid it directly to you or to your landlord or your landlord's agent. If you are a council tenant HB is usually paid as a rebate to your local authority rent account. In Northern Ireland an HB overpayment may take the form of a rebate on your rate account.

18.2   Overpayments can occur when the authority first decides your entitlement or following a change in your entitlement (technically after the authority has revised or superseded an earlier decision). An overpayment can also arise in relation to a payment on account if the authority later decides that it was greater than your entitlement to HB for the relevant period.

18.3   Tribunals dealing with overpayment appeals (except in relation to payments on account) expect the authority to show which revisions or supersessions relate to the overpayment (CH/3439/2004, C3/07-08(IS), C2/10-11(HB)). A tribunal can remedy defective decision-making by the authority (R(IB)2/04), but if the authority hasn't made a revision or supersession or if such changes to entitlement have no legal foundation there is no overpayment.

18.4   The overpayment and recovery of HB creates major difficulties for claimants, landlords and authorities. Many authorities fail to:

(a) follow the correct decision-making process;

(b) notify claimants and landlords correctly;

(c) keep adequate records; or

(d) account for overpayments properly.

As a result they create rent arrears for themselves, debts for claimants and landlords and make inaccurate subsidy claims (DWP S4/2014 para 4(a)).

18.1   AA 75(1), 134(2); NIAA 73(1), 126(1)-(2); HB 99; HB60+ 80; NIHB 96; NIHB60+ 77

18.2   HB 99; HB60+ 80; NIHB 96; NIHB60+ 77

The authority's duties

18.5   When the authority identifies an HB overpayment it should:

(a)   establish the cause;

(b)   determine whether or not it is recoverable;

(c)   identify the period of the overpayment and calculate the amount;

(d)   consider whether or not to recover it;

(e)   determine who to recover it from; and

(f)   notify you and any other person affected such as your landlord (normally within 14 days or as soon as reasonably practicable after that).

18.6   The DWP provides authorities with detailed guidance on these matters and more in its HB Overpayments Guide (2015) (OG) [www]. There is also a good practice guide on recovering HB overpayments [www].

The cause of an overpayment

18.7   The authority must establish the cause of the overpayment to:

(a)   decide whether it is recoverable;

(b)   provide you (and anyone else it should or may recover the overpayment from) with required information;

(c)   claim the correct amount of subsidy from central government; and

(d)   decide the method of recovery in certain cases.

18.8   To establish the cause of the overpayment the authority needs to consider what is the substantial cause of the overpayment viewed in a commonsense way (R (Sier) v Cambridge CC HB Review Board [2001]; [2010] UKUT 57 (AAC) para 19); or who really caused the overpayment ([2011] UKUT 266 (AAC) para 68).

How an overpayment is 'caused'

18.9   The main causes of overpayments are:

(a)   claimant error, e.g. you fail to tell the authority about a change of circumstances which you have a duty to report (but if the authority disputes you reported it then it is a question of fact the tribunal is entitled to decide: no authority's procedures are infallible: [2014] UKUT 23 (AAC)); or

(b)   local authority error, e.g. you tell the authority about a change in your circumstances but it fails to act on this information;

(c)   DWP error, e.g. the jobcentre plus, pension service, or disability and carers service makes a mistaken award of JSA(IB)/ESA(IR), pension credit or income support;

(d)   third party error, e.g. your landlord in receipt of HB gives the authority incorrect information about a rent increase;

18.6   www.gov.uk/government/publications/housing-benefit-overpayments-guide
          www.gov.uk/government/publications/housing-benefit-overpayment-recovery-good-practice

18.8   R (Sier) v Cambridge CC HBRB 08/10/01 CA [2001] EWCA Civ 1523 www.bailii.org/ew/cases/EWCA/Civ/2001/1523.html

(e) no-one's fault, e.g. you get a backdated pay award and this affects your entitlement to HB in the past;

(f) a payment on account turns out to be too great;

(g) HB payment technicalities, e.g. you get a rebate for a future period, but your entitlement is changed before that period; or

(h) other reasons.

More than one cause of an overpayment

18.10 If there is more than one cause of an overpayment, the authority must separate these out (CH/858/2006). This is the case, for example, where you delay telling the authority that your earnings have increased and it then delays acting on that information. The authority should identify the two causes, periods and amounts of the overpayment and make separate decisions about whether the two amounts are recoverable.

Which overpayments are recoverable

Non-recoverable overpayments

18.11 An HB overpayment is not recoverable if:

(a) it arose because of 'official error' by a relevant authority (para 18.13); and

(b) you, someone acting on your behalf, or the person paid the benefit (if different), could not reasonably have been expected to realise it was an overpayment either at the time of receipt of the payment or of any notice relating to that payment (para 18.14).

18.12 All other overpayments are recoverable. This includes:

(a) an overpayment of a payment on account of HB (para 16.23) which is being recovered by deductions from ongoing HB;

(b) an overpayment of HB to a council or NIHE tenant, which was caused by an 'official error' (para 18.13) but which relates to a period in the future;

(c) an overpayment of HB for rates in Northern Ireland caused by a retrospective reduction in regional rates.

Meaning of 'official error'

18.13 An official error is a mistake, whether in the form of an act or omission, made by the authority, the DWP or HMRC (and in Northern Ireland DfC and the former DSD and DEL) or someone on their behalf (such as a contractor or a housing association which verifies HB claims). It does not include cases where you, someone acting on your behalf, or the payee, caused or materially contributed to that error. The test is whether you contributed towards the error, not whether you contributed towards the overpayment (CH/215/2008 at para 28). Overpayment appeals often require consideration of what is and is not an 'official error'. Significant cases are summarised in table 18.1.

18.11   HB 100(2); HB60+ 81(2); NIHB 97(2); NIHB60+ 78(2)

18.12   HB 100(1); HB60+ 81(1); NIHB 97(1); NIHB60+ 78(1); HB 93(3), 100(4); HB60+ 74(3), 81(4); NIHB 90(3), 97(4); NIHB60+ 71(3), 78(4)

18.13   HB 100(3); HB60+ 81(3); NIHB 97(3); NIHB60+ 78(3)

Table 18.1 **Overpayments case law:**
meaning of 'official error'

- *Terminology:* In this context, a 'mistake' is not different from an 'official error' and it is artificial to try and read different meanings into these two terms (CH/943/2003).

- *Previous tribunal decisions:* Official error includes where an earlier tribunal has decided that a DWP/HMRC decision is wrong (CH/943/2003).

- *Overpayment caused by DWP benefit being increased or reinstated on appeal:* Where the overpayment is caused by a DWP benefit being reinstated following an appeal this amounts to an official error ([2015] UKUT 197 (AAC) reversing CH/38/2008).

- *The authority:* In this context includes any part of the authority and is not confined to any department within it (CH/3586/2007).

- *Designated office:* The claimant's circumstances had been repeatedly notified to the housing department. Not to pass the information on to the benefits service or advise the claimant to do so was an official error to which the claimant had not contributed (CH/2567/2007).

- *Whether official bodies talk to each other:* Just because one department of the DWP holds the information it cannot be presumed that another DWP department is also aware of it: 'The claimant's duty is to tell whom she is told to tell' (Hinchy v Secretary of State for Work and Pensions, reported as R(IS)7/05).

- *Failure by DWP to pass on information:* The failure of the DWP to notify the authority that JSA(IB) or income support has ceased is not an official error because the claimant has a duty to notify the authority of this (R (Sier) v Cambridge CC). But this does not apply to pension credit (and some other) cases in which it is the pension, disability and carers service's duty to notify the authority of changes (table 17.2).

- *Failure by DWP to act on a promise:* If the DWP undertook to forward a notice of a change to the authority and then failed to do so, that might amount to official error (CH/939/2004, CH/3761/2005).

- *Failure by the authority to cross-check:* The fact that the claimant disclosed income (etc) in a previous claim (but not in their current claim) does not mean that the authority's failure to cross-check is official error (R(H) 1/04, CH/2794/2004).

- *Failure by the authority to ask a fundamental question about eligibility:* (here, whether the child mainly lived with her mother, the claimant, which it did not) amounted to official error, as can a failure to amend forms CH/4228/2006 and [2014] UKUT 201 (AAC).

T18.1   R (Sier) v Cambridge HBRB see footnote to para 18.8

- *Failure to recognise relevant information on document provided for a different purpose:* There is no general rule that the failure by the authority to recognise information as relevant which was provided for a different purpose cannot be official error: it depends on the particular circumstances (CH/3925/2006).

- *Failure by the authority to check potential changes:* Failure by the authority to check up on potential changes in entitlement to a tax credit is not official error (R(H) 2/04), nor is failure to check up on a potential increase in incapacity benefit (CH/687/2006) or earnings (CH/3/2008).

- *Delay by authority in dealing with a notified change:* In a case in which the claimant notified her increased earnings on 19th April, but her council did not take them into account until 13th May (24 days later), this was quick enough not to constitute official error. In reaching this decision, the commissioner compared the council's duty to act on a change of circumstances with its duty to act on a claim, where there is a time limit of 14 days (para 16.2). The 24 days the commissioner allowed in this case was based on its individual circumstances (CH/858/2006).

- *Delay in applying to the rent officer:* A delay in applying to the rent officer can be an official error (CH/361/2006).

- *Claimant reports wrong amount of benefit due to overpayment deductions:* If the claimant reports the incorrect amount of benefit because the DWP is making deductions, the fact that the authority does not realise the mistake does not amount to an official error (CH/56/08).

- *Claimant's method of notifying changes:* Where a claimant had notified a change by telephone only, and the council had failed to act on it, this did not necessarily mean that the claimant had materially contributed to the error (CH/2409/2005).

Awareness of being overpaid

18.14 An overpayment which arises due to official error is recoverable only if you, someone acting on your behalf, or the person paid (if different), could reasonably have been expected to realise that it was an overpayment – either at the time the payment is received, or at the time of any decision notice relating to it is issued. This test is often considered on appeal. Significant cases are summarised in table 18.2.

18.14   HB 100(2); HB60+ 81(2); NIHB 97(2); NIHB60+ 78(2)

Table 18.2 **Overpayments case law: awareness of being overpaid in official error cases**

- *Purpose of the rule:* The purpose of the rule is to protect a claimant who has relied on being entitled to the payment so that, having innocently spent it, they do not have to repay money they cannot afford (CH/1176/2003).

- *'Was' or 'might be' an overpayment?* The test is whether there was a reasonable expectation that there was an overpayment not whether there might be one (R v Liverpool CC ex parte Griffiths, CH/2935/2005, CH/858/2006).

- *Burden of proof:* The burden of proof (paras 1.45-46) is on the person stating that they could not reasonably have been expected to realise – not on the council stating that they could (CH/4918/2003).

- *What can a person reasonably be expected to realise?* What a particular claimant could have been expected to realise varies according to their knowledge, experience and capacity (R v Liverpool CC ex parte Griffiths). For example, someone who had needed the council's help to fill in his application form may be less likely to realise he was overpaid (CH/2935/2005); someone from a country where (the equivalent of) tax credits are taken into account in a different way (in the assessment of the equivalent of HB) might not realise that they are taken into account as income in the UK (CH/858/2006).

- *Information available to the claimant:* Usually involves considering what the claimant should have realised from previous experience of the scheme and the documents provided by the authority (CH/2554/2002).

- *Receipt of a notice:* Whether a person could reasonably have been expected to realise at the time of any notice, refers to a notice about the award of HB, not the overpayment notice – otherwise the rule would be meaningless (CH/1176/2003).

- *Comprehensible notice:* If a notice of an award contains the basis of the calculation in a reasonably clear manner, and it is clear that there has been a mistake in the claimant's favour, then the overpayment is recoverable – because the claimant could reasonably have been expected to realise (CH/2409/2005).

- *Claimant queries notice but authority continues to pay wrong amount:* Where the claimant queries the decision notice but the council continues to pay, there comes a point where the claimant is entitled to rely on the notice and accept that the council knows best (CH/3240/2007).

- *Reference to wages omitted in the decision notice:* If there was no reference at all to the claimant's wages in the notice, whereas their other income was listed, a 'claimant of normal intelligence' could reasonably be expected to deduce that there had been a mistake and that they were overpaid (CH/2554/2002).

T18.2   R v Liverpool CC ex p Griffiths 14/03/90 QBD 22 HLR 312
         www.rightsnet.org.uk/pdfs/liverpool_griffiths.pdf

■ *Reference to state retirement pension omitted in the decision notice:* If there was no reference at all to the claimant's state retirement pension in the notice, the claimant might have concluded that the pension was being ignored (perhaps because it was disregarded or because everybody of his age received one); and 'a typical claimant cannot reasonably be expected to read or understand the calculations' so they could not reasonably be expected to deduce that they were overpaid (CH/2554/2002).

■ *A disparity between the claimant's declared earnings and the amount on the decision notice:* If this is large (in this case earnings of £210 assessed and notified as less than £50) then it would be reasonable to expect the claimant to realise that they must be being overpaid (CH/2943/2007). For a similar case relating to an incorrect eligible rent, see [2008] UKUT 6 AAC.

■ *The claimant must have some reason to believe the council's figures are wrong:* A claimant cannot be expected to seek advice unless they have some reason to believe the figures are wrong. A tribunal should ask the claimant how they reconciled their own knowledge of their earnings with the figures in the notice, to give them the opportunity to explain why they could not be expected to realise there was an overpayment (CH/2943/2007).

■ *Claimant telephoned to say they thought there was a mistake:* If there has been an official error, and the claimant alleges they telephoned to say they thought there had been, then the council should determine whether they in fact did so before going on to consider if this affects whether the overpayment is recoverable (CH/4065/2001).

■ *Claimant's other actions in relation to the award:* The authority in this case had asked for evidence of earnings for the wrong period. The claimant provided what they asked for, but not other evidence that would have shown his income was higher. His other actions (including telephoning to check things) suggested he was not trying to mislead and there was no reason to suppose he could reasonably have been expected to realise there was an overpayment (CH/1780/2005).

■ *Time of receipt of a payment:* The 'time' of a payment by cheque is fairly narrow, but a telephone call from the council a couple of hours after the claimant received a large HB cheque, advising her it was incorrect, may be soon enough to mean that the claimant was aware at the 'time of receipt' that it was an overpayment (CH/1176/2003).

■ *When the overpayment is a rebate:* If the overpayment is of a rebate, the council may need to consider whether the claimant could reasonably have been expected to realise that there was an overpayment 'at the times when credits were applied to his rent account' (CH/1675/2005).

■ *What a landlord could have realised:* It is not always the case that a landlord knows when a claimant has left their accommodation ([2013] UKUT 232 (AAC)). And in the case of a landlord company or housing association, it is what the whole organisation might reasonably have been expected to have realised that is relevant (CH/4918/2003).

Meaning of 'claimant or third party error'

18.15   You or a third party can only 'cause' an overpayment if you intentionally or unintentionally misrepresent, or fail to disclose, a material fact. However, you may not be expected to disclose a fact if you were given clear advice to the contrary by an official of the authority or the DWP (R(SB) 3/89).

The amount of a recoverable overpayment

18.16   The amount of a recoverable overpayment is the difference between what was paid and what you were entitled to under the regulations. The following rules can reduce the amount of the overpayment.

Underlying entitlement

18.17   When the authority calculates the amount of a recoverable overpayment, it should deduct any amount 'which should have been determined to be payable' in respect of the whole or part of the overpayment period:

(a)   on the basis of the claim as presented to the authority;

(b)   on the basis of the claim as it would have appeared had any misrepresentation or non-disclosure been remedied before the decision; or

(c)   on the basis of the claim as it would have appeared if any change of circumstances (except a change of the dwelling which you occupied) had been notified at the time that change occurred.

This means whatever would have been awarded (to you, or to any partner had they claimed: [2015] UKUT 460 (AAC)) if the authority had known the facts of the case throughout, and all changes of circumstances had been notified on time (including frequent changes: [2015] UKUT 423 (AAC)).

18.18   HB not recovered under this rule is called 'underlying entitlement' to distinguish it from any actual entitlement to HB. The application of the underlying entitlement rule is mandatory but the DWP has expressed concern that some authorities are not considering it when calculating recoverable overpayments (DWP G2/2013, para 16).

Why underlying entitlement can occur

18.19   Underlying entitlement overrides the rules about:

(a)   which partner in a couple (or polygamous marriage) is the claimant;

(b)   late notice of beneficial changes (para 17.11): see example 1; and

(c)   late requests for a reconsideration (para 17.68).

18.16   HB 99; HB60+ 80; NIHB 96; NIHB60+ 77
18.17   HB 104(1); HB60+ 85(1); NIHB 101(1); NIHB60+ 82(1)

The stage at which the authority considers underlying entitlement

18.20   When a recoverable overpayment arises, the authority may already have information enabling it to allow underlying entitlement (as in example 1). And in all cases, unless there is no possibility of underlying entitlement (e.g. you had more than £16,000 throughout the overpayment period), the authority should invite you to provide information and evidence to establish underlying entitlement (OG paras 3.32-3.34) (using the usual rules about obtaining information and evidence: para 5.13) and the onus is on you to do this (R(H) 1/05).

18.21   If underlying entitlement has not been identified when the authority determines and notifies the overpayment, you (or other overpaid person) may ask the authority to reconsider or appeal to a tribunal – and in doing so may include information which establishes underlying entitlement. Once the time limit for appeal has expired (one month which can be increased to 13 months in special circumstances), it is not possible to allow underlying entitlement (OG para 3.37) – unless there has been an official error (para 17.63).

Calculation rules for underlying entitlement

18.22   There are two calculation rules:

(a) only underlying entitlement falling within the overpayment period is used to reduce the amount of the overpayment; and

(b) underlying entitlement may reduce an overpayment to nil, but it can never be used to actually pay money out to you or anyone else.

If you still paid rent to the authority or rates in Northern Ireland

18.23   If you are a council/NIHE tenant and during the period of the overpayment you paid rent above your erroneous liability then the authority may deduct these payments from the recoverable overpayment. The rule applies equally to payments of rates in Northern Ireland.

Examples: Underlying entitlement

1. When there has been late notice of a change

Information: Blythe's non-dependant Gwenyth moved out six months ago, but Blythe did not tell her council until three months ago (and had no special circumstances for the late reporting of this change) so her council removed the non-dependant deduction from three months ago. Today the council discovered that Blythe has undeclared earnings from work over the previous nine months.

Assessment: The underlying entitlement rule means that the council must reduce the amount of the overpayment (due to Blythe's undeclared earnings from work) by the amount it could not award in relation to Gwenyth moving out. This results in a lower recoverable overpayment; it may even reduce the overpayment to nil; but in no circumstances can it result in Blythe getting more benefit.

18.22   HB 104(1); HB60+ 85(1); NIHB 101(1); NIHB60+ 82(1)

18.23   HB 104(2); HB60+ 85(2); NIHB 101(2); NIHB60+ 82(2)

2. Calculation rules

Information: In William's case, there is a recoverable overpayment of £5 per week for weeks 1 to 20 inclusive (20 x £5 = £100), and underlying entitlement (because William did not tell the council about a beneficial change on time) in weeks 11 to 20 inclusive of £15 per week.

Assessment: The authority uses William's underlying entitlement in weeks 11 to 20 inclusive (10 x £15 = £150) to reduce the overpayment (£100). It is enough to reduce the recoverable overpayment to nil but it can't award the remainder of the underlying entitlement to William.

Deductions if you move home within the same authority

18.24   When the authority calculates a recoverable overpayment caused by you moving home within its area, it has the discretion to offset your HB entitlement at the new address against the HB overpayment on your previous property. However, the authority can only use this rule where:

(a)   you were awarded a rent allowance on the old address that you were not entitled to because you had moved; and

(b)   the HB on the old and new home is paid to the same person (e.g. you or the same landlord) by the same authority.

Where the authority deducts this amount it should treat an equivalent amount as having been paid in respect of your new home.

Example: Calculating an overpayment when you move home

Bob gets a rent allowance of £100 a week. He moves to a new home where he gets HB of £110 a week. Bob doesn't tell the authority about the move for three weeks after leaving the earlier address. This results in an overpayment of £300 on the old address.

Bob is entitled to £330 a week on the new address for the same period. The authority may reduce the amount of the recoverable overpayment on Bob's old home by £300, reducing it to nil, and paying Bob the remaining £30 in relation to his new home.

The diminishing capital rule

18.25   The authority should use this overpayment calculation rule if your recoverable overpayment:

(a)   arose due to capital being wrongly taken into account (for any reason); and

(b)   was in respect of a period of more than 13 weeks.

18.24   HB 104A; HB60+ 85A; NIHB 101A; NIHB60+ 82A

18.25   HB 103; HB60+ 84; NIHB 100; NIHB60+ 81

Example: The diminishing capital rule

Thomas failed to declare capital of £16,033. When his council discovers this, there has been a recoverable overpayment for 30 weeks. Throughout that time Thomas got HB of £9 per week, he had no other capital at all, and the figure of £16,033 remained the same.

- In the first 13 weeks, he is not entitled to HB:
  Overpayment: 13 x £9   =   £117

- His capital is then treated as reduced by this amount:
  £16,033 – £117   =   £15,916

- In the second 13 weeks, based on this reduced capital,
  he is entitled to HB of £5 per week, so the overpayment is
  £4 per week. Overpayment: 13 x £4   =   £52

- His capital is then treated as further reduced by this amount:
  £15,916 – £52   =   £15,864

- In the remaining 4 weeks, based on this further
  reduced capital, he is still entitled to HB of £5 per week,
  so the overpayment is still £4 per week. Overpayment: 4 x £4   =   £16

- So the total overpayment of HB for the 30 weeks is   £185

18.26   In such cases, the authority should take the following steps:

(a) at the end of the first 13 weeks of the overpayment period, the authority should treat the capital as reduced by the amount overpaid during those 13 weeks. This gives it an imaginary capital figure which it should use to calculate the overpayment after that;

(b) the authority should do the same again at the end of each 13 weeks until the end of the overpayment period;

(c) but when the authority calculates your HB after the end of the overpayment period, it should use the actual capital (not the imaginary amount).

This rule reflects the fact that if the authority had awarded you less HB due to the capital being taken into account, you might have used some of the capital to pay the rent or, in Northern Ireland, rates.

The discretion to recover

18.27   If an overpayment is 'recoverable' (paras 18.11-12), this means the authority has the discretion to recover it or not recover it (para 1.53). The question of whether an overpayment is recoverable is therefore separate from the question of whether to recover it. The DWP advises the authority that it should have 'due regard' for individual circumstances (OG paras 2.145-147). The authority should look at your case on its individual merits.

18.28   You can ask the authority to use this discretion but you have no right of appeal to a tribunal about this ([2011] UKUT 266 (AAC) para 71). If the authority exercises its discretion unreasonably or irrationally you could instead seek a judicial review – but should obtain advice about this. This was done in a case where an authority sought to recover an overpayment caused by a war pension awarded for a past period – though the outcome was that the court required the authority to think again taking into account relevant considerations and did not ban recovery (R v South Hams District Council ex p Ash).

Who to recover from

18.29   The authority may recover a recoverable overpayment as follows:

(a) if the overpayment was caused by you or the payee, or someone on their behalf (para 18.15), it is recoverable only from the person who caused the overpayment (and if there is more than one such person, it is recoverable from any of them);

(b) if the overpayment was due to official error, and you or the payee, or someone on their behalf, could reasonably have been expected to realise it was an overpayment (para 18.14), it is recoverable only from the person who could reasonably have been expected to realise (and if there is more than one such person, it is recoverable from any of them);

(c) in any other case (e.g. if the overpayment was no-one's fault) it is recoverable from you and (if different) the payee (in other words from either).

18.30   If, for any of the above reasons, the overpayment is recoverable from you, it may also be recoverable from your partner (para 18.32). In some cases, the effect of the above rules is that the authority has a choice about who to recover the overpayment from (para 18.37).

Recovery from you

18.31   The effect of the above rules (para 18.29) is that the authority can recover most overpayments from you. If you die it can recover the overpaid amount from your estate. In fact, the only cases in which the authority cannot recover a recoverable overpayment from you (and can only recover from the payee, typically a landlord or agent) are:

(a) when the payee was the cause of the overpayment (and you played no part in causing it); or

(b) when the payee could reasonably have been expected to realise there was an official error overpayment (and you could not have done so).

Recovery from your partner

18.32   Whenever the authority can recover an overpayment from you (for any of the reasons in para 18.29), it can also recover it from your partner – but only if you were a couple when the overpayment was made and at the time of recovery. A former partner (following

---

18.28   R v South Hams DC ex p Ash 10/05/99 QBD [1999] EWHC Admin 418 32 HLR 405

18.29   AA 75(3); NIAA 73(3); HB 101(2), (3A); HB60+ 82(2), (3A); NIHB 98(2),(3A); NIHB60+ 79(2), (2A)

18.31   HB 101(2),(3A); HB60+ 82(2),(3A); NIHB 98(2),(3A); NIHB60+ 79(2),(3A)

18.32   HB 102(1ZA); HB60+ 83(1ZA); NIHB 99(1A); NIHB60+ 80(1A)

the end of a relationship or death), or a new partner after the period of the overpayment, does not meet these conditions so the authority can't recover the overpayment from them. The authority should separately notify your partner when it is going to recover the overpayment from your partner. In these circumstances your partner has the same rights you do: CH/3622/2006 (para 18.38).

18.33   The rules limit the methods of recovery from your partner to:

(a) making deductions from your partner's future HB (para 18.41); or

(b) making deductions from your partner's future DWP benefits (para 18.45).

Recovery from your landlord or their agent

18.34   The effect of the above rules (para 18.29) is that the authority can only recover the overpayment from your landlord or their agent (the 'landlord') if it was the landlord (rather than you) who was paid the HB; and one of the following also applies:

(a) the landlord caused the overpayment; or

(b) the landlord could reasonably have been expected to realise there was an overpayment (in the case of an official error overpayment); or

(c) the overpayment was no-one's fault – in which case it is recoverable from either you or the landlord; and the mere fact that the landlord knew nothing of the overpayment does not prevent recovery from them: Warwick DC v Freeman.

18.35   In such cases, the authority may recover overpaid HB from the landlord if the landlord was paid the HB, but from the agent if the agent was paid the HB (even if the agent has paid it to the landlord: R(H)10/07 and CH/761/2007). When the authority decides to recover from your landlord or their agent they must be separately notified and have the same rights of appeal as you: CH/3622/2006 (para 18.38).

18.36   However, an authority must not recover HB from your landlord or their agent if:

(a) the landlord/agent tells the authority or the DWP in writing that they suspect there has been an overpayment; and

(b) it appears to the authority that there are grounds for instituting proceedings for an offence in relation to the overpayment, or that a deliberate failure to report a relevant change of circumstances (other than moving home) caused the overpayment; and

(c) the authority is satisfied that your landlord or their agent did not collude with you in the overpayment, nor contribute (through action or inaction) to its period or amount.

This rule supplements the earlier rule (para 18.34) but does not override it: [2013] UKUT 232 (AAC). For example, if your landlord or their agent gets your HB and notifies the authority that you are doing undeclared work, and does so promptly, this rule prevents the authority from recovering the resulting overpaid HB from your landlord or their agent provided that the landlord's warning notice reaches the authority before it discovers the overpayment (CH/2411/2006).

18.34   AA 75(3); NIAA 73(3); HB 101(2),(3A); HB60+ 82(2),(3A); NIHB 98(2),(3A); NIHB60+ 79(2),(3A);
         Warwick DC v Freeman 31/10/94 CA 27 HLR 616
         www.rightsnet.org.uk/pdfs/warwick_v_Freeman.pdf

18.36   AA 75(3); NIAA 73(3); HB 101(1); HB60+ 82(1); NIHB 98(1); NIHB60+ 79(1)

A choice about who to recover HB from

18.37   When the above rules (para 18.29) allow an authority to recover an HB overpayment from more than one person (e.g. you and your landlord or their agent), you have a joint and several liability to repay the overpayment (R(H) 6/06). The authority may choose which of you to recover from. In one case an authority billed two people at the same time, and a commissioner said this was 'unfortunate' but had no lasting effect on the appeal CH/2583/2007).

Appeals about who the authority can recover HB from

18.38   Once the authority has identified who it may recover the overpayment from, and notified them (all) of this, each of the possible targets is a 'person affected' (para 16.6) and may ask the authority to reconsider the decision or appeal to a tribunal.

18.39   A tribunal's jurisdiction is limited to deciding first, the true entitlement for the period in question and second, whether the resultant overpayment is legally recoverable from you and/or someone else. But it does not have the power to decide the third and final stage: how the authority should effect recovery (CH/2298/2007). A tribunal has a duty to decide whether the authority's selection of possible targets for recovery is correctly drawn up – but not whether it is fair or appropriate to recover from you or someone else (R(H) 6/06 and CH/4213/2007). This applies whether the appellant is you or your landlord or their agent (CH/1129/2004). In unreasonable or irrational cases you could instead seek judicial review but you should obtain advice about this.

Methods of recovery

18.40   The authority may recover a recoverable overpayment of HB by any lawful method. This section describes the methods set out in the law, along with other relevant considerations.

Deducting overpaid HB from future awards of HB

18.41   The authority may deduct a recoverable overpayment of HB from your, or your partner's, future award of HB. This deduction is limited in three ways:

  (a) the award of HB must not be reduced below 50p a week;

  (b) the amount of the deduction must not be greater than shown in table 18.3; and

  (c) the authority should consider deducting a lower amount where hardship might otherwise arise.

The first two limits do not apply to deductions from lump sum arrears of HB.

18.41   AA 75(4),(5); NIAA 73(4),(5); HB 102; HB60+ 83; NIHB 99; NIHB60+ 80

Table 18.3 **Maximum weekly deductions from HB (2015-18)**

(a) If you have been found guilty of fraud, or admitted fraud after caution, or agreed to pay an administrative penalty (para 18.73)	£18.50
(b) In any other case	£11.10

Plus, in each of the above cases, 50% of:

(c) any £5, £10, £20 or £25 earned income disregard (table 14.5)

(d) any disregard of regular charitable or voluntary payments (para 13.30)

(e) the £10 disregard of war pensions for bereavement or disablement (table 13.4).

18.42 The deductions from your on-going HB entitlement may leave you with more rent to pay – or rent arrears if you don't pay (table 18.4). Your landlord doesn't have to identify these rent arrears separately from other rent arrears – and they can, for example, lead to your eviction.

18.43 The deductions count as recovery from you, not the landlord. This is true even when the authority pays the HB to your landlord/agent. In such cases the landlord/agent has no right to appeal to a tribunal about the deductions (R(H) 7/04).

Overpayments and rent accounts

18.44 If you are a council or NIHE tenant your rent account can include a record of overpaid HB, but the recovered overpayments do not normally constitute rent arrears – and should not, for example, lead to your eviction (unlike the arrears in para 18.42). Table 18.4 identifies when overpaid HB recovered through the rent account results in rent arrears for you.

Table 18.4 **When recovered HB overpayments create rent arrears**

Rent rebate (local authority/NIHE tenants)

- Recovery by deductions from ongoing HB or arrears of HB (para 18.41): Assuming you do not pay any shortfall then this always creates rent arrears (because at no point has the rent due been paid).

- Recovery by charging your rent account or by sending you a bill (paras 18.44 and 18.51): Recovery by this method does not create rent arrears (R v Haringey ex p Ayub) except if:

T18.3   AA 75(4),(5); NIAA 73(4),(5); HB 102; HB60+ 83; NIHB 99; NIHB60+ 80

T18.4   AA 75(5),(6); NIAA 73(5),(6); HB 95(2),107(1),(2); HB60+ 76(2),88(1),(2); NIHB 92(2),104(1),(2); NIHB60+ 73(2),85(1),(2)
        R v Haringey LBC ex p Ayub 13/04/92 QBD 25 HLR 566
        www.rightsnet.org.uk/pdfs/R_V_Haringey_exp_Ayub.pdf

> (a) the tenancy agreement expressly allows for recovered overpayments of HB to be charged as additional rent; or
>
> (b) following the recovery you fail to say which debt (rent or overpayment) any payments should be attributed to – in which case any payment goes against the earliest debt first.
>
> ## Rent allowance
>
> ■ Recovery by deductions from ongoing HB or arrears of HB (para 18.41): As for rent rebates above.
>
> ■ Recovery from a blameless tenant's HB (paras 18.46-47): This never results in rent arrears for the blameless tenant; and does not result in rent arrears for the tenant to whom the overpayment relates except in the same circumstances as in (a) and (b) above.
>
> ■ Recovery from the landlord by deductions from the landlord's own benefits or by sending the landlord a bill (paras 18.50-51): The tenant to whom the overpayment relates is treated as not having paid the amount of rent which has been repaid (as a recoverable overpayment) so this creates rent arrears.
>
> ■ Recovery by deductions from a guilty landlord's payments (paras 18.48-49): The tenant to whom the overpayment relates is treated as having paid the rent to the value of the deduction.

Recovering overpaid HB from your DWP benefits

18.45   The authority may recover a recoverable HB overpayment by requesting DWP Debt Management to make deductions from your or your partner's DWP benefits. The details of the arrangement are set out in a model service level agreement between authorities and DWP Debt Management (DWP HB G7/2014 Annex). The DWP's Payment Deductions Project (PDP) (A6/2016, U2/2016) is an IT interface that has been designed to make it easier for authorities to recover HB debt from DWP benefits. Recovery from your DWP benefits should only take place if the HB overpayment was due to misrepresentation of, or failure to disclose, a material fact (para 18.15); and only if the authority is unable to recover it from future awards of HB. The DWP benefits from which deduction may be made are set out in table 18.5. Recovery from your partner's DWP benefits may only be made by deductions from: IS, JSA(IB), PC, ESA(IR), PIP and UC.

18.45   HB 102(1), 105, 106; HB60+ 83(1), 86, 87; NIHB 99(1), 102, 103; NIHB60+ 80(1), 83, 84

Table 18.5 **Recovering HB overpayments from your DWP benefits**

A recoverable overpayment of HB may be deducted from:

- income support
- jobseeker's allowance
- employment and support allowance
- personal independence payment
- maternity allowance
- industrial injuries benefits
- widow(er)'s benefits
- bereavement benefits

- retirement pension
- incapacity benefit
- state pension credit
- universal credit
- carer's allowance
- disability living allowance
- attendance allowance
- equivalent EU and Swiss benefits

but not from:

- child benefit
- guardian's allowance
- war pensions

- working tax credit
- child tax credit
- statutory sick, maternity, paternity or adoption pay

Deducting overpaid HB from a blameless tenant's HB

18.46   If your HB was overpaid to your landlord or their agent (the 'landlord'), the authority may deduct it from any other tenant's HB that is paid to your landlord. This is often called 'recovery by schedule' (because it is usually only done in the case of landlords with several tenants on HB) or recovery from a 'blameless tenant' (because the other tenant had nothing to do with the overpayment).

18.47   The authority must notify your landlord that your HB was overpaid and who the blameless tenant is. The blameless tenant is not notified, and your landlord must treat them as having paid rent equal to the amount deducted.

Deducting overpaid HB from a guilty landlord/agent's payments

18.48   Special rules apply to the recovery of rent by a landlord or their agent ('the landlord') and to the information on the authority's decision notice where:

(a)   the overpayment is one for which your landlord has agreed to pay a penalty (para 18.73) or been convicted of fraud; and

(b)   recovery is to be from your landlord; and

(c)   recovery is by deduction from the HB paid by the authority to the landlord for you and you are the tenant to whom the overpayment relates.

18.46   AA 75(5), (6); NIAA 73(5),(6); HB sch 9 para 15(2); HB60+ sch 8 para 15(2); NIHB sch 10 para 15(2); NIHB60+ sch 9 para 15(2)

18.47   AA 75(5), (6); NIAA 73(5), (6); HB 106(2); HB60+ 87(2); NIHB 103(2); NIHB60+ 84(2)

18.48   AA 75(5)(b); NIAA 73(5)(b); HB 107; HB60+ 88; NIHB 104; NIHB60+ 85

18.49   In these circumstances the landlord has no right in relation to the recovered amount against you and must treat your rent as paid by the same amount. The authority must notify you and the landlord of these matters.

Deducting overpaid HB from your landlord's own benefits

18.50   If a recoverable overpayment of HB was paid to your landlord or their agent, the authority may (though this is rare) recover it from your landlord's personal entitlement to:

(a)   HB (in which case the limits in table 18.3 do not apply); or

(b)   DWP benefits (table 18.5) – but only if the overpayment was due to misrepresentation of, or failure to disclose, a material fact.

Recovering HB by sending a bill

18.51   The authority may recover any recoverable overpayment of HB by sending a bill to anyone it can be recovered from (paras 18.29-36). If not paid, the authority can enforce recovery through court action (paras 18.61-67).

Recovering HB by direct earnings attachment (DEA)

18.52   The authority may recover recoverable overpayments of HB by requiring your employer to make deductions from your earnings (or the earnings of any other 'liable person' (someone from whom HB may be recovered: paras 18.29-36) without the need for court action. DWP's Impact Assessment (2011) [www] suggests that this method of recovery is useful if you are no longer in receipt of benefit and refuse to come to a voluntary agreement to repay the debt. The DWP has made available to authorities an information pack on using DEA (HB G2/2014) [www].

18.53   If the authority decides to use this method of recovery it must send a notice to both you and your employer before your employer can make deductions. The employer should tell the authority if they are not your employer or if they think any exemption applies. They should do this within ten days of the day after the notice was sent.

18.54   The authority may vary the notice to decrease or increase amounts or to substitute a new employer for a previous one. Where your employer has to make deductions under more than one notice they should deal with them in date order.

18.50   AA 75(5); NIAA 73(5); HB 106(2); HB60+ 87(2); NIHB 103(2); NIHB60+ 84(2)

18.51   HB 102(1); HB60+ 83(1); NIHB 99(1); NIHB60+ 80(1)

18.52   AA 75(8)-(10); HB 106A; HB60+ 87A, SI 2013 No 384; NIAA 73(8)-(10), NIHB 103A, NIHB60+ 83A, NISR 2016/224
        www.legislation.gov.uk/uksi/2013/384/pdfs/uksifia_20130384_en.pdf
        www.whatdotheyknow.com/request/hbctb_direct_earnings_attachment

18.53   Regs 19, 24 of SI 2013 No 384, Regs 18, 23 of NISR 2016/224

18.54   Regs 25-26, 29 of SI 2013 No 384, Regs 24-25, 28 of NISR 2016/224

18.55   The DEA notice has effect from the next pay-day which falls at least 22 days after the date on which it is given or sent. The amounts to be deducted are set out in legislation (sch 2 of SI 2013 No 384/sch 1 of NISR 2016/224). Your employer may deduct up to £1 for administrative costs. Your net earnings should not be reduced below 60% of protected net earnings.

18.56   Your employer must notify you of the amount of the deductions and pay the amount deducted (excluding that for administrative costs) to the authority. Your employer must also keep records of the people in respect of whom such deductions have been made and the amounts deducted.

18.57   You must tell the authority within seven days if you leave the employment or when you become employed or re-employed. The employer should also tell the authority if you are no longer employed by them. It is a criminal offence to fail to make or pay deductions or to provide information.

The effect of insolvency on recovery

18.58   The DWP's Overpayments Guide (OG paras 7.110-188) provides detailed information on the recovery of overpayments where your insolvency has led to formal measures such as bankruptcy, the making of a debt relief order (DRO) (in England and Wales) or sequestration (in Scotland) [www].

18.59   The DWP's Overpayments Guide (OG paras 7.188) draws particular attention to the implications of the recent Supreme Court's judgments in SSWP v Payne & Cooper (England and Wales) and Re Nortel Companies. The current situation is as follows. If bankruptcy has started or an overpayment has been included in a DRO, the authority cannot recover an overpayment that was decided before the order was granted. The Supreme Court confirmed that the authority cannot recover such overpayments even by making deductions from ongoing HB entitlement. Authorities are told in DWP circular HB/CTB U6/2011 that they should stop such recoveries if they are making them. Once the bankruptcy or DRO is discharged the liability to repay is also discharged except for fraudulent overpayments (HB/CTB U1/2012 para 8).

18.60   The DWP (G10/2013, para 35) (following Nortel) advises authorities that when a debtor is discharged from bankruptcy (or sequestration in Scotland) then any non-fraud debts, where the end date of the overpayment is before the date of the bankruptcy or sequestration order, must be written off and that this must take effect immediately. Its previous advice (following R (on the application of Steele) v Birmingham CC and Secretary of State for Work and Pensions) had been that a benefit overpayment (including an HB overpayment) did not become a fixed liability until such time as the decision maker had made a determination that the overpayment, or part of it, was recoverable under social security legislation.

18.55   Regs 17, 19, 20(9) of SI 2013 No 384, Regs 17, 18, 19(11) of NISR 2016/224

18.56   Reg 21-22 of SI 2013 No 384, Regs 20-21 of NISR 2016/224

18.57   Regs 23, 30 of SI 2013 No 384, Regs 22, 29 of NISR 2016/224

18.58   www.gov.uk/government/publications/housing-benefit-overpayments-guide

18.59   SSWP v Payne & Cooper 14/12/11 UKSC [2011] UKSC 60 www.bailii.org/uk/cases/UKSC/2011/60.html
          Re Nortel Companies 24/07/13 UKSC [2013] UKSC 52 www.bailii.org/uk/cases/UKSC/2013/52.html

18.60   R (on the application of Steele) v Birmingham City Council [2005] EWCA Civ 1824; [2006] 1 W.L.R. 2380
          www.bailii.org/ew/cases/EWCA/Civ/2005/1824.html

Court action

18.61   The DWP advises authorities that legal proceedings should only be considered after attempts to recover by other means have failed and there is good reason to believe you can afford to make repayments (OG paras 7.23). Authorities are told that before pursuing recovery through the courts they should allow your appeal period to run out, allow any outstanding appeal to be decided, send at least two letters requesting repayment and make sure that procedures are in place to check that you are getting all the HB and other benefits you may be entitled to (OG paras 7.20-22). You may find that not all authorities follow this guidance. Court action may take the form of civil proceedings for debt, but the following procedure is simpler for the authority.

The simplified debt recovery procedure

18.62   Authorities have the power to recover HB overpayments by execution in the County Court in England and Wales as if under a court order; and in Scotland as if it were an extract registered decree arbitral (OG paras 7.24-38).

England and Wales

18.63   In England and Wales, this procedure allows a council to register an HB overpayment determination directly as an order of the County Court without the need to bring a separate action. The DWP has provided some much needed guidance on this procedure (OG paras 7.24-38). The authority applies to the court on a standard form (form N 322A) [www], enclosing a copy of the overpayment notice and the relevant fee. The notice must include all the matters in paragraph 18.69 (OG para 5.07). An officer of the court then makes an order and a copy is sent to the authority and to you. Once the order has been made, the normal methods of enforcement are available to the authority – a garnishee order allowing it to obtain money owed to you by a third party; a warrant of execution against goods executed by the county court bailiff; or a charging order, normally against land.

18.64   There is no appeal against the above order, but you or your landlord/agent may apply to the court to set it aside if the overpayment notice was defective or the authority has ignored your HB appeal rights. In the case of other disputes, you should ask the authority to reconsider or appeal to a tribunal (Ghassemian v Borough of Kensington and Chelsea).

Scotland

18.65   In Scotland, an HB overpayment determination is immediately enforceable by the authority as if it were an extract registered decree arbitral (OG paras 7.24). The authority doesn't need to register it with the Sheriff Court. The usual methods of enforcement are available.

18.62   AA 75(7), 76(6); NIAA 73(7)

18.63   www.gov.uk/government/uploads/system/uploads/attachment_data/file/405555/hbopg-part-7-courts-and-civil-procedings.pdf
http://hmctsformfinder.justice.gov.uk/HMCTS/FormFinder.do

18.64   Ghassemain v Kensington and Chelsea LBC 09/06/09 CA [2009] EWCA Civ 743 www.bailii.org/ew/cases/EWCA/Civ/2009/743.html

18.65   AA 75(7)(b)

Time limits

18.66   The authority must start the above procedures within six years in England and Wales (s9 The Limitation Act 1980). This limitation does not apply to any other method of recovery – such as by deductions from future HB (OG paras 7.00-05). In Scotland your council cannot recover overpayments by any method after 20 years (OG paras 7.05).

18.67   This time limit does not affect how far back an overpayment can go. For example, the authority may discover today that it has overpaid you from the beginning of the HB scheme, and may make a determination to recover it. But the further the overpayment goes back, the more difficult it may be for the authority to obtain the evidence needed to prove the overpayment to the court (OG para 7.00). Also, overpayments from before 6th April 2009 fall within the rules which applied before that date: CH/4213/2007.

Overpayment decision notices

18.68   For every recoverable overpayment, the authority should send a decision notice to you and everyone it can be recovered from (paras 18.29-36), because each of these is a 'person affected' (paras 16.68-70) – regardless of who the authority will actually recover it from (R(H) 6/06). The authority should do this within 14 days of the date it made the decision or as soon as reasonably practicable afterwards.

18.69   The authority's notice about the overpayment should contain the following information:

(a)   the fact that there is a recoverable overpayment;

(b)   the reason why there is a recoverable overpayment;

(c)   the amount of the recoverable overpayment;

(d)   how that amount was calculated;

(e)   the benefit weeks to which the recoverable overpayment relates;

(f)   if overpaid HB is to be deducted from future HB, the amount of the deduction;

(g)   any other relevant matters;

(h)   your right to request a written statement, to request the authority to reconsider, and to appeal to a tribunal, and the manner and time in which to do these things.

18.70   A notice must also be issued about your new (lower or nil) entitlement to HB. Both this and the overpayment notice are often inadequate. The main cases about this are summarised in table 18.6.

18.71   The DWP advises authorities that recovery of HB overpayments by deduction from future HB should not begin until one month after notice (unless the overpayment is small) to allow time for an appeal to be made (but advises that it may issue an invoice) (OG paras 4.240 and 4.250).

18.66   s38(1),(11) Limitation Act 1980 as amended by s108 Welfare Reform Act 2012, s7 of The Prescription and Limitation (Scotland) Act 1973

18.68   HB 90(1)(b); HB60+ 71(1)(b); NIHB 86(1)(b); NIHB60+ 67(1)(b)

18.69   HB sch 9 para 15; HB60+ sch 8 para 15; NIHB sch 10 para 15; NIHB60+ sch 9 para 15

Table 18.6 **Overpayments case law: notices and effect on recovery**

- *Failure to give a reason why there is a recoverable overpayment:* To say it was due to a 'change of circumstances' is not itself an adequate explanation as it covers a multitude of possibilities and so does not give the person affected sufficient information to be able to judge whether they have grounds for an appeal (R v Thanet DC ex parte Warren Court Hotels Ltd).

- *Failure to identify the parties the overpayment is recoverable from:* A notice naming only a landlord as the person from whom the overpayment could be recovered was quashed (and so had no effect), because it should have named both the claimant and the landlord (CH/3622/2005, in which the commissioner followed R(H) 6/06).

- *The notices which must be issued and the impact on recoverability:* For an overpayment to be recoverable, notices must be issued about both the new (lower or nil) award of HB and the resulting overpayment. If one (or both) of these is omitted, the overpayment is not recoverable: [2013] 208 (AAC) and R (Godwin) v Rossendale BC.

- *Clarity and completeness of notices:* Decisions must be clear and unambiguous with proper use of statutory language and dates (C3/07-08 (IS)). An authority that issues an incomplete notice may undermine the legal basis of its debt recovery action (Warwick DC v Freeman). But if the defect in the notice is only trivial and no substantial harm has been caused as a result, the authority may be entitled to recover the overpaid benefit (Haringey LBC v Awaritefe).

- *Recovery taken before notice issued:* If, in a 'blameless tenant' case, a council recovers HB before issuing a valid notice, the landlord/agent can apply to the court for repayment of the recovered HB (Waveney DC v Jones).

- *Recovery volunteered before notice issued:* If a landlord/agent voluntarily pays a bill for overpaid HB before the authority has issued a valid notice, they cannot obtain repayment because (unlike in Jones, above) they could have resisted recovery by requesting the authority to reconsider or appealing to a tribunal (Norwich CC v Stringer).

T18.6   R v Thanet ex p Warren Court Hotels 06/04/00 QBD 33 HLR 32 www.rightsnet.org.uk/pdfs/thanet_ex_parte_warren_court.doc
R (Godwin) v Rossendale BC 03/05/02 CA [2002] EWCA Civ 726 www.bailii.org/ew/cases/EWCA/Civ/2002/726.html
Warwick DC v Freeman 31/10/94 CA 27 HLR 616 www.rightsnet.org.uk/pdfs/warwick_v_Freeman.pdf
Haringey LBC v Awaritefe 26/05/99 CA [1999] EWCA Civ 1491 32 HLR 517 www.bailii.org/ew/cases/EWCA/Civ/1999/1491.html
Waveney v Jones 01/12/99 CA 33 HLR 3 www.rightsnet.org.uk/pdfs/Waveney_v_Jones.pdf
Norwich CC v Stringer 03/05/00 CA 33 HLR 15 www.ucc.ie/law/restitution/archive/englcases/norwich.htm

Overpayments and fraud

18.72　　The Social Security Administration Act 1992 creates several offences related to HB fraud. A number of other enactments are also relevant. Previously English and Welsh authorities had the power to prosecute HB fraud cases. From 24th May 2016 the legislation prevents this (except in very limited circumstances). The Single Fraud Investigation Service project (SFIS) [www] brought together fraud staff from local authorities, HMRC and DWP to provide a fraud investigation service across all social security benefits and tax credit (but not CTR). This approach was rolled out nationally from July 2014 and completed in March 2016. The DWP's Fraud and Error Service (FES) has now assumed overall responsibility for the investigation of all benefit and tax credit offences in Great Britain. The Single Investigation Service in the DfC has responsibility for HB fraud work in NI. Prosecutions arising from these fraud investigations are conducted by: the Crown Prosecution Service in England and Wales, the Procurator Fiscal in Scotland and the Public Prosecution Service of Northern Ireland.

Administrative penalties

18.73　　The DWP (FES) (in consultation with the authority) may offer you the chance to pay an 'administrative penalty' rather than face prosecution, if:

(a)　　a recoverable HB overpayment was caused by an 'act or omission' on your part; and

(b)　　there are grounds for bringing a prosecution against you (under the Social Security Administration Act 1992 or any other enactment) for an offence relating to that HB overpayment.

You do not have to agree to a penalty. You can opt for the possibility of prosecution instead. The DWP (FES) is expected to advise the authority of the outcome of an administrative penalty offer [www].

18.74　　The offer of a penalty must be in writing, explain that it is a way of avoiding prosecution, and give other information – including the fact that you can change your mind within 14 days (including the date of the agreement), and that the penalty will be repaid if you successfully challenge it by asking for a reconsideration or appeal (OG para 4.330). You are not normally offered a penalty if the overpayment is substantial or there are other aggravating factors (such as you being in a position of trust).

18.75　　The amount of the penalty is 50% of the recoverable HB overpayment (subject to a minimum of £350 and a maximum of £5,000/(£2000 NI)). For offences that were committed before 8th May 2012 or span that date the penalty is 30% of the recoverable HB overpayment (DWP F6/2012, para 4.2) and the maximum penalty before 1st April 2015 was £2,000.

18.72　AA s 116ZA, SI 2016/511 art 4, SI 2016/519
　　　www.parliament.uk/written-questions-answers-statements/written-question/commons/2015-11-09/15651
　　　www.gov.uk/government/collections/single-fraud-investigation-service

18.73　AA 115A, NIAA 109A; SI 1997/2813; NISR 1997/514, NIOrder 2016/46
　　　Audit Scotland, A review of housing benefit fraud investigation liaison arrangements in Scoland, pp 13-14 (Dec 2016)
　　　www.audit-scotland.gov.uk/uploads/docs/um/hb_investigation_liaison_arrangements_2016.pdf

18.74　AA 115A(2), NIAA 109A(4)-(5)

18.75　AA 115A(3), NIAA 109A(3)

18.76   You may also be offered a penalty where your act or omission could have resulted in a recoverable HB overpayment and there are grounds for bringing a prosecution for a related offence. In these cases the penalty is a fixed amount of £350.

Civil penalties

18.77   In GB the authority may impose a civil penalty of £50 if you:

(a)   negligently make an incorrect statement or representation or negligently give incorrect information or evidence relating to a claim or award and fail to take reasonable steps to correct the error; or

(b)   without reasonable excuse, fail to provide required information or evidence relating to a claim or award or fail to tell the authority about a relevant change of circumstance; and

(c)   in any of these circumstances this results in the authority making an overpayment (wholly after 1st October 2012); but

(d)   you have not been charged with an offence or cautioned.

18.78   The amount of the civil penalty is added to the amount of the recoverable over-payment. If you have been successfully prosecuted for fraud or offered an administrative penalty or caution, the authority cannot issue you with a civil penalty for the same offence. If you want to appeal against a civil penalty you should appeal against the amount of the HB overpayment.

18.76   AA 115A(1A), (3A); NIAA 109A(1A), (3A)

18.77   AA 115C-115D, SI 2012/1990

Chapter 19 **HB for rates**

- HB for rates and other schemes in Northern Ireland: see paras 19.1-2.
- An overview of domestic rates in Northern Ireland (including liability and exemptions and so on): see paras 19.3-12.
- Rate rebates and eligible rates for HB: see paras 19.13-19.
- Rate relief (and how to calculate it): see paras 19.20-30.
- Lone pensioner allowance: see paras 19.31-38.

HB for rates and other schemes in Northern Ireland

19.1   This chapter applies only in Northern Ireland. It describes three schemes that provide help with your domestic rates whether the bill is paid by you or your landlord. The three schemes are: HB for rates, rate relief and the lone pensioner allowance.

19.2   From September 2017, universal credit (UC) is expected to be introduced for new working age claimants in some areas (paras 1.15-16). A new rate rebate scheme (described in *Help with Housing Costs Volume 1,* chapter 22) replaces HB and rate relief for UC claimants. HB and rate relief continue for all other claims.

Rates overview

19.3   Domestic rates are the form of local taxation in Northern Ireland. Rates are a tax on residential properties known as dwellings (which for convenience we also refer to as 'your home'). Responsibility for paying them normally falls on the occupier: see paragraph 19.7. Land and Property Services (LPS) are responsible for the billing and collection of the tax.

Table 19.1 **Domestic rates: key considerations**

(a) Which dwelling is being considered?
(b) What is the capital value (or social sector value) for that dwelling?
(c) What is the aggregate rate poundage in that district?
(d) Who is liable for the rates?
(e) Is the dwelling exempt from rates altogether?
(f) Do they qualify for a disability reduction?
(g) Do they qualify for full or partial HB on their rates?
(h) Do they qualify for rate relief on any remaining rates?
(i) Do they qualify for lone pensioner allowance on any remaining rates?

Dwellings and annual rates

19.4   The domestic rate is an annual bill. One rates bill is issued per dwelling, unless the dwelling is exempt (para 19.8). A 'dwelling' means any house, flat, houseboat or mobile home, etc, whether lived in or not.

19.5   The amount of your rates bill depends first on the capital value set by LPS, assessed as the open market sale value of your home on 1st January 2005 (capped to a maximum of £400,000). If you are a NIHE or registered housing association tenant the capital value is substituted by a 'social sector value', calculated by the DFC based on the rent you pay for your home.

19.6   The amount of annual rates is calculated by multiplying the capital value (or £400,000 if the cap applies: para 19.5) by the rate in the pound ('rate poundage') for the year. The capital value and aggregate rate poundage for each district is shown on the bill and can be found on the LPS website.

Liability for rates

19.7   The rates bill goes to the owner or occupier of the dwelling. For example:

(a) if you are a NIHE or housing association tenant the rates bill goes to your landlord, who recovers the cost by increasing the overall amount of rent you pay;

(b) if you are a private tenant the rates bill may go to you, or your landlord may add it to your rent (para 19.11);

(c) if you are an owner occupier the rates bill is sent to you.

Note that if you are a tenant and your landlord has paid the rates bill, then they have in effect included the amount in your rent whether or not it was a conscious decision to do so.

Exemptions

19.8   Certain dwellings are exempt from rates. This is not automatic – you must make an application to Land and Property Services. An occupied dwelling is exempt if the landlord is a registered charity. There are very few other exemptions and they mainly relate to unoccupied properties.

Disability reductions

19.9   Your rates bill is reduced by 25% if your home has been adapted or extended because of the disability of anyone who lives there. The reduction is not automatic: you must make an application to Land and Property Services.

Rate rebates, rate relief and lone pensioner allowance

19.10   If you are liable for rates on a dwelling that is your normal home (including, if you are a tenant, where your rent includes an amount towards your rates: para 19.11) then you can get any or all of rate rebate, rate relief or lone pensioner allowance. But you cannot get rate rebate or rate relief (but can get lone pensioner allowance) if you are:

19.6   www.dfpni.gov.uk/lps/

19.10   NICBA 129(1)(a); NIHB 8(1)(a),9(1); 10(1),53(1); NIHB60+ 8(1)(a); 9(1),10(1)

(a)   in certain circumstances, a migrant or recent arrival in the UK (chapter 20); or

(b)   a full-time student (for exceptions see table 22.1).

19.11   A person is eligible for all three of these schemes whether they pay rates direct to Land and Property Services, or via the rent they pay their landlord. If you are a tenant and your landlord pays the rates bill then they have in effect included the amount in your rent whether or not it was a conscious decision to do so. The only time that your rent does not include rates is if you receive the rates bill in your own name.

19.12   However, if you are a tenant, your rate rebate, rate relief or lone pensioner allowance cannot be awarded until a rates bill is issued. Once it has, your rate rebate and rate relief are awarded retrospectively provided you notify the NIHE within one month of receiving it; this time limit can be extended in special circumstances. Otherwise your benefit is awarded according to the usual HB rules (paras 5.45-49). If you are claiming lone pensioner allowance, the award starts from the date your rates liability commenced, or the date you qualify if later.

Rate rebates and eligible rates

What are rate rebates?

19.13   A rate rebate (HB for rates) reduces the amount of rates you pay. It is worked out in a similar way to your HB for rent. It is funded by subsidy payable to Land and Property Services or NIHE. To find out where to apply for a rate rebate, see paragraph 1.28 and table 1.6.

Eligible rates

19.14   Your eligible rates is the figure used in calculating your entitlement to rate rebate (HB for rates). It is calculated by working through the following steps:

1.   Start with the annual rates due on your home (paras 19.5-6) after any capping that may apply.

2.   If you are entitled to a disability reduction (para 19.9), use the rates figure after that has been made.

3.   If you are a joint occupier apportion the result.

4.   Convert it to a weekly figure (as described in para 6.34).

Note that unlike HB for rent, there is no power to restrict the eligible rates if your home is too expensive or too large.

Impact of rates changes on eligible rent

19.15   If your rent includes an amount for rates (para 19.11), a change in the rates (such as the new amount applying from each April, or following the award of a disability reduction) means your eligible rent changes too. Since there is no duty on you or your landlord to advise of changes to rates, the NIHE alters your HB for rent and rates automatically when advised by Land and Property Services.

19.11   NIHB 12(2), 13(3)(b),(6); NIHB60+ 12(2), 13(3)(b),(6)

19.14   NIHB 11(1)(a), 12(3), 78(3); NIHB60+ 11(1)(a), 12(3), 59(3)

19.15   NIHB 12(1),(2); 84(2)(a),(b); NIHB60+; 12(1),(2),65(2)(a),(b)

Example: Calculation of eligible rates

A dwelling has a capital value of £135,000 in an area where the rate poundage is £0.0057777 per £1 of capital value. Capping does not apply so the annual rates payable are:

 £135,000 x 0.0057777   =   £780.00

The weekly eligible rates (to the nearest 1p) are therefore:

 £780.00 ÷ 365 x 7   =   £14.96 if paid separately from rent or

 £780.00 ÷ 52   =   £15.00 if paid along with rent.

Apportionment of eligible rates

19.16   Your eligible rates figure is apportioned if:

(a) you occupy only part of a rateable unit (for example, if you are a lodger or live with others in a multi-occupied property). In this case only the proportion of the rates payable for your accommodation is eligible for HB;

(b) if you are jointly liable to pay rates with one or more other occupiers – for example if you have a joint tenancy (see paras 8.12-13 and 9.7);

(c) part of the rateable unit is for business use – such as a shop with a flat above. This is done in the same way as for eligible rent (para 8.90).

Calculating rate rebate

19.17   The method of calculating your rate rebate is given in paragraphs 6.2-7 and 6.35-36 and see examples at the end of this chapter. As with your HB for rent, non-dependant charges may apply (table 6.4) and see paragraphs 6.9-20 for details.

Awarding rate rebate as a credit or as a payment

19.18   A rate rebate is awarded as a credit to your rates account except only that the NIHE may choose (at its discretion) to pay your HB for rates as an allowance (along with any HB for rent) if:

(a) your rent includes an amount for rates (para 19.11); and

(b) you qualify for HB for rent, or would do but for any non-dependant deduction or the deduction made because you have excess income (i.e. the 'taper': para 6.6).

19.19   When HB is paid as an allowance, it is paid either to you or your landlord following the same rules as HB for rent (paras 16.20-22 and 16.34-66). But if your total HB (for rent and rates) is £2 per week or less it can be paid four-weekly; and if it is less than £1 per week it can be paid every six months.

19.16   NIHB 12(2),(4)-(6), 72(1)(a),(b),(8)(b),(10); NIHB60+; 12(2),(4)-(6), 53(1)(a),(b),(8)(b),(9)

19.18   NIHB 87(2),88,89(5); NIHB60+ 68(2),69,70(5)

Rate relief

What is rate relief?

19.20   The rate relief scheme was introduced in Northern Ireland on 1st April 2007 following changes in the assessment of domestic rates from being based on an outdated historic rental value to a recent open market capital value. Because of the way rate rebates are calculated, you get no financial benefit from a change in your rates. The rate relief scheme gives you an extra reduction to compensate for this.

19.21   Rate relief is not part of the HB scheme, and is funded from the rates themselves rather than from government subsidy. It is possible for you to qualify for rate relief even if you do not qualify for HB; and since the same information is required for both, a full assessment is always carried out.

Who gets rate relief?

19.22   Your rate relief is considered automatically (so no claim is needed) if you:

(a)   qualify for a rate rebate (HB); but

(b)   you still have rates to pay – other than any amount arising from a non-dependant deduction or recovery of an overpayment.

So if you already qualify for maximum HB (para 6.2) for rates, including where you are repaying an overpayment, you cannot get rate relief. In any other case where you have made a claim for, and are awarded a rate rebate, you also get rate relief. If you do not qualify for a rate rebate but you still have rates to pay you can claim rate relief separately.

Calculating rate relief

19.23   Rate relief is calculated in the same way as your rate rebate – except that:

(a)   your rate relief is worked out on the amount of rates remaining after rate rebate has been granted – ignoring any non-dependant deduction;

(b)   if you have a pension age claim and/or if you qualify for a carer premium your applicable amount is higher (para 19.24);

(c)   if you have a pension age claim the upper capital limit is £50,000 (tariff income applies as in HB);

(d)   the taper percentage used in the calculation is 12% of your excess income;

(e)   the deductions for non-dependants and the income bands that apply to them are different to HB for rent (see table 6.4).

Examples of the calculation are given at the end of this chapter.

19.22   NISR 2007/203; NISR 2007/204; NISR 2007/244; NISR 2011/43

19.24 Your applicable amount is calculated the same way as for HB except:

(a) the rate of the carer premium is £41.94;

(b) if you or your partner have attained state pension credit age (para 1.24) but are aged under 65 your personal allowance is £183.25 if you are single or a lone parent, £267.58 if you are a couple;

(c) if you or your partner are aged 65+ your personal allowance is £198.48 if you are a single claimant or a lone parent, £283.97 if you are a couple.

Awarding rate relief

19.25 Your rate relief is used to reduce the amount of rates you pay. If you are an owner occupier or a private tenant, it is credited to your rates account by Land and Property Services. If you are a NIHE or housing association tenant, it is paid to your landlord and so reduces the overall rent and rates you pay.

Reconsiderations and appeals

19.26 The rules about how you can get a written statement of reasons, request a reconsideration, and request an appeal, are the same as if you were claiming HB for rent (paras 16.67-90). Although rate relief is not a social security benefit, an appeal tribunal nonetheless deals with your appeal and, whenever practicable, deals with your rate relief appeal at the same time as your HB appeal.

Overpayments of rate relief

19.27 Overpaid rate relief can be recovered in the same circumstances as any overpaid HB for rent (paras 18.11-15).

19.28 Any recoverable overpayment of rate relief can be recovered by any lawful method, but the main methods used are:

(a) charging the amount back to your rates account;

(b) deducting it from any future rate relief award you are entitled to.

19.29 A recoverable overpayment of rate relief can be charged back to your rates account. But this method is not normally used if you are a NIHE or housing association tenant, except where the account is now closed (for example following a death or a move) and there remains sufficient credit on the account to make a recovery from it.

19.30 A recoverable overpayment of rate relief can be deducted from your future rate relief award. If you have an ongoing award the maximum rate of deduction is limited to the amounts in table 18.3. But this limit does not apply to deductions from lump sum arrears of rate relief. Any deductions to recover rate relief overpayments are additional to those to recover HB overpayments.

19.24   NISR 2007/203, Reg 17(2)(c); NISR 2007/244; NISR 2011/43

19.25   NISR 2007/203; NISR 2007/204

19.26   NISR 2007/203; NISR 2007/204

19.27   NISR 2007/203; NISR 2007/204

Lone pensioner allowance

What is lone pensioner allowance?

19.31 Lone pensioner allowance was introduced in Northern Ireland on 1st April 2008 following a review of domestic rating policy by the Northern Ireland Executive, which concluded that single people over 70 required further assistance to help with rates charges. In some respects it is similar to the single person discount within council tax but applies only to people aged 70 or above. You may qualify for lone pensioner allowance whether or not you qualify for HB or rate relief.

19.32 Lone pensioner allowance is not part of either the HB or rate relief schemes and is funded by the Northern Ireland Executive.

Who gets lone pensioner allowance?

19.33 If you are liable for rates on your normal or only home, aged 70 or over, and you live alone (but see para 19.34 for details of limited exceptions) you will receive lone pensioner allowance. The allowance is not means tested; but it is not awarded automatically, you must make a claim for it either alongside your HB and/or rate relief or separately. If you qualify for full HB and/or rate relief you cannot also get lone pensioner allowance since it is based on the rates you still have left to pay.

Living alone

19.34 In limited circumstances, even though someone else lives in your household, you can still be treated as living alone and thus qualify for lone pensioner allowance. This applies if:

(a) the person living with you is a resident carer (conditions apply);

(b) the person living with you is aged less than 18;

(c) you are receiving child benefit for the person who lives with you; or

(d) the person living with you is severely mentally impaired (conditions apply).

Calculating lone pensioner allowance

19.35 Since the lone pensioner allowance is not means tested, if you qualify you receive a flat rate 20% reduction on the rates you have to pay. If you also qualify for rate rebate (HB), rate relief or a disability reduction the allowance is applied to the amount of rates left to pay. If you do not qualify for any other kind of reduction the allowance is applied to your full rates charge. Examples of lone pensioner allowance calculations are at the end of this chapter.

Awarding lone pensioner allowance

19.36 Like rate relief, lone pensioner allowance is used to reduce the amount of rates you pay on your home. If you are an owner occupier or a private tenant, it is credited to your rate account by Land and Property Services. If you are a NIHE or housing association tenant, it is paid to your landlord and so reduces the overall rent and rates you have to pay.

Overpayments of lone pensioner allowance

19.37   An overpayment of lone pensioner allowance is only likely to occur if you no longer live alone (such as if a new partner moves in) or you no longer have rates to pay on your home (for example, if you move). An overpayment of lone pensioner allowance cannot be recovered from any HB or rate relief you are entitled to unless you agree to this but it can be recovered by any other lawful method. If you are an owner occupier or a private tenant the recovery is usually made by charging the amount back to your rates account. If you are a NIHE or housing association tenant, and the account is now closed (for example following a death or a move) there may be sufficient credit on the account or assets in an estate to make a recovery. If you later re-qualify for lone pensioner allowance, recovery can be made by deducting the overpayment from any lump sum arrears of your new award.

Appeals

19.38   If you want to appeal a decision relating to lone pensioner allowance it is considered by the Valuation Tribunal; you must appeal within 28 days of being notified of the decision. Note that this differs from the usual time limit of one month for both HB and rate relief appeals.

Examples: Rate rebate, rate relief and lone pensioner allowance

A claimant without a non-dependant

A couple in their 40s have no non-dependants. They are not on JSA(IB), ESA(IR) or income support. Their income exceeds their applicable amount by £20 per week. Their eligible rates are £15 per week.

Rate rebate (HB for rates)	£
Eligible rates	15.00
minus 20% of excess income (20% of £20.00)	– 4.00
equals weekly rate rebate	11.00
Rate relief	
Rates due after rate rebate	4.00
minus 12% of excess income (12% of £20.00)	– 2.40
equals weekly rate relief	1.60

A claimant with a non-dependant

A single claimant in her 50s has a non-dependant son living with her. The claimant is not on JSA(IB), ESA(IR) or income support. Her income exceeds her applicable amount by £10 per week. Her eligible rates are £18.00 per week. Her son works full-time with gross income of £450 per week.

Rate rebate (HB for rates)	£
Eligible rates	18.00
minus non-dependant deduction	– 9.90
minus 20% of excess income (20% of £10.00)	– 2.00
equals weekly rate rebate	6.10

Rate relief	
Rates due after rate rebate – ignoring non-dependant deduction	2.00
minus 12% of excess income (12% of £10.00)	– 1.20
equals weekly rate relief	0.80

Lone pensioner allowance

A person aged 72 lives alone and has a weekly rates charge of £18. She does not receive either HB or rate relief.

	£
Weekly rates to pay	18.00
Minus lone pensioner allowance (20% of £18)	– 3.60
Net amount to pay	14.40

If the same person receives £10 per week HB and £2 per week rate relief:

Weekly rates to pay	18.00
Minus HB	– 10.00
Minus rate relief	– 2.00
Rates left to pay	6.00
Minus lone pensioner allowance (20% of £6)	– 1.20
Net amount to pay	4.80

Chapter 20 **Migrants and recent arrivals**

- ■ The rules that apply to migrants: see paras 20.1-8.
- ■ How the decision is made: see paras 20.9-22.
- ■ The immigration control test, asylum seekers and refugees: see paras 20.23-37.
- ■ The habitual residence test: see paras 20.38-52.

20.1 This chapter is about when you are eligible for HB if you are a person from abroad. It covers everyone, whether you are from the British Isles, Europe or the rest of the world, and whether you are arriving in the UK for the first time or returning after a time abroad.

Which rules apply

20.2 If you have recently arrived in the UK, there are three main rules which affect whether you are eligible for HB:

(a) the immigration control test;

(b) the right to reside test; and

(c) the habitual residence test.

Table 20.1 shows when each of those rules apply to you. There are also further rules if you are seeking asylum or a refugee.

Table 20.1 **Migrants and recent arrivals: eligibility for HB**

A national of	Test you have to satisfy
The British Isles (para 20.5)	Habitual residence
The EEA including Croatia (table 20.2)	Right to reside (and in some cases also habitual residence)
Macedonia and Turkey	Right to reside and habitual residence
The rest of the world	Immigration control and habitual residence

20.3 For clarity, this guide treats the above three tests as separate (though in the law they are intertwined: paras 20.17-21). The guide also avoids the term 'person from abroad', because it is often used informally to describe someone who has recently arrived in the UK (whereas in the law it has a narrower meaning).

Eligibility of nationals of different parts of the world

20.4   This section identifies which rules apply to you depending on your nationality, followed by a straightforward example of each.

Nationals of the British Isles (the Common Travel Area)

20.5   The 'British Isles' (a geographical term, roughly meaning all the islands off the North-West of the continent) is also known in immigration law as the 'Common Travel Area'. They both mean:

     (a)   the United Kingdom (England, Wales, Scotland and Northern Ireland);

     (b)   the Republic of Ireland;

     (c)   the Isle of Man; and

     (d)   the Channel Islands (all of them).

If you are a national of any part of the British Isles you only have to satisfy the habitual residence test (paras 20.38-52) to be eligible for HB.

Nationals of the European Economic Area

20.6   Table 20.2 lists all the countries in the European Economic Area (EEA) plus Switzerland, which UK law treats as being part of the EEA. The EEA includes all of the European Union (EU) states and some others. The EEA includes Croatia, which joined the EU on 1st July 2013. If you are an EEA national, the rules for eligibility are described in chapter 21.

Table 20.2 **The European Economic Area (EEA)**

The EEA states (apart from Ireland and the United Kingdom) are:

Austria	Belgium	Bulgaria
Croatia	Cyprus	Czech Republic
Denmark	Estonia	Finland
France	Germany	Greece
Hungary	Iceland	Italy
Latvia	Liechtenstein	Lithuania
Luxembourg	Malta	Netherlands
Norway	Poland	Portugal
Romania	Slovakia	Slovenia
Spain	Sweden	Switzerland

Nationals of the rest of the world

20.7   In this guide this means any country not mentioned above (paras 20.5-6). It also applies to you if you have applied for asylum or to enter the UK solely on humanitarian grounds, whether or not your application has been determined.

20.6 and T20.2   EEA 2(1) definition: 'EEA state'

20.8   If you are a national of the rest of the world you have to satisfy the immigration control test (paras 20.23-37) and also the habitual residence test (paras 20.38-52) to be eligible for HB.

Examples: Eligibility for HB

1. A British citizen

A British citizen has been living abroad for 12 years. During that time she gave up all her connections in the UK. She has now just come 'home' and has rented a flat here.

The only test that applies to a UK national is the habitual residence test. As described later, it is unlikely that the above claimant satisfies that test to begin with (unless she was living and working in an EEA state). She might well satisfy that test in (say) three months time. So for the time being she is not eligible for HB.

2. National of the EEA

An Italian national has been working in the UK for several years. He has recently taken a more poorly paid job.

He passes the right to reside test because he is working. So he is eligible for HB.

3. National of the rest of the world

An Indian national arrived in the UK six months ago to be with her family. She was given leave to enter and remain, and was granted leave by the Home Office without any conditions, in other words her leave did not include a 'no recourse to public funds' condition, so she is able to claim benefits. She now claims HB.

The two tests that apply to a national of the rest of the world are the immigration control test and the habitual residence test. As described later, she passes both tests. So she is eligible for HB.

Decision-making

20.9   This section covers general matters relevant to this chapter and chapter 21, including decision-making and claims, and how the law and terminology work.

DWP and authority decisions: passport benefits

20.10   If you receive any of the following benefits you are exempt from the habitual residence test (para 20.38-52) and right to reside test (chapter 21):

   (a)   income-based jobseeker's allowance (but see para 21.27 for exceptions);

   (b)   income-related employment and support allowance;

   (c)   income support;

   (d)   any kind of state pension credit (guarantee credit or savings credit).

The above is true only if the DWP has decided (in full possession of the facts) that you are eligible for one of the benefits mentioned (and not, say, in a case where you wrongly continued to receive one of the benefits).

20.10   HB 10(3B)(k),(l); HB60+ 10(4A)(k); NIHB 10(5)(l),(m); NIHB60+ 10(5)(l)

20.11   If the DWP has decided that you are not eligible for one of the above benefits, this decision is not binding on the authority – but a considered decision by the DWP carries weight.

Claims and couples

20.12   If you are a couple, it can matter which partner is the HB claimant. The rules in this chapter apply to each partner individually. So if partner A is eligible under the rules, but partner B is not, it is necessary for partner A to be the claimant (for you to get HB at all). If the 'wrong' partner claims the authority must give you a 'not entitled' decision; in such a case it would be good practice to explain this and invite a claim from your partner.

20.13   Once a claim is made by the 'correct' partner, the claim is assessed (e.g. income, applicable amount, etc) in the usual way. The applicable amount includes the personal allowance for a couple even though only one of them is entitled (GM para C4·218). If your partner is a non-EEA spouse the couple allowance may count as public funds and this may affect your immigration status (para 20.15).

Partners and national insurance numbers

20.14   Normally both members of a couple must have or have applied for a national insurance number (para 5.16), but an exception applies if one of you requires 'leave' from the Home Office (table 20.3 and paras 20.24-26) but does not have it (for example if they have not applied for leave or it has expired). In these cases, the normal rule does not apply to that member. In such cases the DWP advises authorities that they should assign a dummy number (GM D1·284-286).

20.15   The above and the rule in para 20.13 are only rules about eligibility for HB. This guide cannot guarantee that it is safe, in immigration terms, for that partner to be part of your HB claim. The council/NIHE or DWP may inform the Home Office, although they are not obliged to do so (GM para C4·219).

HB claim forms

20.16   Most HB claim forms ask you (the claimant): (a) your nationality and (b) whether you have entered the UK within the past two years. These two questions are intended to act as a trigger for further investigation in appropriate cases. If you

(a)   are a British citizen, and

(b)   did not enter the UK within the past two years,

you are unlikely to fall foul of these rules (since two years in the UK is almost always sufficient to pass the habitual residence test).

Law, terminology and how the tests overlap

20.17   The tests used in deciding your eligibility for HB are contained in a mixture of immigration, European and HB law as follows.

20.12   HB 8(1)(b), 10(1); HB60+ 8(1)(b), 10(1); NIHB 8(1)(b), 10(1); NIHB60+ 8(1)(b), 10(1)

20.14   HB 4(c); HB60+ 4(c); NIHB 4(c); NIHB60+ 4(c)

20.18   The 'immigration control test' (para 20.23) may stop you from getting HB (and many other benefits) if you are from outside the EEA depending on your immigration status.

20.19   HB law (constrained by European law) then stops certain other people including EEA nationals from getting HB (and many other benefits):

(a) The 'habitual residence test' (para 20.38) is in HB law and applies regardless of your nationality. It treats you as not being liable for rent/rates – which means you do not qualify for HB.

(b) The 'right to reside test' applies if you are an EEA national (table 20.2). It is also in HB law, but what the right to reside means is in the Immigration (European Economic Area) Regulations 2006 (which apply to the whole of the UK). HB law says that if you do not pass this test then you do not pass the habitual residence test (and so, as described in (a), you cannot get HB).

20.20   If you pass the immigration control test then you also pass the right to reside test. There is only one exception: if you are a national of Macedonia or Turkey (para 20.28) you pass the immigration control test but do not pass the right to reside test unless you have 'leave' – 'temporary admission' (table 20.3) is not sufficient (Yesiloz v LB Camden). But without exception if you have a right of abode, right to reside or leave from the Home Office (table 20.3) you pass the right to reside test.

20.21   If you pass the right to reside test then in most cases you also pass the habitual residence test – but there are a few exceptions: mainly if you are not in work or if you have retired without having worked in the UK (see paragraphs 21.26-32).

Immigration law terms

20.22   A basic understanding of immigration law terminology is useful (particularly in relation to the immigration control test). Table 20.3 lists the key terms and defines them in a way that is useful for HB decision making.

Table 20.3 **Simplified immigration law terminology**

Immigration rules

The legal rules approved by parliament which UKIV officers use to decide whether a person should be given permission ('leave') to enter the UK.

UK Immigration and Visas (UKIV)

The Home Office agency responsible for immigration control and determining asylum applications (including asylum support).

Leave and temporary admission

Leave is legal permission to be in the UK. Leave can be for a fixed period (limited leave) or open ended (indefinite leave). Both can be granted with or without a 'no recourse to public

---

20.18   Immigration and Asylum Act 1999 s115 (applies to the whole of the UK)

20.19   HB 10(1)-(3); HB60+ 10(1)-(3); NIHB 10(1)-(3); NIHB60+ 10(1)-(3)

20.20   Yesiloz v Camden LBC [2009] EWCA Civ 415 www.bailii.org/ew/cases/EWCA/Civ/2009/415.html

funds' condition, and this nearly always applies if you have been given limited leave. Leave can be varied provided the application is made before it has expired (para 20.26).

A person who has been granted open ended leave without any conditions is said to have 'indefinite leave to remain', also known as settled status.

Temporary admission is not in itself a form of leave, it is merely the discretion allowed by UKIV which allows time for you to do something – such as apply for asylum or leave – without falling foul of the law. Since it is not a form of leave, it does not confer a right to reside.

Public funds

Nearly all tax credits and non-contributory benefits (including HB and passport benefits) count as public funds. So does a local authority homelessness duty or acceptance on its housing waiting list.

Sponsorship and maintenance undertaking

These terms go together. Someone (typically an elderly relative) may be granted leave to join a family member on the understanding that this 'sponsor' will provide for their support and/or accommodation.

Some (but not all) sponsors are required to sign a written agreement (a maintenance undertaking) as a condition of granting leave and if they do the person they sponsor is excluded from HB (but see para 20.28 for exceptions).

Illegal entrant and overstayer

These both refer to someone who needs leave to be in the UK but does not have it and has not been granted temporary admission. An illegal entrant is someone who entered the UK without applying for leave and an overstayer is someone who was granted leave which has since expired.

Right of abode and right to reside

'Right of abode' is a term that describes someone who is entirely free of any kind of immigration control. It applies to all British citizens and some citizens of Commonwealth countries, but not necessarily to other forms of British nationality. Non-British nationals can apply to have this status confirmed in their passport.

'Right to reside' is a wider term that describes anyone who has legal authority to be in the UK. It therefore includes everyone with the right of abode, plus anyone who has any form of leave (including if your leave is granted with 'no recourse to public funds') or is from the EEA and has a right of residence. 'Right to reside' is sometimes used informally to mean right of abode (because it sounds less archaic).

The immigration control test

20.23 If you are from a country outside the EEA you have to pass the immigration control test to get HB. (You also have to pass the habitual residence test: paras 20.38-52.)

20.24 The purpose of the test is to stop you getting benefit if:

(a) you require 'leave' (table 20.3) but do not have it – e.g. you are an illegal entrant or overstayer; or

(b) you have been granted leave but with a 'no recourse to public funds' condition (but see paras 20.27-28 for exceptions); or

(c) you have been granted leave as a result of a maintenance undertaking (i.e. you are a sponsored immigrant, but see paras 20.27-28 for exceptions); or

(d) you have been granted temporary admission while your application to the Home Office is being decided – for example if you are an asylum seeker.

People who pass the immigration control test

20.25 You pass the immigration control test regardless of your nationality if:

(a) you hold a passport containing a certificate of entitlement to the 'right of abode' (table 20.3) in the UK;

(b) you have 'indefinite leave to remain' (also called settled status);

(c) you have any form of leave whether limited or indefinite (table 20.3), but only if it is not subject to a public funds condition or a maintenance undertaking (table 20.3) – although certain exceptions apply (paras 20.27-28);

(d) you applied for asylum and you have been granted refugee status, humanitarian protection or discretionary leave (paras 20.33-34);

(e) you are not an asylum seeker and you have been granted permission to claim HB as a victim of domestic violence by UK Immigration and Visas (para 20.37).

The authority normally needs to see your passport or other Home Office documentation to confirm the above.

20.26 If you have limited leave you can apply for it to be extended before it expires. Provided your application is made in time and in the correct form, you are still treated as having leave until 28 days after the decision is made on your application, and so you pass the immigration control test until then. Authorities often wrongly terminate benefit in these cases.

People with no recourse to public funds who are entitled to HB

20.27 The general rule is that if your UK visa is subject to a public funds condition or a maintenance undertaking (table 20.3) you fail the immigration control test (para 20.24). The only exceptions are in paragraph 20.28.

20.24   IAA99 115(9)

20.26   Immigration At 1971 s3C

20.28   You are not affected by the general rule (para 20.27) and pass the immigration control test (and see also paras 20.20 and 20.29) if:

(a) you are a national of Macedonia or Turkey and have been granted 'leave' by the Home Office – including leave with a 'no public funds' condition: [2015] UKUT 438 (AAC) (but see para 20.20);

(b) you were admitted to the UK as a result of a maintenance undertaking (a 'sponsored immigrant'), but you have been resident for five years or more;

(c) you were admitted to the UK as a 'sponsored immigrant' and have been resident for less than five years and your sponsor (or all of your sponsors if there are more than one) has died;

(d) you are the former partner of a British citizen or of a person with settled status (table 20.3) and have been granted permission to claim HB under the Domestic Violence Concession (para 20.37).

20.29   In the first three cases you must also be habitually resident to be entitled to HB but not in the fourth (para 20.40).

Asylum seekers

20.30   You are an asylum seeker if you have applied to be recognised as a refugee (para 20.33) under the United Nations Convention because of fear of persecution in your country of origin (typically on political or ethnic grounds).

20.31   While your asylum application is being processed you fail the immigration control test and are disqualified from HB, although there are some limited exceptions (para 20.32). If you are disqualified you may be able to get help with your maintenance and accommodation from the Home Office asylum support scheme.

20.32   If you are an asylum seeker the general rule in paragraph 20.31 does not apply and so you may be eligible for HB (although all of these cases are rare) if:

(a) you are a couple where your partner is eligible (para 20.12) – in this case any Home Office support counts as income (GM para C4.128); or

(b) you have been granted discretionary leave (para 20.33) (e.g. if you are aged under 18 and unaccompanied by an adult); or

(c) you are a national of an EEA state (para 20.6) in which case the rules in chapter 21 apply.

Refugees and others granted leave on humanitarian grounds

20.33   Following your asylum application the Home Secretary may:

(a) recognise you as a refugee (i.e. accept your claim for asylum) and grant leave; or

(b) refuse asylum but grant humanitarian protection (which is a form of leave) or discretionary leave (see circular HB/CTB A16/2006 for details of when these might apply); or

(c) refuse asylum and not grant leave.

20.28   IAA99 115(1),(3),(9); SI 2000 No. 636 reg 2(1), sch paras 2-4; SI 2013 No 458; NISR 2000 No. 71 reg 2(1), sch paras 2-4

20.34 If leave is granted it is normally for an initial period of 30 months, and then one further period of 30 months, after which you can normally apply for settled status. If you have been granted refugee status, humanitarian protection or discretionary leave you pass the immigration control test and the habitual residence test (including during your first two periods of limited leave). So you are eligible for HB from the date your status is confirmed. If you are granted refugee status (but not in other cases), then your dependants are granted leave as well so they are also eligible for HB.

Evacuees

20.35 Evacuees are people granted exceptional leave to enter the UK in response to a specific humanitarian crisis (e.g. war, famine, natural disaster). They are often British nationals without full UK citizenship. In appropriate circumstances, the UK government may grant discretionary leave to those affected, normally on a temporary basis.

20.36 Evacuees are only eligible for HB if or when they become habitually resident. Temporary exceptions have been made in response to a specific crisis (e.g. the programme for vulnerable British citizens living in Zimbabwe and Montserrat residents fleeing the volcanic eruption) but there are none that currently apply.

Destitution domestic violence concession

20.37 If you were originally granted limited leave as the partner of a British citizen or a person with settled status (table 20.3) but your relationship has broken down because of domestic violence, you can apply for permission to claim public funds (benefits) for up to three months while the Home Office considers your application to settle in the UK. This is known as the Victims of Domestic Violence Concession (or 'Destitution Domestic Violence Concession' (DDVC)) [www]. If you have been granted this concession you are entitled to HB (i.e. you are exempt from the habitual residence test). The DDVC is not available to EEA family members but in certain circumstances you have a right to reside under the EEA regulations if you have suffered domestic abuse: see para 21.23(e).

20.34   HB 10(1),(3B)(g),(h),(hh); HB60+ 10(1),(4A)(g),(h),(hh); NIHB 10(1),(5)(g),(h),(i); NIHB60+ 10(1),(5)(g),(h),(i)

20.37   10(3B)(h)(ii); HB60+ 10(4A)(h)(ii); NIHB 10(5)(h)(ii); NIHB60+ 10(5)(h)(ii); rule 289A of the immigration rules
        www.gov.uk/government/publications/application-for-benefits-for-visa-holder-domestic-violence

The habitual residence test

Who has to pass the habitual residence test

20.38   The habitual residence test applies if you are a national of:

(a) the British Isles; or

(b) the rest of the world (apart from the EEA).

It does not normally apply if you are an EEA national unless you are not active in the labour market (e.g. not working or looking for work). All the rules that apply if you are an EEA national including these exceptions are dealt with in chapter 21.

20.39   The purpose of the test is to stop someone claiming benefit immediately they enter the UK (for example, if you have a right of abode in the UK but have never lived here or have not lived here for a long time).

Habitual residence and eligibility for HB

20.40   To get HB you (the claimant) must be either exempt from the habitual residence test or be actually habitually resident (there are no exceptions). You are exempt from the habitual residence test if:

(a) you (or your partner) are entitled to a passport benefit (para 20.10);

(b) you are a former asylum seeker who has been granted by the Home Office;

- refugee status,

- humanitarian protection, or

- discretionary leave (paras 20.25 and 20.33);

(c) you have been granted leave by the Home Office under the destitution domestic violence concession (para 20.37);

(d) you are an 'economically active' EEA national (para 21.8) or the family member of an economically active EEA national (para 21.22); or

(e) you have been deported to the UK from another country (para 20.41).

If you are exempt from the habitual residence test you also pass the right to reside test. In any other case you must be actually habitually resident (paras 20.42-52).

People deported to the UK from another country

20.41   If you are a British citizen or a person with a right of abode or settled status (table 20.3) who is deported to the UK from another country you are exempt from the habitual residence test and are entitled to HB.

20.38   HB 10(2); HB60+ 10(2); NIHB 10(2); NIHB60+ 10(2)

20.40   HB 10(3B)(za)-(zc),(g),(h),(hh),(i),(k),(l); HB60+ 10(4A)(za)-(zc),(g),(h),(hh),(i),(k); NIHB 10(5)(za)-(zc),(g),(h),(i),(j),(l),(m); NIHB60+ 10(5)(za)-(zc),(g),(h),(i),(j),(l)

The meaning of habitual residence

20.42   To be eligible for HB you must be 'habitually resident' in the British Isles (para 20.5). What counts as habitual residence is a 'question of fact' (a phrase used to mean that the term is not defined in the regulations). It is decided by looking at all the facts in your case; no list of considerations can be drawn up to govern all cases. The DWP gives general guidance on this (GM paras C4.87-106).

20.43   There are two elements to 'habitual residence':

(a) 'Residence': You must actually be resident, a mere intention to reside being insufficient; and mere physical presence is not residence.

(b) 'Habitual': There must also be a degree of permanence in your residence in the British Isles (GM C4.80), the word 'habitual' implying a more settled state in which you are making your home here. There is no requirement that it must be your only home, nor that it is permanent, provided it is your genuine home for the time being.

Losing habitual residence

20.44   Habitual residence can be lost in a single day. This applies if you leave the UK intending not to return but to take up long-term residence in another country.

Gaining habitual residence

20.45   You cannot gain habitual residence in a single day. If you have left another country with the intention to settle in the UK you do not become habitually resident immediately on arrival. Instead there are two main requirements (R(IS) 6/96):

(a) your residence must be for an 'appreciable period of time'; and

(b) you must have a 'settled intention' to live in the UK.

'Appreciable period of time' and 'intention to settle'

20.46   There is no fixed period that amounts to an appreciable period of time (CIS 2326/1995). It varies according to the circumstances of your case and takes account of the 'length, continuity and nature' of your residence (R(IS) 6/96).

20.47   Case law (CIS 4474/2003) suggests that, in general, the period lies between one and three months, and that a decision maker needs 'powerful reasons to justify a significantly longer period'. That time would have to be spent making a home here, rather than merely studying or on a temporary visit.

20.48   As suggested by the DWP (GM C4.85-86), factors likely to be relevant in deciding what is an appreciable period of time, include:

(a) the length and continuity of your residence;

(b) your reasons for coming to the UK;

(c) your future intentions;

(d) your employment prospects (para 20.49); and

(e) your centre of interest (para 20.50);

although no one factor is absolutely decisive in every case.

20.49   In considering your employment prospects, your education and qualifications are likely to be significant (CIS 5136/2007). An offer of work is also good evidence of an intention to settle. If you have stable employment here it is presumed that you reside here, even if your family lives abroad.

20.50   Your centre of interest is concerned with the strength of your ties to this country and your intention to settle. As suggested by the DWP (GM C4.105), this can be shown by:

(a)   the presence of close relatives;

(b)   decisions made about the location of your family's personal possessions (e.g. clothing, furniture, transport);

(c)   substantial purchases, such as furnishings, which indicate a long term commitment; and

(d)   the membership of any clubs or organisations in connection with your hobbies or recreations.

Temporary absence and returning residents

20.51   Once your habitual residence has been established, the following general principles apply (in each case unless other circumstances over-ride them):

(a)   if you are a UK or EEA national (only), it resumes immediately on return from a period of work in another EEA member state (Swaddling v Chief Adjudication Officer);

(b)   and, in all cases, it resumes immediately on your return from a single short absence (such as a holiday or visiting relatives).

20.52   In considering whether you regain your habitual residence following a longer absence, or repeated absences, the following points need to be considered:

(a)   the circumstances in which your habitual residence was lost;

(b)   your intentions – if your absence was always intended to be temporary (even in the case of longer absences) you are less likely to lose your habitual residence than someone who never originally had any intention of returning;

(c)   your continuing links with the UK while abroad;

(d)   the circumstances of your return. If you slot straight back into the life you had before you left, you are likely to resume habitual residence more quickly.

20.51   Swaddling v Chief Adjudication Officer ECJ C-90/97www.bailii.org/eu/cases/EUECJ/1999/C9097.html

Chapter 21 **EEA nationals**

- Introduction: see paras 21.1-6.
- EEA nationals and the right to reside: see paras 21.7-33.
- Croatian nationals: see paras 21.34-41.

Introduction

21.1   This chapter is about when you are entitled to HB if you or a member of your family are a citizen of an EEA member state (an 'EEA national'). EEA member states are listed in table 20.2. This chapter does not apply if you are a British or Irish citizen (para 20.5), if you have settled status (table 20.3), or if you are a citizen of a European country which is not part of the EEA (para 20.6).

21.2   If you are an EEA national you are entitled to HB if:

(a) you are 'economically active' (para 21.3) and you have a right to reside (paras 20.21 and 21.7-23); or

(b) you are not economically active, and

- you have a right to reside; and

- you are habitually resident in the British Isles.

The requirement to have a right to reside does not violate your right to family life (Mirga v SSWP) and although it constitutes discrimination it is justifiable and so is lawful (Patmalniece v SSWP). If you are a Croatian national further rules apply (paras 21.34-41). If you are a couple see paragraphs 20.12-13 for how all these rules apply to you.

21.3   'Economically active' means you are working or you are temporarily out of work due to sickness or unemployment. In certain circumstances you can be treated as if you are working if you have worked in the UK for at least one year. See also paragraph 21.8.

Decision making and terminology

21.4   If you are an EEA national general matters such as making your claim, how the law works, decision making and an explanation of the technical terms used in the law and administration are in paragraphs 20.9-22. In particular, it describes how decision making is carried out if you receive a passport benefit, but see also paragraph 21.27 if you receive JSA(IB).

21.5   The law about entitlement to HB if you are an EEA national is very complex so case law develops rapidly. How the rules are interpreted is likely to continue changing.

21.6   If you are an EEA national you have to show you have a 'right to reside' in the UK to get HB. But if you are a worker, a former worker (including if you are temporarily unemployed

21.2   HB 10(3),(3B)(za)-(zc); HB60+ 10(3),(4A)(za)-(zc); NIHB 10(3),(5)(za)-(zc); NIHB60+ 10(3),(5)(za)-(zc)
    Mirga v SSWP [2016] UKSC 1 www.bailii.org/uk/cases/UKSC/2016/1.html
    Patmalniece v SSWP 16/03/11 UKSC [2011] UKSC 11 www.bailii.org/uk/cases/UKSC/2011/11.html

or retired), self-employed or the family member of someone who is any of these (paras 21.9-23) you are exempt from this test and entitled to HB.

EEA nationals and the right to reside

21.7   This section (paras 21.8-33) is about whether you are entitled to HB if you are an EEA national. However, if you are a Croatian the rules in this section only apply if:

(a)   you are self-employed (paras 21.9 and 21.36);

(b)   you have completed one year employed in authorised work (para 21.39).

For all other rules for Croatians, see paragraphs 21.34-41.

Who has a right to reside

21.8   If you are an EEA national (para 20.6) you have a right to reside if you:

(a)   are self-employed (paras 20.9-11);

(b)   are a worker (paras 20.12-16);

(c)   are self-employed but temporarily unable to work due to sickness (para 21.17);

(d)   are a worker who has retained your worker status while temporarily out of work;

(e)   are a family member as defined in table 21.1(a)-(c) of the above;

(f)   are a retired worker or the family member of a retired worker (para 21.20);

(g)   are, in certain circumstances, a long-term resident, parent with a child in education, student or a self-sufficient person; or

(h)   the family member of a person in (g).

Details of each of these categories are given in the following paragraphs. In immigration law, the first six groups are sometimes called 'economically active' because you are engaged in the labour market. If you are economically active, you are entitled to HB without further conditions. If (g) or (h) apply you must also be habitually resident (paras 20.42-52) to get HB.

Self-employed people

21.9   If you are an EEA national and you are self-employed you have a right to reside and you are entitled to HB (including if you are a Croatian national, see para 21.36).

21.10   Your self-employment must be 'real', and have actually begun, but unlike the requirement for workers it seems that the ten-hour threshold (para 21.15) does not apply and your self-employed status can continue even where there is no current work, provided you continue to look for it: [2010] UKUT 451 (AAC). A seller of The Big Issue who buys the magazine at half price and sells it has been found to be in self-employment: [2011] UKUT 494 (AAC).

21.11   If you are self-employed you have a legal duty to register with HMRC within three months of starting your business – even if you think you won't earn enough to pay tax/national insurance. However, just because you are registered it does not necessarily mean that HMRC accepts you are self-employed (since their job is to collect money, without perhaps worrying unduly about the niceties of its origins). On the other hand, the fact that you have not registered does not mean that you are not self-employed: CIS/3213/2007.

21.8   EEA 6(1), 14(1); HB 10(3),(3B)(za)-(zc); HB60+ 10(3),(4A)(za)-(zc); NIHB 10(3),(5)(za)-(z); NIHB60+ 10(3),(5)(za)-(zc)

Workers

21.12   If you are an EEA national you have a right to reside and you are entitled to HB if you are a 'worker' (para 21.13). But if you are a Croatian national, see paragraph 21.34.

21.13   You are a worker if you are currently engaged in remunerative work in the UK, which is

(a) 'effective and genuine'; and

(b) not 'on such a small scale as to be purely marginal and ancillary'.

'Remunerative' here has its ordinary English meaning: broadly payment for services you provide. (It does not have the same technical meaning as in paragraph 6.19.)

21.14   The following are relevant to whether your work is 'effective and genuine':

(a) the period of employment;

(b) the number of hours worked;

(c) the level of earnings; and

(d) whether the work is regular or erratic.

21.15   The number of hours worked is not conclusive of your worker status but it is relevant: CH/3733/2007. The European Commission considers ten hours to be sufficient [www] although this may not be enough when the other factors here are considered – and not doing ten hours does not automatically exclude you. The factors always have to be considered together.

21.16   The fact that your job is poorly paid or the fact the that you have to claim, say, tax credits, is not enough on its own to stop you from qualifying as a worker. You can be a 'worker' even if your work is paid 'cash in hand': [2012] UKUT 112 (AAC).

Examples: Right to reside as worker

A Spanish national works in the UK as a cleaner in a garage for two hours a night on two nights a week. He is mainly in the country to study English. So he probably does not pass the right to reside test as a worker.

An Icelandic national works in the UK as a legal translator doing variable hours (depending on whether it is term time or holiday time) but averaging six hours a week over the year. She has been doing this for three years, and her hourly rate is substantial. It is therefore quite possible that she passes the right to reside test as a worker.

Retaining worker/self-employed status while out of work

21.17   If you are an EEA national (but see para 21.36 if you are Croatian) you can retain your worker or self-employed status (and therefore your right to reside and entitlement to HB) if:

(a) you are temporarily unable to work due to sickness or injury. 'Temporarily' is decided objectively (rather than to your intention): De Brito v Home Secretary;

21.15   http://eur-lex.europa.eu/legal-content/EN/TXT/PDF/?uri=CELEX:52002DC0694&from=on

21.17   EEA 6(2),(2A),(3)-(7); HB 10(3B)(za); HB60+ 10(4A)(za); NIHB 10(5)(za); NIHB60+ 10(5)(za)
        De Brito v Home Secretary CA [2012] www.bailii.org/ew/cases/EWCA/Civ/2012/709.htm
        Saint Prix v SSWP ECJ (2014) www.bailii.org/eu/cases/EUECJ/2014/C50712.html

(b) you are on sick leave or maternity leave, with the right to return under your contract – or you stopped work because of pregnancy (or its 'aftermath') and intend to return to work or start another job within a reasonable period of no more than 52 weeks: Saint Prix v SSWP and [2015] UKUT 502 (AAC);

(c) you have worked for more than one year and are registered unemployed at the Jobcentre;

(d) you have worked for less than one year and are registered unemployed at the Jobcentre in which case your retained status lasts for only six months (after which you become a jobseeker: para 21.26);

(e) you are involuntarily unemployed and have started vocational training; or

(f) you are voluntarily unemployed in order to follow vocational training relating to your previous employment.

Item (a) includes self-employment but items (b)-(f) only apply to former employees who have worked in the UK. In the case of items (c) and (d) (registered unemployed with the Jobcentre), you must provide evidence that you are seeking work and have a genuine prospect of being engaged; and in the case of item (c), after six months unemployment the DWP says you must provide 'compelling evidence' of this, although in reality this means no more than provide evidence itself: [2016] UKUT 372 (AAC).

21.18   You do not necessarily have to be entitled to ESA to qualify as being 'unable to work due to sickness or injury' (CIS 4304/2007). Likewise you don't have to qualify for JSA or national insurance credits to be 'registered unemployed' (CIS 184/2008). Small gaps between leaving your employment and registering as a jobseeker can be ignored: [2013] UKUT 163 (AAC).

EEA nationals with the permanent right of residence

21.19   If you are an EEA national you have a right to reside and you are entitled to HB if you have a 'right of permanent residence' in the UK, as defined by the EEA regulations. You have this right if:

(a) you are a retired worker (para 21.20) or the family member (table 21.1 (a)-(d) of a retired worker; or

(b) you are a 'long-term resident' (para 21.21).

But in the case of (b) you must also be habitually resident.

21.20   You are a retired worker (para 21.19) or the family member of a retired worker if:

(a) you or your family member has retired (at retirement age or at early retirement) after working in the UK for at least 12 months – and have been continuously resident in the UK for more than three years. In counting this 12 months, any period of involuntary unemployment registered with the Jobcentre, or period out of work due to illness, accident or some other reason 'not of [your] own making', is counted as a period of employment; or

(b) you have retired (at retirement age or at early retirement) and your spouse or civil partner is a UK national; or

---

21.19   EEA 5, 15(1)(a)-(f); HB 10(3B)(zc); HB60+ 10(4A)(zc); NIHB 10(5)(zc); NIHB60+ 10(5)(zc)

21.20   EEA 5(2),(3) 15(1)(c),(d),(e); HB 10 (3B)(zc); HB60+ 10(4A)(zc); NIHB 10(5)(zc); NIHB60+10(5)(zc)

(c) you have ceased working as a result of permanent incapacity; and either

   ■ the incapacity is the result of an accident at work or an occupational disease which entitles you to ESA, incapacity benefit, industrial injuries benefit or some other pension payable by a UK institution; or

   ■ you have continuously resided in the UK for more than two years; or

   ■ your spouse or civil partner is a UK national;

(d) you are a former family member of a deceased worker or self-employed person who has retained the right to reside in the way described in para 21.22(d).

21.21   You are a 'long-term resident' if you have lived in the UK for a continuous five-year period by using your EEA right to reside (and not, for example, as a British citizen): McCarthy v Secretary of State for the Home Department. And a period of residence counts as 'continuous' despite absences, so long as:

(a) in any one year, the total length of your absence(s) from the UK is no more than six months, and this can be longer if your absence is due to compulsory military service; or

(b) the total period of absence is not more than 12 months – so long as the reason is pregnancy, childbirth, serious illness, study, vocational training, a posting in another country, or some other important reason.

Once you have acquired a permanent right of residence it can only be lost after an absence from the UK of more than two years.

EEA family member rights

21.22   If you are the 'family member' of an EEA national who has acquired the right to reside you may also acquire a right to reside (and therefore a right to HB) through them. You are an EEA family member if you satisfy the conditions in table 21.1. You do not need to be an EEA national yourself (although you can be): instead your rights depend on the status of the person you are accompanying (e.g. worker, self-employed, student). If you are an EEA family member (table 21.1) you have a right to reside if:

(a) the person you are accompanying is a worker, self-employed person, student or a self sufficient person;

(b) the person you are accompanying is a person with a permanent right to reside (para 21.19) (whether through residence or retirement);

(c) you have lived in the UK for a continuous period of five years under a right to reside (whether as a family member or otherwise);

(d) the person you accompanied is a worker or self employed person who has died, and

   ■ you were living with them immediately before their death, and

   ■ either the worker or self-employed person had lived continuously in the UK for at least the two years immediately before their death or their death was a result of an accident at work or occupational disease; or

(e) you are a former family member with a retained right of residence (para 21.23).

21.21   EEA 3; McCarthy v Secretary of State for the Home Department [2010] EUECJ C-434/09 www.bailii.org/eu/cases/EUECJ/2010/C43409_0.html

21.22   EEA 14(2), 15(1)(b),(d),(e); HB 10(3)(3B)(zb); HB60+ 10(3)(4A)(zb); NIHB 10(3)(5)(zb); NIHB60+ 10(3)(5)(zb)

Table 21.1 **Who is an EEA family member**

You are an EEA family member if you accompany an EEA national who is self-employed, a worker, a student or a self-sufficient person and you are:

(a)   their spouse or civil partner (until divorce/dissolution, not mere separation or estrangement);

(b)   a direct descendant of that person (e.g. a child or grandchild) or of their spouse or civil partner, and you are

■   aged under 21; or

■   dependent on him/her or their spouse or civil partner (for example, because you are studying or disabled);

(c)   a dependent direct relative in ascending line (e.g. a parent or grandparent) or of their spouse or civil partner;

(d)   some other family member who has been admitted to the UK on the basis that you are:

■   their partner (in the benefit sense, instead of being their spouse or civil partner); or

■   a dependent household member of that person in their country of origin; or

■   a relative who is so ill that you strictly require personal care from that person.

Note:

If the EEA national you accompany is a student:

■   if you are not their dependent child you do not count as a family member during the first three months of their (i.e. the student's) residence; and/or

■   if you only fall within category (d) you only count as a family member if you have been issued with a residence card, family permit or registration certificate by the Home Office.

Former EEA family members with retained rights

21.23   If you are a former EEA family member you nevertheless retain your family member rights if:

(a)   you are the child of a former EEA worker who is in education in the UK;

(b)   you are the parent who is the primary carer of a former EEA worker's child that is in education in the UK;

(c)   the EEA national you accompanied has died, and

■   you were living with them as their family member for at least one year immediately before they died; and

■   you are not an EEA national yourself;

T21.1   EEA 7(1),(2),(4), 8(2)-(5)

(d) you are the separated spouse or registered civil partner of an EEA worker who is living in the UK but you have not yet divorced (or dissolved your civil partnership);

(e) you are a non-EEA national former spouse/civil partner who has divorced (or had your partnership dissolved) and either:

- your marriage/civil partnership lasted at least three years and you both lived in the UK for at least a year before the marriage ended, or

- there was domestic violence, or

- there is a child from the relationship and either custody or access (you must have one or the other) needs to take place in the UK.

Generally, if you are a partner who is not married or in a civil partnership you lose your family member rights if the relationship ends. However, if the relationship has ended because of domestic violence and your former partner is an EEA national you may be able to get leave to remain or a right to reside: this is a new and complicated area of law.

Primary carer of a child in education in the UK

21.24   If you are the child of an EEA migrant worker and in education in the UK, or you are the child's primary carer (parent, grandparent, guardian), you have a right to reside and are entitled to HB provided that you are also habitually resident. This right to reside is sometimes called an 'Ibrahim/Teixeira' right (after the case that first established it) and you qualify for it as a child/primary carer if:

(a) the child has started a course of education in the UK, (e.g. primary or secondary school, or beginning a college or university course); and

(b) a parent of that child has been, at some time, an EEA worker (including a Croatian while working on the worker authorisation scheme).

The child has the right to reside while finishing the course of education, and the primary carer of the child (whether an EEA citizen or not) also has the right to reside. But you can only acquire this right through being a worker and not as a self-employed person: [2014] UKUT 401 (AAC). And if you are subject to immigration control and the other parent has a right to reside in the UK and can care for your child, you do not acquire the right to reside through being the primary carer: Hines v Lambeth LBC.

Non-EEA parents of a child who is a UK citizen

21.25   If you are a non-EEA national who is the parent of a child who is a UK citizen you have a right to reside in the UK under the EEA regulations. This right is sometimes referred to as a 'Zambrano' right after the case that first established it. However, this right to reside

21.23   EEA 10(2)-(6)

21.24   EEA 15(A)(1)-(4),(5); HB 10(3); HB60+ 10(3); NIHB 10(3); NIHB60+ 10(3);
Harrow LBC v Ibrahim and Secretary of State for the Home Department [2010] EUECJ C-310/08
www.bailii.org/eu/cases/EUECJ/2010/C31008.html
Teixeira v Lambeth LBC and Secretary of State for the Home Department [2010] EUECJ C-480/08
www.bailii.org/eu/cases/EUECJ/2010/C48008.html
Hines v Lambeth LBC [2014] EWCA Civ 660 www.bailii.org/ew/cases/EWCA/Civ/2014/660.html

21.25   EEA 15A(4A); HB 10(3A)(bb),(e); HB60+ 10(4)(bb),(e); NIHB 10(4)(bb),(e); NIHB60+ 10(4)(bb),(e);
Sanneh v SSWP CA [2015] www.bailii.org/ew/cases/EWCA/Civ/2015/49.html

(unlike the others above) cannot be used to help you qualify for HB. (The HB regulations prohibit this and have been upheld as valid by the Court of Appeal but you may qualify for other financial support from social services: Sanneh v SSWP.)

EEA job seekers

21.26   You count as an EEA job seeker (as defined by the EEA regulations) if:

(a)   you entered the UK seeking work, or you are seeking work immediately after your retained worker status as a registered unemployed person (para 21.17) has expired; and

(b)   you can provide evidence that you are seeking employment and have a genuine chance of being engaged.

21.27   If you meet the conditions in paragraph 21.26 you are entitled to register as unemployed and claim JSA(IB) but no award can be made during your first three months' residence in the UK. You are not entitled to HB so long as you remain an EEA jobseeker (para 21.26) unless you have some other right to reside (i.e. other than as a jobseeker) described above (paras 21.7-24). However, you are protected from this rule if you were getting both JSA(IB) and HB on 31st March 2014, in which case you remain entitled to HB until such time as either your JSA(IB) ends or you make a new claim for HB (paras 2.1 and 17.22).

Students and other economically inactive but self-sufficient people

21.28   You have a right to reside as an EEA national if you were admitted to the UK on the basis that you were self-sufficient. The rules about self-sufficiency apply if you are 'economically inactive', including if you are a student (but with some differences). If you have a right to reside as self-sufficient (paras 21.29-32), whether or not you are a student, you must also be habitually resident (paras 20.38-52) to be entitled to HB. You must have your own resources to be considered self sufficient: [2014] UKUT 32 (AAC).

21.29   If you are an EEA student you have the right to reside if:

(a)   you are currently studying on a course in the UK;

(b)   you signed a declaration at the beginning of the course that you were able to support yourself without social assistance (which means HB and any passport benefit); and

(c)   the declaration was true at the time it was signed and for the foreseeable future; and

(d)   you have comprehensive health insurance for the UK (access to NHS treatment is not enough: Ahmad v Home Secretary).

21.30   In practice, this means that if you are an EEA student you are unlikely to be entitled to HB. However, it is possible to qualify for HB if your circumstances have changed since you started your course (e.g. your source of funds has unexpectedly dried up) – but you will also have to satisfy the rules for students in chapter 22.

21.26   EEA 6(1),(4)-(6)

21.27   HB 10(3A)(b),(l); HB60+ 10(4)(b); NIHB 10(4)(b),(m); NIHB60+ 10(4)(b); SI 2013/3196 Reg 2; SI 2014/539 Reg 3; NISR 2013/308 Reg 2; NISR 2014/98 Reg 3

21.29   EEA 4(1)(c),(d),(2),(4), 6(1)(d),(e), 14(1); HB 10(3); HB60+ 10(3); NIHB 10(3); NIHB60+ 10(3); Ahmad v Home Secretary [2014] EWCA Civ 998 www.bailii.org/ew/cases/EWCA/Civ/2014/988.html

21.31   If you are economically inactive but not a student you have a right to reside if you:

(a) have sufficient resources not be an 'unreasonable burden' on the social assistance system; and

(b) have comprehensive health insurance.

21.32   The fact that your income is so low that you qualify for social security benefits does not automatically disqualify you but in practice you are likely to be refused HB. However, whether you are an 'unreasonable burden' is a matter of judgment and discretion (paras 1.52-53). DWP guidance acknowledges this and suggests that if you have been resident in the UK for some time, the fact that you have been self-sufficient until now is a relevant factor in deciding whether you are an 'unreasonable burden' as is the length of time you are likely to be claiming (GM paras C4.123). For example, if your funds have been temporarily disrupted you may still qualify.

Transitional exceptions

21.33   If you are an EEA national (including if you are a Croatian) you do not need a right to reside to qualify for HB if you were entitled to HB on 30th April 2004, and have since remained continuously entitled to one or more of the following benefits: HB, IS, JSA(C), JSA(IB), state pension credit or council tax benefit (prior to its demise on 31st March 2013). This is now rare.

Croatian nationals

21.34   The remainder of this chapter only applies if you are from Croatia. These rules have applied since 1st July 2013 when Croatia joined the European Union. If you are from Croatia you must have a right to reside to get HB, but unlike other EEA nationals the circumstances in which you can have a right to reside are more limited because there are restrictions on your right to work and you have limited rights if you lose your job.

Right to reside

21.35   If you are a Croatian national you have a right to reside (and so are eligible for HB) if you:

(a) are self-employed (para 21.36);

(b) are employed in authorised work (para 21.37);

(c) have completed your one year qualifying period in authorised work (para 21.39) and have a right to reside that would qualify you for HB if you were from any other EEA country (paras 21.7-33) (for example, if you were working);

(d) are in paid employment and exempt from worker authorisation in any of the ways listed in table 21.2; or

(e) are, in limited circumstances, a primary carer of a child in education (para 21.24).

21.31   EEA 4(1)(c),6(1)(d),14(1); HB 10(3); HB60+ 10(3); NIHB 10(3); NIHB60+ 10(3)

21.33   CPR sch 3 para 6(4); NICPR sch 3 para 6(3)

21.35   EEA 4(1)(a),(b), 6(1)(b),(c); SI 2013 No 1460 regs 2(3),(4),(5), 5

Self-employed people

21.36 If you are a Croatian who is self-employed you qualify for HB in exactly the same way as any other EEA national (paras 21.9-11). There are no further conditions and you do not need Home Office authorisation to run your business. However, you must be currently self-employed; it is not enough that you were self-employed in the past: R (Tilianu) v SSWP. But you may remain self-employed despite the fact that your work has currently dried up ([2010] UKUT 451 (AAC)) – even, in the short term, if you have claimed JSA: [2011] UKUT 96 (AAC).

Authorised work

21.37 If you are a Croatian you can usually only take up work (as an employee) which has been 'authorised' by the Home Office until you have completed 12 months in continuous lawful employment (para 21.40). Authorised work is limited to certain specified occupations and in most cases you must meet other further conditions. Unless the work you propose to do falls into the 'highly skilled' category, the numbers of places that are authorised by the Home Office are subject to strict quotas.

21.38 If you are a Croatian it is not enough for you to have been a worker in the past to get HB, you must meet one of the conditions in paragraph 21.35.

Completing the 12 month qualifying period

21.39 After you have completed your 12 month qualifying period in lawful employment you are no longer required to be authorised to work and you can acquire the right to reside in exactly the same way as any other EEA national (paras 21.8-33).

21.40 During your qualifying period your employment only counts as 'lawful' if you hold the appropriate authorisation document and are complying with any conditions set out in it (CIS/3232/2006 and CJSA/700/2007).

21.41 You are treated as having completed your 12 month qualifying period if you were in lawful employment at the beginning and end of that period and any intervening periods in which you were not do not, in total, exceed 30 days.

21.36   R (Tilianu) v SSWP [2010] EWCA Civ 1397 www.bailii.org/ew/cases/EWCA/Civ/2010/1397.html

21.37   SI 2013 No 1460 Reg 5

21.40   SI 2013 No 1460 Reg 2(3),(4),(5)

21.41   SI 2013 No 1460 Reg 2(5)

Table 21.2 **Croatians exempt from worker authorisation**

You are a Croatian national who is exempt from worker authorisation if:

(a) you have leave to enter the UK (table 20.3) which is not subject to any condition restricting your employment;

(b) you have worked in the UK in lawful employment for an uninterrupted period (para 21.39) of 12 months (whether that period started on, before or after 1st July 2013 when the work authorisation rules started);

(c) you have dual nationality either as a British citizen or a citizen of another EEA state, other than Croatia;

(d) your spouse, civil partner or partner is either a British citizen or a person with settled status (table 20.3);

(e) you have acquired a permanent right of residence (para 21.19);

(f) you are a family member (para 21.22) of an EEA national (other than a Croatian who is subject to worker authorisation) who has a right to reside in the UK;

(g) you are the spouse/civil partner/partner or a child aged under 18 of a person who has 'leave' to enter the UK (table 20.3) provided the terms of that leave allows them to work;

(h) you are the spouse/civil partner/partner or direct descendant of a Croatian who is subject to worker authorisation, provided that in the case of a direct descendant you are aged under 21 or dependent on that worker;

(i) you meet the Home Office criteria to enter the UK under the highly skilled migrant programme and hold a registration certificate that states that you have unrestricted access to the UK labour market;

(j) you are a student who works for no more than 20 hours per week and you hold a registration certificate which allows you to work for up to 20 hours per week;

(k) you have been posted to work in the UK by an organisation that is based in another EEA member state; or

(l) you are a diplomat or the family member of a diplomat.

T21.2   SI 2013 No 1460 Reg 2(2)-(20); HB 10(3); HB60+ 10(3); NIHB 10(3); NIHB60+ 10(3)

Chapter 22 **Students**

- General rules and who counts as a student: see paras 22.1-8.
- Which students can get HB: see paras 22.9-18.
- How student loans, grants and other income are assessed: see paras 22.19-32.

General rules

22.1   This chapter explains the HB rules which apply if you are a student or your partner is. They apply in addition to the rules in the rest of this guide.

Working age HB claims

22.2   In working age HB claims:

(a) you can get HB if you are an eligible student;

(b) you can get HB if your partner is a student but you are not;

(c) eligible students include:

- part-time students;
- students under 21 who are not in higher education;
- students with a child or young person in their family;
- many students with a disability; and
- some others (see table 22.1);

(d) your income from a student loan, grant and so on is taken into account (unless you are on a passport benefit).

This chapter gives the details of these and related rules.

Pension age HB claims

22.3   In pension age HB claims:

(a) all students and partners of students can get HB;

(b) all the kinds of student income in this chapter are disregarded.

But see paras 22.12-15 for rules that can apply to you.

Who is a student

22.4   You count as a student if:

(a) you are 'attending or undertaking a course of study at an educational establishment'. This could be a university, college or school, and the DWP says it can include any other

---

22.2   CBA 130(1)(a), 137(2)(i); HB 56; NICBA 129(1)(a), 133(2)(i); NIHB 53

22.3   CBA 130(1)(a); HB60+ 2(1) definitions: 'training allowance', 'course of study', 'sandwich course', 'student', 8(1)(e), 29(1); NICBA 129(1)(a); NIHB60+ 2(1), 8(1)(e), 27(1)

educational establishment 'used for the purposes of training, education or instruction' (GM C2 annex A para C2.04); or

(b)   you are on JSA and attending or undertaking an employment-related course.

You do not have to be getting a student loan or grant to count as a student, but you do not count as a student if you are getting a government training allowance.

22.5   You count as a student from when your course begins to when it ends, or you abandon it or are dismissed from it. This includes:

(a)   all term-times and vacations within the course (but not the vacations after it ends, or between two different courses);

(b)   periods of work experience in a sandwich course; and

(c)   absences while you remain registered with your educational establishment (for example, because you are sick or caring for someone, or for other personal reasons): O'Connor v Chief Adjudication Officer.

Full-time and part-time students

22.6   You count as a full-time student if you are on the following courses:

(a)   sandwich courses (courses with a period of work experience);

(b)   in England and Wales, courses funded by the Department for Education, Welsh Ministers, or Skills Funding, which require more than 16 hours per week of guided learning;

(c)   in Scotland, courses up to and including Scottish Higher level or SCOTVEC level 3 at a college of further education, which require more than:

- 16 hours per week of classroom or workshop based programmed learning; or
- 21 hours per week of those and other structured learning supported by teaching staff.

Information relating to (b) and (c) should be in the learning agreement (or a similar document) signed by you and your educational establishment.

22.7   For other courses there is no all-embracing definition of who counts as a full-time or part-time student. Your council should decide this by considering the nature of the course, the number of hours you are required to attend, how the educational establishment describes the course, and the amount and nature of any student loan or grant you receive (GM chapter C2 annex A para C2.08). Information about student courses and qualifications is available online [www].

22.8   But if you are on a modular course, you only count as full-time during the periods you are registered as full-time, or re-taking an exam or module from a full-time period.

22.4-5   HB 2(1) definition: 'training allowance', 53(1) definitions: 'course of study', 'sandwich course', 'student', 'qualifying course'; HB60+ 2(1); NIHB 2(1), 50(1); NIHB60+ 2(1)
           O'Connor v Chief Adjudication Officer 03/03/99 CA [1999] EWCA Civ 884 1 FLR 1200

22.6   HB 53(1) definitions: 'college of further education', 'full-time course of study', 'full-time student', 'higher education'; NIHB 50(1)

22.7   https://www.gov.uk/what-different-qualification-levels-mean

22.8   HB 53(2)-(4); NIHB 50(2)-(4)

Eligibility for HB

22.9   The basic conditions for getting HB are summarised in table 2.1. This section explains the additional student rules. Table 22.1 gives the list of eligible students.

Table 22.1   **Eligible students**

Working age HB claims

In working age HB claims, you are an eligible student if you are in one or more of the following groups:

(a)   you are on JSA(IB), ESA(IR) or IS;

(b)   you are in supported accommodation and on UC (see para 2.13);

(c)   you are on a part-time course (see paras 22.6-8);

(d)   you are under 21 and are on a course which is not higher education (in other words your course is up to and including GCSE A level or BTEC/SCOTVEC National Diploma or Certificate level 3), or you are aged 21 and you are continuing such a course;

(e)   you are a lone parent (see table 4.1);

(f)   you are in a couple and are responsible for one or more children or young persons (see paras 4.4-19);

(g)   you are a single claimant and are responsible for a foster child placed with you by a local authority or voluntary organisation;

(h)   you qualify for a disability premium or severe disability premium (see paras 12.31 and 12.38);

(i)   you would qualify for a disability premium except that the DWP has disqualified you from incapacity benefit because you are treated as capable of work;

(j)   you are accepted by the DWP as having had limited capacity for work for ESA purposes for 28 weeks or more (ignoring breaks of up to 12 weeks), or as having been incapable of work for incapacity benefit purposes for 28 weeks or more (ignoring breaks of up to eight weeks);

(k)   you have a UK grant which includes an amount for deafness (this applies from the date you requested this);

(l)   you are unable to get a student loan or grant following an absence from your studies which was due to sickness or to providing care, and was agreed by your educational establishment. But this only applies from when your sickness or caring responsibility ends to the day before you resume your studies, and only for a maximum of one year.

Pension age HB claims

In pension age HB claims, all students are eligible for HB.

T22.1   CBA 130(1)(a); HB 56; NICBA 129(1)(a); NIHB 53

Single claimants and lone parents

22.10   If you are a single student:

(a) in working age HB claims, you can only get HB if you are an eligible student. All lone parents and some single claimants are eligible students: see table 22.1;

(b) in pension age HB claims, all students can get HB.

Couples

22.11   If you are a couple:

(a) in working age HB claims, you can only get HB if at least one of you is:

  ▪   an eligible student: see table 22.1; or

  ▪   not a student.

  You cannot get HB if you are both ineligible students;

(b) in pension age HB claims, all students and partners of students can get HB.

In working age HB claims, if one of you is an ineligible student the other one has to be the HB claimant (see para 5.4 for how to change which partner in a couple is the claimant). In other working age HB claims, and all pension age HB claims, either of you can be the HB claimant (see para 5.3). In all cases the calculation of your HB takes into account the income (including student income in working age claims) and capital of both of you.

Occupying your home (students and trainees)

22.12   Chapter 3 gives the rules about occupying your home. Further rules for students are in paras 22.13-17. Unlike the rest of this chapter, paras 22.13-15 also apply to trainees on a government sponsored or approved training course.

22.13   If you are a single claimant or lone parent, and are an eligible student (table 22.1) or a trainee (para 22.12), the following applies when your term-time accommodation is different from your normal home:

(a) if you are liable for mortgage interest on your normal home, you cannot get HB (even if you pay rent on your term-time accommodation);

(b) if you are liable for rent on your normal home, you can only get HB there (even if you also pay rent on your term-time accommodation);

(c) if you are liable for rent on your term-time accommodation but are not liable for rent or mortgage interest on your normal home (for example because it is your parent's home), you can only get HB on your term-time accommodation. (See also para 22.16.)

22.14   If you are in a couple, you can get HB on two homes (paras 3.10-15) if:

(a) at least one of you is an eligible student (table 22.1) or a trainee (para 22.12);

(b) occupying two homes is unavoidable; and

(c) awarding HB on two homes is reasonable.

22.10   HB 54,56; NIHB 51,53

22.11   CBA 136(1); HB 8(1)(e), 54,56(1); HB60+ 8(1)(e); NICBA 132(1); NIHB 8(1)(e), 51,53(1); NIHB60+ 8(1)(e)

22.12   HB 2(1) definition: 'student', 7(18) definition: 'training course'; HB60+ 2(1), 7(18); NIHB 2(1), 7(18); NIHB60+ 2(1), 7(18)

22.13   HB 7(1),(3); HB60+ 7(1),(3); NIHB 7(1),(3); NIHB60+ 7(1),(3)

For example, this could be because one of you is renting term-time accommodation for a course which is a long way from your normal rented home.

22.15   Whether you are a single claimant or lone parent or in a couple, you can get HB on your normal home during a temporary absence (paras 3.38-39 and 3.60) if you (the claimant) are an eligible student (table 22.1) or a trainee (para 22.12). For example this could apply if you are staying somewhere in connection with your studies and can't get HB there. But this rule can't apply at the same time as the rules in paras 22.13-14.

Examples: Student eligibility for HB

The examples are about working age HB claims, and the claimants meet the basic conditions for getting HB (see table 2.1).

1. A single student

A single student does not fall within any of the groups in table 22.1.

■   She cannot get HB: see para 22.10.

2. A single student with a disability

A single full-time student is registered as blind, so he qualifies for a disability premium.

■   He can get HB: see table 22.1(h).

3. A lone parent student

A student is a lone parent with two children.

■   She can get HB: see table 22.1(e).

4. A couple: one is a student

One partner in a couple works. The other is a full-time student and does not fall within any of the groups in table 22.1.

■   They can get HB, but the non-student has to be the HB claimant: see para 22.11.

5. A couple: both are students

A couple are both full-time students. Neither of them falls within any of the groups in table 22.1.

■   They cannot get HB: see para 22.11.

6. The couple have a baby

The couple in example 5 have a baby.

■   They can get HB, and either of them can be the HB claimant: see para 22.11.

Exceptions for term-time accommodation

22.16   Paragraphs 22.13-14 describe when you can get HB on term-time accommodation which is not your normal home. But in working age HB claims, if you are a full-time student you cannot get HB there while you are absent from it in your summer vacation (see para 22.18), unless the absence is due to hospital treatment or is less than one complete benefit week.

22.14   HB 7(6)(b); HB60+ 7(6)(b); NIHB 7(6)(b); NIHB60+ 7(6)(b)

22.15   HB 7(16)(iv),(viii),(17); HB60+ 7(16)(iv),(viii),(17); NIHB 7(16)(iv),(viii),(17); NIHB60+ 7(16)(iv),(viii),(17)

22.16   HB 55; NIHB 52

Exceptions for student accommodation

22.17   Student accommodation means:

(a)   accommodation you rent from the educational establishment you are attending. This includes accommodation it in turn rents from another educational establishment, an education authority, or under a long tenancy (a tenancy with a lease of more than 21 years), but not accommodation it rents from someone else; or

(b)   accommodation an educational establishment has arranged to provide to you in order to 'take advantage of' (abuse) the HB scheme (see also para 2.59).

In working age claims, if you are a full-time or part-time student you cannot get HB there during your 'period of study' (see para 22.18), unless you are in one or more of groups (c) to (k) in table 22.1. And if you are the partner of a full-time or part-time student, the same applies during their period of study.

Period of study and summer vacation

22.18   Your 'period of study' means:

(a)   all the period you count as a student (see para 22.5) apart from summer vacations; but

(b)   in courses requiring more than 45 weeks of study in a year (for example many postgraduate courses), all the period you count as a student. In these cases you do not count as having summer vacations.

Student income

22.19   The rules about how income is assessed are in chapters 13 and 14. This section gives the additional rules for student loans, grants and other income. Information about the amounts of loans, grants and so on is available online [www].

22.20   In pension age HB claims, all the kinds of student income in this section are disregarded. The rest of this chapter applies only to working age HB claims. But all your income is disregarded if you are on a passport benefit (see paras 13.3 and 13.5).

Student loans

22.21   A student loan can include:

(a)   a fee loan towards your fees. This is disregarded; and/or

(b)   a maintenance loan towards your living expenses. Part of this is counted as your income: see paras 22.22-24.

22.17   HB 53(1) definition: 'education authority', 57,58; NIHB 50(1), 54,55

22.18   HB 53(1) definitions: 'last day of course', 'period of study'; NIHB 50(1)

22.19   England: www.gov.uk/student-finance
          www.practitioners.slc.co.uk/policy-information/student-support-information-notices.aspx
          Scotland: www.saas.gov.uk/
          Wales: www.studentfinancewales.co.uk
          Northern Ireland: www.studentfinanceni.co.uk
          NHS and social work: www.nhsbsa.nhs.uk/students.aspx

22.20   HB 54; HB60+ 29(1); NIHB 51; NIHB60+ 27(1)

22.21   HB 64(1), 64A; NIHB 61(1), 62

22.22 Most UK students in higher education are eligible for a maintenance loan. Higher education means degree courses, postgraduate courses, teacher training courses, training courses for youth and community workers, BTEC/SCOTVEC Higher National Diploma or Certificate, and other courses at level 4 and above. The main groups who cannot get a maintenance loan are part-time students, students on nursing and midwifery diploma courses (but students on NHS-funded courses can get a reduced maintenance loan), students aged 60 or over at the start of the course; and students in Scotland aged 50 or over at the start of the course (unless you are under 55 and intend to work after completing the course).

22.23 If you are eligible for a student maintenance loan:

(a) you are counted as receiving it at the maximum level applicable to you for the year. This includes:

- any additional loan you could get for extra weeks and so on;
- any contribution you, your partner or your parents have been assessed as being able to make (see also para 22.27);
- in Scotland, a young student's bursary;

(b) it is taken into account as your income (not capital) as described in table 22.2.

22.24 The rules in para 22.23 apply if you get a maintenance loan. They also apply if you could get a maintenance loan by 'taking reasonable steps' to do so. Religious beliefs are unlikely to be accepted as preventing you from doing so (CH/4422/2006).

Table 22.2 **Assessing student maintenance loans**

If you are eligible for a student maintenance loan (see paras 22.22-24), your income from it is calculated as follows.

(a) Start with the maximum amount of student maintenance loan you could receive for the year (see para 22.23). But in the case of a postgraduate master's degree loan, start with 30% of the maximum amount (the other 70% is disregarded). And disregard the whole amount of a special support loan.

(b) Subtract £693. This is a standard annual disregard of £303 towards travel and £390 towards books and equipment.

(c) Average the result over the weeks in the period from:

- the first Monday in September,
- or in Scotland, the first Monday in your academic year if it begins in August;

to:

- the last Sunday in June,
- or in your final year (or only year in a one-year course), the last Sunday in your course.

22.23   HB 53(1) definitions: 'contribution', 'student loan', 56(1),(3),(4); NIHB 50(1), 53(1),(3),(4)

22.24   HB 56(3); NIHB 53(3)

T22.2   HB 40(7)-(9), 53(1) definitions: 'academic year', 'last day of course', 64, 64B; NIHB 37(3)-(7), 50(1), 61

In 2016-17 there are 42 weeks from 5th September 2016 to 25th June 2017, and in 2017-18 there are also 42 weeks from 4th September 2017 to 24th June 2018.

(d) Then subtract £10. This is a standard weekly disregard (see also para 13.45).

(e) This gives your income for each of the weeks described in step (c).

(f) But in your first year, the income calculated as above is not taken into account until your course begins (CIS/3735/2004).

Notes

■   If you are a couple and are both eligible for a student maintenance loan, the calculation applies separately for each of you (you each get the disregards at steps (b) and (d)).

■   If your course does not start in the autumn, the period used in step (c) is all of your academic year apart from weeks falling wholly or partly in the 'quarter' containing your longest vacation. But the 'quarters' are January to March, April to June, July to August, and September to December (even though these aren't all three months).

■   If you abandon or are dismissed from your course, any student loan you have received continues to be taken into account as calculated above, but the £10 disregard in step (d) does not apply after you have left.

Example: A student assessment (2016-17 academic year)

One partner in a couple is a full-time student in the first year of a degree course at a university outside London. He receives a student maintenance loan of £5,330 (£5,150 plus £180 for two extra weeks), which is the maximum he could receive as an English student. He also receives a fee loan. The other partner is self-employed for an average of 35 hours per week, and has net profit of £90 per week. They are eligible for HB because the non-student is the claimant (see para 22.11). They have no other income, and their capital is below £6,000. Their eligible rent is £130 per week.

Student income

The fee loan is disregarded (see para 22.21). The maintenance loan is assessed as follows (see table 22.2):

(a) He receives £5,330, which is the maximum amount applicable to him.

(b) Subtract £693, leaving £4,637.

(c) Average over the 42 weeks from 5.9.16 to 25.6.17: £4,637 ÷ 42 = £110.40.

(d) Subtract £10, leaving £100.40.

(e) This is his weekly income from the maintenance loan.

(f) It is ignored from 1st September 2016 to when his course begins. It is then his income until 25th June 2017.

Amount of HB

From when the course begins to 25th June 2017 (unless their circumstances change) their HB is calculated as follows (see paras 6.2-6):

- Student maintenance loan   £100.40 pw
- Self-employed net profit (£90) minus standard earned income disregard for a couple (£10) and additional earned income disregard (£17.10)   £62.90 pw
- Total income   £163.30 pw
- Applicable amount (for a couple aged 18 or over but under SPC age)   £114.85 pw
- Excess income (£163.30 – £114.85)   £48.45 pw
- Eligible rent   £130.00 pw
- Minus 65% of excess income (65% of £48.45)   £31.49 pw
- Amount of HB   £98.51 pw

Student grants

22.25 A student grant means any kind of educational grant, award, scholarship, studentship, exhibition, allowance or bursary, whether it is paid by a local authority, a government department, an employer or someone else.

22.26 If you receive a grant:

(a) the amount you receive is taken into account as your income. This includes:
- a maintenance grant towards your living expenses,
- any amounts for the living expenses of a child or adult dependant,
- any additional amounts you get for extra weeks and so on,
- any contribution you, your partner or your parents have been assessed as being able to make (see also para 22.27);

(b) but some kinds of grant, and most amounts for extra expenses are disregarded.

The details are in table 22.3.

Making contributions to your student loan or grant

22.27 If you or your partner have been assessed as being able to contribute to your student loan or grant, the contribution is:

(a) included when the loan or grant is assessed (see paras 22.23 and 22.26);

(b) disregarded from your or your partner's other earned or unearned income.

Parental contributions are also included when your loan or grant is assessed (see also para 13.43).

22.25   HB 53(1) definition: 'grant'; NIHB 50(1)

22.26   HB 53(1) definitions: 'contribution', 'grant income'; NIHB 50(1)

22.27   HB 64(1),(4)(a)(iii),(b)(ii), 66,67; NIHB 61(1),(4)(a)(iii),(b)(ii), 64,65

Table 22.3　**Assessing student grants**

If you receive a grant (see paras 22.25-26), your income from it is calculated as follows.

Assessments and disregards

(a) Disregard the whole amount of the following grants:

- special support grant (awarded to students on means-tested benefits),
- education maintenance allowance (EMAs), and 16-19 bursary fund payments which replaced EMAs in England (awarded to students in non-advanced education). These are also disregarded in the assessment of your capital,
- parent's learning allowance (awarded for dependants),
- higher education bursary (awarded to care-leavers).

(b) For other grants, start with the total amount of grant you receive for the year (see para 22.26).

(c) If you are not eligible for a student maintenance loan (see para 22.22), subtract £693. This is a standard annual disregard for travel and books and equipment (it applies even if amounts for these are deducted at step (d)).

(d) Subtract all amounts included in your grant for:

- any disability you have,
- child care costs,
- travel,
- books and equipment,
- tuition or examination fees,
- maintenance of two homes,
- term-time residential study away from your educational establishment,
- anyone outside the UK who is not included in your application amount.

(e) The result counts as your income.

(f) It is averaged over the period(s) described in (g) to (k).

Amounts for child or adult dependants

(g) If you are eligible for a student loan (see para 22.22), apart from the reduced loan for an NHS-funded degree student, average amounts in your grant for a child or adult dependant over the same period as the student loan (see table 22.2).

(h) But if you receive a mandatory government grant (and aren't eligible for a student loan), or a grant for a nursery and midwifery diploma course or an NHS-funded degree course, average amounts in your grant for a child or adult dependant over the whole academic year (52/53 weeks).

(i) In any other case, the rules in steps (j) and (k) apply.

T22.3　HB 40(7)-(9), 53(1) definition: 'grant income', 59; NIHB 37(3)-(7), 50(1), 56

Other amounts

(j) Average other amounts in your grant (apart from disregarded amounts) over the weeks from the first Monday to the last Sunday in the period they cover:

- for many grants this means your 'period of study' (see para 22.18),

- for a care-leaver's grant it means your summer vacation.

(k) But if you are a sandwich student, omit any weeks wholly or partly in your period of work experience.

Notes

- If you are a couple and both receive a grant, the calculation applies separately for each of you.

- If you abandon or are dismissed from your course, any amount you have received which falls within step (g) continues to be taken into account as calculated above.

Using other income to supplement a student loan or grant

22.28   If you have income from a student loan or grant, you may qualify for an extra disregard towards your expenditure. This is calculated as follows:

(a) work out your expenditure for the year on the items in table 22.3(d), but only include expenditure which is necessary for you to attend your course;

(b) add together the following figures:

- £693,

- your higher education bursary (if you get one),

- the amounts subtracted from your grant (if you get one) for the items in table 22.3(d);

(c) if the total of (a) is greater than the total of (b), you qualify for a disregard equal to the difference. In practice this is averaged over the year (or a more appropriate period) to give the weekly amount of the disregard.

But this disregard can only be made from income 'intended' for this purpose (CIS/3107/2003), for example if you have to take a part-time job to pay for your travel. It cannot be made from the student loan or grant, or from income you would have anyway.

Repaying a student loan

22.29   If you are repaying a student loan, your repayments cannot be deducted in the assessment of your income. But in England, Scotland and Wales, payments you receive from the Teacher Student Loan Repayment Scheme are wholly disregarded.

22.28   HB 63; NIHB 60

22.29   HB 40(1), sch 5 para 12; NIHB 37(1)

Access funds, learner support funds and financial contingency funds

22.30   Educational establishments can make payments to students from 'access funds' or 'learner support funds', and Welsh Ministers can make payments to students from 'financial contingency funds'. These are sometimes called hardship payments. They are assessed as follows:

(a)   payments towards your living costs (see para 22.31) are counted as your income or capital as appropriate. But if they are income (in other words regular payments):

- the whole amount is disregarded if they are paid before your course begins, or to tide you over until you receive your student loan,

- £20 per week is disregarded in other situations (see also para 13.45);

(b)   payments for anything else (for example course-related expenses) are disregarded as income and as capital for 52 weeks.

22.31   In paras 22.30 and 22.32, your living costs mean rent (other than any part of the rent which is not eligible for HB, or not met by HB because of a non-dependant deduction), council tax (in Northern Ireland rates), water charges, household fuel, food or ordinary clothing or footwear.

Sports Council awards

22.32   Sports Council awards are assessed as follows:

(a)   payments towards your living costs (see para 22.31) are counted in full as your income or capital as appropriate;

(b)   payments for anything else (including vitamins, minerals or performance-enhancing dietary supplements) are disregarded as income, and as capital for 26 weeks.

22.30   HB 53(1) definition: 'access funds', 65,68(2),(4); NIHB 50(1), 63,66(2),(4)

22.32   HB 2(1) definition: 'sports award', sch 5 para 59, sch 6 para 50; NIHB 2(1), sch 6 para 61, sch 7 para 49

Chapter 23 **Subsidy**

- General rules about subsidy for HB expenditure, local schemes, and administration: see paras 23.1-8.
- The effect of HB overpayments on subsidy: see paras 23.9-25.
- The effect of high rents etc on subsidy: see paras 23.26-40.

General rules

23.1 This chapter explains how much the DWP pays councils in Great Britain to run the HB scheme. This is called subsidy. (For the separate rules about grants towards discretionary housing payments see paras 25.17-18.)

23.2 The DWP pays councils subsidy for each financial year (1st April to 31st March) towards their:

(a) HB expenditure: see paras 23.3-4; and

(b) HB administration: see para 23.5.

The balance of the council's costs are met from the council's general fund in England and Scotland, or its council fund in Wales.

Subsidy for HB expenditure

23.3 The DWP pays each council subsidy towards the HB it pays in the financial year:

(a) this equals 100% of all HB lawfully paid;

(b) except that a lower amount (or no subsidy) is paid for:

- additional HB paid under a local scheme: see para 23.4,
- some overpayments of HB: see paras 23.9-25, and
- some payments of HB relating to high rents etc: see paras 23.26-40.

Lawfully paid HB includes rebates, allowances and payments on account (see chapter 16). It also includes payments made in the financial year for an earlier financial year. But each amount of HB can only get subsidy once.

Subsidy towards local schemes

23.4 If the council runs a local scheme for war disablement and bereavement pensions (see paras 13.18-19):

(a) first the council's annual subsidy is calculated (see para 23.3), but including only the HB that would be awarded if it did not run a local scheme;

23.3   AA 140(6), 140B(1); SO 11(2),(3), 12(1)(a), 13, 14, 19(1)(h), 20

23.4   SO 12(1)(c),(4)

(b) then this is increased to take account of the local scheme. The increase equals the lower of:

  ▪ 0.2% of the council's annual subsidy,

  ▪ 75% of the additional HB awarded in the year as a result of the local scheme.

Subsidy for HB administration

23.5 The DWP also pays each council subsidy towards part of its HB administration costs in the financial year (for example staffing, accommodation, training and computers). The amounts for 2017-18 are in circulars S10/2016; S9/2015 (E); S10/2015 (S); S11/2015 (W). The DWP calls this a 'cash-limited specific grant'. It is separate from the grant for council tax rebate (CTR) administration, which is paid to councils by the DCLG in England, or by the Scottish or Welsh Government.

Subsidy claims, payments and overpayments

23.6 To get subsidy, councils have to claim it from the DWP. They may not get their full amount of subsidy if they do not:

(a) claim it on time using the correct procedures;

(b) provide the information and evidence required by the DWP; and

(c) get their final subsidy claim certified by their auditor by 30th November.

The Secretary of State for Work and Pensions has a discretion to recover subsidy which was overpaid, or was claimed in breach of the subsidy rules: R (Isle of Anglesey County Council) v SSWP, R (Lambeth LBC) v SSWP.

Subsidy law and guidance

23.7 The law about HB subsidy is in:

(a) sections 140A-140G of the Social Security Administration Act 1992 (which gives the legal framework); and

(b) the Income-related Benefits (Subsidy to Authorities) Order 1998, SI 1998 No.562 (which gives the detailed rules).

When the subsidy rules change in relation to a financial year, the Order is usually amended at the end of that year, but DWP guidance usually gives advance warning. DWP guidance is in its Subsidy Guidance Manual (which is reissued each year) and the 'S' series of circulars [www].

Subsidy and HB decision-making

23.8 When councils make decisions about awarding HB, or recovering overpaid HB, they have a duty to apply HB law fairly, objectively and impartially. If a decision means the council has to use its judgment (see para 1.52), it must not allow the subsidy rules to affect this. For

---

23.5   AA 140B (4A),SO 12(1)(b), sch 1

23.6   SO part II
        R v Anglesey CC v SSWP 30/10/03 QBD [2003] EWHC 2518 Admin www.bailii.org/ew/cases/EWHC/Admin/2003/2518.html
        R (Lambeth LBC) v SSWP 20/04/05 QBD [2005] EWHC 637 Admin www.bailii.org/ew/cases/EWHC/Admin/2005/637.html

23.7   www.gov.uk/government/publications/housing-benefit-subsidy-guidance-manual-2015-to-2016
        www.gov.uk/government/collections/housing-benefit-for-local-authorities-subsidy-circulars

example, although backdated HB qualifies for 100% subsidy, decisions about 'good cause' (see paras 5.56-57) are subject to certification by the council's external auditor (DWP Subsidy Guidance Manual paras 307-308). But if a decision allows the council to use its discretion (see para 1.53), it may take its own financial position (including the effect of the subsidy rules) into account as one factor: R v Brent LBC HBRB ex parte Connery. For examples see paras 10.27, 18.27-28 and 23.12.

Overpayment of HB

23.9 This section describes how much subsidy the DWP pays councils towards overpayments of HB.

Subsidy categories

23.10 For subsidy purposes, HB overpayments fall into the categories shown in table 23.1. The table also summarises the amounts of subsidy paid. The details for each category are in paras 23.13-25.

23.11 The rules about which HB overpayments are recoverable do not always correspond to the subsidy categories, but in broad terms:

(a) departmental error and authority error/administrative delay overpayments may or may not be recoverable: see the rules about official error overpayments in paras 18.10-14;

(b) other overpayments are usually recoverable: see paras 18.11-12 and 18.15.

Table 23.1 **Overpayments subsidy categories**

Subsidy category	Amount of subsidy
(a) Departmental error overpayments	100%
(b) Payment on account overpayments	100%
(c) Duplicate payment overpayments	25%
(d) Technical overpayments	Nil
(e) Authority error/administrative delay overpayments	100%, 40% or nil depending on certain thresholds
(f) Claimant error, fraudulent and other overpayments	40%

Notes

In broad terms:

- subsidy in categories (a) to (c) is paid only on unrecovered overpayments;
- subsidy in categories (e) and (f) is paid whether the overpayments are recovered or not.

Detailed rules about the categories, amounts, etc are in paras 23.13-25.

23.8   R v Brent LBC ex p Connery 20/10/89 QBD 22 HLR 40

T23.1   AA 140(6); SO 11(2), 13, 18, 19(1)(e)-(i)

Deciding subsidy categories

23.12   The council decides which category each HB overpayment falls into for subsidy purposes. To ensure councils do this correctly, and claim the correct amount of subsidy, their external auditors are instructed that 'testing of overpayments needs to provide assurance that overpayments are correctly classified and fairly stated, recognising that there is a subsidy incentive to misclassify overpayments, for example, to code a technical error overpayment (nil subsidy) as an eligible [claimant error, etc] overpayment (40% subsidy) or, at or near one of the [authority error/administrative delay] thresholds, not to code a local authority error at all' (Audit Commission, Certification Instruction BEN01 (06-07) para 35).

Departmental error overpayments

23.13   For subsidy purposes, a 'departmental error overpayment' means one caused by a mistake of fact or law (whether in the form of an act or omission):

(a) by the DWP or HMRC or someone providing services to them; or

(b) in a decision of a First-tier or Upper Tribunal.

This does not include an overpayment to which the claimant, or someone acting on the claimant's behalf, or the payee, materially contributed (see para 23.24(c)). And it does not include an overpayment caused because a court interprets the law differently from how the DWP or HMRC or a tribunal interpreted it (see para 23.24(d)).

23.14   Subsidy on these overpayments is 100% of:

(a) the total departmental error overpayments in the year;

(b) minus the total departmental error overpayments recovered in the year (whether they were overpaid in the year or in a previous year).

This means the council does not qualify for subsidy towards the amount it recovers.

Payment on account overpayments

23.15   A 'payment on account overpayment' means one caused when a payment on account is greater than the amount of HB a claimant qualifies for (see paras 16.23-28).

23.16   Subsidy on these overpayments is 100% of:

(a) the total payment on account overpayments in the year;

(b) minus the total payment on account overpayments recovered in the year (whether they were overpaid in the year or in a previous year).

23.12   SO 18(4)

23.13   SO 18(4)

23.14   SO 18(b)(i),(2),(3), 19(1)(e)

23.15   SO 18 (7B)

23.16   SO 18(1)(f)

Duplicate payment overpayments

23.17   A 'duplicate payment overpayment' means one caused when:

(a) a duplicate payment of HB is issued because the first one was (or was alleged to have been) lost, stolen or not received; but

(b) the first one is in fact cashed.

23.18   Subsidy on these overpayments is 25% of:

(a) the total duplicate payment overpayments in the year;

(b) minus the total duplicate payments recovered in the year (whether they were issued in the year or in a previous year).

Technical overpayments

23.19   A 'technical overpayment' means one caused because:

(a) a council tenant's liability for rent ends (for example their tenancy ends) or reduces; but

(b) HB has already been credited to their rent account for a period after it ended or reduced.

23.20   No subsidy is paid on these overpayments.

Authority error/administrative delay overpayments

23.21   For subsidy purposes:

(a) an 'authority error overpayment' means one caused by a mistake of fact or law (whether in the form of an act or omission) by the council;

(b) an 'administrative delay overpayment' means one caused by a delay (rather than a mistake), but only when the council:

- is notified of a change of circumstances, and

- has the information and evidence it needs to make a decision on it, but

- fails to make the decision before the next HB payment date.

These do not include an overpayment to which the claimant, or someone acting on the claimant's behalf, or the payee, materially contributed (see para 23.24(c)). And they do not include an overpayment caused because a court interprets the law differently from how the council interpreted it (see para 23.24(d)).

23.22   These overpayments are combined for subsidy purposes. The amount of subsidy (see para 23.23) depends on:

(a) the total authority error and administrative delay overpayments in the year;

(b) as a percentage of the total HB paid in the year. (This means HB which qualifies for 100% subsidy: see para 23.3.)

23.17   SO 18(1)(a)

23.18   SO 18(1)(a), 19(1)(i)

23.19   SO 18(7),(7A)

23.20   SO 18(2)(b)

23.21   SO 18(6),(6ZA)

23.22   SO 18(1)(e),(6A)

23.23   If the above percentage is:

(a)   not more than 0.48% (the lower threshold), 100% subsidy is paid on all authority error and administrative delay overpayments in the year;

(b)   more than 0.48% but not more than 0.54% (the higher threshold), 40% subsidy is paid on all these overpayments;

(c)   more than 0.54%, no subsidy is paid on any of these overpayments.

In cases (a) and (b), the council qualifies for this subsidy even if it recovers some or all of these overpayments.

Example: Subsidy for authority error and administrative delay overpayments

A council's annual expenditure on correctly paid HB is £10,000,000.

So its lower threshold is £48,000 and its higher threshold is £54,000 for that year (see para 23.23).

If the total authority error and administrative delay overpayments in that year are:

- ■   £45,000, the council gets subsidy of 100% of this, which is £45,000;
- ■   £50,000, the council gets subsidy of 40% of this, which is £20,000;
- ■   £55,000, the council gets no subsidy for this.

Claimant error, fraudulent and other overpayments

23.24   Any other overpayment qualifies for 40% subsidy, whether it is:

(a)   a 'claimant error overpayment'. This means one caused by the claimant, or someone acting on the claimant's behalf, failing to provide required information or evidence;

(b)   a 'fraudulent overpayment'. This means one where the claimant has been found guilty of an offence, made an admission under caution, or agreed to pay a penalty as an alternative to prosecution (see para 18.73);

(c)   an overpayment that would count as departmental error (see para 23.13) or authority error/administrative delay (see para 23.21), except that the claimant, someone acting on the claimant's behalf, or the payee, materially contributed to it;

(d)   an overpayment caused because a court interprets the law differently from how the DWP, HMRC, a tribunal or the council interpreted it (see paras 23.13 and 23.21);

(e)   an overpayment caused by a third party, for example a landlord, whether or not they are the payee; or

(f)   any other overpayment not included in paras 23.13-23.

23.23   SO 18(1)(e),(6A)

23.24(a)   SO 18(4A)

23.24(b)   SO 18(5),(5A)

23.24(c),(d)   SO 18(4),(6)

23.24(e),(f)   SO 18(1)(b)(iii),(2)

23.25   Subsidy is 40% of the total of these overpayments in the year. The council qualifies for this subsidy even if it recovers some or all of these overpayments.

High rents etc

23.26   This section describes the subsidy limitations which apply when HB is paid for:

(a) exempt accommodation: see paras 23.28-31;

(b) temporary accommodation for homeless people: see paras 23.32-38;

(c) council tenants in certain circumstances: see para 23.39; and

(d) rent referral cases which the council fails to refer to the rent officer: see para 23.40.

23.27   The DWP pays councils 100% subsidy on all other payments of HB (see para 23.3) regardless of how high the claimant's eligible rent is, so long as it is correctly assessed. In practice this applies in most HB cases, because most HB cases do not fall within any of the rules in para 23.26. In particular, local housing allowance (LHA) cases never fall within these rules. (For how eligible rent is assessed, see chapters 7 to 11.)

Exempt accommodation

23.28   'Exempt accommodation' is defined in paras 10.3-6. The rules for exempt accommodation are as follows:

(a) details of the claimant's eligible rent are referred to the rent officer (see paras 10.28-31);

(b) the rent officer's determinations are not binding on the assessment of the claimant's eligible rent (see paras 10.37 and 23.8);

(c) but the subsidy limitations in paras 23.29-30 apply if:

  ■ the rent officer's determinations include a 'significantly high rent' or 'exceptionally high rent' determination (see paras 10.42 and 10.44), and

  ■ the claimant's eligible rent is higher than these.

For exceptions for registered housing associations see para 23.31.

Subsidy limitations for exempt accommodation

23.29   The subsidy limitations for exempt accommodation apply to the part of the claimant's HB which is attributable to:

(a) the excess of the claimant's eligible rent;

(b) over the exceptionally high rent (EHR) determination (if there is one); or

(c) over the significantly high rent (SHR) determination (if there is no EHR).

23.30   Subsidy on HB attributable to this excess is:

(a) 100% when the claimant falls into the protected groups of people who:

  ■ could formerly afford their accommodation (see paras 7.31-33), or

  ■ have had a death in their household (see paras 7.34-36);

23.25   SO 18(1)(b)(iii),(c),(d),(2), 19(1)(ea),(f)

23.28-31   SO 13, 16, sch 4

(b) 40% when:

- the claimant or someone in their household is considered vulnerable (see para 10.23), and

- there is no suitable cheaper alternative accommodation the claimant can reasonably be expected to move to (see paras 10.24-25);

(c) nil in any other situation. For example, when there is no suitable alternative accommodation to make a comparison with (see paras 10.17-20), or when the amount by which the council has restricted the claimant's eligible rent still leaves an excess (see paras 10.15-16).

In all these cases, 100% subsidy is paid on HB not attributable to the excess. The example illustrates this.

Example: Subsidy for exempt accommodation

A claimant is renting exempt accommodation. The rent officer has provided an exceptionally high rent (EHR) determination of £170 per week. But the council decides her eligible rent is £200 per week. This is because she falls into a vulnerable group and there is no suitable cheaper alternative accommodation she can move to. The claimant is not on a passport benefit and qualifies for HB of £80 per week.

Subsidy is calculated as follows (see paras 23.29-30):

- the excess of her eligible rent over the EHR is £30 per week.

- First subsidy is calculated on the HB attributable to this excess: this is 40% of £30   £12 pw

- Then subsidy is calculated on the HB not attributable to the excess: this is 100% of £50   £50 pw

- Total subsidy   £62 pw

Note: If the landlord was a registered housing association and the council did not consider the rent unreasonably high, the council would get subsidy of 100% of the claimant's HB (see para 23.31), which is £80 per week.

Registered housing association exempt accommodation

23.31 When the landlord of exempt accommodation is a registered housing association (see para 7.10), the subsidy limitations in paras 23.29-30 only apply if the council considers:

(a) that the claimant's rent is unreasonably high; or

(b) in pension age HB claims, that the accommodation is unreasonably large.

This is because details of the claimant's rent can only be referred to the rent officer in these circumstances (see table 10.3).

Temporary accommodation for homeless people

23.32   The subsidy limitations in paras 23.36-38 apply to accommodation:

(a) which is provided to prevent the claimant being or becoming homeless, or for the related purposes in part 7 of the Housing Act 1996 or part 2 of the Housing (Scotland) Act 1987;

(b) where the claimant's rent is payable to;

- ■ an authority that administers HB ('an LA'), or

- ■ a registered housing association (paras 7.9-11) ('an HA');

(c) which falls within one of the descriptions in paras 23.33-35; and

(d) which isn't exempt accommodation (paras 10.3-6).

If it is exempt accommodation, see instead paras 23.28-31.

LA and HA board and lodging accommodation

23.33   For subsidy purposes this means accommodation:

(a) where the claimant's rent includes a charge for at least some meals which are cooked or prepared, and also consumed, in the accommodation or in associated premises; or

(b) which is in a hotel, guest house, lodging house or similar establishment.

But is doesn't include accommodation in a hostel (para 7.22) or care home (table 7.2).

LA and HA licensed accommodation

23.34   For subsidy purposes this means accommodation which an LA or HA itself rents from someone else other than under a lease (i.e. usually under a licence agreement). In this case, the subsidy rules depend on whether the accommodation is self-contained. 'Self contained' means the claimant's household doesn't have to share a kitchen, toilet or bathroom with another household.

LA and HA leased accommodation and HA owned accommodation

23.35   For subsidy purposes this means accommodation which:

(a) an LA or HA itself rents from someone else under a lease, but in the case of English LAs the lease must be for ten years or less and the accommodation must be outside the LA's Housing Revenue Account; or

(b) an HA owns.

But is doesn't include accommodation an LA owns.

23.32   SO 17(1), 17A(1), 17B(1), 17C(1)

23.33   SO 11(1), 17(1)(b)(i), 17B(1)(b)(i)

23.34   SO 17(1)(b)(ii),(4), 17A(1)(b)(i), 17B(1)(b)(ii), 17C(1)(b)(ii)

23.35   SO 17A(1)(b)(ii),(iii), 17C(1)(b)(i),(ii)

Subsidy limitations for temporary accommodation

23.36   Subsidy on temporary accommodation (paras 23.32-35) is limited on a weekly basis to:

(a) the claimant's entitlement to HB in the week;

(b) the 'maximum amount' (see para 23.37);

(c) the 'cap' figure of;

  ■ £500 if the accommodation is in one of the following London broad rental market areas: Central, Inner East, Inner North, Inner South East, Inner South West, Inner West and Outer South West;

  ■ £375 if the accommodation is elsewhere.

For further subsidy details, see circulars S1/2011, S5/2011 and G10/2012.

Before April 2017 authorities received a temporary accommodation management fee in HB subsidy. This was an amount per household of £40 for London authorities and £60 for other authorities. From April 2017 this has been removed (DWP S5/2017). In England this element of HB subsidy has been replaced by the DCLG's flexible homelessness support grant [www]. In Scotland and Wales funding is now available through authorities' block grants. Except for the removal of the temporary accommodation management fee, the DWP expects HB subsidy paid on temporary accommodation to continue under the existing rules (until the claimant is awarded or migrated to UC) (DWP S5/2017).

23.37   The 'maximum amount' (para 23.36(b)) is based on January 2011 local housing allowance (LHA) figures for the broad rental market area the accommodation is in:

(a) for board and lodging accommodation (para 23.33) and non-self-contained licensed accommodation (para 23.34), the maximum amount is the January 2011 LHA figure for one-bedroom self-contained accommodation;

(b) for self contained licensed accommodation (para 23.34) and leased and HA-owned accommodation (para 23.35), the maximum amount is 90% of the January 2011 LHA figure for the appropriate size of dwelling (para 23.38).

23.38   The appropriate size of dwelling (paras 23.37(b)) depends on the number of rooms, counting both bedrooms and living rooms, in the claimant's accommodation (not the size of their household). If their accommodation contains:

(a) one or two rooms, the appropriate size is one-bedroom self-contained accommodation;

(b) three rooms, the appropriate size is a two-bedroom dwelling

(c) four rooms, the appropriate size is a three-bedroom dwelling

(d) five or six rooms, the appropriate size is a four-bedroom dwelling

(e) seven or more rooms, the appropriate size is a five-bedroom dwelling (in January 2011 there were LHA figures for five-bedroom dwellings).

The law says this because other rooms in the claimant's accommodation must be regarded as living rooms (even if they are in fact bedrooms).

23.36   SO 13, 17(2),(5), 17A(2), 17B(2), 17C(2), sch 8;
                www.gov.uk/government/publications/flexible-homelessness-support-grant-2017-18-to-2018-19

23.37-38   SO 17(3),(5), 17A(3),(4), 17B(3), 17C(3),(4)

Example: subsidy for leased temporary accommodation

A London council houses a homeless family in a house outside London which it holds on a three year lease. The claimant's rent is payable to the London council and the claimant is entitled to HB of £260 per week. The house has three bedrooms and one living room, making four rooms in all. So the January 2011 LHA figure for a three-bedroom dwelling is used to calculate subsidy (paras 23.37-38). In the area the house is in, this figure is £180 per week.

Subsidy is therefore 90% of the January LHA figure, i.e. £162 per week.

Council tenants

23.39   The following subsidy limitations can apply to council tenants (see para 8.4), but in practice they are rare. The DWP's Subsidy Guidance Manual gives further details and exceptions:

(a)   The 'rent rebate subsidy limitation scheme' applies in England and Wales only. If a council increases its tenants' rents by more than its central government guideline rent increase, no subsidy is payable on the HB attributable to the excess (DWP circulars S6/2015 and S7/2016). (Rents on local authority homes provided under the Affordable Rents model are exempt from this control.)

(b)   The 'disproportionate rent increase rule' applies in Wales and Scotland only. If a council increases rents to its tenants on HB more than it increases its other rents, subsidy on the difference is restricted.

(c)   Limitations on 'modular improvement schemes' apply throughout Great Britain. If a council offers its tenants the right to select optional services, no subsidy is payable on the amount of HB attributable to these.

(d)   Limitations on 'rent payment incentive schemes' apply throughout Great Britain. If a council makes payments (in cash or kind) to reward tenants for paying their rent on time, the total value of such payments is deducted from the amount of subsidy paid to the council.

Failure to make a rent referral

23.40   'Rent referral cases' are described in paras 10.28-53. If the council:

(a)   is required to refer an HB case to the rent officer during the year;

(b)   but fails to do so before the date its final subsidy claim has to be submitted for that year,

no subsidy is paid for any of the HB awarded in the year for that case. Some councils have lost a significant amount of subsidy for this reason: R (Isle of Anglesey County Council) v SSWP, R (Lambeth LBC) v SSWP.

23.39   SO 11(2), 13, 15, 15A, 19(1)(a),(c),(2),(3), 20A, sch 4A

23.40   SO 13, 16, sch 4 para 6; R (Anglesey) v SSWP and R (Lambeth) v SSWP see footnote 23.6

Chapter 24 **Support for mortgage interest**

- Summary and terminology: see paras 24.1-5.
- Who can get SMI: see paras 24.6-15.
- Calculating your qualifying benefit: see paras 24.16-26.
- Your eligible housing costs: see paras 24.27-45.
- Waiting periods, time limits and other rules: see paras 24.46-62.

Summary and terminology

24.1 This chapter describes how social security benefits can help you meet:

(a) interest on a mortgage or other loan to buy your home;

(b) interest on a loan for certain repairs and improvements to your home;

(c) certain other housing costs that HB can't meet.

It only gives the rules for claims made on or after 1st October 2010.

24.2 This help is not part of the HB scheme, but is administered separately by the DWP, and in Northern Ireland by the DFC. Some of the rules are different from HB but many are similar. These differences and similarities are described throughout this chapter.

'Support for mortgage interest' (SMI)

24.3 We use this term as a generic description for all the kinds of payment in this chapter.

'Qualifying benefits'

24.4 You have to be claiming one of the qualifying benefits to get SMI. They are JSA(IB), ESA(IR), IS and guarantee credit.

Eligible housing costs

24.5 This means the amount of help your qualifying benefit can provide towards SMI. The amount is based on a standard rate rather than what you actually pay, and there are rules limiting how much it can be and (in some cases) when your SMI starts or stops. Your eligible housing costs are included in your qualifying benefit's applicable amount, but can be reduced if you have one or more non-dependants.

Who can get SMI

24.6   You can only get SMI if:

(a) you claim one of the SMI qualifying benefits;

(b) you meet the conditions for the particular one you are claiming; and

(c) you are entitled to it – or would be once your eligible housing costs have been included.

SMI qualifying benefits

24.7   The SMI qualifying benefits are:

(a) guarantee credit;

(b) income-based JSA;

(c) income-related ESA; and

(d) income support.

The basic conditions for these are in paras 24.8-14, but this guide does not give every detail. (Different rules apply if you are on UC: see *Help with Housing Costs Volume 1*.)

Basic conditions for guarantee credit

24.8   The main conditions for getting guarantee credit are that:

(a) you (or your partner if you have one) must have reached state pension credit age (para 1.24);

(b) you must not be in an excluded group (para 24.14); and

(c) your income (including tariff income) must be lower than your applicable amount (once your eligible housing costs have been included in it) see para 24.17.

There is no upper capital limit, but you are counted as having tariff income if your capital is above £10,000 (para 24.19).

Basic conditions for JSA(IB), ESA(IR) and IS

24.9   The main conditions for getting JSA(IB), ESA(IR) or IS are that:

(a) you (and your partner if you have one) must be under state pension credit age (para 1.24);

(b) you (and your partner) must not be in 'remunerative work' (para 24.10);

(c) you must meet one of the additional conditions for the benefit you are claiming (paras 24.11-13);

(d) you must not be in an excluded group (para 24.14);

(e) your capital must not be above £16,000 (para 24.19);

(f) your income (including tariff income) must be lower than your applicable amount (once your eligible housing costs have been included in it): see para 24.17.

You are counted as having tariff income if your capital is above £6,000 (para 24.19).

24.10 'Remunerative work' means work of at least:

(a) 16 hours per week for you (the claimant);

(b) 24 hours per week for your partner.

The rules about this are the same as in paras 14.69-72, apart from the different number of hours for your partner.

Income-based JSA

24.11 To get JSA(IB) you (and in some cases both you and your partner) must meet the labour market conditions. Broadly these are that you must be 'available for work' and 'actively seeking work' and not be disqualified (for example if you gave up a job without good reason).

Income-related ESA

24.12 To get ESA(IR) you must be accepted by the DWP as having limited capability for work (or for work and work-related activity): see para 12.25.

Income Support

24.13 To get IS you must be capable of work (with some exceptions) but if you are in one of the groups listed below, you are not expected to meet the labour market conditions for JSA. You can get income support if you are:

(a) entitled to statutory sick pay;

(b) a lone parent with a youngest child aged under five;

(c) a single claimant or lone parent who is fostering a child aged under 16;

(d) pregnant and either incapable of work due to the pregnancy or there are 11 weeks or less before the baby is due;

(e) a woman who has given birth to a baby not more than 15 weeks ago;

(f) a person aged under 19 (in some cases aged under 21) in non-advanced full-time education and you have no-one acting as parent for you or (in certain circumstances) you are unable to live with your parents;

(g) a carer entitled to carer's allowance, or caring for a person who has claimed attendance allowance or disability living allowance in the last 26 weeks;

(h) a refugee learning English (in certain circumstances);

(i) a prisoner on remand or awaiting sentence (in this case you are only eligible for the housing costs element of IS); or

(j) a juror or witness required to attend court or a tribunal.

This is not an exhaustive list: there are other less common categories, such as if you are sick or disabled and met the conditions for IS prior to April 2011 (i.e. transitional cases).

Excluded groups

24.14   You may be excluded from getting a qualifying benefit (and therefore from getting SMI) if you are a migrant or recent arrival in the UK, or are a student. These rules are similar to those that apply to HB (chapters 20 to 22) but there are some differences.

How to start a claim for a qualifying benefit

24.15   You can start your claim for a qualifying benefit by a telephone call to the national number: 0800 055 6688 for JSA/ESA/IS; 0800 99 1234 for pension credit. A claim for JSA/ESA/IS can also be started online. In Northern Ireland, claims for these benefits must be made in writing at the local Social Security Agency office.

Calculating your qualifying benefit

24.16   The weekly amount of your qualifying benefit equals:

(a) your weekly applicable amount (para 24.18);

(b) minus your weekly income (para 24.19).

24.17   The most important difference from HB is that your applicable amount includes your eligible housing costs (para 24.27) after any non-dependant deductions have been made (para 24.20). The calculation can mean your qualifying benefit includes all, some or none of your eligible housing costs: see examples.

Examples: Support for mortgage interest

(a) A single home-owner on ESA(IR)

His ESA(IR) includes a work-related activity component, and he has no other income or capital. His eligible housing costs (towards mortgage interest) are £40 per week, and he has completed his SMI waiting period (para 24.46). His ESA(IR) is calculated as follows:

- Applicable amount:

personal allowance	£73.10
work-related activity component	£29.05
eligible housing costs	£40.00

- He has no income to deduct
- Weekly amount of ESA(IR)   £142.15

His ESA(IR) meets the whole of his eligible housing costs. He is also likely to qualify for maximum CTR (para 24.25).

(b) A non-dependant moves in with him

The adult daughter of the above home-owner moves in and a non-dependant deduction of £95.45 applies for her. This reduces his eligible housing costs from £40 to nil (but is not used to reduce any other part of his applicable amount). His ESA(IR) is now calculated as follows:

- Applicable amount:

  personal allowance   £73.10

  work-related activity component   £29.05

  eligible housing costs   £0.00

- He has no income to deduct

- Weekly amount of ESA(IR)   £102.15

His ESA(IR) no longer meets any of his eligible housing costs. He is now likely to qualify for maximum CTR but with a non-dependant deduction (para 24.25).

(c) A home-owner couple on guarantee credit

They have state and private pensions totalling £250 per week and have capital of £4,000. Their eligible housing costs (towards mortgage interest) are £24.80 per week, and they don't have to complete an SMI waiting period (para 24.46). Their guarantee credit is calculated as follows:

- Applicable amount:

  personal allowance   £243.25

  eligible housing costs   £24.80

- Minus their weekly income   – £250.00

- Weekly amount of guarantee credit   £18.05

Their guarantee credit meets only part of their eligible housing costs. But they qualify for maximum CTR (para 24.25).

(d) Their capital increases

The capital of the above couple increases to £18,750. So they have tariff income of £18 per week, which increases their total income to £268 per week. Their guarantee credit is now calculated as follows:

- Applicable amount:

  personal allowance   £243.25

  eligible housing costs   £24.80

- Minus their weekly income   – £268.00

- Weekly amount of guarantee credit   £0.05

This cannot be awarded because it is less than 10p. But it means they have underlying entitlement to guarantee credit, so they still qualify for maximum CTR even though their capital is over £16,000 (para 24.25).

Applicable amounts

24.18   Your applicable amount is made up of a personal allowance, any premiums and components you qualify for, and an amount for your housing costs. Table 24.1 gives the details and shows the differences from HB.

Table 24.1 **SMI qualifying benefits: applicable amount**

The conditions for the personal allowance, premiums and components are the same as in HB (chapter 12) as are the amounts (table 12.1) except as mentioned below.

Guarantee credit

Your applicable amount is the total of the following that apply to you.

(a)   A personal allowance for yourself, or for you and your partner if you are a couple – but the amount for people over 65 is the same as for people under 65.

(b)   Severe disability premium.

(c)   Carer premium.

(d)   Your weekly eligible housing costs (para 24.27) after any deduction has been made for non-dependants (para 24.20).

JSA(IB), ESA(IR) and IS

Your applicable amount is the same as above plus any of the following that apply to you.

(e)   Enhanced disability premium for adults.

(f)   Disability premium – JSA(IB) and IS only.

(g)   Work-related activity component or support component – ESA(IR) only, and in the case of a couple only if you are both under state pension credit age.

Note: You can't be awarded a personal allowance for children/young persons, a family premium, a disabled child premium, or an enhanced disability premium for children/young persons. This is because children and young persons are covered by child tax credit, which is disregarded in the assessment of your income.

Income and capital

24.19   Your (and your partner's) income and capital assessed in a similar way to HB (chapters 13 to 15):

(a)   the main differences for income are in table 24.2;

(b)   the main difference for capital is that you can get guarantee credit (but not JSA(IB), ESA(IR) or IS) even if your capital is over £16,000;

(c)   the only difference for tariff income (para 15.5) is that for guarantee credit it is calculated on all of your assessed capital (not just the first £16,000).

Table 24.2 **SMI qualifying benefits: assessing income**

The main differences from HB are as follows. These apply to all the qualifying benefits except as mentioned below.

Earned income

- Your self-employed earnings are averaged over one year or a more appropriate period. Reasonable expenses include debts.

Earnings disregards

- There is no child care disregard or additional disregard (paras 14.63 and 14.68).

- For JSA(IB), IS and guarantee credit, the standard disregard for lone parents is £20 (table 14.5(b)).

- For ESA(IR), the standard disregard can only be £120 if you are in permitted work (table 14.5(a)), or £20 in other cases (i.e. when your partner works part-time or is in one of the special occupations in table 14.5(f), or you work as a councillor).

- For guarantee credit, you can't qualify for a £20 standard disregard (table 14.5(d)) through the old fitness for work test or just through getting paid national insurance credits for incapacity.

Income from social security benefits and tax credits

- For JSA(IB), ESA(IR) and IS, statutory sick, maternity, paternity and adoption pay (table 14.1) count as unearned income, so the earnings disregards don't apply to them.

- For JSA(IB), ESA(IR) and IS, arrears of any benefits only count from the day they are paid and then for the same length of time as the period they cover.

- But for guarantee credit, the rules about the above are the same as for HB, and this also applies to JSA(IB) and IS if you are in a couple and one of you is over state pension credit age.

- Child tax credit is disregarded in full.

- There is no carry over of any unused earnings disregard to working tax credit (para 14.61(c),(d)).

- Only £10 is disregarded from widowed parent's allowance (table 13.2(n)).

Other income

- Maintenance for an adult counts in full.

- Payments made by a mortgage protection policy to cover costs not covered by SMI are ignored completely.

Assessing weekly income

- Your income is generally treated as being paid to you on the first day of your benefit week (para 24.22) in which it is due – or on the day it was due if this was before you made your claim.

- Income is converted to a weekly amount in the same way as for HB (para 6.37) except that for all claims annual amounts are simply divided by 52.

Non-dependant deductions

24.20   An amount can be deducted from your eligible housing costs if you have one or more non-dependants residing with you. The rules about whether this deduction is made, and if so how much it is, are the same as in HB (para 6.11).

Minimum benefit

24.21   If the weekly amount of your JSA(IB), IS or guarantee credit calculated as above is less than 10p, then it is not awarded. But for guarantee credit, if the amount is between 1p and 9p you count as having 'underlying entitlement' (and this affects your entitlement to CTR: para 24.25).

Your benefit week

24.22   The SMI qualifying benefits are assessed on a weekly basis. Your benefit week is:

(a) for JSA(IB), the seven days ending on your pay day (para 24.23);

(b) for ESA(IR) and IS, the seven days ending on the day before your pay day;

(c) for guarantee credit, the seven days ending on your pay day if it is paid in arrears, or starting on your pay day if it is paid in advance.

Your pay day

24.23   Your pay day is decided by the last two digits of your national insurance number as follows (though there are some exceptions for old claims):

- 00 to 19   –   Monday
- 20 to 39   –   Tuesday
- 40 to 59   –   Wednesday
- 60 to 79   –   Thursday
- 80 to 99   –   Friday

Qualifying benefits and CTR

24.24   Council tax rebates (CTR) help you pay your council tax in Great Britain, and are administered by the council that sends your council tax bill. For full details see *Help with Housing Costs Volume 1*.

24.25   You qualify for maximum CTR if:

(a) you are on guarantee credit, or have underlying entitlement to it (para 24.21) – even if your capital is over £16,000; or

(b) you are on JSA(IB), ESA(IR) or IS – but this can depend on the details of the CTR scheme in your area.

Getting 'maximum CTR' means your CTR covers the whole of your council tax apart from any amounts for non-dependants (these are usually much lower than in HB). See earlier examples.

24.26   Otherwise (depending on the circumstances) you could qualify:

(a)   for maximum CTR if your CTR applicable amount is lower than the applicable amounts used to calculate JSA(IB), ESA(IR), IS or guarantee credit (table 24.1); or

(b)   for some CTR in many other situations.

Eligible housing costs

24.27   Your qualifying benefits can cover three types of eligible housing costs. These are:

(a)   interest on a loan taken out to purchase your home (e.g. a mortgage or other loan);

(b)   interest on a loan taken out to pay for certain repairs and improvements on your home;

(c)   other miscellaneous housing costs not eligible for HB (ground rent, rent for Crown tenants, certain service charges payable by leaseholders etc: table 7.2).

Further details are given in the rest of this chapter.

Eligible mortgages and home loans

24.28   Your loan is eligible if:

(a)   it is taken out to buy the home you and your family normally occupy (para 3.2) or to increase your share of the equity (such as buying out the share of your former partner or a sitting tenant or purchasing the freehold of a leasehold property); or

(b)   it is taken out to repay a loan that would have qualified as above.

For exceptions see paras 24.29-31.

Disqualified mortgages and home loans

24.29   All or part of your loan is disqualified if:

(a)   any part of it was more than you needed to buy the home (e.g. any part of the loan was used to purchase other goods, or to repay accrued interest); or

(b)   the loan was taken out or increased while you were on benefit (para 24.30) though in this case there are some exceptions (paras 24.32-34).

Taking out or increasing a mortgage or home loan while on benefit

24.30   If your loan was taken out during a 'relevant period' it is disqualified from help. A relevant period is a period:

(a)   when you were entitled to JSA(IB)/ESA(IR)/IS/guarantee credit;

(b)   when you were living as a member of a family of someone who was entitled to JSA(IB)/ESA(IR)/IS/guarantee credit; or

(c)   up to 26 weeks between two of either of the above periods.

For exceptions about what counts as a relevant period see para 24.31, and for exceptions for certain kinds of loan see para 24.32.

24.31 The rule about a relevant period is modified as follows:

(a) if you are claiming IS it does not include periods on guarantee credit;

(b) if you are claiming JSA(IB) it does not include periods on guarantee credit, but it also includes periods on JSA(C) (although DWP guidance suggests it should not when you or the family member you were living with was entitled to JSA(C));

(c) if you are claiming ESA(IR) or guarantee credit, 'member of family' means your partner only.

Eligible new or increased mortgage and home loans

24.32 Certain new or increased loans are eligible for assistance even if you take one out during a relevant period (para 24.30). Your new or increased loan is eligible if:

(a) it was used to buy a home that is better suited than your former home to the special needs of a disabled person. The disabled person need not be a member of your family but they must have qualified as disabled at the time the loan was taken out;

(b) it was used to buy a new home because it was needed to provide separate sleeping accommodation for two children of the opposite sex who are aged 10 or over but under 20 and are members of your family;

(c) it was used to pay off your original loan (e.g. a remortgage);

(d) the original home was sold to pay off an eligible loan and the loan was taken out to buy a new home even if this was some time later; or

(e) it was used to buy a home and in the week before, you were in receipt of HB or of 'other' housing costs (para 24.27(c)) in your JSA(IB), ESA(IR), IS or guarantee credit.

In the case of the last three items, although the loan is eligible, the amount of SMI you can receive is subject to the limits in paras 24.33-34.

24.33 If the loan was taken out to repay your original loan or after your original home was sold (para 24.32(c) and (d)), then any increase in housing costs is not eligible. For example, if your original loan was for £50,000 and your new loan is for £60,000 then only £50,000 of housing costs are eligible.

24.34 If the loan was taken out immediately after being on HB or help with other housing costs (para 24.32(e), then to begin with the amount of help is limited to the amount of support you were previously receiving (e.g. if you were getting £50.00 HB per week this would be the maximum help you could receive). However, if the standard rate of interest subsequently increases you become entitled to a proportional increase.

Loans for repairs and improvements

24.35 You cannot get help to cover the cost of repairs or improvements (i.e. any bills for those repairs), nor for variable service charges in leasehold accommodation.

24.36 However, if your loan was taken out to cover the cost of certain qualifying repairs and improvements (including a loan to cover a leasehold variable service charge) it is eligible. Any type of borrowing is eligible but you must have used it to pay for the repairs or improvements within six months of taking it out.

Qualifying repairs and improvements

24.37   If you took out a loan for repairs and improvements it only qualifies for help if the repairs and improvements were for one or more of the items listed in table 24.3 and the works were undertaken to maintain the fitness of the home for human habitation. If a loan is also for other repairs and improvements not listed in table 24.3, only the proportion that is in respect of qualifying items is covered.

Table 24.3 **Qualifying repairs and improvements**

The following items are qualifying repairs and improvements (para 24.37).

Measures to provide

- a bath, shower, wash basin, sink or lavatory, and necessary associated plumbing, including the provision of hot water not connected to a central heating system;
- ventilation and natural lighting;
- drainage facilities;
- facilities for preparing and cooking food;
- insulation;
- electrical lighting and sockets;
- storage facilities for fuel or refuse.

Repairs

- to an existing heating system;
- of unsafe structural defects.

Other measures

- damp proofing measures;
- measures to make your home better suited to the needs of a disabled person, as in para 24.32(a);
- measures to provide sleeping accommodation, as in para 24.32(b).

The amount of eligible housing costs

24.38   Once your eligible housing costs have been identified the weekly amount is calculated and included as part of your applicable amount. The calculation is as follows:

(a) Any eligible loans are added together (e.g. separate loans for home purchase and eligible repair).

(b) A restriction is made if the total exceeds the upper limit (para 24.39) or if the costs are otherwise considered excessive (para 24.40). If there is more than one eligible loan and together they exceed the upper limit the restriction is applied proportionately to each.

(c) Each loan (or each restricted loan) is multiplied by the standard rate of interest (para 24.44) and then divided by 52 to give a weekly amount and, if there is more than one, they are added together.

(d) From this total the appropriate deductions (if any) are made for any non-dependants (para 24.20).

(e) The resulting figure is included in the calculation of your applicable amount (table 24.1).

The upper limit on eligible loans

24.39   The upper limit on eligible loans is:

(a) £200,000 in the case of claims for JSA(IB), ESA(IR) or IS.

(b) £100,000 in the case of claims for pension credit.

Restrictions on excessive costs

24.40   Whether or not the upper limit applies, your housing costs can be restricted if:

(a) the home you occupy is larger than is reasonably required by you and your family (including any foster children) and any non-dependants, having regard to any suitable alternative accommodation; or

(b) the area in which your home is located is more expensive than other areas in which suitable alternative accommodation exists; or

(c) the amount that is eligible is higher than the cost of suitable alternative accommodation in your area.

When the DWP is making a decision about any of the above, the area over which the comparison is made should not be too wide and the capital value of your home must be ignored. In certain circumstances, a restriction cannot be applied or must be delayed (paras 24.41-43).

24.41   A restriction cannot be made (even if suitable accommodation is available) when it is not reasonable to expect your household to look for other accommodation. In deciding this, similar considerations apply as in HB exempt accommodation cases (paras 10.24-25).

24.42   If it is reasonable to expect your household to move, your housing costs cannot be restricted for the first 26 weeks if you were able to meet the repayments when they were entered into. This can be extended for a further 26 weeks if you are using your 'best endeavours' to find somewhere cheaper. In calculating the 26 week period, the 12 week linking rule applies (para 24.53).

24.43   If a restriction applies, any excess over the amount of loan you would need to obtain suitable alternative accommodation is disallowed. So if the equity in your home is sufficient to buy a new home outright, there may be no entitlement.

The standard rate of interest

24.44   As at 1st April 2017 the standard rate of interest is 3.12%. The standard rate of interest is set in line with the Bank of England average mortgage rate. Future changes will only be triggered when the standard rate and the Bank of England published average mortgage rate differ by at least 0.5%.

24.45   The standard rate applies to all claims covered in this chapter, regardless of whether the actual interest rate paid by you is more or less. If the standard rate is more than the actual interest rate, any excess payments are nonetheless credited to your mortgage account.

Waiting periods and time limit of awards

What the waiting period is and when it applies

24.46   If you are claiming JSA/ESA/IS, even if there is entitlement you will not normally receive SMI towards any housing costs during the first 39 weeks of your claim (known as the 'waiting period').

24.47   But if your waiting period began before 1st April 2016, it is 13 weeks (not 39 weeks).

24.48   The waiting period does not apply if:

  (a)   your partner has attained the qualifying age for state pension credit or, for JSA only, you have;

  (b)   your claim is for payments as a Crown tenant, under a co-ownership scheme or for a tent (para 24.27).

24.49   If you are entitled to JSA/ESA/IS during your waiting period without your housing costs included (i.e. because your income is less than your personal allowance plus any premiums and components) then your award is increased to include your housing costs when the waiting period ends.

24.50   If you are only entitled to JSA/ESA/IS once your housing costs are included then your 'nil award' can be increased at the end of your waiting period to include your housing costs provided you are treated as entitled, otherwise you will have to make a fresh claim. You are treated as entitled if throughout that period you were entitled to JSA(C), ESA(C), incapacity benefit or statutory sick pay or were awarded national insurance credits for sickness or unemployment. You are also treated as entitled in certain other situations.

Time limit for JSA claims

24.51   If you are claiming JSA, your award of housing costs is time limited (para 24.52) unless your claim (or linked claim) began before 4th January 2009 (para 24.53).

24.52   If your JSA claim began on or after 4th January 2009, the maximum length of your housing costs award is 104 weeks. In calculating the 104 week limit the waiting period is ignored. Any two or more periods that are linked to an award that first began on or after 4th January 2009 will count as a continuous award.

Linking rules (JSA, ESA, IS)

24.53   If you are claiming JSA/ESA/IS, breaks in your claim can affect entitlement to SMI when you reclaim (paras 24.46 and 24.51). However, there are special rules (known as the 'linking rules') which treat you as having a continuous award. There are two main linking rules that affect your award of SMI. These are:

  (a)   where a repeat claim for a qualifying benefit is made within 12 weeks (104 weeks in certain circumstances if you were claiming ESA and returned to work), your claims are linked and treated as being continuous (whether or not your waiting period had been served when your previous claim ended);

24.46-47   SI 2015/1647

(b)   where SMI was previously in payment and you or your partner move into work (or certain kinds of training) a 52 week linking period applies, and you are treated as having been continuously in receipt of SMI from day one of any repeat claim.

24.54   In addition to the main rules above, any periods you spend on ESA(IR) or IS are treated as entitlement to each other; so, for example, if you moved off ESA(IR) and onto JSA(IB), any time spent on ESA(IR) would be treated as time on JSA(IB). Likewise, any periods spent on these benefits by your partner or former partner also count. There are also a number of other less common linking rules.

24.55   The linking rules affect your entitlement to SMI as follows:

(a)   your linked claim counts as time served towards the waiting period and if SMI was already in payment at the end of your previous claim it can be paid immediately; and

(b)   if you are a jobseeker who has exhausted your 104 weeks' entitlement you cannot re-qualify for a further 104 weeks by simply breaking your claim and reclaiming.

24.56   If you are claiming JSA the only way you can can re-qualify for SMI once your 104 week entitlement has been exhausted is to:

(a)   leave JSA for over 12 weeks if you are not working, or over 52 weeks if you move off benefit and into work; and

(b)   make a new claim for JSA and serve a new 39 week waiting period for SMI.

If both of these conditions are met you qualify for a fresh 104 week period of entitlement.

Other matters

Moving home, two homes and temporary absence

24.57   As with HB, there are rules about when you can claim for two homes, during a temporary absence and during a move into a new home:

(a)   SMI can be paid in certain circumstances for a period before you move into a new home. The rules are the same as in paragraphs 3.24-28 (waiting for disability adaptation or local welfare assistance, and leaving care);

(b)   SMI can be paid for up to 13 or, in some cases, 52 weeks when you are temporarily absent. The rules are the same as in paragraphs 3.29-47;

(c)   SMI can be paid in certain circumstances if you have commitments on two homes. The rules are same as in paragraphs 3.21, 3.43 and 22.14 (unavoidable liability, fear of violence, students and trainees).

Mortgage interest run-on

24.58   The mortgage interest run-on scheme mirrors extended payments if you get help with your housing costs through JSA/IS/ESA instead of HB (paras 17.46-53). The conditions are the same as for 'qualifying income related benefits' in table 17.7 except that, instead of the fourth bullet, any qualifying benefit received must include an amount for housing costs within your applicable amount. Payment is automatic provided you have notified the DWP/Jobcentre Plus office that you have started full-time work.

24.59   If you are entitled, the run-on is for four weeks. The amount paid is the same as any housing costs award you were previously being paid, or the amount of JSA/ESA/IS you received if lower (para 24.16). Payment counts as an award of JSA/ESA/IS, so you qualify for maximum CTR (para 24.25).

Paying your SMI

24.60   Your SMI is normally paid direct to your lender – except in the case of an SMI run-on which is paid to you instead. Your lender can opt out of the direct payment scheme but this is virtually unheard of.

Appeals about SMI

24.61   Most decisions about your SMI can be reconsidered and then appealed to a tribunal. The rules – including the basic one month time limit – are similar to those described in chapter 16. But you can only appeal to a tribunal after requesting a reconsideration, and there are other minor differences.

Planned changes

24.62   The government plans that SMI payments will change in 2018 from an award of benefit to an interest-bearing loan secured on your home (Summer Budget 2015).

Chapter 25 **Other help with housing costs**

- Discretionary housing payments (DHPs) towards your rent or service charges: see paras 25.1-18.
- Welfare supplementary payments in Northern Ireland: see paras 25.19-33.
- Local welfare assistance schemes: see paras 25.34-36.
- Direct payments from DWP benefits towards your rent or mortgage arrears or hostel charges: see paras 25.37-55.

Discretionary housing payments

25.1   This section describes how the council/NIHE can award you a discretionary housing payment (DHP) if you are entitled to HB or a UC housing costs element and need further help towards your rent or related housing costs.

25.2   DHPs are not part of the HB scheme, but are administered by the same councils as HB, and in Northern Ireland by the NIHE.

The law and guidance on DHPs

25.3   The Acts of Parliament governing DHPs are the Child Support, Pensions and Social Security Act 2000 and its Northern Ireland equivalent. The details of the DHP scheme are in the Discretionary Financial Assistance Regulations SI 2001/1167 and its Northern Ireland equivalent (see appendix 1). DWP guidance for councils is in its Discretionary Housing Payments Guidance manual (DHPGM) [www].

Who can get DHPs

25.4   To get a DHP you must meet the conditions in paras 25.5-6. But DHPs are discretionary. This means the council doesn't have to award you a DHP even if you meet the conditions. And some councils are more willing to award DHPs than others. So while it is worth asking about and/or claiming a DHP, you shouldn't rely on getting one.

Basic conditions

25.5   In Great Britain the conditions for getting a DHP are that:

(a) you are entitled to HB or a UC housing costs element;

(b) you are liable for rent (in any kind of social or private sector letting); and

(c) you 'appear… to require some further financial assistance… in order to meet housing costs'.

25.3   CPSA 69,70; NICPSA 60,61; SI 2001/1167; NISR 2001/216
         www.gov.uk/government/publications/discretionary-housing-payments-guidance-manual

25.5   DFA 2; NIDFA 2; NISR 2016/432

In Northern Ireland the same conditions apply, but you can only get a DHP if your eligible rent is reduced due to the LHA or rent referral rules (paras 9.4 and 10.37-38), you get less HB due to the abolition of the family premium (para 12.19), or your HB has been reduced due to the benefit cap (to the extent that the reduction is not met by a WSP: para 25.22-27).

Requiring financial assistance

25.6   DHP law doesn't define what requiring 'some further financial assistance' means. The DWP says you usually need to demonstrate you 'are unable to meet housing costs from [your] available income' or 'have a shortfall as a result of the welfare reforms' (paras 1.15-17 of DHPGM). But your (and your family's) circumstances don't have to be 'exceptional' or causing you 'hardship'. And the council/NIHE shouldn't take account of any DLA mobility component you or your partner receive, or have a fixed rule or policy that it always takes account of any DLA care component or equivalent PIP component (Hardy v Sandwell MBC).

Housing costs

25.7   DHP law doesn't list which 'housing costs' you can get help with. They clearly include rent and any eligible service charges you pay (para 8.52). The DWP says (para 1.12 of DHPGM) they can also include:

(a)   rent in advance;

(b)   deposits; and

(c)   other lump sum costs associated with a housing need such as removal costs.

For exceptions see para 25.10.

Uses for DHPs

25.8   In Scotland you will get a DHP regardless of your circumstances to cover the whole of any reduction due to the social renter size criteria (paras 8.15-26). The only exceptions is if you don't meet the basic conditions (i.e. your HB has been reduced to nil after the reduction has been applied) [www].

25.9   In any other case in Great Britain DHPs can be used to help with:

(a)   reductions in your HB due to the following:

  ▪   the benefit cap (para 6.21),

  ▪   in England and Wales, the social renter size criteria (para 8.15),

  ▪   the private renter LHA rules (para 9.4),

  ▪   the social or private renter rent referral rules (paras 10.37-38),

  ▪   the income taper (para 6.6),

  ▪   non-dependant deductions (para 6.9);

(b)   similar reductions in your UC (DWP circular G8/2016);

25.7   R (Hardy) v Sandwell MBC 30.3.15 [2015] EWHC 890 (Admin); www.bailii.org/ew/cases/EWHC/Admin/2015/890.html

25.8   www.parliament.scot/ResearchBriefingsAndFactsheets/S5/SB_16-50
          _Scotland_Act_2016_Discretionary_Payments_and_New_Benefits.pdf

(c) a shortfall in your rent to prevent your household becoming homeless while the housing authority explores other options;

(d) a rent deposit or rent in advance if you are getting HB/UC on your present home and are waiting to move into a new home;

(e) the gap between the end of your UC for housing costs and the start of your HB when you move into specified supported accommodation (para 17.31);

(f) other gaps in your entitlement to HB or UC for housing costs, e.g. because of the limits on backdating (para 5.50).

These are examples, and DHPs can be used in other situations. Examples (a) to (d) are based on DWP guidance (paras 2.3-4 of DHPGM) and for (e) and (f) see para 25.14.

Exceptions

25.10   You can't get a DHP to help with any of the following:

(a) service charges that are ineligible for HB (para 8.67) or (if you aren't on HB) for UC;

(b) any charges for water, sewerage or allied environmental services;

(c) any liability for council tax, or in Northern Ireland rates;

(d) increases to cover rent arrears which are not eligible for HB (para 8.87);

(e) reductions in any benefit due to the recovery of an overpayment of HB/UC, or to sanctions relating to jobseekers, child support or benefit offences.

DHP claims

25.11   You can make your DHP claim in any way the council/NIHE agrees to (e.g. in writing or by telephone) or someone can claim on your behalf if this is reasonable. Some councils have a special DHP form you can use. You should provide information and evidence you are asked for when you claim. And if your circumstance change in a way that could affect your DHPs, you (and the person they are paid to if this is different) should tell the council/NIHE about this.

DHP awards

25.12   DHPs can be awarded for a fixed period, an open-ended period or as a lump sum. The council/NIHE can start or stop your award when it thinks fit. This means you may have to reclaim, possibly several times, if you need DHPs for more than a short period.

DHP amounts and limits

25.13   When DHPs are awarded for a period, the following limits apply:

(a) if you are on HB, the weekly total of your HB and DHP must not be greater than the weekly amount of:

  ▪ your actual rent,

  ▪ minus any service/support charges that are ineligible for HB (para 8.67);

25.10   DFA 3; NIDFA 3

25.11-12 DFA 5,6; NIDFA 5,6

25.13   DFA 4; NIDFA 4

(b) if you are on UC, the monthly amount of your DHP must not be greater than your UC housing costs element. In other words, it must be greater than the monthly amount of:

- your actual rent,

- minus any service/support charges that are ineligible for UC (see *Help with Housing Costs Volume 1*).

If you are on HB in specified supported accommodation (para 2.13) the limit (a) applies, but the law is not completely clear about this if you are also on UC.

25.14 The above limits don't apply when DHPs are awarded:

(a) as a lump sum (e.g. towards a deposit or rent in advance); or

(b) 'for past housing costs (arrears of rent) on the ground that [you are] currently receiving full housing benefit' (Gargett v Lambeth LBC para 32).

Payments and overpayments

25.15 The council/NHE can pay your DHP to you, or to someone else if appropriate (e.g. someone acting on your behalf or your landlord). It also has a discretion to recover overpayments of DHPs that are due to you (or someone else) not giving correct information, or due to an error it has made.

Decisions, notifications and appeals

25.16 When you claim a DHP the council/NIHE must decide whether or not to award you one. It must give you written notice of its decision, including reasons, as soon as reasonably practicable. You can ask the council/NIHE to review its decision if you disagree with it, but the detailed rules about reconsiderations don't apply. You can't appeal to a tribunal, but in limited circumstances you may be able to apply for judicial review (para 1.54).

DHP expenditure: government grants and limits

25.17 In Great Britain the DWP makes grants to councils towards their expenditure on DHPs. This is separate from HB subsidy. The details are in the Discretionary Housing Payments (Grants) Order SI 2001/2340. In 2016-17 the amounts for each council are in circular HB S1/2016 and the total for all councils is £150 million. In 2015-16 it was £125 million: circular HB S1/2015. The council has to claim this grant by 30th April in the following financial year, but doesn't have to submit audited accounts.

25.18 The council doesn't have to spend the exact amount of its grant on DHPs; it can spend less or more. In England and Wales the maximum it can spend in any year is two and a half times the amount of its grant for that year. This limit doesn't apply in Scotland, and the Scottish Government provides additional funding for councils in the expectation that they will use DHPs to mitigate the reductions in HB/UC due to the social sector size criteria rules [www].

25.14　R (Gargett) v Lambeth LBC [2008] EWCA Civ 1450; www.bailii.org/ew/cases/EWCA/Civ/2008/1450.htm

25.15　DFA 8; NIDFA 8

25.16　CBA 73(14); SI 2001/1167; NISR 2001/216

25.17-18　CPSA 70; SI 2001/2340; SI 2014/2918; SSI 2014/298; http://tinyurl.com/mql2p9t

Welfare supplementary payments in Northern Ireland

25.19   In Northern Ireland, welfare supplementary payments (WSPs) can help people affected by recent changes in HB and other social security benefits. This section describes how WSPs can help with your rent if your HB is reduced as a result of the benefit cap or the social renter size criteria ('bedroom tax').

25.20   WSPs are not part of the HB scheme and are administered by the DFC in conjunction with the NIHE.

The law and guidance on WSPs

25.21   The primary legislation governing WSPs is the Welfare Reform (Northern Ireland) Order SI 2015/2006. Relevant details are in the Welfare Supplementary Payments Regulations (Northern Ireland) 2016 NISR 2016/178, the Welfare Supplementary Payment (Amendment) Regulations (Northern Ireland) 2017 NISR 2017/28, and the Housing Benefit (Welfare Supplementary Payment) Regulations (Northern Ireland) 2017 NISR 2017/35.

WSPs for the benefit cap

25.22   The benefit cap is explained in paras 6.21-32. It was introduced in Northern Ireland on 31st May 2016 (the 'old' benefit cap) and reduced on 7th November 2016 (the 'new' benefit cap). But in each case, this usually starts affecting your HB from a later date (para 6.31). WSPs can be awarded for the old benefit cap, the new benefit cap, or both (paras 25.23-27).

25.23   You qualify for benefit cap WSPs if:

(a) you are a lone parent or couple with at least one child or young person in your family (para 4.14);

(b) your HB is reduced as a result of the benefit cap;

(c) you have been entitled to welfare benefits since 31st May 2016 or 7th November 2016 (para 25.24); and

(d) your home is in Northern Ireland (para 25.25).

25.24   To get WSPs for:

(a) the old benefit cap, you (or your partner) must have been entitled to one or more welfare benefits since 31st May 2016;

(b) the new benefit cap, you (or your partner) must have been entitled to one or more welfare benefits since 7th November 2016.

This means any of the welfare benefits in table 6.6(a). If you were a couple who separated on or after 31st May 2016 and met condition (a) or (b) when you separated, you continue to meet condition (a) and/or (b) whenever your former partner does.

25.21   SI 2015/2006 arts 137, 137A; NISR 2016/178 (as amended by NISR 2016/389); NISR 2017/28 part 2; NISR 2017/35

25.22-27   NISR 2016/178 regs 1-4A, 13-16

25.25 You can only get benefit cap WSPs if you are present and normally resident in Northern Ireland. But during a temporary absence from Northern Ireland you can get them for:

(a) up to 13 weeks if your absence is to receive medical treatment; or

(b) up to four weeks if your absence is for any other reasons;

so long as your absence is unlikely to exceed 52 weeks. And you can only get them for the first four weeks you are in prison (in Northern Ireland or elsewhere).

WSPs for the old benefit cap

25.26 WSPs for the old benefit cap are awarded from the first day your HB is reduced as a result of it. To begin with, they equal the amount of your benefit cap reduction (table 6.6), so you don't lose any money. After that, they go down if your benefit cap reduction goes down, but can never go up (until you qualify for WSPs for the new benefit cap). They end when your HB ends or (if earlier) when your benefit cap reduction ends, and can't start again (unless you qualify for WSPs for the new benefit cap).

WSPs for the new benefit cap

25.27 WSPs for the new benefit cap are awarded from the first day your HB is reduced as a result of it. To begin with, they equal the amount of your benefit cap reduction (table 6.6), so you don't lose any money. After that, they go down if your benefit cap reduction goes down, but can never go up. They end when your HB ends or (if earlier) when your benefit cap reduction ends or (in all cases) on 31st March 2020, and can never start again.

WSPs for the social renter size criteria

25.28 The social renter size criteria are explained in paras 8.15-26. They were introduced on 20th February 2017. WSPs can be awarded whenever your HB is affected by size criteria (paras 25.29-31).

25.29 You qualify for size criteria WSPs if:

(a) you rent from the NIHE or a registered housing association;

(b) your HB is reduced because your home has more bedrooms than the size criteria allow (table 11.1); and

(c) your home is in Northern Ireland (the rules about temporary absence are the same as for HB: para 3.29).

You can't get size criteria WSPs if you rent from any other landlord.

25.30 Size criteria WSPs are awarded from the first day your HB is reduced as a result of the size criteria. They equal the amount of the reduction in your HB (paras 8.22-23), so you don't lose any money. Whenever the reduction in your HB goes up or down, your size criteria WSPs go up or down by the same amount. With one exception (para 25.31), they continue for as long as you qualify for them, and start again whenever you qualify for them again.

25.31 Size criteria WSPs end if:

(a) you move to another home rented from the NIHE or a registered housing association;

25.28-31   NISR 2017/28 regs 1-7, 14

25.32   NISR 2016/178 reg 2; NISR 2017/28 regs 2(1),(5), 7, 15

(b) your move is not a 'management transfer' arranged by your landlord(s); and

(c) your new home has even more bedrooms (compared with what you are allowed following your move) than your old home did (compared with what you were allowed before your move).

WSP awards and appeals

25.32 You are awarded WSPs without having to make a claim. The DFC uses information provided by the NIHE, and by your landlord if you rent from a registered housing association. You can ask the DFC to review your award if you think it is wrong. You can't appeal to a tribunal but may be able to apply for judicial review (para 1.54).

WSP payments and overpayments

25.33 WSPs are paid four weekly in arrears. They are paid to you (or someone on your behalf) or to your landlord or agent if your HB is paid to them (but not a private landlord/agent unless they are registered with the Landlord Registration Scheme). Overpayments of WSPs are nearly always recoverable – from you and/or the person they were paid to. The methods include making deductions from future payments of WSPs, HB, some other social security benefits, or earnings.

Local welfare assistance/discretionary support

25.34 You may be able to get help from:

(a) a local welfare assistance scheme in England;

(b) the Welsh Discretionary Assistance Fund;

(c) the Scottish Welfare Fund; or

(d) discretionary support in Northern Ireland.

These are not part of the HB scheme. They are administered by local councils and partially replace the former Social Fund. In England many councils have their own name for the scheme.

25.35 To get help you normally have to be 'in need' and without the money to meet the need. But the schemes and funds are discretionary, so you have no right to help. Payments can be a grant or a loan but many councils provide help only (or mainly) on a non-cash basis.

25.36 In general terms you may be able to get help to:

(a) avoid becoming homeless;

(b) avoid entering institutional care (e.g. residential care, hospital or prison);

(c) set up home after leaving institutional care; or

(d) meet a crisis and avoid harm.

In Scotland you cannot get a grant or loan for rent or mortgage payments, rent in advance, repair costs or any housing costs that could be covered by a DHP. Similar exclusions apply in Northern Ireland but you may get a loan for rent in advance to secure a tenancy. In England and Wales local councils set their own rules but in practice similar exclusions are likely to apply.

25.33 NISR 2016/178 regs 4(7)-(9), 11; NISR 2017/28 regs 4-13, schs 1, 2; NISR 2017/35 regs 4-13, schs 1, 2

Direct payments from DWP benefits

25.37   This section describes how the DWP can make deductions from your social security benefits in order to make direct payments towards rent or mortgage arrears or hostel charges. It gives the rules for Great Britain. Similar rules apply in Northern Ireland but some of the details differ.

25.38   Direct payments are not part of the HB scheme, but are administered by the DWP, and in Northern Ireland by the DFC. The DWP/DFC call them 'third party payments'.

The law and guidance on direct payments

25.39   The law about direct payments is in schedule 9 of the Social Security (Claims and Payments) Regulations SI 1987/1968 and schedule 8A of its Northern Ireland equivalent (see appendix 1). DWP guidance for landlords and mortgage lenders is in *How to Apply for Third Party Payments* and the *Third Party Payments Creditor/Supplier Handbook* [www]. Guidance for councils is in GM D1.570-689.

What direct payments can be used for

25.40   The DWP can make direct payments:

(a) to your landlord towards arrears of rent including service charges;

(b) to your mortgage lender towards mortgage arrears;

(c) to your landlord, if you live in a hostel, towards essential services that are not eligible for HB.

They are designed to encourage your landlord or mortgage lender to let you stay in your home rather than evict you because of arrears. They can only be made for your current home, not for rent arrears, etc on a former home. (This guide does not give the rules about when direct payments can be used for other purposes, but these are summarised in para 25.55).

When direct payments can be made

25.41   The basic conditions for making direct payments are in para 25.42 and further details are in the rest of this section. But direct payments are discretionary. This means the DWP doesn't have to make them even if all the conditions are met, though in practice it usually does.

Basic conditions

25.42   The DWP can only make direct payments if:

(a) you or your partner are getting a qualifying benefit (para 25.43);

(b) either:

- you or your partner are also getting HB (or live in a hostel and have claimed HB), or

- your qualifying benefit includes support for mortgage interest (chapter 24); and

---

25.39   SI 1987/1968 35(1) and sch 9, NISR 1987/465 34A(1) and sch 8A
          www.gov.uk/government/uploads/system/uploads/attachment_data/file/236163/tpp-new-creditor-guide.pdf
          www.gov.uk/government/uploads/system/uploads/attachment_data/file/417640/third-party-payments-handbook-march-2015.pdf

25.42   SI 1987/1968 sch 9

(c)   the direct payments are for the dwelling you occupy as your home.

There are also further conditions for each kind of direct payment: see paras 25.45-48.

Qualifying benefits

25.43   Direct payments can only be made if you or your partner are:

(a)   on state pension credit (SPC) – whether this is guarantee credit or savings credit or both;

(b)   on income support (IS);

(c)   on income-based JSA;

(d)   on income-related ESA;

(e)   on contribution-based JSA and are also entitled to JSA(IB) at the same rate; or

(f)   on contributory ESA and are also entitled to ESA(IR) at the same rate.

The last two apply because in these circumstances you are paid JSA(C)/ESA(C) rather than JSA(IB)/ESA(IR). (Different rules apply if you are on UC: see *Help with Housing Costs Volume 1.*)

Benefits from which deductions can be made

25.44   When the DWP makes a direct payment, it deducts the same amount from your qualifying benefit (para 25.43). But if the amount of your SPC, IS or JSA(IB) is insufficient to make the deduction, the DWP can make it from any retirement pension, JSA(C), incapacity benefit or severe disablement allowance you or your partner get (whether this is paid separately or together with your SPC/IS/JSA(IB)).

Direct payments for rent arrears

25.45   The DWP can make direct payments to your landlord for rent arrears if:

(a)   you meet the basic conditions (para 25.42);

(b)   you have rent arrears (para 25.46) of:

■   at least four times your weekly rent, or

■   if you live in a hostel (para 7.22) at least £100; and

(c)   either:

■   the arrears have accrued or persisted over at least eight weeks and your landlord has requested direct payments, or

■   they have accrued or persisted over less than eight weeks and the DWP considers it is in your and your family's overriding interests to make direct payments, or

■   you live in a hostel and are eligible for direct payments of service charges (para 25.48).

When this applies to you, your HB must also be paid to your landlord (para 16.40).

25.43-44   SI 1987/1968 sch 9 para 1(1) definition: 'specified benefit', (2),(3)

25.45   SI 1987/1968 sch 9 para 5(1),(1A),(2)

25.46   For the above purposes (para 25.45), both 'rent' (also called 'gross rent') and 'rent arrears':

(a)   include all the following (whether or not they are eligible for HB):

- your rent (or licence fee, etc: table 7.1),

- any service or other charges included in your rent, and

- any separate charge made by your landlord for water or services;

(b)   but do not include:

- any fuel charge that is not eligible for HB and varies more than twice a year,

- any unpaid non-dependant charge, or

- any unpaid amount relating to a former home.

The amounts in (b) are also ignored when calculating the period over which your rent arrears have accrued or persisted.

Direct payments for mortgage arrears

25.47   The DWP can make direct payments to your mortgage lender for mortgage arrears if:

(a)   you meet the basic conditions (para 25.42);

(b)   you have mortgage arrears; and

(c)   during the past 12 weeks you:

- haven't paid your mortgage lender at all, or

- have paid them less than eight times the weekly amount of your eligible housing costs (para 24.38).

Direct payments for hostel charges

25.48   The DWP can make direct payments to your landlord for hostel charges if:

(a)   you meet the basic conditions (para 25.42);

(b)   you live in a hostel (para 7.22); and

(c)   your hostel charges include an amount for fuel, meals, laundry and/or cleaning (other than communal areas).

This can apply whether or not you have arrears of rent or other charges. When it does apply, your HB must also be paid to your landlord (para 16.40).

Amounts deducted from your benefits

25.49   Paras 25.51-52 explain how much is deducted from your social security benefit and paid to your landlord or mortgage lender as a direct payment. Paras 25.53-55 give the limits that can affect this.

25.46   SI 1987/1968 sch 9 paras 1(1) definition: 'rent', 5(7)

25.47   SI 1987/1968 sch 9 para 5(1),(1A),(2)

25.48   SI 1987/1968 sch 9 para 4A

25.50   All the amounts in the rest of this section are given as weekly figures. The standard amount of £3.70 (para 25.51) is 5% of the personal allowance for a single person aged 25-plus (table 12.1) rounded up to the next multiple of 5p. It only changes when the personal allowance changes.

Amount for rent or mortgage arrears

25.51   The amount deducted as a direct payment for rent or mortgage arrears is:

(a) the standard amount of £3.70; plus

(b) (in rent arrears cases) the amount of any fuel and/or water charges that are included in your rent and that aren't eligible for HB;

(c) (in mortgage arrears cases) the amount of your eligible housing costs (para 24.38).

Once all your rent or mortgage arrears are cleared, the amount in (b) or (c) can continue to be deducted as a direct payment if this is in the 'interests of [your] family'.

Amount for hostel charges

25.52   The amount deducted as a direct payment for hostel charges equals the amount of your charges for fuel, meals, laundry and/or cleaning (other than communal areas). This is calculated as described in paras 8.32 and 10.51 or, if your HB hasn't yet been awarded, the DWP should estimate it.

Limits to amounts for rent arrears

25.53   Once the amount for rent arrears has been calculated (para 25.51):

(a) it is reduced whenever necessary to leave you receiving 10p a week of your qualifying benefit (para 25.43);

(b) if it is higher than 25% of:

- ▪ your qualifying benefit's applicable amount,
- ▪ plus (if you are on CTC) your CTC and child benefit,

it is reduced to that 25% unless you consent to a higher amount.

Limits when there is more than one direct payment

25.54   Amounts can be deducted from your DWP benefits to make direct payments for other purposes, and in many cases they equal or include a standard amount of £3.70. If more than one direct payment applies to you:

(a) the maximum deduction for standard amounts is £11.10 (3 x £3.70);

(b) the total deduction is reduced whenever necessary to leave you receiving 10p a week of your qualifying benefit (para 25.43).

25.50   SI 1987/1968 sch 9 paras 1(1) definition: '5%', 3(2),5(6)

25.51   SI 1987/1968 sch 9 paras 2,5(6),(7)

25.52   SI 1987/1968 sch 9 para 4A(3)

25.53   SI 1987/1968 sch 9 para 2(2)

25.54-55   SI 1987/1968 sch 9 paras 8,9

25.55   If the above limits mean that only some direct payments can be made, they are made in the following order of priority:

(a) rent or mortgage arrears;

(b) fuel;

(c) water;

(d) council tax;

(e) unpaid fines;

(f) child support;

(g) repayments of refugee integration loan;

(h) loan repayments to certain affordable credit lenders (credit unions);

(i) tax credit overpayment debts and self assessment debts.

Appendix 1 **Legislation**

England, Wales and Scotland

Main primary legislation (Acts)

The Social Security Contributions and Benefits Act 1992

The Social Security Administration Act 1992

The Child Support, Pensions and Social Security Act 2000

The Welfare Reform Act 2007

The Welfare Reform Act 2012

The Welfare Reform and Work Act 2016

Main secondary legislation (Regulations and Orders)

SI 2006/213	The Housing Benefit Regulations 2006
SI 2006/214	The Housing Benefit (Persons who have attained the qualifying age for state pension credit) Regulations 2006
SI 2006/217	The Housing Benefit and Council Tax Benefit (Consequential Provisions) Regulations 2006
SI 1997/1984	The Rent Officers (Housing Benefit Functions) Order
SI 1997/1995	The Rent Officers (Housing Benefit Functions) (Scotland) Order
SI 2001/1002	The Housing Benefit and Council Tax Benefit (Decisions and Appeals) Regulations
SI 2001/1167	The Discretionary Financial Assistance Regulations
SI 2014/1230	The Universal Credit (Transitional Provisions) Regulations 2014

Recent secondary legislation: housing benefit

The following is a list of amendments etc (or otherwise relevant) to the main regulations from 1st April 2016. This list is up to date as at 1st April 2017.

SI 2016/242	The Social Security Benefits (Adjustment of Amounts and Thresholds) Regulations 2016
SI 2016/233	The Social Security (Scottish Rate of Income Tax etc.) (Amendment) Regulations 2016
SI 2016/511	The Welfare Reform Act 2011 (Commencement No 28) Order 2016
SI 2016/519	The Social Security Administration Act 1992 (Local Authority Investigations) Regulations 2016
SI 2016/624	The Housing Benefit and State Pension Credit (Temporary Absence) (Amendment) Regulations 2016
SI 2016/732	The Children and Young People (Scotland) Act 2014 (Consequential Modifications) Order 2016
SI 2016/743	The Social Security (Treatment of Postgraduate Master's Degree Loans and Special Support Loans) (Amendment) Regulations 2016
SI 2016/909	The Benefit Cap (Housing Benefit and Universal Credit) (Amendment) Regulations 2016
SI 2016/1179	The Rent Officers (Housing Benefit and Universal Credit Functions) (Local Housing Allowance Amendments) Order 2016
SI 2017/204	The Employment and Support Allowance and Universal Credit (Miscellaneous Amendments and Transitional and Savings Provisions) Regulations 2017
SI 2017/213	The Housing Benefit and Universal Credit (Size Criteria) (Miscellaneous Amendments) Regulations 2017
SI 2017/252	The Universal Credit (Housing Costs Element for claimants aged 18 to 21) (Amendment) Regulations 2017
SI 2017/260	The Social Security Benefits Up-rating Order 2017
SI 2017/297	The Pensions Act 2014 (Commencement No10) Order 2017
SI 2017/329	The Social Security (Scottish Infected Blood Support Scheme) Regulations 2017
SI 2017/376	The Social Security (Restrictions on Amounts for Children and Qualifying Young Persons) Amendment Regulations 2017
SI 2017/422	The Pensions Act 2014 (Consequential, Supplementary and Incidental Amendments) Order 2017
SI 2017/581	The Employment and Support Allowance (Miscellaneous Amendments and Transitional and Savings Provision) Regulations 2017

Recent commencement orders: universal credit

The following is a list of commencement orders from 1st April 2016 affecting the roll-out of universal credit full service and consequent phasing out of housing benefit for new working age claims. This list is up to date as at 1st April 2017.

SI 2016/394	The Welfare Reform and Work Act 2016 (Commencement No 1) Regulations 2016
SI 2016/407	The Welfare Reform Act 2012 (Commencement No 27 and Transitional and Transitory Provisions and Commencement No 22, 23 and 24 and Transitional and Transitory Provisions (Modification)) Order 2016
SI 2016/596	The Welfare Reform Act 2012 (Commencement No 13, 14, 16, 19, 22, 23 and 24 and Transitional and Transitory Provisions (Modification)) Order 2016
SI 2016/610	The Welfare Reform and Work Act 2016 (Commencement No 2) Regulations 2016
SI 2016/910	The Welfare Reform and Work Act 2016 (Commencement No 3) Regulations 2016
SI 2016/963	The Welfare Reform Act 2012 (Commencement No 19, 22, 23 and 24 and Transitional and Transitory Provisions (Modification)) Order 2016
SI 2017/57	The Welfare Reform Act 2012 (Commencement No 11, 13, 16, 22, 23 and 24 and Transitional and Transitory Provisions (Modification)) Order 2017
SI 2017/483	The Welfare Reform Act 2012 (Commencement No 9 and 21 and Transitional and Transitory Provisions (Amendment)) Order 2017
SI 2017/584	The Welfare Reform Act 2012 (Commencement No 19, 22, 23 and 24 and Transitional and Transitory Provisions (Modification)) Order 2017

Northern Ireland

Main primary legislation (Acts and Acts of Northern Ireland Assembly)

The Social Security Contributions and Benefits (Northern Ireland) Act 1992

The Social Security Administration (Northern Ireland) Act 1992

The Child Support, Pensions and Social Security Act (Northern Ireland) 2000

The Welfare Reform Act (Northern Ireland) 2007

The Welfare Reform Act (Northern Ireland) 2015

The Welfare Reform (Northern Ireland) Order SI 2015/2006

The Welfare Reform and Work (Northern Ireland) Order 2016 SI 2016/999

Main secondary legislation (Statutory Rules and Orders)

NISR 2006/405   The Housing Benefit Regulations (Northern Ireland) 2006

NISR 2006/406   The Housing Benefit (Persons who have attained the qualifying age for state pension credit) Regulations (Northern Ireland) 2006

NISR 2006/407   The Housing Benefit (Consequential Provisions) Regulations (Northern Ireland) 2006

NISR 2008/100   The Housing Benefit (Executive Determinations) Regulations (Northern Ireland) 2008

NISR 2001/213   The Housing Benefit (Decisions and Appeals) Regulations (Northern Ireland) 2001

NISR 2001/216   The Discretionary Financial Assistance Regulations (Northern Ireland) 2001

NISR 2016/226   The Universal Credit (Transitional Provisions) Regulations (Northern Ireland) 2016

Recent secondary legislation: housing benefit

The following is a list of amendments etc (or otherwise relevant) to the main regulations from 1st April 2016. This list is up to date as at 1st April 2017.

NISR 2016/55   The Benefit Cap (Housing Benefit) Regulations (Northern Ireland) 2016

NISR 2016/110   The Social Security Benefits (Adjustment of Amounts and Thresholds) Regulations (Northern Ireland) 2016

NISR 2016/147   The Social Security (Scottish Rate of Income Tax etc) (Amendment) Regulations (Northern Ireland) 2016

NISR 2016/176   The Employment and Support Allowance (Amendment of Linking Rules) Regulations (Northern Ireland) 2016

NISR 2016/230   The Housing Benefit (Miscellaneous Amendments) Regulations (Northern Ireland) 2016

NISR 2016/236   The Universal Credit (Consequential, Supplementary, Incidental and Miscellaneous Provisions) Regulations (Northern Ireland) 2016

NISR 2016/258   The Housing Benefit (Amendment) Regulations (Northern Ireland) 2016

NISR 2016/310   The Housing Benefit (Abolition of the Family Premium and date of claim) (Amendment) Regulations (Northern Ireland) 2016

NISR 2016/326   The Housing Benefit (Amendment No 2) Regulations (Northern Ireland) 2016

NISR 2016/375   The Benefit Cap (Housing Benefit and Universal Credit) (Amendment) Regulations (Northern Ireland) 2016

NISR 2016/432   The Social Security (Miscellaneous Amendments) Regulations (Northern Ireland) 2016

NISR 2017/1   The Housing Benefit and State Pension Credit (Temporary Absence) (Amendment) Regulations (Northern Ireland) 2017

NISR 2017/9   The Housing Benefit (Executive Determinations) (Amendment) Regulations (Northern Ireland) 2017

NISR 2017/51   The Employment and Support Allowance (Consequential Amendments and Transitional and Savings Provisions) Regulations (Northern Ireland) 2017

NISR 2017/56   The Social Security Benefits Up-rating Order (Northern Ireland) 2017

NISR 2017/62   The Social Security (Income-related Benefits) (Amendment) Regulations (Northern Ireland) 2017

NISR 2017/66   The Pensions (2015 Act) (Consequential, Supplementary and Incidental Amendments) Order (Northern Ireland) 2017

NISR 2017/70   The Housing Benefit and Universal Credit (Size Criteria) (Miscellaneous Amendments) Regulations (Northern Ireland) 2017

Recent secondary legislation: other commencement orders etc

The following is a list of commencement orders and other secondary legislation from 1st April 2016 relating to housing benefit. This list is up to date as at 1st April 2017.

NISR 2016/56   The Social Security (Information-sharing in relation to Welfare Services etc.) Regulations (Northern Ireland) 2016

SI 2016/325   The Welfare Reform (Northern Ireland) Order 2015 (Commencement No 5) Order 2016

NISR 2016/374   The Welfare Reform and Work (Northern Ireland) Order 2016 (Commencement No 1) Order 2016

Recent secondary legislation: welfare supplementary payments

The following is a list of secondary legislation from 1st April 2016 relating welfare supplementary payments so far as they relate to compensation for loss of housing benefit. This list is up to date as at 1st April 2017.

NISR 2016/178   The Welfare Supplementary Payments Regulations (Northern Ireland) 2016

NISR 2016/389   The Welfare Supplementary Payment (Benefit Cap) Regulations (Northern Ireland) 2016

NISR 2017/35   The Housing Benefit (Welfare Supplementary Payment) Regulations (Northern Ireland) 2017

NISR 2017/28   The Welfare Supplementary Payment (Amendment) Regulations (Northern Ireland) 2017

Appendix 2 **Selected weekly benefit rates from April 2017**

	£
Attendance allowance	
Higher rate	83.10
Lower rate	55.65
Bereavement benefits	
Widowed parents allowance (standard rate)	113.70
Bereavement allowance (standard rate)	113.70
Bereavement support payment (higher rate)	80.77
Bereavement support payment (lower rate)	23.08
Child benefit	
Only or older/oldest child	20.70
Each other child	13.70
Carer's allowance	
Claimant	62.70

Disability living allowance/Personal independence payment

Care component	*Daily living*	£
Highest rate	Enhanced	83.10
Middle rate	Standard	55.65
Lowest rate	–	23.10
Mobility component	*Mobility component*	
Higher rate	Enhanced	58.00
Lower rate	Standard	22.00

Employment and support allowance (contributory)

Personal allowances	£
Under 25/lone parent under 18	57.90
18 or over/under 25 (main phase)	73.10
Couple both under 18 with child	87.50
Couple both over 18	114.85
Components	
Work-related activity	29.05
Support	36.55

	£
Guardian's allowance	16.70

Incapacity benefit

Short-term lower rate (under pension age)	80.25
Short-term higher rate (under pension age)	95.00
Long-term rate	106.40
Spouse or adult dependant (where appropriate)	61.80
Increase for age higher rate (under 35)	11.25
Increase for age lower rate (35-44)	6.25

Industrial disablement pension

20% disabled	33.94
For each further 10% disability up to 100%	16.97
100% disabled	169.70

Jobseekers allowance (contribution-based)

Aged under 18 to 24	57.90
Aged 25 or more	73.10

Maternity and paternity pay and allowance

Statutory maternity, paternity and adoption pay	140.98
Maternity allowance	140.98

Retirement pension

New state pension (flat rate)	159.55
Old state pension single person (basic rate)	122.30
Old state pension couple (basic rate)	195.60

Severe disablement allowance

Basic rate	75.40
Age-related addition	
Higher rate	11.25
Middle and lower rate	6.25

Statutory sick pay

Standard rate	89.35

For details of other benefit rates from April 2017 (including means-tested benefits, tax credits and war pensions) see Circular A12/2016.

Appendix 3 **Qualifying age for state pension credit**

Date of birth	Date qualifying age for state pension credit is reached
Before 6th April 1950	On reaching age 60
6th April 1950 to 5th May 1950	6th May 2010
6th May 1950 to 5th June 1950	6th July 2010
6th June 1950 to 5th July 1950	6th September 2010
6th July 1950 to 5th August 1950	6th November 2010
6th August 1950 to 5th September 1950	6th January 2011
6th September 1950 to 5th October 1950	6th March 2011
6th October 1950 to 5th November 1950	6th May 2011
6th November 1950 to 5th December 1950	6th July 2011
6th December 1950 to 5th January 1951	6th September 2011
6th January 1951 to 5th February 1951	6th November 2011
6th February 1951 to 5th March 1951	6th January 2012
6th March 1951 to 5th April 1951	6th March 2012
6th April 1951 to 5th May 1951	6th May 2012
6th May 1951 to 5th June 1951	6th July 2012
6th June 1951 to 5th July 1951	6th September 2012
6th July 1951 to 5th August 1951	6th November 2012
6th August 1951 to 5th September 1951	6th January 2013
6th September 1951 to 5th October 1951	6th March 2013
6th October 1951 to 5th November 1951	6th May 2013
6th November 1951 to 5th December 1951	6th July 2013
6th December 1951 to 5th January 1952	6th September 2013
6th January 1952 to 5th February 1952	6th November 2013
6th February 1952 to 5th March 1952	6th January 2014
6th March 1952 to 5th April 1952	6th March 2014
6th April 1952 to 5th May 1952	6th May 2014
6th May 1952 to 5th June 1952	6th July 2014
6th June 1952 to 5th July 1952	6th September 2014
6th July 1952 to 5th August 1952	6th November 2014

6th August 1952 to 5th September 1952..6th January 2015

6th September 1952 to 5th October 1952..6th March 2015

6th October 1952 to 5th November 1952..6th May 2015

6th November 1952 to 5th December 1952..6th July 2015

6th December 1952 to 5th January 1953..6th September 2015

6th January 1953 to 5th February 1953..6th November 2015

6th February 1953 to 5th March 1953..6th January 2016

6th March 1953 to 5th April 1953..6th March 2016

6th April 1953 to 5th May 1953..6th July 2016

6th May 1953 to 5th June 1953..6th November 2016

6th June 1953 to 5th July 1953..6th March 2017

6th July 1953 to 5th August 1953..6th July 2017

6th August 1953 to 5th September 1953..6th November 2017

6th September 1953 to 5th October 1953..6th March 2018

6th October 1953 to 5th November 1953..6th July 2018

6th November 1953 to 5th December 1953..6th November 2018

6th December 1953 to 5th January 1954..6th March 2019

6th January 1954 to 5th February 1954..6th May 2019

6th February 1954 to 5th March 1954..6th July 2019

6th March 1954 to 5th April 1954..6th September 2019

6th April 1954 to 5th May 1954..6th November 2019

6th May 1954 to 5th June 1954..6th January 2020

6th June 1954 to 5th July 1954..6th March 2020

6th July 1954 to 5th August 1954..6th May 2020

6th August 1954 to 5th September 1954..6th July 2020

6th September 1954 to 5th October 1954..6th September 2020

6th October 1954 or after..On reaching age 66

Index

References in the index are to paragraph numbers (not page numbers), except that 'A' refers to appendices, 'T' refers to tables in the text and 'Ch' refers to a chapter.

S